Mass Mediations

Mass Mediations

*New Approaches to Popular Culture
in the Middle East and Beyond*

EDITED BY

Walter Armbrust

UNIVERSITY OF CALIFORNIA PRESS

Berkeley   Los Angeles   London

University of California Press
Berkeley and Los Angeles, California

University of California Press, Ltd.
London, England

© 2000 by the Regents of the University of California

Library of Congress Cataloging-in-Publication Data

Mass mediations : new approaches to popular culture in the Middle
East and beyond / edited by Walter Armbrust.
    p.   cm.
    Includes bibliographical references and index.
    ISBN 0-520-21926-0 (pbk : alk. paper)
    1. Mass media—Middle East.   2. Popular culture—Middle East.
I. Armbrust, Walter.
P94.65.M628M37   2000
302.23'0956—dc21
                                    99-43224
                                        CIP

Manufactured in the United States of America

09 08 07 06 05 04 03 02 01 00

10 9 8 7 6 5 4 3 2 1

The paper used in this publication meets the minimum requirements of ANSI/NISO
Z39.48-1992 (R 1997) (*Permanence of Paper*).

CONTENTS

ILLUSTRATIONS

PREFACE

Mass Mediations examines popular culture broadly, in terms of economics, politics, conventions of taste and aesthetics, and performance. The "popular" is an integral part of a wide cultural spectrum, not a set of practices to be opposed to "elite" culture. High/low distinctions such as those commonly made in the West are sometimes part of cultural discourse in Middle Eastern societies, but they rarely operate in a strictly analogous fashion. Our focus, therefore, is less on what popular culture is than on what it does in its mass-mediated forms, namely, to create new scales of communication and, consequently, new dimensions of modern identity.

A wide variety of media are considered, including recorded music (as well as live performance), television, cinema, and print media ranging from mass-circulation weeklies to postmodern novels. All the material examined here is underrepresented in scholarship on the Middle East. This volume therefore helps to fill gaps in the regional literature. Growing excitement over new communications technologies makes it easy to overlook the historical depth of mass media in the Middle East. Consequently, we include several chapters that analyze historical dimensions of mass-mediated culture. Of course, the very idea of a Middle East is itself a political issue. We respond to this concern by addressing transnational dimensions of Middle Eastern identities that challenge conventional assumptions about the region and its relation to Western societies.

Relations between metropolitan societies and the colonized are an important part of contemporary history. However, on many levels the unfolding of modernity in colonial and postcolonial societies has scarcely been described or analyzed. The literature on Middle Eastern popular culture is so impoverished partly because concerns about Western power and Western representational practices have overwhelmed analyses of non-Western modernities that can be understood in their own terms. The scale of social practice with which this book is most concerned, therefore, is one at which important expressions of modernity occur for large numbers of people but one which has thus far eluded extensive analysis.

Most of the chapters in this volume initially took shape at two conferences in 1995, the American Anthropological Association (AAA) meeting and the Middle East Studies Association (MESA) meeting, both in Washington, D.C. The AAA panels, titled "Expressive Culture in the Middle East: Modernity, National Community, Transnational Contexts," were conceptualized by myself and Ted Swedenburg, and several of the papers benefited from comments by Lila Abu-Lughod, who was discussant for half of the papers (I was discussant for the other half). The papers for the MESA panel, titled "Public Culture in the Arab Middle East II: Transnational Contexts," received valuable comments from Joel Beinin. Several of the papers were also presented at a symposium, "The Politics of Culture in Arab Societies," at Princeton University in spring 1996. The symposium took place as part of the program of the Institute for the Transregional Study of the Middle East, North Africa, and Central Asia, under the directorship of Abdellah Hammoudi. As the essays underwent their metamorphosis from conference papers to book chapters they benefited from comments by Susan Ossman and Gregory Starrett. We also thank University of California Press editor Lynne Withey for her guidance and patience. Finally I wish to thank all the contributors to the volume for their excellent contributions and for their patience. Roberta Dougherty played a crucial role in the final round of copyediting and in preparing the index. Turning the papers into a book has been a lengthier process than any of us foresaw, but in the end I hope all will agree that the whole volume is greater than the sum of its parts.

NOTE ON TRANSLITERATION

In Arabic transliterations long vowels and emphatic consonants are not differentiated in the text from their closest English equivalents. The ayn and
hamza are used. Some Egyptian and Syrian colloquialisms have been used
where the authors deem appropriate, or where correct transliteration of a
text (within the limits of the simplified transliteration system used in this
volume) demands it.

ONE

Introduction
Anxieties of Scale

Walter Armbrust

Mass Mediations examines the role of mass-mediated popular culture in defining the scale and character of social interaction in the Middle East. Mass media are now as ubiquitous in Karachi and Cairo as they are in Dearborn and Los Angeles. Few question their importance in the contemporary process of constructing the boundaries of social identity. Although mass media potentially raise as many questions as sociological ingenuity can devise, in this volume we address primarily the larger, more inclusive issues that lend themselves to questions of scale: modernity, nationalism, and globalization. Our goal is to examine these issues of general relevance in ethnographic and historical detail. By examining a broad set of analytic issues in fine-grained regionally oriented perspective, we hope to shed light on the complex phenomenon of mass media without inevitably forcing the analysis into a common scale—specifically, the global—or reducing the analysis of modernity to a tension between global and local cultural forms. In particular, constructing the local so as to preclude consideration of the nation-state as a viable framework for modern social action risks analytic distortion. Together the chapters herein suggest that modernity need not be associated definitively with either nationalism (as it often has been) or globalization (which is increasingly taken to signal the irrelevance of the nation-state).

THE MIDDLE EAST

Our regional focus is the Middle East, which for the past two decades has been a lightning rod for anxieties about the reality of conceptual boundaries. In the wake of Edward Said's *Orientalism* (1978) the very idea of a Middle East has come under suspicion. For some the Middle East as a cultural entity is a prime example—perhaps *the* prime example—of how European discourse created the definitively non-Western and thereby defined the Western by distinguishing it from an opposite created by political and social convention. Area studies programs are a postwar manifestation of this kind of logic, and consequently, in the wake of Said's critique, Middle East–oriented projects—and to a much lesser extent area studies in general—are often frowned on. By adopting this particular regional perspective, we are not trying to revive a much-criticized analytic framework. However, the Middle East, precisely because of the passions and ambiguities it evokes, is an ideal forum for considering the role of mass media in both creating and transcending the boundaries that define scales of social action. A quick perusal of the volume's contents shows that the area focus ranges from Pakistan (Richard Murphy) to Dearborn (Andrew Shryock)—not the Middle East of cold war era area studies—and that all the chapters make reference to relations that go beyond their immediate environs. Framing the volume around such a disputed entity as the Middle East helps to draw attention to the issues of scale, cultural conditions (modernity, or for some, postmodernity), and contemporary history. This is all to the good; it is precisely the volume's purpose.

But in another sense one perhaps ought to question the ongoing deconstruction of this region. There is an institutional politics of analytic scale that has to a great extent delegitimized the Middle East as a regional analytic framework. This delegitimization is based on a false presumption that in a larger academic context the area concept is dead—allegedly superseded by more robust global comparative approaches, which are institutionally based in academic disciplines or international studies centers rather than the old area studies framework. But, in fact, the area concept is alive and well for some. In the past decade those who have written about Latin America, Africa, or Asia have benefited from institutional investment that is massive compared to investment in Middle East–oriented knowledge.[1] African, Asian, and Latin American specialists can criticize the area studies framework now axiomatically disparaged as the critique of *Orientalism* steadily hardens into orthodoxy. But they can do so while enjoying a steady supply of area-specific jobs. Of course, academics who study the Middle East would also like to be able to have their cake and eat it too—to acknowledge the limits and insufficiencies of the area concept without having to participate in a rhetoric of dissolving the institutional framework within which they work. In contemporary academia one should be able to engage in both cross-regional comparison within a discipline and cross-disciplinary comparison within an area studies framework. Disciplinary and regional perspectives are by no means mutually exclusive.

Nonetheless, the past two decades have been increasingly marked by an anti–area studies rhetoric, though it is often informal rhetoric and it has never been followed to its logical conclusion on the institutional level. The critique of area studies occurred in the context of a gradual crystallization of transregional analysis, now often conflated with "globalization." This happened in conjunction with a clear pattern of institutional shift toward identifiable area specializations *other than the Middle East.* "Area studies" became a stick used to beat Middle East specialists in particular. If connections between power and the production of knowledge are truly a prominent academic concern, it would seem imperative to ask whether the recent shift in institutional backing of area specialties was entirely due to intellectual priorities. What role do interests shaped by national criteria play in the reshaping of academic institutions? Surely a very substantial one. This is not to say that there is a neat correspondence between national interest and institutional priorities. The point is that the politics of presence *and* absence at the institutional level are closely tied to the politics of the nation-state. A growing institutional interest in transnational phenomena is not necessarily even connected to scales of interaction at the "global" level; it is quite clearly connected to interactions that affect the United States. These interactions vary in character and intensity. What ties them all together is the nation-state as an analytic and practical framework.

For example, one might speculate that commercial interest in Latin America and Asia—currently areas of intense academic interest—is obvious. Latin American and Asian markets and, increasingly, productive capacity are important to the economic future of the United States. Although commercial interest need not be strictly national (and probably never was), the congruence of national ethnic categories, commercial interest, and institutional response to precisely these interests and categories does not suggest the imminent irrelevance of the nation-state. American academic interest in Africa is more complex. African resources and markets are clearly on the horizon of commercial interest, but the main impetus to increasing interest in African studies is, in many cases, less the importance of Africa than the politics of relations between African-Americans and the dominant population of European descent. Whether increased attention to Africa stems from the efforts of African-Americans to put their concerns on the intellectual agenda or from a growing appreciation for the commercial potential of African markets, it would be deceptive to think of institutional attention to Africa as the product of global or transregional forces to the exclusion of national considerations.

Of course, the United States has commercial interests in the Middle East as well. But from a national policy perspective—regardless of any considerations of such issues as human rights or sound economic development—U.S. Middle East policy could not be more successful than it is now. The price of the oil so crucial to our consumption habits is at a historic low. Money spent on oil is conveniently recycled into the metropolitan economy by cooperative Arab states. The large and influential constituents of American society who see the Middle East through the lens of Israeli politics[2] observe a continuing occupation of Palestinian territory that goes virtually unchallenged on an international level. Both Iraq and Iran are preoccupied with trying to break free of American-sponsored economic and political embargoes; both states provide continuing pretexts for maintaining an American military presence in the region. With the demise of the Soviet Union, American backing of Islamic insurgency directed from the Pakistani frontier can be conveniently forgotten. In the Maghreb a simmering Algerian civil war threatens no vital "American" resources, and thus the conflict, for all practical purposes, does not exist in the American media. On the domestic front there is no effective Arab-American or Muslim-American pressure to put any other Middle Eastern issues into the political discourse.

One could plausibly argue that the Middle East absorbs the lion's share of American foreign policy attention. What is increasingly difficult to argue is the notion of a strong academic institutional connection between imperial ambition and the exercise of power. Making the power/knowledge nexus so crucial to Said's *Orientalism* into a "seminal event" (Hajjar and Niva 1997, 4) for Middle East specialists has been a Faustian bargain. If academic scrutiny of the Middle East helps to construct the cultural basis for imperial domination, we should now be witnessing a diminution of American interference in the region, and of course nothing could be farther from the truth. Middle East particularism as an institutional construction is on the wane (to the benefit of Asian, Latin American, and African particularisms). The withering of academic interest in the Middle East has often been abetted by the field of Middle East studies itself, a substantial portion of which embraced the idea that the very existence of a discipline of Middle East studies in the United States was antithetical to the interests of those living in the region.[3] That portion of the field has gotten its wish. But the result is that precisely the "expertise" deemed dubious by left-leaning academics interested in the Middle East has been privatized and removed from the scrutiny of academics. As institutional commitment to the production of academic knowledge of the Middle East wanes, openly partisan private foundations designed to influence Middle East policy flourish.[4] Universities were the institutions most likely to hire individuals who questioned the political status quo vis-à-vis the Middle East. As Irene Grendzier put it, "The mainstream [of Middle East studies] has never been the only stream, nor the one in which the most creative, insightful and urgent intellectual work is to be found. Generally speaking, however, those who have resisted the canons of orthodoxy have not been the ones to shape the dominant motifs of research" (1997, 11). A mainstream reduced to a trickle is even less likely to produce a critical mass of scholars who oppose the canons of political orthodoxy.

Commercial interest, although not the only element structuring Middle East studies in the United States, could still conceivably revive the fortunes of Middle East studies. But with matters running so smoothly in the Middle East (from a purely cynical perspective of national interest), there is little potential for intensification of U.S. commercial exploitation of the region, hence little incentive for increased institutional investment in studying it. In Latin America, Asia, and Africa, where prospects for intensification of commercial activity are far greater, U.S. institutional investment is correspondingly higher. But whether or not local knowledge is necessary to promote commercial or national interest depends on how interests are defined. It is no coincidence that the one region of the world in which the United States has recently gone to war is also an area of *decreasing* institutional importance in academia. The Gulf War was first and foremost a conflict to defend national interests, whether or not one agrees with the way those interests were defined.[5]

In the end we have nothing to gain from accepting globalization as the logical antithesis of either a national or a regional focus. Even some of the prominent figures in globalization discourse are less hostile to the area concept than many Middle East specialists who are encouraged by contemporary institutional realities to steer clear of obvious manifestations of area interest. For example, Arjun Appadurai, an early advocate of transnational approaches to cultural studies, is well aware of the dangers of throwing the area studies baby out with the post-Orientalist bathwater:

> Left-wing critics of area studies, much influenced by the important work of Edward Said on orientalism, have been joined by free-marketeers and advocates of liberalization, who are impatient with what they deride as the narrowness and history fetish of area-studies experts. . . . Bedeviled by a certain tendency toward philology (in the narrow, lexical sense) and a certain over-identification with the regions of its specialization, area studies has nonetheless been one of the few serious counterweights to the tireless tendency to marginalize huge parts of the world in the American academy and in American society more generally. (1996, 16–17)

The Middle East, a charter member of institutionalized area studies, and more recently the scapegoat for those who oppose it, is now a serious candidate for marginalization. The Gulf War and ongoing American threats of military action are not a product of dubious area expertise but of general, willful, ignorance. Middle East exceptionalism truly is a danger, but casting an area focus as a choice between a myopic outdated antimethodology and complete surrender to globalization is no way to remedy the situation.

Mass Mediations therefore fills a general need for continuing a viable regional literature situated in relation to more generalized intellectual and institutional concerns. The intellectual agenda currently most prevalent points toward a global analytic framework thrown into relief by various forms of interaction at more localized scales but explicitly not at the level of the nation-state. This intellectual agenda, however, does not correspond to institutional priorities. It is our own national framework—cultural, political, and economic—that dictates the institutional presence or absence of regional studies and the shape of academic disciplinary discourses. The chapters in this volume help to qualify and focus debates over scales of social interaction and their significance to our analyses. On the whole they suggest that global/local tensions are the crucial frame of analysis if one decides to make them so. But the decision to make them so is as embedded in institutional and power relations as any other discourse.

This volume also answers a more specific need to address the effect on Middle Eastern societies of mass media and related phenomena such as mass consumption. This inevitably requires attention to connections between the Middle East and metropolitan societies. We therefore hope to capture something of the complex transitions between scales of social interaction without, however, taking globalization rhetoric as a universalizing master narrative. This is because globalization is part unfinished agenda and part sociological reality.

AND BEYOND

In the United States the study of transnational immigrant populations, a growth area in all relevant academic disciplines, focuses on exactly the same areas as the wider job market: Latin America, Africa, Asia. The overarching rationale for this is that transnational and transregional considerations now take priority over social phenomena understood as relevant primarily within national and area boundaries. But the categories we actually study, as distinct from the rhetoric of non-place-specific analytic frameworks, are defined by a national criterion: the U.S. census. A well-known strategy of colonial domination, enumeration of social types "helped to ignite communitarian and nationalist identities that in fact undermined colonial rule" (Appadurai 1996, 117). In the contemporary United States enumeration also forms the basis of political activity. Over the past decade there have been hundreds of job openings for the study of American immigrant communities, virtually all of them structured around U.S. census categories. The reasons for this are complex. Some of the rapid increase in positions that study those particular American immigrant communities can be accounted for by changes in academic culture. Students are increasingly viewed as paying customers (rather than the products of academic business) who must be satisfied; because more of the customers are now of Hispanic, Asian, or African origin, courses must be offered that are tailored for those markets. The logic of this pattern is hardly free of national considerations. The groups in question are the most rapidly growing ethnic populations *within the United States*. A truly global analytic framework would demand greater attention to such places as the Middle East, South and Central Asia, Oceania, and Europe. But the zones of ambiguity (according to the enumerative categories of the census) are not necessarily slated for greater institutional investment.[6] "Globalization" is less about an interconnected world than it is about the complex ways that the world is apprehended from the United States.[7]

Middle Eastern immigrant communities—invisible in the U.S. census, and almost equally so in terms of institutional investment—are the focus of two chapters in *Mass Mediations*. Andrew Shryock's "Public Culture in Arab Detroit" makes a powerful case that even relatively mobile transnational communities still must contend with a powerful imperative to reterritorialize—to become rooted in a place and in national institutions. Anthony Shay's "The 6/8 Beat Goes On" looks at popular music in the Iranian community of Los Angeles. Although motives for relocating to the United States are complex in both communities, as is the class and ethnic makeup of both communities, the Iranian community of Los Angeles can be properly described as an "exile community" (see Naficy 1993), the members of which cannot necessarily maintain movement back and forth from the country of origin to the United States. The population of Arab Dearborn, by contrast, has much less difficulty maintaining contact with its countries of origin. In the short term the result is that Iranian Los Angeles possesses a higher degree of autonomy in media production than Arab Dearborn. Shay notes that entire genres of Iranian popular music essentially moved offshore after the Islamic Revolution, and the market for this music is the Iranian-American immigrant community as well as Iran itself. Traditional vernacular genres and "classical" music (insofar as such distinctions can be applied to Iranian music) as well as modernized variants of Iranian music flourish in Los Angeles. The decisive factor in this autonomous Iranian production in the United States is the considerable sense of isolation the community feels as a result of the political reality of the Islamic Revolution.

In Dearborn modern Arabic music (and indeed most media content) comes from its countries of origin,[8] while another segment of the local cultural scene depends on local (American) financing. Shryock shows how American financing is contingent on certain types of cultural content: culture that invokes a sense of the "folkloric" (rather than the modernity constructed by most Arabic cultural products in the Middle East); and Arabic culture presented in English. Whether the two communities, Iranian Los Angeles and Arab Dearborn, can preserve the sense of cultural difference essential to theories of transnationalism depends largely on a continued influx of immigrants. In Dearborn modern Arabic media and cultural products appeal mainly to first-generation immigrants who still speak Arabic.

Iranian Los Angeles is a newer community—substantially a post-1978 community—and is also more affluent than Arab Dearborn. These factors give Iranian Los Angeles certain advantages in maintaining a cohesive community outside of national institutions. Whether this remains true for second and third generations of Iranian immigrants is an open question. But the juxtaposition of the two communities presented in Shryock's and Shay's chapters does not suggest a generalizable pattern of transnational or globalized culture outside the influence of a steadily withering nation-state.

GLOBALIZATION

Currently the presumption that global interaction will inevitably take precedence over all other frameworks for organizing social life dominates discussions of modernity. Most who write on globalization make a distinction between consciousness of the phenomenon and the reality of global systems of economics and, to some extent, politics and culture. Global, or at least transregional, systems are far from new, and the reality of such systems inspires little dispute. Janet Abu-Lughod (1989), Immanuel Wallerstein (1974), and Eric Wolf (1982), among others, have outlined various ways that transregional economic systems of various scales have operated long before the twentieth century. However, consciousness of globalization as a crucial framework for social action is generally thought to be a quite recent phenomenon, and the significance of this phenomenon is a much more contentious issue. Advocates of globalization as an analytic strategy assume that the roots of global consciousness in its contemporary form extend no deeper than the latter half of the twentieth century, or perhaps even to only the past three decades when digital technology became prevalent. Globalization discourse posits a new and unique configuration of these two broad tendencies—the intensification of interconnectedness due to the expansion of world economic systems and the consciousness of that interconnectedness. All analyses of globalization are necessarily vague on the exact relationship between the reality of world systems and the consciousness of these systems, because all analyses are forced to recognize at some level the unevenness of the institutional and technological infrastructures that make possible a relationship between an expanding world system and consciousness of it. Mike Featherstone, for example, qualifies his analysis of globalization processes:

> For many of the people in the world the consciousness of the process of globalization, that they inhabit the same place, may be absent, or limited, or occur only spasmodically. . . . At the same time there are clearly systemic tendencies in social life which derive from the expansive and integrating power of economic processes and the hegemonizing efforts of particular nation-states or blocs. (1996, 70–71)

But, however qualified, globalization discourse also implies an underlying technological determinism: those parts of the world that have not yet been assimilated into the global system will be assimilated at a later date. Resistance is futile. Communications technology and media—phenomena emphasized throughout this book—play a crucial role in creating globalization. The ultimate effects of assimilation to the global system, however, are hotly disputed. Cultural homogenization is by no means assumed. Rather, discussion of globalization revolves around a tension between the apparent homogenizing tendency of globalized modes of production and consumerism (with media again playing a crucial role) and the creation of localized cultural enclaves. Consumerism and its associated media phenomena labeled "global" are usually Western, or at least metropolitan.

As Ella Shohat and Robert Stam put it, the global distribution of power, dominated by Western Europe, the United States, and Japan, "still tends to make the First World countries cultural 'transmitters' and to reduce most Third World countries to the status of 'receivers'" (1996, 147). Shohat and Stam do not emphasize the theme of metropolitan domination of global media. Rather, they focus on the potential for both nonmetropolitan media (in which some industries are actually quantitatively superior to Western production, if not more profitable) and new forms of media to challenge metropolitan hegemony. Their metropole is one in which spectatorial habits in "an increasingly transnational world, characterized by nomadic images, sounds, goods, and peoples, . . . impacts complexly on national identity, communal belonging, and political affiliation" (Shohat and Stam 1996, 164).

In the same vein, Ted Swedenburg's "Sa'ida Sultan/Danna International" addresses an instance of transnational media flow that is nonhierarchical—not from a metropolitan producer to a Third World receiver. Rather, the flow is horizontal between two nonmetropolitan nations, from Israel to Egypt.[9] The impact of Sa'ida Sultan, a transsexual singer of Yemeni origin who became popular in Cairo through underground cassette tapes, was indeed complex. But Swedenburg's analysis of Sultan does not suggest media "nomadism" so much as a mélange of sound and image calculated to appeal to a niche market consisting of Israel's gay subculture and, to a somewhat lesser extent, disaffected Mizrahim who chafe at Israel's European-dominated social hierarchy. As in many of the contributions in *Mass Mediations*, Swedenburg finds it useful to discuss a transnational phenomenon through national categories. Egyptian youth were certainly not the niche the singer was trying for. But Sa'ida Sultan's border crossing is nonetheless quite locatable: the singer is highly suspect in Egyptian public culture and rather contentious in Israeli society. She serves to mark important borders between and within the two societies; she does not necessarily blur these boundaries in any way.

Katherine E. Zirbel's "Playing It Both Ways" provides another view of transnational media consumption. Zirbel examines two Egyptian performance communities that relate quite differently to both global and national trends. The Cairene community of Muhammad 'Ali Street exists largely outside the influence of global culture markets and has experienced both the state's favor and, more recently, its disfavor. Muhammad 'Ali Street performers had their day on the national stage but were never of interest in metropolitan venues. The other community is Upper Egyptian, marginal within Egypt, and precisely the sort of phenomenon favored in metropolitan "world beat" music that seeks to present itself as alternative to dominant metropolitan trends. For Shohat and Stam, metropolitan audiences who experience such culture "are reminded of the limits of their own knowledge and indirectly of their own potential status as foreigners" (1996, 165). But Zirbel's Upper Egyptians' music was in fact recorded *entirely for the benefit of* foreigners. Within Egypt this music might not have been recorded at all, though it may well have been (and still is) performed at weddings and on holidays. But the ability of the music to remind metropolitan listeners of their own potential marginality is strictly a mirage. "Westerners describe such music as a quirky kind of disco music that is consistently off kilter" (Zirbel, this volume). For them the music is essentially a brand of exoticism, purchased entirely by reference to their own culture. These Upper Egyptian musicians perform in a niche market every bit as circumscribed and locatable as the gay subculture to which Swedenburg's Sa'ida Sultan markets herself. But Sa'ida Sultan's market understands her: her image is predicated on a series of sly insider jokes. In the case of these "Gypsy" musicians, as this community is marketed, the effectiveness of the music is predicated on the audience's inability to understand either it or its place in the "authentic" Egyptian culture they imagine it represents.

Philip Schuyler's "Joujouka/Jajouka/Zahjoukah" looks at a musical phenomenon similar to that of Zirbel's "Gypsies." In Schuyler's case the "world beat" marketing of a Moroccan ensemble is the primary focus, whereas in Zirbel's case the phenomenon is relevant to one community of musicians and the main focus is on contrasting the two communities to each other in relation to the state. The Master Musicians of Jajouka hail from a small Arabic-speaking village near Tangier. They are "master musicians" only in the imagination of their Western patrons. Like the Egyptian "Gypsies," the Jajouka musicians are quite marginal in Moroccan terms. Music of the Jajouka musicians is more plausibly nomadic than that of Zirbel's Upper Egyptians, at least insofar as "ownership" of the music is slightly ambiguous. The ambiguity arises from disputes between the Jajouka musicians' principal Moroccan patron and the various Westerners—but particularly Brian Jones of the Rolling Stones—over how to market the music and who gets the profits from their albums. Schuyler's analysis of the Jajouka phenomenon suggests none of the displacement or subversion implied by Shohat and Stam's celebration of nonmetropolitan performance in metropolitan venues. The Master Musicians of Jajouka are very much whatever metropolitan audiences want to read into them, including an association with paganism attributed on largely ideological grounds by various Western scholars as a survival from either Berber or Roman culture (Hammoudi 1993, 30–31). Judging by the Jajouka phenomenon as related by Schuyler, "world music" makes the most sense in terms of metropolitan tastes for exoticism. These tastes are interesting in their own right but are hardly new, and their existence hardly depends on a global stage. This is not to say that complex syntheses of musical styles are not intentionally created all the time by musicians (witness Sa'ida Sultan, or American jazz, or modernist appropriations of imagined primitivism such as Stravinsky's *Rite of Spring*). But the horizons of musical audiences are always both circumscribed and changeable under the right circumstances.

THE FUTILITY OF RESISTANCE

The most conspicuous loser in discussions of global consciousness is the nation-state, which many consider outmoded as a framework for experiencing modernity.[10] In both the popular media and academia the demise of the nation-state is thought by some to be an uncompleted process, but the general trajectory toward its dissolution is an article of faith. This is true across a wide spectrum of writing. For example, popular publications such as *Wired*, a trade magazine that shills for the computer industry, regularly extol the virtues of globalization: "Ultimately the migration of culture is not monolithic but mosaic, flowing over and around borders, washing away strict definitions, surging into new social spaces created by the tools of the age" (Couch 1997, 214). More thoughtful (and less obviously business oriented) voices often concur. The anthropologist Michael Kearney puts the matter in terms that readers of *Wired* would find familiar: "Globalization entails a shift from two-dimensional Euclidean space with its centers and peripheries and sharp boundaries, to a multidimensional global space with unbounded, often discontinuous and interpenetrating sub-spaces" (1995, 549).[11]

There is much evidence close at hand to support such observations. Our own media generate globalization discourse relentlessly; our universities echo it, albeit with an avowedly alternative agenda. However, the ready availability of globalization discourse to metropolitan consumers in particular should also be a reason to be cautious about such pronouncements. Much globalization rhetoric is prescriptive. To adopt globalization as an analytic framework may be to make it a self-fulfilling prophecy. It has become difficult to separate globalization as an agenda of economic determinism

(Ferguson 1992) from globalization as a practice of modern identity (Friedman 1995), or globalization as a postmodern culture of media consumption (Baudrillard 1995). The totality of these agendas is like flypaper: even if one rejects them, one is still forced to argue against them. Cultural practice not done in consciousness of globalization becomes an affirmation of the local in response to the pressure of the global.

An example of how globalization discourse treats attempts at resistance can be found in the relative lack of attention in metropolitan circles to *Sharaf*, a novel by the Egyptian writer Sonallah Ibrahim (1997). In this novel Ibrahim explicitly criticizes globalization. *Sharaf* is a prison narrative centering on Sharaf, an unemployed Egyptian youth, and an older Egyptian man named Dr. Ramzi. Sharaf is the ultimate commodity fetishist; much of his speech in the novel takes the form of lists of "global" products, all of which come to Egypt from the industrialized metropole—the West or newly industrialized Asia. He has been culturally deprogrammed by commoditization and thereby turned into a passive consumer. When a British tourist lures the boy into a movie theater, later into his apartment, and then tries to rape him, Sharaf resists (his name means "honor") and accidentally kills the man.

Sharaf contrasts explicitly with Dr. Ramzi, who is the ultimate global pirate, an Egyptian who left the country when the nationalist Nasser regime imposed state control on the economy. Dr. Ramzi spends his life dismantling the industrial capacities of Third World nations so that "global" (metropolitan-based) companies can take their place. When sent to Egypt to dismember the nationalized pharmaceuticals industry, Dr. Ramzi rebels. His company, in league with corrupt Egyptian officials eager to cash in on the sell-off to multinational corporations, frames Dr. Ramzi, who ends up in prison next to Sharaf. In this way Ibrahim's narrative engineers a meeting between Dr. Ramzi, the agent of globalization, and Sharaf, the human product of global processes.

In the course of the novel the warden allows the prisoners to watch the national soccer team compete in the World Cup. Islamic fundamentalists— a large component of the prison's population—cannot stand this open worship of secular nationalism. They start a riot. A new warden comes to the prison and imposes harsh discipline. The new prison master knows Dr. Ramzi from long ago, before Ramzi left the country to work as a global raider. One of the things the warden knows is that the young Dr. Ramzi had a love for the theater. The warden agrees to relax his grip on the prison only if Ramzi writes a play and entertains him and the guards. Ramzi's play, in which Sharaf performs, is a bitter criticism of globalization. The prisoners' performance of Ramzi's play causes another riot, after which Ramzi gets tortured to the point of insanity. By the end of *Sharaf*, Dr. Ramzi roams the prison reciting long lists of multinational atrocities, a counterpoint to

Sharaf's recitations of consumer brand names. Nobody listens to the "insane" Dr. Ramzi. Sharaf ends the novel precisely where he began: with a man, an older and stronger prisoner, trying to rape him. This time Sharaf submits, abandoning the honor suggested by his name, the defense of which landed him in prison in the first place. In the final scene we find Sharaf shaving his legs in preparation for becoming his rapist's "wife."

This is no nationalist allegory of the type analyzed by Fredric Jameson (1986). Ibrahim's message is direct and angry: We—the Third World, but in this case particularly Egypt—are being screwed by metropolitan nations in the name of the new global economy. Although the novel openly discusses globalism, in globalist discourse *Sharaf* would most often make the most sense as an expression of localism. But Ibrahim's localism is of a particular kind: it argues for the defense of national institutions, scathingly criticizing the privatization policies of the post-Nasser era that facilitate the penetration of global capital. The novel argues for a national project rooted in the Nasser era, which is remarkable for a writer who was among the many intellectuals imprisoned in the period.[12] Ibrahim's invocation of the Nasser period as a comparatively healthy counterpoint to the current rush to liquidate state-supported institutions in favor of global capitalist enterprises finds a receptive audience.

However, in globalization discourse forthright advocacy of national institutions is frowned on. More often nationalism is portrayed as an anachronistic urge rather than as an intellectual position: "Maimed bodies and barbed wire in Eastern Europe, xenophobic violence in France, flag waving in the political rituals of the election year here in the United States—all seem to suggest that the willingness to die for one's country is still a global fashion" (Appadurai 1996, 159–60).[13] Obviously, when put this way, nationalism is not a fashion many would be eager to buy into. Consequently, a novel like *Sharaf* fares poorly in the realm of "world" literature. *Sharaf*'s entry into the discourse of "world" literature is also hindered by Ibrahim's habit of writing in Arabic, unlike more prominent Third World authors who write in English or in other metropolitan languages that, compared to Arabic, translate relatively easily into English. Arabic is a "weak language" in global terms. The volume of material translated into Arabic far exceeds the volume of material moving the other way (Asad 1993, 191). The languages of globalization are English first, followed by other European languages. All else is "local." Even works advanced in globalization discourse as "counter-hegemonic" in various senses are overwhelmingly works in English or other European languages.[14] Consequently, a novel such as Ahdaf Soueif's *In the Eye of the Sun* (1992), which depicts the lives of Egyptians living in England, has a better chance of being considered important than Ibrahim's *Sharaf* precisely because Soueif lives outside of Egypt and writes in English. Postcolonial literary theorists—close allies of academic globalists—consider

the appropriation of English by non-Europeans to be a salutary and necessary antidote to an alleged European silencing of non-European vernacular languages. The "empire writes back" (Ashcroft, Griffiths, and Tiffin
1989) in order to subvert European power. Karin Barber, in the context of
African literature, calls for a reconsideration of the assumption that postcolonial writing must first subvert colonial languages to effectively challenge metropolitan power. An emphasis on European-language works by
metropolitan scholars amounts to a "definitive theoretical lockout" of in-
digenous-language expression in colonized countries by postcolonial theorists (Barber 1995, 4).

> The model proposed by postcolonial criticism—the model in which colonial
> glottophagia silences the native until he or she masters and subverts the col-
> onizer's language—is based on a fundamental misconception, almost a will to
> ignorance. By casting the indigenous as always and only outside or under-
> neath the "mainstream" literary discourses of modern Africa, it turns a blind
> eye to what is in fact the actual mainstream, the cultural discourses of the ma-
> jority, in most of Africa. (Barber 1995, 11)

The "will to ignorance" to which Barber refers is not irrelevant to the Jajouka or "Gypsy" phenomenon described here by Schuyler and Zirbel. And
Barber's criticism applies equally to Middle Eastern literature and media.
Sophisticated modern works not easily pigeonholed into the "exotic" or
"folkloric" categories are not as celebrated in the United States as are authors who write in metropolitan languages. This includes works by authors
such as Ibrahim, who writes in Arabic and, so far, is not often translated into
English.[15] The same is true of cinema.[16]

One of the virtues of Ibrahim's *Sharaf* is that it highlights this imbalance
by insisting that any attempt to understand globalization is subsumed by the
powerful economic forces that, while enormously complex, are in fact not
global at all but rather locatable in the metropolitan core that defines such
places as Egypt as a periphery.[17] Increasingly the dominant voice in globalization rhetoric, if not analysis, is a metropolitan profit-driven business
agenda—the homogenizing bogeyman in the global/local dialectic. Opponents of globalization are often dismissed in the press as dinosaurs or
dangerous radicals. *Wired* crystallizes the dismissive attitude of the business
community toward anyone who seems not to be getting with the globalized
technological program. In a photo essay titled "Change Is Good" (*Wired*
6.01, January 1998, 182–83), the magazine juxtaposes two pictures. One is
a stark black-and-white photo of a stern Muslim scholar—male, in a knit-
ted skullcap, prayer mat hanging on the wall, Persian writing on a black-
board behind him, attention focused on a paper on which he is writing with
a pen. The other photo is of a girl, probably about eight years old, sitting in
front of her Macintosh computer. Her stuffed bunny sits on the machine,

and her hands are on the keyboard as she looks backward at the camera. Golden sunlight streams through a window in the background of the scene. She is unbearably cute. The two photos are linked by a caption in large, bold letters that cross both pages: "The true learning revolution." The caption sets up the comparison between the old man's austere patriarchal Islamic learning and the girl's gentle enlightenment. On the girl's side the "true learning revolution" phrase is completed in smaller print. The "true revolution" (as opposed to the delusional backward Islamic one featured in large type on the opposite page) "is not just computers in the classroom— it's networking students, teachers, and parents together." And if the reader (or viewer in this case) is not yet fully networked, or "wired" as the magazine might put it, the publication features numerous advertisements from vendors eager to connect another customer to the global network.

Several contributions to *Mass Mediations* take constructions of nationalism rather more seriously than globalization rhetoric suggests is warranted. Joel Gordon's chapter on the film *Nasser 56* suggests a potent nostalgia for the nationalist project. Gordon notes that the film steers clear of Nasser's nationalization and import-substitution policies, emphasizing instead the much less controversial Suez crisis. There is, of course, no guarantee that audiences separate one kind of nationalism from another. Although the actual policies of Nasser still mark numerous fault lines within Egyptian society—between classes, generations, and regions of the country—Gordon writes that everyone was eager to take credit for the film, "notwithstanding the obvious irony of a state-funded film glorifying nationalization in the age of privatization and championing a charismatic, idolized ruler in an era of political malaise." The film does not occur in a vacuum. Egyptian history is in vogue in the Egyptian media; historical visions flourish alongside all the obvious signs of globalization. A visitor to Cairo could easily consider the satellite dishes sprouting like mushrooms all over the city to be a sign that Egypt has moved fully into global culture. But Ibrahim's angry *Sharaf* and the popularity of *Nasser 56* suggest a wide spectrum of public culture within which nationalist imagery can form an effective bulwark against metropolitan globalization.

Christa Salamandra's "Consuming Damascus" examines a Middle Eastern state that attempts to construct the "local" as a national community that is to some extent outside the reach of global capital. Baathist Syria has had decidedly mixed results in its efforts to preserve a distinctively Syrian identity. Although Syria has been more reluctant than Egypt to pave the way for the entry of global capital by dismantling national institutions, nonetheless modes of social distinction geared to state institutions have lost prestige. "Mere consumption" takes the place of such modernist engines for constructing national identity as a university education. Many Syrians aspire to the same sort of globalized life as Ibrahim's Dr. Ramzi—the Nasserist-turned-multinational raider. In Syria the consumption patterns in question include leisure practices that revolve around public display in restaurants and hotels, as well as representations of "Old Damascus" in literature and television serials. All of these juxtapose highly self-conscious constructions of "Damascene" and "foreign" cultures in ways that appear eclectic and cosmopolitan but which are meaningful primarily on local terms.

"Old Damascus" is a construct of nostalgia. Richard Murphy's "The Hairbrush and the Dagger" also shows how nostalgia is deployed in national narratives. Pakistani media invoke it in quite locally (nationally) specific ways but nonetheless ways that imply a multiplicity of perspectives within nationalist discourse. The subject of Murphy's chapter, a state-produced television serial called *Muhasira* (Siege), in which the author acted the part of a Western journalist, would seem at first glance a poor candidate to illustrate multiple viewpoints. In principle the program was an exercise in chauvinism, a rejection of any possibility that Muslims and Hindus could coexist peacefully. *Muhasira* depicts a monthlong Indian army siege of a mosque in disputed Kashmir province, the result of which, not surprisingly, is that Kashmir is shown to have been wrongly divided from Muslim Pakistan at partition. But beneath the uncompromising surface of the serial Murphy finds a highly nuanced mediated debate "about social, political, and historical registers of truth." Such debates are the ground on which Pakistani modernity is constructed, both with regard to the definitively non-Pakistani (Indian) and with regard to the much more problematic internal terrain of class and regional difference.

In "'Beloved Istanbul'" Martin Stokes discusses the ambiguous and troubled nature of modernity in contemporary Turkey. Stokes's chapter makes an excellent contrast with subthemes that run through several other chapters in this volume. Like Swedenburg's "Sa'ida Sultan," Stokes's focus is a transsexual singer—Bülent Ersoy, a conservatory-trained but popular singer not highly approved in official circles. The focus of Stokes's analysis is sonic and literary representations of a city—Istanbul—that many take to be emblematic of the entire state. In this respect the chapter belongs with those by Salamandra (Damascus) and Murphy (Lahore). The chapter also revolves around the importance of nostalgia, which occupies a large place in the contributions by Zirbel, Gordon, Shay, Murphy, and me.

Stokes is not writing about the transnational flow of culture here but about the uncoupling of modernity from nationalism in contemporary Turkey. The "classical" voice in modern Turkey is prized for clarity, whereas Ersoy deliberately distorts her singing, thereby risking the disapproval of Turkish officialdom. The Ersoy performance analyzed by Stokes is no arabesk piece marketed to new immigrants to the city; rather, it is a new version of a 1948 nationalist classic, "Beloved Istanbul." Its text was written by a foremost republican poet; the music originally performed by a well-known musical modernizer who straddled the Ottoman and republican periods. Stokes shows how Ersoy's rendition of the song—considered scandalous by many—articulates with the surprising popularity of a postmodern novel by Orhan Pamuk. Postmodernity in Turkey, however, requires a confrontation with history rather than the schizophrenic fragmentation of the self that Westerners sometimes associate with the idea of postmodernity (Harvey 1989, 53–54). As Stokes writes, "In a society in which the state of being modern is cast so insistently in terms of forgetting, and in which the modern is so organically connected to the institutions of the nation-state, remembering becomes both a problem and a matter of cultural elaboration." Among all the boundaries being blurred—sexual and musical in the case of Ersoy, literary realism in the case of Pamuk's *Kara Kitab*—the most significant of all is the one constructed between the present and the Ottoman past. Paradoxically the compromising of the modernist project in Turkey opens up new horizons for the development of Turkish nationalism.

"Beloved Istanbul" and *Kara Kitab,* unlike Murphy's *Muhasira,* Salamandra's depiction of constructions of "Old Damascus," and the historical interpretations of *Nasser 56* described by Gordon, are not straightforward nationalist texts. However, none of these texts can be understood without a nuanced explication of the social conditions surrounding their production and consumption. Though the social conditions are complex, the texts are nonetheless still nationalist, and still quite vital. All of them suggest resistance to the dominant themes of globalization, which either advocate the demise of the nation-state or predict its occurrence. Commercial interest in such a hostile depiction of nationalism is understandable. Murphy's chapter, and Shryock's even more so, also makes reference to the congruence of commercial, political, and academic thinking about the relationship of globalization to both nationalism and modernity. This congruence demands further comment.

Academics who see globalization as the crucial frame of reference for understanding the contemporary world—many of them self-described leftists or at least opponents of the metropolitan status quo—are well aware of the correspondence between their analytic strategies and commercial interests that openly try to make globalization a self-fulfilling prophecy. Appadurai (1996, 18 ff.), for example, distinguishes between the ethical dimension of globalization and its analytic dimension, which he sees as too strong to ignore. However, the ethical implications of a withering of the nation-state put him in "mixed company" with the political right, which also celebrates the expected demise of the nation-state. Appadurai and many others (e.g., Marcus 1996a) find hope in a postnationalist world, because for them the nation-state has been a conspicuous failure at promoting such values as "the protection of minorities, the minimal distribution of democratic rights, and the reasonable possibility of the growth of civil society"

(Appadurai 1996, 19). Consequently, the long-term ethical possibilities inherent in the demise of the nation-state are thought to outweigh the immediate fact of commercial benefit from globalization as well as the fact that such benefit is quite devoid of ethical considerations.[18]

However, putting an ethical spin on globalization substitutes one prescriptivism—an optimistic progressive one—for another openly commercial agenda. In the short term hopeful progressive globalization agendas are clearly losing ground to the amoral commercial agenda. American social activists since Abbie Hoffman (1971) have believed that in the long run the energy of decentralized communication networks can be harnessed for their own ends. A recent example can be found in *Connected* (Marcus 1996a), a volume of academic analyses of media—particularly the Internet—that places "strong value on the new, on left-liberal activism, on the desire for grass-roots media experimentation at the level of everyday life and commitment to change" (Marcus 1996b, 13).[19] But the volume explicitly backs away from analysis of "the great organizational changes within corporate capitalism that are accommodating technological changes in media" (Marcus 1996b, 16). One essay in Marcus's volume notes that the main forces behind creating the Internet are the state and the military (Kirshenblatt-Gimblett 1996, 24–28), but, as in the other essays, the analysis does not ultimately integrate that fact with the goal of exploring how the Internet can be used to create new types of community.[20]

The global consciousness that actually exists in the world—as opposed to global systems that reach much farther back in history than the consciousness to which contemporary commentators refer—is highly compatible with regimes of flexible capitalist accumulation described by David Harvey (1989, 147 ff.) and now celebrated by the corporate-controlled U.S. media. Jonathan Friedman describes the outcome of this consciousness as

> a global class structure, an international elite made up of top diplomats, government ministers, aid officials and representatives of international organizations such as the United Nations, who play golf, dine, take cocktails with one another, forming a kind of cultural cohort. This grouping overlaps with an international cultural elite of art dealers, publishing and media representatives, the culture industry VIPs who are directly involved in media representations and events, producing images of the world and images for the world. The news is made by them, very much about them and communicates their visions of reality. . . . It is from these quarters that much of the globalization discussion has emerged, from the economic "global reach" to the cultural "global village." (1995, 79–80)

This is similar to Shryock's observation (in this volume) that "the people who produce, distribute, and consume the transnationalism rhetoric most devotedly belong to the academy, the corporate elite, and government: social bodies that, in their modern forms, are designed to exceed the limits of any human community they can imagine." Friedman notes that this globalization is not hegemonic or homogeneous, a point also vigorously made by Appadurai (1996, 17). But where Appadurai and others[21] see disjuncture providing interstitial spaces within which new social forms can flourish, Friedman insists on a simultaneous project of global systematization that encompasses global fragmentation. In other words, the turmoil suggested by Appadurai's (1996, 27–47) use of the term "disjuncture" is actually quite systematic and works to the advantage of elites in the cosmopolitan "global class structure" to which Friedman alludes. Friedman implies that by emphasizing processes that occur in and around the boundaries of cultural categories—processes such as hybridization or creolization—we make globalization a self-fulfilling prophecy. Practices that do not fit the model can be simply omitted from an analysis.

The omission of nonconforming practices from analyses of modernity (or alternatively, the neutralization of such practices by assigning them to the category of the "local" in distinction to the global) involves a striking selectivity. For example, in summer 1997 an Egyptian television station broadcast a prerecorded "world music awards" program. Each recipient of an award—most of whom were well known in the United States and Europe (the "Macarena" figured prominently)—performed a brief rendition of his or her hit song. The categories appeared at first to be arranged by nation: "most popular song in France" during the past year, "most popular song in Germany," "most popular song in the United States," and so on. But some awards made it plain that the organizing principle for the event was not national popularity but market organization. The ceremony did not include "most popular song in Zaire" or "most popular song in Nigeria," and so forth, but "most popular song in Africa." Except for Japan and Hong Kong, it was "most popular song in Asia." One might assume that the smaller markets were lumped together, and in some cases that may have been true. But in some cases the omitted markets were quite large and quite well acquainted with mass-mediated music.

There was no category in the program for the Middle East. This was not necessarily because the Middle Eastern market is small but more likely because it is small for those record companies. Although a few of the "world music" productions performed in the program were known in Cairo (particularly the "Macarena"), the most popular songs in Cairo the previous year had been mainly those made for an Arabic-speaking market outside the reach of the metropolitan record companies. "Ifrid" (Just Suppose), by a rising young Egyptian star known simply as Hakim, was getting a great deal of play in summer 1997. The market for these songs was not necessarily defined strictly by national borders, but there were (and have been for decades) clear demarcations between the national scope of songs and their Arabic-language scope. Technology plays a part in defining these markets. Satellite television funded by Saudi Arabia but based in Europe has become economically important in the business. But most Egyptians do not receive satellite television, and although the phenomenon of the satellite dish is spreading in Egypt, the extent of the satellite market is still far more limited than that of the state-dominated television system. By summer 1997 one could receive nine terrestrial stations in Cairo, all of them run by the state. Arabic-language music videos broadcast on these stations were crucial in defining the market for music in Egypt. National radio (very conservative in its selection of music) was another factor in shaping the availability of music. And below the broadcast level many songs are disseminated on cassettes.

Clearly there is a spectrum of scales relevant to the practice of music in Cairo. The music itself has undoubtedly changed over the years, although the direction of change is very much open to question (Danielson 1996). But the global scale is not necessarily decisive in the Egyptian musical market, and definitions of the "local" may in fact correspond to the national. One could certainly ask whether patterns of musical consumption in Cairo point toward convergence with global patterns, but such research might not inevitably lead to the conclusion that the global is becoming the "decisive framework for social life" (Featherstone and Lash 1995, 1–2). The state, an unregulated music industry rife with piracy, and live performance contexts largely geared to family events and rites of passage may lend distinctiveness to the practice of music in Cairo. To label these practices "local" in distinction to the sort of globalization manifested in the "world music awards" collapses a whole range of analytic possibilities to the point of insignificance—including the possibility that in Egypt the nation-state is still (or perhaps in some ways more than it had been in the recent past) a potent player in the construction of musical taste and musical habits. Joel Gordon's contribution to this volume suggests that the state also remains a key player in the cinema. None of this means that the phenomenon of globalization so heavily promoted in academia is entirely misplaced; it does suggest that the "local" category posed dialectically to globalization might have a life of its own—even a life within the supposedly obsolete nation-state framework.

GLOBAL AHISTORICISM

Another reason for caution about globalization is that it puts too high a premium on the newness of the phenomenon of transregional connection. Appadurai, for example, argues for "a general rupture in the tenor of intersocietal relations in the past few decades" (1996, 2). Migration and media create "mobile texts" (1996, 9) of an unprecedented sort. But are such phenomena really so unprecedented?

The career of an Egyptian dancer named Tahiyya Kariyuka suggests otherwise. Kariyuka took her stage name from the Carioca dance, which swept across the world in 1933, when Fred Astaire and Ginger Rogers immortalized the "Brazilian" Carioca in their film *Flying Down to Rio*. Like the Jajouka phenomenon described in this volume by Schuyler, or the "Gypsy" music of Upper Egyptian performers described here by Zirbel, the Carioca was geared more to American and European fantasies of exotic foreignness than to anything "Brazilian."[22]

When the film and the dance became an international hit in the 1930s, Cairo was a bit less out of the global first-run cinema loop than it is now. One of the film's first published advertisements in the Egyptian press showed Fred and Ginger grinning insouciantly seated amid massed chorus girls. The fashion for Carioca spread. In September 1934 another magazine displayed a *raqisat kariyuka*, a Carioca dancer, as the caption said on its back cover.[23] Shortly thereafter an Egyptian dancer named Badawiyya Muhammad Karim took the stage name Tahiyya Kariyuka. None of the images—those of the film, its advertisements, the "Carioca dancer" on the magazine, or Tahiyya Kariyuka herself—bore very much resemblance to each other. They were linked only by a common name and vaguely Latin American associations.

On the surface the creation in the United States of a "Brazilian" dance with no real connection to Brazil, and its adaptation in Egypt still another step or two from its original imagined inspiration, seems a perfect illustration of the workings of "global flows" across variously defined boundaries, be they national, ethnic, or confessional (Appadurai 1990). In one sense the migration of the Carioca stands out mainly by its precociousness; most commentary on globalization focuses on developments of the past three or four decades at most (or an even shallower time frame for some), whereas the Carioca moved across the globe sixty years ago. The Carioca might therefore be seen as an example of "modest precursors" (Appadurai 1990, 2) to the decentralized free-flowing world of the present, dominated by migration and transnational media.

But perhaps the Carioca was noteworthy for more than its precociousness. The quick dissemination of the phenomenon well before the advent of digital media suggests that the often-stated link between globalization and electronic media is overhyped. As mentioned above, few people object to the notion that transregional or even world systems are a long-standing phenomenon. World systems precede digital communication by centuries, not just by decades. What makes globalization of contemporary interest is some undefinable (because so variable) combination of increased intensity in the operations of world systems and consciousness of them. Tahiyya

Kariyuka's status in this respect is ambiguous. Her link to the "Brazilian" Carioca dance was a conscious choice, and for a time must have implied an obvious public association of foreign exoticism with a specific Egyptian dancer. The film that made the fashion popular was clearly present in Egypt, as the advertisements show, and was clearly the source of the dancer's name. But how long did the association last? Current generations of Egyptians are mostly unaware that the Carioca was a faux-Brazilian world fashion of the 1930s. Tahiyya Kariyuka's eventual fame did not stem from her renown as an importer of Latin American exoticism but from her film roles as a *mu'allima*—a small merchant of traditional Cairene neighborhoods—in Egyptian films that were remembered much longer than *Flying Down to Rio*.

Friedman (1995) notes a similar ambiguity in the spread of the American television serial "Dallas" to Nigeria. Nigerians consume an American product, but the product is used to define local social hierarchies that have nothing to do with America. Consequently the cosmopolitan who is amused by the ironies of social miscommunication created by a Nigerian viewing of an American serial is the real representative of globalism and, in Friedman's (1995, 73) opinion, of modernity. It also takes a cosmopolitan perspective to trace the migration of the faux-Brazilian American Carioca dance to Tahiyya Kariyuka the Egyptian dancer.

Friedman reminds us that imported objects have always been naturalizable to the point that origins are irrelevant at the level of social practice. Pasta came to Italy from China, and is therefore an element of global processes, but to modern Italians it has no cultural significance as a global phenomenon (Friedman 1995, 74). How many of the phenomena that now appear to be clear manifestations of globalization will ultimately resemble, in cultural terms, Italian pasta with its Chinese origins or Tahiyya Kariyuka's commandeering of the Carioca?[24] Many practices and objects are hybrid creations in terms of global processes, but they appear to be evidence of globalization only from a modern cosmopolitan perspective that views such practices as culturally discrete in the first place. This is the Achilles' heel of globalization theory—that its novelty is a projection from a certain perspective. In the past fifty years the world has indeed been characterized by a high degree of migration, but so too did Europe once experience waves of migration from the East over hundreds of years. Still Europe developed its own self-identity. The novelty of globalization is predicated on the ability of media to maintain a sense of connection among places, people, and things in motion. This might be the case, but close inspection of migratory phenomena often reveals a more complex process of forgetting, or creating cultural memories that may have little use for the modern cosmopolitan perspective of globalization.

The final three chapters in *Mass Mediations* explore the development of media-generated modernity well before the digital age. Roberta Dougherty's "Badi'a Masabni, Artiste and Modernist" shows the complexity of nationalist imagery from the 1930s. The "carnival of national identity" is a series of comic sketches—in prose and in caricatured images—that look at first glance like an eclectic hodgepodge of elements: Europeans, popular entertainers, singers who later became part of the expanding "heritage" (Shawan 1981) of Egyptian music, and politicians are all part of the mix. The sketches are mock courtroom scenes that are very much addressed to the presence of the occupying British colonial administration. They hardly suggest the stunned silence to which postcolonial theorists allude, but of course these narratives were not postcolonial: they were being produced in great quantity long before the British were finally expelled from Egypt. Of course, neither were these texts "literature" in the sense normally understood by metropolitan literature departments. Some of the figures to whom these sketches allude *were* well-known litterateurs; Dougherty's study demonstrates how complexly they were embedded in the popular culture of the period. Images of the politician, the singer, the nightclub impresaria, and the British official are all juxtaposed to one another in a sophisticated mix of linguistic registers. Significantly, the registers in question were Arabic, a language that was in no way silenced by the pressure of colonial discourse. In the context of sub-Saharan African literatures, Barber urges us to acknowledge "the full presence of texts in indigenous languages . . . not as a shadowy, vaguely delineated, value-laden 'oral heritage' in the background, but as a modern, mainstream, heterogeneous, hybrid and changing mode of discourse, created and recreated daily by the majority of the population" (1995, 25). Although the iconic value of "oral heritage" is rather different in an Arabic-speaking context than in African literature, this is still excellent advice. Dougherty demonstrates precisely the modernity that the above passage invokes and suggests, furthermore, that the roots of this modernity lie much deeper than the digital age.

The second of the final three chapters is "American Ambassador in Technicolor and Cinemascope" by Robert Vitalis. Like Dougherty, Vitalis takes a longer historical view than contemporary preoccupations with global frameworks would suggest. He examines the politics and economics of the Egyptian film industry before its nationalization in the 1960s, demonstrating that the economic crisis Egyptian filmmakers found themselves in by the mid-1950s was *not* caused entirely, or even predominantly, by the hegemony of American and European cinemas. Records of communication between U.S. film industry representatives and the U.S. government indicate that by the early 1950s foreign (mostly American) films were screened in a small minority of theaters and that there is every reason to believe that Egyptian films were more profitable than foreign films. The economic problems of the Egyptian cinema therefore had less to do with foreign competition from the United States and Europe than has commonly been assumed. It is not that American films were ever absent from the Egyptian market, but it is also not the case that foreigners controlled the market. Vitalis makes a convincing case that the Egyptian cinema, far from being crippled by unfair foreign competition, was actually unable to meet the demand of the local market. The Egyptian cinema should be understood as segmented: foreign films competed for only a part of the market, and film production in the end was hampered more by poor market organization than by foreign domination.[25] The implications of this segmentation have been hidden by a systematic attention to the most accessible segments of the market—the parts most conducive to the confirmation of globalization theory.

Vitalis's argument makes an intriguing comparison to Shryock's analysis of Arab Dearborn. Globalist rhetoric of the present overemphasizes the attraction of Arabic-language material for Arab immigrants to the United States, just as postcolonial theorists axiomatically disparage the ability of nonmetropolitan vernacular culture to flourish despite—or alongside— metropolitan culture. The result in both cases is to make the foreign segment of each market stand for a much more complex whole. Both Shryock and Vitalis contextualize their analyses in relation to world systems, but their conclusions contest the prominence given to "nomadic" global flows of culture. Vitalis cautions against forgetting "what is most basic to the story: Cairo and Alexandria were colonial cities with a distinctive cultural landscape." Shryock reminds us that Dearborn also has a distinctive cultural landscape. All the contributions to this volume help to recover something of this distinctiveness that is lost in the implicit universalism of globalism.

"The Golden Age before the Golden Age" is my own contribution to the volume. It addresses a point made by Vitalis—that Egyptian films historically had a strong inherent advantage over their foreign competition. Cinema was part of a vernacular culture elaborated in countless films, songs, articles, and images, all of which deserve to be taken more seriously. The sources for much of this vernacular culture were many, and the way it was constructed constantly changed, but at the same time it becomes naturalized to the point that origins become secondary to its local (often national) significance. The "nomadic" character of all the elements that make up a Tahiyya Kariyuka are like the figures described in the chapter—entertainers such as the singer Layla Murad or the comedian Najib al-Rihani. Their hybrid origins may or may not be part of their intertextually elaborated identity. But in a global perspective vernacular culture tends to disappear in favor of a well-regulated exoticism that paradoxically obscures real difference.

CONCLUSION: NEW APPROACHES TO POPULAR CULTURE

The focus of this introduction has been on mass mediation and what it implies for the scale of social action, for the character of modern societies, and for sociological analysis. The chapters themselves all address mass media in the context of popular culture, which is, of course, a potentially problematic term. Scholars everywhere have had to hash and rehash distinctions between culture of "the folk," "mass culture," and "elite culture." Popular culture has been cast in terms of preliterate "tradition" opposed to literate modernity (a dichotomy that almost all academics today reject). Popular culture can be populist culture—populist in the sense of political movements (Islamist, for example, or nationalist, or Nasserist). And in a Middle Eastern context popular culture has often been, and continues to be, associated with unmediated oral vernacular culture. For example, a proposed conference on Middle Eastern popular culture at Oxford categorizes popular culture as

1. Oral poetry performed/written down in the vernacular (especially Arabic, but other Middle Eastern languages also).
2. Artistic prose in the vernacular (e.g., hero cycles).
3. Tribal oral narrative.
4. Folk or traditional stories.
5. Drama or other forms of performance in the vernacular. ("Middle Eastern Popular Culture" 1998)

All the chapters in this volume would have to be shoehorned into category number five, "Drama or other forms of performance in the vernacular." And for many of them this would be quite a stretch (Danna International? public culture in Damascus? the mock courts presided over by the dancer Badiʻa Masabni?). But, in fact, the popular culture analyzed in this volume is far more closely intertwined with the lives of contemporary Middle Easterners than is the popular culture of four of the five categories devoted to forms of vernacular culture not directly addressed here.

In the end there is no all-purpose definition of popular culture. Trying to arrive at one would be a waste of time. The forms of popular culture should arise from ethnography, not from preconceived packages. The contributions to this volume all address what might be described as art and "entertainment," which, in their mass-mediated forms, we all refer to in everyday life as popular culture. Some of the material analyzed here can be mapped onto the sorts of high/low cultural distinctions commonly made in the West, but much of it cannot, and there is, in any case, a widespread recognition that the most interesting thing about cultural distinctions is never their inherent character but the process of differentiating one set of practices from another. In the end a focus on popular culture gives the volume an internal consistency, but no author in the volume would be satisfied to have his or her chapter described as merely an attempt to legitimate or define the study of popular culture in the Middle East. One aspect of our claim to newness in our approach to popular culture is that we want to shift our focus away from what it is and toward a focus on what it does. What it does is to create new scales of communication and new dimensions of modern identity.

I have consciously not invoked a commonly used neologism that articulates with a great deal of the material analyzed here. This term is "public culture," the key concept of a very influential journal by the same name. Arjun Appadurai and Carol Breckenridge, the founders of the movement and the journal, neatly encompassed much of what might be called "popular culture" by focusing on the local production and reception of transnational forms of culture (Breckenridge and Appadurai 1988). The idea of public culture has increasingly crystallized around the analysis of flows of people, objects, and cultural practices, which are taken to constitute a pluralized modernity no longer seen as something created in Europe and disseminated to the rest of the world. But as much of the above discussion argues, public culture and its attendant concern with transnationalism and cultural flows have become a hegemonic insight. "The global produces the local" has become an orthodoxy—one that most observers would characterize as a productive one, but nonetheless an orthodoxy that is beginning to think for would-be cultural analysts rather than a framework that helps them to think in ways they otherwise might not have.

All the contributions presented here can claim to have escaped the straitjacket of the Oxford popular culture conference. However, none of us can claim to have transcended the globalist perspective or to have overturned it. That is part of the anxiety of scale to which the volume responds. The mediated popular culture analyzed in this book falls somewhere below the radar of transnational culture but can never be understood in isolation. This is perhaps a form of popular culture that mediates the homogenizing tendencies of global culture and the fragmentation of localism. The scale of such a mediation might well be described as national, and predictions of its demise may prove to be premature.

NOTES

1. This is, of course, not the same issue as that of the overall institutional health of non-European studies. The point is that, relatively speaking, the huge disparities in the vitality of area-defined academic specialization can be observed very easily in the job market. Jobs created during the past decade for specialists in the favored areas—particularly Latin America, Asia, and Africa as well as U.S. ethnic community derivations of the same—outnumber those earmarked for Middle East specialists

many times over. Anthropology provides an excellent example. The November 1997 *American Anthropological Association Newsletter* advertised 60 tenure-track positions, of which 7 were earmarked for Asia specialists, 13 for Latin Americanists, 11 for Africanists, and 3 for Native Americanists. For Middle East specialists: 0. The three Native Americanist positions advertised for this one month—numerically the smallest area-defined category in the total—are equal to the number of Middle East positions advertised in the entire 1998–99 academic year. The 1998–99 academic year offered the largest number of potentially entry-level Middle East positions in a single year since at least the early 1990s. Jobs in academic departments may or may not have explicit connections to institutionalized area studies, and might or might not be associated with novel institutional affiliations such as ethnic studies. But whether it is in a department or an interdisciplinary center, a job for a Latin Americanist or an Asianist is by definition not a job for someone who studies the Middle East. Middle East specialists are therefore forced to choose between selling themselves as "generalists" or casting themselves as academic dinosaurs laboring within a soon-to-be-extinct (for Middle East specialists at any rate) area framework. To make matters worse, not only are new jobs for Middle East specialists not being created, but old Middle East specialist positions will often not be replaced with the same specialization. Lisa Hajjar and Steve Niva note, "A MESA survey of faculty in the U.S. indicated that an estimated 27 percent of the Middle East positions at private colleges and universities and 36 percent at public institutions would not be refilled" (1997, 9 n. 30). Given this planned erosion of existing Middle East specialization, combined with the near-lockout of Middle East specializations in area-specific positions for certain disciplines (roughly half the jobs listed in the sample *AAA Newsletter* cited above and often an even higher proportion of the total), the future for Middle East area studies looks grim. Barring the unlikely event that Middle East specialists are disproportionately hired in non-area-specific jobs, we can expect to see a continuing decrease in the institutional presence of Middle East specialists.

2. Aside from those who see a pro-Israeli stance as beneficial to American interests according to various political/economic/military standards, the segment of American society that tends to strongly define the region primarily through the fortunes of Israel include American Zionists and dispensationalist Christians who see the Second Coming of Christ as inextricably tied to the conversion of the Jews once they have all been gathered in modern-day Israel (Hardy 1994). Americans only casually interested in the region also tend to see the Middle East through the Arab-Israeli conflict because of heavy media coverage of the conflict, to the disadvantage of any other issue conceivably connected to the area.

3. Indeed, it is often Middle East specialists themselves who argue, implausibly, that their institutional marginalization is the well-deserved fruit of their own intellectual backwardness. The apparent self-loathing of some Middle East specialists is rarely, if ever, expressed in print. It is part of what Paul Rabinow (1986), in the slightly different context of the politics of fieldwork, called "corridor talk." By this he meant "those domains that cannot be analyzed or refuted, and yet are directly central to hierarchy" (1986, 253). In the past two decades the hierarchy of academic area specializations has been restructured to the disadvantage of Middle East specialists. Middle East specialists themselves, largely in informal "corridor" contexts, have been complicit in this restructuring.

4. An example is the pro-Israeli Washington Institute for Near East Policy, which supplies American politicians with Middle East "expertise" unambiguously hostile to Arab interests. There are no left-leaning or pro-Arab organizations with anything remotely approaching the resources of the Washington Institute.

5. Contrary to Baudrillard's (1995) characterization of the Gulf War as a creation of the media, the conflict made perfect sense in old-fashioned terms of defending crucial resources—crucial according to national criteria. The resources in question, of course, were not actually "ours" in any sense. The official reason for the war—to defend Kuwaiti sovereignty—was without credibility. I do not mean to defend the war. The point is that the political rationale for the war was clear and conventional: it was about oil. Baudrillard's emphasis on media-constructed consumption as the paramount factor in the war is reasonable insofar as the media is an expression, and perhaps a partial cause, of the high-consumption suburban design of American cities. As a component in a culture of consumption, the media is as dependent on oil as the automobile. Energy was the root of the war, not media. Disputes over resources such as oil are very conventional in terms of national interests. If there was a role for media consumption in the war it was, at most, with regard to the mechanics of the conflict. The media, owned by corporations that may be part of a putatively transnational "mediascape" (Appadurai 1996, 35) but that are still linked to national interests, was little more than a glossy propaganda machine working in the interests of one nation, the United States. The propaganda machine that sanitizes the true nature of war might be a feature of the twentieth century (Fussell 1989), but it was certainly not a novel feature of the Gulf War.

6. For example, jobs for the study of Arab or Muslim immigrants are rare, if not completely absent. There are individuals who study Arab- or Muslim-American communities, but their jobs are not necessarily structured around those subjects, and in terms of the formal criteria for new positions Arab- and Muslim-Americans have been virtually invisible, while the number of jobs for the study of the ethnic communities defined by the national census has increased dramatically.

7. Europe shows a pattern similar to the United States in the sense that its "near abroad" (the Mediterranean, in this case including, obviously, substantial portions of the cold war "Pakistan to Morocco" definition of the Middle East) receives higher priority than the rest of the globe (Rogan 1997).

8. But see Rasmussen (1996) for an analysis of how a musical aesthetic specific to Arab America has developed in Dearborn. Langlois (1996) shows how Algerian Rai music in France became autonomous from Rai production in Algeria. As in the Iranian case discussed here by Shay, political crisis contributed to the differentiation of French and Algerian musical styles.

9. Of course, Israel's relationship to metropolitan societies is vastly different from Egypt's. Indeed, with a substantial European population, relatively open access to metropolitan markets, and political support in the United States so strong that large transfers of capital take place almost entirely on Israel's terms (rather than with the crippling conditions attached to aid transferred to "Third World" nations like Egypt), Israel can easily be seen as a quasi-metropolitan state. But the singer Sa'ida Sultan—the subject of Swedenburg's chapter—is of Yemeni origin and is not part of mainstream Israeli society. It would therefore be misleading to characterize her as intrinsically connected to the quasi-metropolitan aspects of Israel.

10. The literature premised on the demise of the nation-state and consequent rise of globalization is enormous and rapidly expanding. Globalization (e.g., Appadurai 1996; Chatterjee 1993; Featherstone and Lash 1995; Wilson and Dissanayake 1996) is the overarching analytic framework of this literature. Within this framework a number of related topics have been elaborated, such as exile and diaspora cultures (Naficy 1993; Pieterse 1995), transnationalism (Basch, Glick-Schiller, and Blanc 1994; Marcus 1993), hybridity (Bhabha 1994), and the apparently decentralized medium of the Internet (Marcus 1996a). Globalization and its related agendas also thoroughly dominate the academic job market, as well as popular (usually business-oriented) publications, guaranteeing that globalization discourse will continue to be reproduced in the short to medium term.

11. Rouse (1995) highlights a rhetoric similar to that of *Wired* in advertisements by the MCI long-distance telephone company. Furthermore, the MCI advertisement "seems at once to echo and recode the work of Jean-François Lyotard (1984) and David Harvey (1989)" (Rouse 1995, 355). Again, as with Shohat and Stam (1996) or Appadurai (1996), the focus of Rouse's and Kearny's analysis centers on possibilities for harnessing or escaping the hegemony of new media and the capitalism that drives them. All are aware of the congruence of business and academic rhetoric; all assume an ultimately different significance of globalization than would the typical business analysis.

12. For more on Sonallah Ibrahim and his works, see Mehrez 1994. Two chapters of Mehrez's book are devoted to Ibrahim.

13. This is not to say that the attitude of commentators on globalization is uniform with respect to the potential of the nation-state to form a meaningful cultural identity. For example, Featherstone (1996) leaves the door open for nationalism as a still-potent frame of reference. Rouse (1995) characterizes the current moment, as least in the United States, as one of national/transnational dialectic. The general tenor of most discussion is toward viewing the world as a dialectic between homogenizing economic processes and fragmenting cultural identities formed increasingly outside the control of nation-states.

14. Said (1990) argues that European languages, English in particular, can, indeed must, be co-opted by those with a counterhegemonic agenda. Ahmad (1992b) disputes this point vehemently. See also Ngugi wa Thiong'o (1986) for an argument in favor of Third World writers breaking free of European-language media and thereby potentially limiting their audience to a national scale.

15. To date only *Tilka al-ra'iha*, Ibrahim's first novel, has been translated into English (Ibrahim 1971). He has, however, fared better in French, into which three of his five major works have been translated (Mehrez 1994, 151 n. 3).

16. See my own contribution to this volume (chap. 13). Although the Arabic-language films most often seen by Arabic speakers living in the Middle East are overwhelmingly Egyptian, the English-language literature on Egyptian cinema is quite limited. Khan (1969) has written on the Egyptian cinema, but his book is now dated. As in literature, the situation is better in other European languages (Lüders 1989; Thorval 1975; Wassef 1994), and there has been considerable publication in Arabic. But the predominant trend has been to conflate Egyptian cinema with "Arab" cinema (Arasoughly 1996; Khayati 1996; Landau 1958; Shafik 1998), or even "Arab and African" cinema (Khelil 1994; Malkmus and Armes 1991), giving

the misleading impression that Arab films circulate freely in an Arabic-speaking market or, in the latter case, that Arab and African films are somehow linked. In fact, outside the Egyptian cinema Arabic-language films are heavily dependent on either state funding (in the case of Syrian films and those of a few other Arab countries) or, more commonly, financing from metropolitan institutions (e.g., most Palestinian and North African films). The only films that circulate freely in the Arab world are precisely the Egyptian commercial films that are most likely to be ignored in metropolitan literature. Conflating Egyptian with other Arabic-language films creates a larger pool of "good" (by metropolitan standards) films to be analyzed. From our own metropolitan perspective it is those films that become "the Arab cinema," when in fact the "Arab cinema" in question is heavily skewed toward films made to be marketed to metropolitan audiences and with metropolitan financing.

17. By contrast, most academic commentary assumes that core-periphery distinctions are not as useful as they once were and that inequalities between regions are fragmented (e.g., Featherstone 1995, 12–13).

18. Of course, the political right (excluding some of its religious adherents) does not recognize a distinction between the accumulation of wealth and moral or ethical concerns. Harvey (1989) describes the mechanism of capitalist "flexible accumulation" that erodes the relevance of nation-states as a frame of analytic reference and, not coincidentally, diminishes possibilities for promoting many of the ethical concerns Appadurai mentions.

19. Appadurai's (1996, 27–47) "scapes" (of ethnicity, media, technology, capital, and ideology) are a similar prescription for providing an alternative to the nation-state.

20. With the exception of an interview with Paul Sagan, director of an interactive news project at Time-Warner (Laughlin and Monberg 1996), *Connected* says almost nothing about the commercial aspects of the Internet. Of course, commercial interests are now the driving force behind the medium's development. Most electronic messages are exchanged between machines rather than people, and generally for the purpose of managing money. And regarding the parts of the Internet that humans do use, its commercial proponents do not hesitate to advocate its promise. Esther Dyson (1995), for example, believes that the point of the medium is not "content" but the ability of "content" to attract readers to advertising. The logic, of course, is not unlike that of American television.

21. For example, Homi Bhabha emphasizes the creativity of liminality: "What is at issue is the performative nature of differential identities: the regulation and negotiation of those spaces that are continually, *contingently*, 'opening out,' remaking the boundaries, exposing the limits of any claim to a singular or autonomous sign of difference—be it class, gender or race. . . . It is, if I may stretch a point, an interstitial future, that emerges *in-between* the claims of the past and the needs of the present" (1994, 219).

22. The choreographer of the Carioca dance was Hermes Pan. The Carioca number was the finale, and for many the most memorable part, of the film. Pan's vision of the Carioca revolved around the novel idea of Astaire and Rogers performing the dance with their foreheads touching (Thomas 1984, 91).

23. The first photo was in *al-Kawakib* (April 23, 1934, 12–13), which was published by Dar al-Hilal, one of Egypt's oldest and most distinguished publishing

houses. The April 23 notice announced the imminent opening of the film at the Royale Theater. No advertisements for *Flying Down to Rio* ever appeared in *al-Kawakib*. The magazine with the "Carioca dancer" on the back was *al-Ithnayn* (September 10, 1934), which was also published by Dar al-Hilal.

24. Friedman's (1995, 86–88) solution to this problem is to emphasize the long-term process of systematizing global relations of production and consumption but to reject the notion that globalization—the consciousness of these relations and the ability to live within them—extends beyond a thin stratum of cosmopolitan elites who occupy an individualized, self-regulated, "identity space" of modernity.

25. Profits from Egyptian films did not find their way back to the studios that made them. The main reason for this was the chronically weak relationship between film producers and distributors. Separation between producers and distributors prevented the horizontal and vertical industrial integration that characterized Hollywood film production during the heyday of the studio era (before antitrust legislation in the late 1940s broke up this arrangement). For the Egyptian cinema this was particularly relevant to the ability of the industry to exploit Arabic-speaking markets outside Egypt. This was where crucial profits without serious foreign competition could potentially have been made were it not for the unfavorable arrangements among film producers, studios, and foreign distributors.

TWO

Public Culture in Arab Detroit
Creating Arab/American Identities
in a Transnational Domain

Andrew Shryock

*The shared economic infrastructure of advanced industrial society and its in-
escapable implications will continue to ensure that men are dependent on culture,
and that culture requires standardization over quite wide areas, and needs to be
maintained and serviced by centralized agencies. In other words, men will continue
to owe their employability and social acceptability to sustained and complex training, which cannot be supplied by kin or local groups. This being so, the definition of
political units and boundaries will not be able to ignore with impunity the distribution of cultures. By and large, ignoring minor and innocuous exceptions, the nationalist imperative of the congruence of political unit and of culture will continue
to apply. In that sense, one need not expect the age of nationalism to come to an end.*
ERNEST GELLNER, *Nations and Nationalism*

Gellner made the above prediction in 1983, when the age of nationalism,
in scholarly circles at least, was just beginning. Benedict Anderson's *Imagined Communities*, originally published in the same year, turned nationalism
into an anthropological obsession, with the result that modernity—a quality both Anderson and Gellner ascribed to nationalism in the West—was finally recognized as a legitimate object of ethnographic research. The topics that consumed anthropology in the 1980s (reflexivity, political
economy, historicity, postcolonialism, and popular culture) were framed,
more explicitly than ever before, in relation to metropolitan, Western-de-
rived social forms. The nationalist imperative was never far from view, even
if there was always something vaguely "imaginary" about it.

The trend continues. Yet today Gellner's vision of endless nationalism is
often treated as unlikely and uninteresting in roughly equal degrees. Metropolitan intellectuals of all sorts, along with businesspeople and politicians, are now drawn to *post*modern, *trans*national images of community.

As a site of cultural reproduction, the nation-state no longer seems big enough; its peculiar resources—industries, workforces, currencies, identities, ideologies—are constantly spilling across its boundaries. This is certainly true of "popular culture," the vast network of information, narratives, and artistic performances conveyed by television, VCR, CD, cassette tape, film, and print technologies. Among anthropologists the study of popular culture is now identified closely with transnational approaches,[1] a development more unusual than it might at first appear. The media in which popular culture travels evolved alongside the nation-state; indeed, they exist everywhere in symbiotic relationships with ruling elites. According to Gellner and Anderson, these relationships produce shared, literate, self-consciously modern cultures that exist (or hope one day to exist) under the protection of their own national governments.

The kinks in the model are obvious. Elites are not motivated solely by national interests, and the demand for CNN, Rai music, and Hindi films is not limited (any longer at least) to Americans, Algerians, and Indians. Popular culture flows across international borders alongside (and often more freely than) the people who consume, produce, and distribute it. The neat cultural boundaries favored by nationalists are now hopelessly blurred by a popular imagination that, the advertisers and analysts assure us, is virtually global in scope.

> Through the experience of everything from food, to culinary habits, music, television, entertainment, and cinema, it is now possible to experience the world's geography vicariously, as a simulacrum. The interweaving of simulacra in daily life brings together different worlds (of commodities) in the same space and time. But it does so in such a way as to conceal almost perfectly any trace of origin, of the labour processes that produced them, or of the social relations implicated in their production. (Harvey 1989, 300)

David Harvey's cautionary note—that public culture obscures the means of its own production—is well worth remembering. At a time when prominent advocates of transnational approaches seem to be bedazzled by the wonderful, mixed-up agglomeration of cultural commodities that the global market makes available to them, it is important to realize (1) that commercial goods originate in places, (2) that mass media and international markets are fragile, highly complex forms of organization that connect places, (3) that media and markets are variously secured by, dependent on, and answerable to the power of states, which govern places, and (4) that contemporary states are nationalist in design. Once these conditions are granted, what becomes of the transnational domain in which popular culture circulates so freely? How do we locate it? Is it just another simulacrum, a kind of "virtual reality" that feeds on the global appetites of metropolitan consumers? Is the transnationalization of popular culture a response to political and economic changes that disconnect people (as well as media and markets) from "original" places?

In this chapter I approach these issues by way of Detroit's Arab community, a large immigrant/ethnic population whose public culture flourishes amid a dense array of (trans)national attachments. In Arab Detroit the relationship between nation and culture is continually rendered problematic by the need to reterritorialize a community that exists across states, between identities, and out of place. The forces that sustain popular culture in Arab Detroit, I argue, are animated by a thoroughly modern, nationalist discourse. In its American forms this discourse is still powerful enough to assimilate, effectively contain, and even "celebrate" the transnational domains that materialize within it.

A MAP OF SORTS: A QUICK INTRODUCTION TO ARAB DETROIT

The Detroit area is home to America's largest, most highly concentrated population of Arab immigrants. There are now roughly two hundred thousand people of Arab descent living in and around the city.[2] Arabs have been coming to Detroit since the late nineteenth century, and they continue to arrive in the thousands each year. The vast majority are from Lebanon, Palestine, Yemen, and Iraq. Initially they were drawn by Michigan's booming automobile industry; today they are often refugees of war or victims of political oppression and economic hardship. They come to Detroit to live among the large networks of kin and fellow villagers that now exist there. As of 1995 Arab-Americans composed Michigan's second-largest (and fastest-growing) minority population.[3] Indeed, certain parts of Metro Detroit have acquired an unmistakably Arab aspect. Barbara Aswad's description of East Dearborn captures the vibrant feel of America's largest Lebanese enclave:

> As one walks along the streets in the Lebanese Muslim community in Dearborn, one feels transplanted back to the Middle East. Fifty or more Lebanese shops line both sides of a six-block stretch of Warren Avenue, where eight years ago there were only eight. Five bakeries and eight restaurants emit the culinary smells of the Middle East. There are also twelve fruit and vegetable markets, two supermarkets, two beauty salons, numerous doctors, dentists, and a pharmacist, a furniture shop, real estate, insurance, and printing office, auto shops, a clothing store, Arabic bookstores, a publishing company, an Arab social service agency, the Islamic Institute for Knowledge, and a Shi'i mosque. Signs are in both Arabic and English. There is much activity on this strip. Men sometimes sit at tables on the sidewalk, women usually cover their heads, and many wear Muslim and village attire. Children are seen rushing to religious and Arabic classes at the Institute. (1992, 167)

The area along Warren Avenue—which now has 117 Arab-owned businesses[4]—is only one of several distinct Arab populations in Metro Detroit.

Highly assimilated middle- and upper-class Christians, whose parents and grandparents came to America from Greater Syria before the fall of the Ottoman Empire, can be found in Detroit's northern and eastern suburbs; Iraqi Chaldeans, a close-knit community of Aramaic-speaking Catholics who own the majority of Detroit's small grocery and liquor stores, live mostly in Detroit, Southfield, and Bloomfield Hills; Palestinian professionals, mostly Christians from the West Bank village of Ramallah, have settled in Livonia; Palestinians from the Jerusalem suburb of Beit Hanina and Yemenis, both of peasant backgrounds, live together in Dearborn's South End, a neighborhood that lies in the shadow of the Ford Rouge Plant and boasts its own mosque and business district.

This broad range of lifestyles and levels of assimilation has made the Detroit Arab community hard to represent, both intellectually and politically. Despite its proximity to the University of Michigan, which houses one of the best Middle East studies centers in the country, very few Middle East scholars have worked in Arab Detroit. It seems too big, too diffuse, too resistant to characterization—too "over here." The small body of research that accumulated in the 1970s and 1980s took up the difficult task of determining the size, internal composition, and history of Detroit's major Arab immigrant populations (e.g., Abraham and Abraham 1983; Aswad 1974); it was descriptive in nature, and the patterns it located have since been woven into the popular narratives of identity and experience Arab Detroiters tell the outside world.

A more visible (and generally less accessible) tradition of self-representation is found in the lucrative trade in Arab cultural commodities. Detroit is awash in Arabic-language videos, cassette tapes, television and radio programs, books, newsletters, daily and weekly newspapers, and magazines, as well as "Middle Eastern" grocery stores, bakeries, pastry shops, and restaurants. Non-Arab Detroiters are nowadays quite familiar with Lebanese cuisine, but the trade in Arab cultural commodities has been oriented, until very recently, toward Arabic speakers. It is fragmented along national, village, and sectarian lines in ways most non-Arabs can hardly understand, and attempts to weave this flow of goods and images into a common fabric of Arab-American ethnic identity have been made, by and large, only in the English-speaking sectors of the Arab community.

The differences between Arabic- and English-speaking styles of cultural production add to the daunting complexity of Arab Detroit as an object of study. As I argue throughout this chapter, both styles are tied closely to the idea of national communities. The English-speaking style, however, is more consciously attuned to the themes of ethnicity, multiculturalism, and diversity that circulate in the larger society. Its agenda is the creation of a new identity that is equally "Arab" and "American." The result is a double-bound (but not quite hybrid) field of public culture that, for all its inherent contradictions, allows a growing number of Arab Detroiters to attach themselves to popular American models of community even as they cultivate what are imagined to be essentially Arab ones.

BEFORE WE GO TRANSNATIONAL: (UN)PACKING OUR THEORETICAL BAGGAGE

There is clearly something in the idea that distance lends enhancement, if not enchantment, to the anthropological vision.

EDWIN ARDENER, *The Voice of Prophecy*

If Arab Detroit is too close, too "in-between" to attract the attention of Middle East area scholarship, it is now suddenly *near* enough to attract the attention of anthropologists, among whom distance is losing its visionary charms. With the steady growth of global communication and transportation networks, the ethnographer's ability to move through remote, physically distant worlds is no longer unusual; in fact, it is not even a necessary component of anthropological practice. Today most American anthropologists do their Ph.D. fieldwork in North America (Givens and Jablonski 1995, 11–12); and with the growing appeal of theory and historicism to the discipline, more and more fieldwork is being done in the library, the archive, and (just as likely) the coffeehouse.

As ethnographers settle down, the "natives" become increasingly mobile. They regularly enter—indeed, they suffuse—urban culture in the metropolitan West, where "remote areas," now unexpectedly near, are sold to us as ethnic villages, cultivated as political constituencies, mined for cheap labor, developed as points of entry into foreign markets, or cordoned off as crime-ridden slums. These new immigrant communities are not bereft of singularity. One could hardly mistake Arab Detroit for New York's "Little Brazil" (Margolis 1994) or Los Angeles's "New Persian Empire" (Naficy 1993). Still, it is hard to conceptualize this singularity using the old logic of place. Among Arabs in Detroit, a popular alternative idiom is one anthropologists are leaving behind: "distance." Coming to America and becoming American are acts that require movement: specifically, movement in an occidental direction. Arab immigrants are often called *mughtarabeen*, or people who go West, and the Arab community in Detroit calls itself *al-jaliya*, a term that conjures up images of an ethnic enclave living far from its place of origin.

The idea of an ancestral place—expressed in terms of nostalgia, estrangement, and enduring obligations—is a leitmotiv of immigrant experience. It is especially strong among Arab Detroiters, most of whom trace their origins to about a dozen peasant villages in Lebanon, Palestine, Yemen, and Iraq. The new idiom of transnationalism, however, often seems designed to swamp these imaginative yet somehow too simple communions in a wash of cultural flows, fragmentation, mix-up, deterritorialization, and other splintering metaphors. The rhetoric is relentless; one sees it everywhere, and everywhere it accentuates the same litany of themes.

> Migrations are producing cultural heterogeneity; diasporic conditions for increasing and increasingly large groups of people are redefining geographic loyalties and commitments; rapid and spreading urbanization is transforming traditional social relations and conceptions of selves; the communications revolution is redefining local and global relations, and the constitution of subjects. Identities, in the light of these dramatic changes, are tending increasingly to cut across traditional political boundaries. (Goldberg and Zegeye 1995, 3)

Clearly, this is a metanarrative. Why, in our postmodern age, does it not inspire greater incredulity? On close inspection the conditions described in this passage are not as novel as they seem. The "new world" they conjure up bears an uncanny resemblance to Henry Ford's Detroit, circa 1920: a city teeming with immigrant labor, intermingled diasporas, transnational associations, rampant urbanization, and new political identities. Communities of this sort are perhaps more common today, and the global processes that create them occur at a more dizzying pace. But the power globalization rhetoric now enjoys among social scientists, historians, and litterateurs springs from other sources.

Like most big narratives, the globalization story "has as its latent or manifest purpose the desire to moralize the events of which it treats" (White 1987, 14). The sense of disruption and the lack of closure that mark the transnational metanarrative are *positively valued* by many of the analysts who invoke them (Clifford 1988; Appadurai 1991; Bhabha 1994), and this celebratory tone reflects the increased tactical mobility Western intellectuals (and the college-educated metropolitan classes) bring to their ongoing management of the borderlands between human communities. Although the most articulate proponents of transnational studies often hail from the "elite sectors of the postcolonial world" (Appadurai 1993, 411)—a quick glance at almost any issue of *Public Culture* will prove this point—the sudden appearance of the "Third World in the First" (Rafael 1993) has not provoked the latest round of moralistic, transnational storytelling. Rather, it is the relentless spread of metropolitan social forms into postcolonial domains that makes global systems (and narratives of globalization) possible. As the structures, practices, and attitudes that define modernity are imposed on wider territories and larger numbers of people, "new alignments made across borders, types, nations, and essences are rapidly coming into view" (Said 1993, xxv).

But the emerging view is still notoriously fuzzy, with the result that, *for the metropolitan intellectual,* (1) cultural forms are no longer convincingly old or new—invented traditions flourish alongside cultural schemas of demonstrable antiquity—and (2) human communities are no longer categorically Other. Instead, they can be alien and admissible, remote and near to hand, all at the same time, all in the same place. This has not made ethnography harder to do; nor has it "liberated" anthropology from its traditional fascination with local worlds. In his discussion of advertising agencies in Trinidad, for instance, Daniel Miller (1995a) suggests that local advertisers profit from the demand for global consumer products by convincing foreign companies that imported goods will not sell there unless they are attached to tastes and desires unique to the island. Only commercials produced in Trinidad, they argue, can secure such attachments. This lucrative exercise in "cultural translation," undertaken on behalf of highly deterritorialized, transnational corporations, is not unlike the work of anthropologists, who profit from their ability to ground knowledge of humanity—itself a metropolitan, highly deterritorialized construct—in knowledge of *particular* human communities. That is why ethnography, more than most disciplines, is well placed to "reveal the internal contradictions and differences that emerge when one insists that the global form is always to be located also in its specific local manifestation" (Miller 1995a, 9).

The "desire to moralize" that animates *critical* brands of transnational storytelling[5] has little to do, then, with a Bakhtinian carnival of identities supposedly unleashed by collapsing boundaries and withering states. It alerts us, instead, to new hegemonies capable of (re)bounding local and translocal identities alike. The globalizing logic that Richard Wilk detects in the staging of beauty pageants in Belize is, not surprisingly, the logic behind almost all forms of cultural representation now available to the ethnographer: those made by groups and individuals, by selves and others, in public and in private.

> The global stage does not consist of common content, a lexicon of goods or knowledge. Instead it is a common set of formats and structures that mediate between cultures; something more than a flow of things, or of the meanings attached to things, or even the channels along which those things and meanings flow. . . . [T]he connections between localities are created by widespread and common forms of contest for the exercise of power over *what* to produce, consume, watch, read and write. These contests follow channels that put diversity in a common frame, and scale it along a limited number of dimensions, celebrating some kinds of difference and submerging others. (Wilk 1995, 111)

Arabs in Detroit, for instance, bear countless marks of Otherness. Their political and religious beliefs, their ideas about gender and family life, their ways of doing business—all differ markedly from those of the larger society.

Yet for all their peculiarities Arab immigrants come to Detroit already immersed in modern institutions: nation-states, public schools, secular universities, consumer-oriented market economies, and the (rather narrow) spectrum of political ideologies that accompany these forms. The result is a disorienting mix of similarity and difference, an open cultural flow in which metropolitan social forms, hegemonic and imperfectly shared by immigrants and locals alike, become the context in which mainstreams are continually re-created. Labor, commodities, and ideas circulate in these mainstreams, which are also called communities. Unlike Said's "new alignments," however, which coalesce across "borders, types, nations, and essences," I argue that Arabs in Detroit use precisely these typological ideas to build communities that cohere despite (and because of) their problematic relationship to place.

POPULAR CULTURE IN ARABIC-SPEAKING DETROIT: REFLECTED IMAGES FROM ELSEWHERE

In all frankness, the world today has seen the end of military conflict (except for local regions in which the flames of war have not yet gone out). With the end of the Cold War polarization, the contest among nations has become a nationalistic and cultural struggle even before it is an economic one, inasmuch as each nation has returned to itself, deriving its power at the expense of others. From all this we conclude that, as an Arab community, we need urgently to protect ourselves and our place under the sun because history shows no mercy. The means to this end is the preservation of our language, our culture, our heritage . . . and we are honored to promote this goal and bolster our community's efforts to protect our place, our future, and our civilization. (Berry 1995a, 3; my translation)

With these words of introduction, Ahmad Berry launched his new magazine, *Panorama*, a glossy monthly that mixes news of Arab Detroit with that of Lebanon and the larger Arab world. Berry is producer, host, and owner of Arabic Time Television, one of the six local networks and sixteen independent Arabic-language programs currently shown on Dearborn Cable Vision. Arabic Time Television (*al-Fatra al-'Arabiyya*) is on the air for two hours, six nights a week, on Ethnic Access Channel 23. In 1995 it was rated the number one Arabic program in a nonscientific, in-house poll conducted by Cable Vision Industries (CVI), and the publication of *Panorama* magazine, despite the lofty rhetoric of national survival, is Berry's attempt to capitalize on this success by extending his small media empire into the realm of print. The feature stories advertised on the inaugural cover page of *Panorama* include the following: "Arabic Time TV Ranks First among Dearborn Cable Programs." The magazine's second issue consists mostly of materials recycled from other Arabic and English periodicals (as did the first issue); the space given to advertising is much greater; and the back cover carries free publicity for the moneymaking operation *Panorama* is designed to promote:

Advertising with

The No. 1

Arabic Time Television

Is A Wise Choice

Few would question this wisdom. The Arabic-language TV scene, which draws advertising dollars from Metro Detroit's pool of five thousand Arab-owned businesses,[6] is by far the most lucrative arena of popular culture in Arab Detroit. Berry's success in this market is based on his keen entrepreneurial spirit, but it also depends on more peculiar factors: (1) the tradition-oriented, conservative—or, more exactly, conservationist—agenda he endorses in his *Panorama* editorials; and (2) his ability to build media networks that subsist on materials that are recycled and copied (often without permission) from state-financed, government-controlled media sources in the Arab world. Berry's career is made in the transnational domain. Like Arab Detroit's other TV impresarios, he profits from his access to Arab national media and, more important, from his location outside the jurisdiction of the Arab governments that control these media.

ARABIC TV IN DEARBORN:
HOW IT STARTED AND THE SHAPE IT'S IN

When Cable Vision Industries came to Dearborn in 1981, it had fifty-four channels—far too many to fill. According to Jackie Kaiser, CVI program manager, the idea of an ethnic access channel was originally floated with Dearborn's Italian and Polish communities in mind. No one expected Arab immigrants to use the service. Yet the Italians and Poles, for all the proddings of CVI and Dearborn's Italian mayor, failed to put together viable programming. It was Lebanese and Chaldean programmers who eventually monopolized Ethnic Access. Today all of the channel's shows are in Arabic. The Arabs surprised CVI management again by producing their own, Arabic-language advertising, thereby turning a nonprofit community service channel into a very healthy cash cow. CVI altered its format accordingly. Today the 5:00 P.M. to 1:00 A.M. time slots are leased. Shows scheduled between 1:00 P.M. and 5:00 P.M. are broadcast free of charge. The sixteen afternoon shows are supplied by local mosques, religious associations, and Lebanese social clubs; in the evening the six networks, all produced by individuals, take over.[7] I have been watching Arabic television in Dearborn since 1990, and I am still fascinated by three qualities of the programming that, I would argue, are broadly characteristic of popular culture in Detroit's Arabic-language "mainstream."

(1) *With scattered exceptions, all programming is in Arabic.* The monolingual nature of Arabic TV might seem commonsensical at first, but it runs counter to linguistic patterns dominant in the community. The majority of Arab Detroiters are bilingual; many Chaldeans are trilingual (speaking English, Arabic, and Aramaic); and tens of thousands of Arab Detroiters speak only English. The latter population is an obvious growth market, but no local programmers are attempting to cultivate it as an audience. Arab Detroit's two most successful newspapers—the *Arab-American News* and the *Chaldean Detroit Times*—went bilingual in the 1980s, and the parade of small Arab journals and magazines that march in and out of print are mostly English/Arabic ventures as well. Ahmad Berry's *Panorama*, for instance, is bilingual. The programming on his Arabic Time Television, however, has not yet been affected by this trend.

(2) *All the shows are locally produced, but they consist almost entirely of imported programming.* To call the programming "imported" is a courtesy. Much of it is pirated, and copyright law (as understood in the United States) is thoroughly ignored by the impresarios of Arabic TV. In an average night of viewing, one might see a Syrian soap opera, an Egyptian movie, a Lebanese variety show, an Iraqi sports program, and several shows in which a local host introduces footage from overseas. The material is copied on videocassette, and the granular, jumpy quality of the tape suggests that the duplicates are themselves nth-generation copies. But techniques are steadily improving. Berry's Arabic Time Television, for instance, has lately become a time-delayed version of Future Television (*Talafiziyun al-Mustaqbal*), a popular Lebanese network. It is commonly said in Dearborn that Future Television employs one of Berry's relatives, who sends high-quality videocassette copies of network programming to Detroit. Before Berry airs this material, he superimposes the Arabic Time Television logo over it. Whether this practice is (or is not) as illegal as it looks—Berry assured me that Future Television approved of his borrowings—it is standard operating procedure on Ethnic Access.

Recycled material is not the only fare available to Ethnic Access viewers. Occasionally the impresarios appear on-screen to interview Arab celebrities and political dignitaries who visit Detroit. Some programs have local anchormen who present summaries of Middle Eastern news, most of it derived from Arabic media abroad. TV Orient, a Chaldean network, regularly features interviews with people important in the local Arab community: school administrators, candidates for public office, bilingual teachers, doctors, and social workers, among others. TV Orient also produces *Afrah al-jaliya* (Community Celebrations), a popular show that consists of video highlights from local Chaldean weddings. The Detroit-based shows are low-budget affairs, and they account for a small proportion of programming in CVI's leased time slots. The impresarios make their profit from videocopying; indeed, their programs could not survive without it.

(3) *Programming is overwhelmed by, and virtually incidental to, advertising.* Commercials take up half the airtime on local Arabic networks. Indeed, commercials are what makes the programming local, and the top three networks in Dearborn—Arabic Time Television, Sada al-'Arab (The Arab Echo), and TV Orient—make their money by shooting commercials for Arab-owned businesses, which they aired at a market average of $300 per business per month in 1995. According to CVI monitors, spot checks of Arabic programming show that commercials consume about twenty-seven minutes per hour (compared to an industrywide average of twelve minutes per hour). In a CVI telephone poll many Dearborn viewers stated that they enjoyed the commercials, and I have been told many times that the commercials are more fun to watch than the regular programming, which is only in part a criticism of regular programming. In a community heavily involved in small business, the ads on Ethnic Access are a means of competition and a measure of accomplishment directed at the audience that counts most. The people who appear in the commercials are well known to the community—they may, in fact, be fellow villagers or even kin—and the conclusion the Lebanese or Chaldean viewer draws from watching the ads is often a reassuring one: I am surrounded by a robust economic community of people like myself; almost all my needs (food and clothing, health care, aluminum siding, floral arrangements, and cellular phones) can be met within this community.

A SPECIAL RELATIONSHIP:
THE IMPRESARIOS WIN A TRANSNATIONAL TV TURF WAR

Though I have never been able to obtain reliable figures, the financial arrangement between CVI and the Arabic media impresarios is no doubt mutually favorable. The power of the impresarios became clear to everyone in 1995, when they kept Arab Network of America (ANA), a Saudi-backed subscriber station, out of the Dearborn market, lobbying for Dubai TV instead. Dubai had no desire to solicit local advertising, whereas ANA did. Moreover, ANA officials hinted that, should they enter the Dearborn market, they would sue local producers who videocopy and illegally broadcast ANA programming, a course of action that would quickly drive the impresarios out of business. After complex negotiations, CVI opted for Dubai TV, thereby protecting its local leased programming even as it added hundreds of monthly subscribers to its new Arabic satellite service.

The decision to do business with Dubai TV reinforced other trends as well. It ensured that Arabic programming in Dearborn would remain over-

whelmingly monolingual (relatively speaking, ANA has more English programming than Dubai TV, but neither has much). Since Dubai TV has no
American-produced programs (whereas ANA has several), the decision
also continued the tendency for popular culture in Detroit's Arabic-speaking mainstream to be state generated, tradition cultivating, homeland oriented, generally disengaged from the society that surrounds it, and inaccessible (or simply unappealing) to the English-speaking children and
grandchildren of Arab immigrants.

THE IMPRESARIOS TALK BACK:
AHMAD BERRY AND NABEEL HAMOUD EXPLAIN WHAT THEY DO

The trends I discuss above are recognized and widely criticized by the viewers of Ethnic Access, by CVI officials, and (oddly enough) by Arab media
impresarios themselves. There is general agreement, for instance, that the
shows on Ethnic Access are imitative, poorly made, cut to pieces by advertising, and insufficiently attuned to community life in America. "Everybody
watches it," a Palestinian friend responded when I asked him about Ethnic
Access TV, "but nobody likes it. The Lebanese and Chaldeans feed us
garbage. We eat it. There is nothing else."

Such remarks are colored, quite obviously, by nationalist prejudice. Yet
even among Lebanese immigrants, there is a strong tendency to describe
the impresarios as sham operators (*ghishshasheen*); certainly the impresarios
describe each other this way, and the accusations sting. In the second issue
of *Panorama*, Berry responded by claiming the high ground for himself,
loudly criticizing the "deceit and scamming" (*al-kidhab wa-al-shatara*) that
infect the business community he serves. "The word of honor," he com-
plained in his editorial, is "a thing of the past" (Berry 1995b, 4).

In Arab Detroit media talk is morally charged. During my interviews with
Berry and his principal rival, Nabeel Hamoud, producer of Sada al-'Arab
TV, I was struck by the idealistic, often judgmental language they used to
describe their careers, their audience, and the constraints their audience
imposes on their work. It was a surprisingly uniform idiom. When I asked
Hamoud and Berry how they got into the TV business, for instance, neither
said anything about learning to use a camera. They were eager, instead, to
explain that they were litterateurs by nature and training. Nabeel Hamoud
writes poetry, song lyrics, essays, and plays; Ahmad Berry does likewise.
Both men called my attention to their college degrees, which were not in
communications.

The point was clear: it is membership in the intellectual elite—not experience on the set or in the studio—that qualifies these men to "transmit"
Arab culture, even if their efforts are focused on the somewhat plebeian
medium of television. Both men present themselves as teachers who must

educate an immigrant community that, in their eyes, is unsophisticated and ill prepared to compete in the "contest among nationalisms" (*al-sira' bayn al-qawmiyyat*) that defines identity in the modern age. Television is simply the most effective pedagogical tool available to them in Detroit. According to Hamoud,

> We [Lebanese in Dearborn] are from a rural background. Most of us do not like to read. The old people are illiterate. People from Bint Ijbayl or Tibnayn [villages in South Lebanon] don't buy newspapers and books. They like images and sounds and music and singing. Television is the way to influence these people. That is why I created Sada al-'Arab. It is the best way for me to serve my community. My message has been the same since I began in 1984: to make our Arab community always united and stronger. Media is like education. It never ends. As long as I'm capable, I will do this work. My responsibility is to the community and my own work and to provide better Arabic media for this community. Whoever has a talent, I would expect the same of him.

The community, as Hamoud imagines it, is Arabic speaking. Its unity and strength are part of the unity and strength of the Arab people. The reality that is gradually taking shape before Hamoud's eyes—that of an English-speaking Arab community that flourishes beyond and (in many ways) apart from the Arab world—is hard to confront. The TV impresarios, in their role as "educators," are understandably averse to this Americanizing trend. When I asked Berry and Hamoud why they did not provide more English programming, they found the question unsettling. Did I really expect them to compete with American TV, with its superior variety, quality, and advertising revenues?

"If you want English programs, you can watch them anywhere," Berry told me. "If you want Arabic shows, you watch the programs we produce. Arabic is what I offer my viewers. We have tried English programming in the past, . . . but in our experience, no one wants to watch English programs on Arabic Time TV. We are 95 percent Arabic, and I think it should stay that way."

I suggested that Arabic is not the only link to the audience. Shared experiences in Detroit might also provide a basis on which to build a viewership, and much of that shared experience, especially among the young, the second- and third-generation immigrants, the U.S. educated, is conveyed in the English language. The English-speaking market is growing, I argued, and Arabic TV could benefit greatly by tapping into it. Nabeel Hamoud agreed that the dominance of English (and the ongoing loss of Arabic speakers) is a fact of life in Detroit, but he did not think it was right to exploit this trend, thereby speeding it along.

> The people in charge determine something like this. Sada al-'Arab TV specifically is playing a great role in making the younger generation attracted to

Arabic television. We have special shows for kids: cartoons, kiddie shows, educational shows. We concentrate on upbeat music from the Arab world, directed at teenagers. We also give the older generation some oldies from Egypt, like Umm Kulthum and 'Abd al-Wahhab. So all members of the family have something in Arabic that is appropriate for their age.

The Arab family in Dearborn stands as a metaphor for the Arab community in America; it can be held together by its commitment to a shared, ancestral language. The official ideology of the Arab media impresarios invariably upholds this nationalistic fusion of culture and language. For Berry and Hamoud, the loss of the Arabic-speaking market means, quite simply, the end of what they do.

Yet beneath the urgent appeals to cultural preservation, there are more practical reasons for the absence of English-language programming. First of all, the impresarios would have to produce this programming themselves, and (as we have already seen) they are slow to produce original programming of any kind.

"The TV networks in the Arab world," Berry told me, "are supported by the government and advertising money from very big companies. Private ones. National ones. They can afford to produce serials and movies and news shows. I do not have this kind of support. I am one man."

The financial argument seems compelling at first glance, but Hamoud attributed the dearth of locally produced programming to other causes. When I asked him if anyone had ever tried to put together a Lebanese-American soap opera based on daily life in Dearborn, he took a document out of his bottom desk drawer. It was a tattered copy of a script called "Jaliyatna al-'aziza" (Our Dear Community). Hamoud wrote it several years ago, and he has not yet succeeded in producing it for television. The reasons for his failure are not financial; they are rooted, he explained, in the very nature of the diaspora community his play was designed to represent.

> I am reluctant to say this, but I must tell the truth. The Lebanese here are villagers. They are very conservative and religious. The sophisticated people do not come to Detroit, just the peasant people. And this means our community does not have enough talent to produce artistic programming. We lack writers and actors. I have seen this myself. I tried to produce "Our Dear Community," but no one would come to rehearsals on time, and they all kept fighting for more money. This is the peasant way. I gave up. I could not tell the truth in my play because our people cannot hear criticism. Do you want to discuss the problem of drugs, or sex, or not respecting parents? The community will forbid you; they will say, "Why are you making us look bad? People in Lebanon will see this. The Americans will see this and say we are criminals." And for us, acting is dirty work anyway. It is shameful. No family wants their sons or daughters to be actors. In Dearborn, everyone knows everyone. Everyone talks. So it is difficult to put real life on television.

The moral universe Hamoud describes has been laid out for me countless times by Arab Detroiters, most of whom come from peasant backgrounds. It turns on a commonly felt sense of deficiency, a belief that Detroit's Arab community is only a fragment of the Arab nation in its proper fullness. The best in Arab culture, says the common wisdom, is always found elsewhere. It flourishes under the patronage of the Arab states, which give their prestige and financial backing to a popular (yet properly sophisticated) culture that transcends the limits of peasant sensibilities.

This, in a nutshell, is Gellner's model of nationalism, with its necessary relationship between nation making and the emergence of popular culture. Yet in Metro Detroit the Arabic-speaking mainstream is not held together and standardized by centralized agencies of the state. It exists between states and (to a surprising degree) beyond legal systems. In the absence of direct government control and investment, Detroit's Arab media impresarios can finance their nationalizing projects through advertising alone, and this requires a *symbiotic* relationship with local businesses built on a *parasitic* relationship with the media products of Arab states.

There is something vaguely unsatisfying about this transnational relationship, for viewers, impresarios, and CVI officials alike. Each party suspects the others of impropriety or low standards. Yet all are willing to defend the status quo, since the Ethnic Access channel effectively turns a community into a market. It does so by appealing to the immigrant's sense of distance from an original place. When the impresarios claim to be fostering "our language, our heritage, and our civilization" in Detroit, few accept the rhetoric at face value. Like the videocopies that show up on their TV programs, the Arab culture the impresarios advocate is a second- or third-order reproduction, a display of something that by all accounts lives "authentically" (and better) elsewhere. Popular culture in Detroit's Arabic-speaking mainstream is marked, at every turn, by its vexed relationship with place: do we belong "here" or "there"? Hamid Naficy, reflecting on the exilic condition of the Iranian community in Los Angeles, suggests that questions like these are not easily answered:

> All cultures are located in place and time. Exile culture is located at the intersection and in the interstices of other cultures. Exile discourse must therefore not only deal with the problem of location but also the continuing problematic of multiple locations. . . . Exilism is doomed to failure unless it is also rooted in some form of specificity and locality, even essentialism of some strategic sort. This distinguishes exile from other cultural expressions that are based on difference. Without such rootedness, exile discourse, like all other oppositional or alternative discourses, will be co-opted and commodified through defusion and diffusion. In the cultural domain, as in literature and film, specificity, locality, and detail are all. (1993, 2–3)

The Arabic-speaking mainstream in Detroit confronts the problem of location by imagining itself as a *jaliya*, a word that (in Detroit) is always incorrectly translated as "community." It actually signifies something akin to "colony" or "enclave," and it serves to position Arab Detroit between a larger society to which it naturally belongs (the Arab world) and a surrounding society to which it is external and alien (America). This model of the Arab community, which is dominant among newly arrived immigrants, sustains the twenty-two Arabic-language programs on Ethnic Access. It cannot sustain the identities of Arab Detroiters who no longer feel alien or external to American society, who express their alienation and externality in characteristically American terms, or who feel *especially* strange only in the company of newly arrived Arab immigrants. These individuals belong, by and large, to Arab Detroit's English-speaking mainstream, and the popular culture they create is radically at odds with the goals of the Arab media impresarios.

PUBLIC CULTURE IN ARAB DETROIT'S ENGLISH-SPEAKING MAINSTREAM: PLAYING TO A NEW AUDIENCE

ACCESS is a human services organization committed to the development of the Arab-American community in all aspects of its economic and cultural life.

Our staff and volunteers have joined forces to meet the needs of low income families, to help newly arrived immigrants adapt to life in America, and to foster among Americans a greater understanding of Arab culture as it exists both here and in the Arab world.

To achieve these goals, ACCESS provides a wide range of social, mental health, educational, artistic, employment, legal and medical services.

ACCESS is dedicated in all its efforts to empowering people to lead more informed, productive, and fulfilling lives.

ACCESS MISSION STATEMENT, 1995

Whereas public culture in Arabic-speaking Detroit is made beyond the reach of centralized, state-controlled agencies, its production in Arab Detroit's English-speaking mainstream is increasingly dominated by a single, government-funded organization: ACCESS, the Arab Community Center for Economic and Social Services, located in Dearborn. The Arab community's successful entry into Detroit's ethnic arts scene in the late 1980s was engineered and overseen by ACCESS staff. As the manifesto above suggests, the cultural politics underlying this move were framed by the assumption that Arabs are part of American society: they must adapt to it, and they must help Americans to understand Arab culture[8] by explaining how that culture is shaped both "here" and "there." The rhetoric is consistent with every trend in the popular shift toward multiculturalism, diversity, and pluralism.

It is consistent because, unlike the jaliya-based nationalism of Detroit's Arabic-speaking mainstream, ACCESS is part of the complex ideological machinery America's business, political, and intellectual elites use to manage and incorporate the nation's "special populations."

A BRIEF HISTORY OF ACCESS:
HOW A LITTLE BUREAUCRACY CAN BE A GOOD THING

ACCESS began in 1971 as a storefront operation run by laid-off auto workers and activists who wanted to provide social services to Arab immigrants in Dearborn. By 1995 ACCESS had grown into one of Metro Detroit's largest, most effective nonprofit human service organizations. Its annual dinner, which regularly draws two thousand people, is the biggest of any Arab-American organization, and the familiar signs of mainstream acceptance are abundantly on display there: U.S. Senators Levin, Riegle, and now Abraham frequently attend the event, as do the mayors of Dearborn and Detroit, their respective superintendents of schools, corporate bigwigs from Ford, GM, and Chrysler, candidates for public office, and a bevy of lesser notables on the local chain of command.

The admittance of ACCESS into the political mainstream was originally based on the organization's ability to turn a community into a constituency, with political support being traded for social welfare dollars. Today almost all of ACCESS's $5 million annual budget comes from state and federal funding sources, with additional contributions from Michigan-based corporations, the United Way, and a community telethon. In 1971 the founders of ACCESS were leftist radicals. The current executive director, Ishmael Ahmed, was a Maoist; other staff and board members belonged to a mix of communist, socialist, and anarchist groups. The demands of mainstream politics have long since pushed ACCESS away from the revolutionary fringe, but the close association between ACCESS and the dole remains a source of stigma in the Arab community. For many years a common criticism of ACCESS (made both in and outside the Arab community) was that it "gets Arabs hooked on welfare" and that its progressive ideals translate, in the final analysis, to the distribution of U.S. government surplus cheese.

The critics failed to see the radical impact ACCESS's administration of government programs was having on its character as an organization. Within a decade ACCESS had been bureaucratized and professionalized; it had cultivated institutional alliances and networks of political patronage that no other Arab community organization could match. In the late 1980s, when ACCESS expanded its programming into the public arts realm, it was well placed to exploit the scant federal, state, and corporate funds set aside for cultural programming in America's minority communities.

ACCESS CULTURAL ARTS:
HOW TO SUCCEED IN THE REPRESENTATION BUSINESS

When discussing ACCESS's public arts programming, the operational strengths of the organization must be kept in mind, as these are frequently overshadowed by the personal reputation of Sally Howell, founder of the ACCESS Cultural Arts Program and its director from 1987 to 1995. Howell has a degree in Middle East studies; she has lived in Israel, Egypt, Yemen, and Jordan; and she speaks Arabic. She is not an Arab, however, and for this reason her success is commonly attributed (by Arabs and non-Arabs alike) to all the qualities Arab immigrants are said to lack. I am often told by Arab friends that Howell has "organizational skills" that Lebanese (or Palestinians, or Yemenis, or Chaldeans) do not; that her vision of the community is holistic, not clannish or sectarian; that she has a firsthand understanding of the methods and standards of "white people"; or, more intangible still, that she has a sense of possibility that extends beyond "big talk, dreaming, and scheming."

I asked Howell how she interpreted this way of talking about her success. Her answer, an impromptu analysis of the "cultural representation business," served both to confirm and deny the validity of her image in Arab Detroit.

> I think the thing I bring to this job which gives me a clear advantage is the fact that I can write a good, competitive grant. Very few people in our community can do that, and if they could, they wouldn't be working for my salary. They'd move into the mainstream. That leaves WASPy "do-gooders" like me, who have this volunteeristic mentality which a lot of people in the community find utterly bizarre. But that's good, because a lot of the big granting agencies are run by people like me. I speak their language. I can tell them what they want to hear, as well as what they *need* to hear. That's incredibly important. In the [immigrant] Arab community, I've noticed that most people just don't know how to represent their culture to a non-Arab audience. It's likely to come across as arrogant, or defensive, or second rate, or just weird. A lot of people [among Arabs] just assume that no one [among Americans] would want to know about them, right? Or they don't know *how* they are different from most Americans—or if they do, they don't want to talk about it in public—so they haven't developed effective ways for telling Americans what's unique or special about Arab culture. That's the biggest disadvantage. Because really there's this huge opening right now for effective cultural representations of almost any "special" group. Schools, museums, city and state governments, companies—they all want to develop new audiences or deal with new immigrant populations. I just tap into that agenda.

If these observations are read simply as the opinions of a non-Arab (and identity politics demands such a reading), they will be easily misunderstood. The same views, more strenuously expressed, can be heard among

Detroit's Arab-American activists and intellectuals. The mainstays of the "cultural representation business," grant writing, interpretive work linking heterogeneous communities, the creation of funding relationships between "special populations" and institutions of the larger society: these are projects Detroit's newly arrived Arab immigrants are rarely equipped (and seldom concerned) to handle. It is American-born Arabs and their non-Arab allies who dominate the cultural representation business, and they do so using the skills and intellectual habits they have acquired as members of the (same) metropolitan, English-speaking, college-educated, managerial class. If Sally Howell's prominence within this stratum of identity brokers is often ascribed to her non-Arabness, the perception is an optical illusion. More significant by far is her ability to "tap into" the multicultural agendas of America's dominant funding agencies.

During her tenure at ACCESS, Howell oversaw roughly $2 million worth of public arts programming, most of it supported by grants from government agencies, big business, and private foundations: the National Endowment for the Arts (NEA) and the National Endowment for the Humanities (NEH), the Michigan Council for the Arts and Cultural Affairs, the Michigan Humanities Council, the United Way, the Lila Wallace/Reader's Digest Fund, the Ruth Mott Fund, Dayton Hudson's Corporation, Ford Motor Company, and others. Unlike the "one man" approach that prevails among the Arabic TV impresarios, Howell used these resources to build a programming infrastructure whose upkeep is shared by dozens of local scholars, Arab artists, community volunteers, and mainstream institutions. The ACCESS Cultural Arts Program oversees the Museum of Arab Culture, teacher workshops and curriculum consulting for Detroit area schools, artist referrals, a performing arts series, the Aliya Hassen Library (with its five thousand books, periodicals, and videotapes on the Arab world), and ongoing ethnographic and historical research projects on Arab Detroit.

In 1991 Howell gave official shape to her informal network of volunteers and consultants by establishing the Arab-American Arts Council (AAAC). The council consists of about thirty members, Arab and non-Arab, most of whom are English-speaking, college-educated professionals. It specializes in events typically described as "high profile," most notably Fann wa Tarab: An Evening of Art and Musical Ecstasy, a biennial event featuring leading Arab-American musicians, visual artists, and poets. Fann wa Tarab is always held at a prestigious venue—the Detroit Institute of Arts, for instance—and the flurry of newspaper articles and radio interviews that accompanies the event is designed, quite specifically, to celebrate Arab musical, literary, and artistic achievement in America.

Whether high profile or low, ACCESS cultural arts programming has had a considerable impact on the popular image of Arabs in Detroit, who, even in today's climate of "diversity," are widely viewed as a politically suspect minority that can and *should* be excluded from public discourse. This relentless experience of marginalization leads many Arab-Americans to doubt it is actually *they* who are being recognized when inclusion finally comes.

"If you told me ten years ago," said ACCESS executive director Ahmed, "that we would be doing joint projects with the Detroit Institute of Arts, I'd have said you're crazy. That wasn't even a fantasy for us back then. Sally made us realize it was possible and . . . it wouldn't have happened without her. A lot of these big-time organizations aren't comfortable working with Arabs, but they can work with Sally; so that gives ACCESS an inside track."

Yet movement down that track is being funded and sped along by the most mainstream elements of American society: big government, big business, and the educational establishment. Without ACCESS as an institutional base, Howell's programming ideas (and her role as "white cultural ambassador" for Arab Detroit) would hardly impress these benefactors. Excellent programs have failed to attract funding in the past. In the early 1980s several Arab cultural organizations sprang up in Detroit—most notable among them, the Arab-American Media Society (1980–86), which produced high-quality musical performances, lectures, poetry readings, and a nationally distributed radio program, "Arabesques." Unlike ACCESS, however, the Arab-American Media Society could not institutionalize itself *within* the domain of American identity politics. It was not tied to important patronage networks in the state or federal government, a condition that forced it to court the erratic largesse of the Arab Gulf states; nor (with a part-time staff of four people) could it organize, stand for, or administer a critical mass of Detroit's Arab community. Despite the obvious quality of its work, the Arab-American Media Society eventually fell apart.[9] In Arab Detroit, as in other American immigrant and ethnic communities, the big funders of public culture expect a specific range of payoffs for their investment. Their support goes to institutions that interweave audiences, constituencies, markets, and identities in consistent, ideologically useful ways. This logic can be seen in every facet of ACCESS cultural arts programming.

HOW ACCESS SPENDS THE MONEY:
PROGRAMMING PATTERNS AND WHAT THEY MEAN

The Rockefeller Foundation
Partnerships Affirming Community Transformation (PACT)
This Request for Proposals

In communities across the United States, changing demographies and increasing local diversity are leading to more contact across racial and ethnic groups. Daily, through public conversations and the media, Americans hear that they are ill equipped to contend with this contact, that divisiveness and confusion are frag-

*menting the American experience. Yet their actual experience often contradicts this
message, as communities struggle, with varying degrees of success, to discover, understand and engage the multilayered differences that characterize contemporary life
in this country. The exploration of who America is — and will become — is informed
by the energy and drive of communities tapping into deep reserves of concern and
creativity to make a better life. Often the power of the arts and humanities is facilitating transformations within these communities.*

*Against this backdrop, the Rockefeller Foundation announces its second Request
for Proposals for PACT: Partnerships Affirming Community Transformation. This
round of PACT is focused on issues of race and ethnicity, whether explicitly and directly or as embedded in community issues such as education, economic opportunity
and violence prevention. PACT is designed to identify, learn from and affirm the
work of communities that are developing new ideas about America, about changing
concepts of American identity and democratic values in a society increasingly defined by multiple pluralities rather than majorities. Specifically, PACT seeks efforts
that engage culture and the arts to understand deeply rooted hopes and fears, discover and articulate shared values, stimulate and sustain change and mobilize diverse forces to transform communities.*

FUNDING INFORMATION RECEIVED BY ACCESS, MAY 1996

Whether "newly arrived" or "native born," Arabs are encouraged to play a
very particular brand of identity politics in Detroit's public spaces. This politics is often described as "inclusive"; it is driven by relentless appeals to diversity and pluralism, yet its ultimate goal is the "appropriation" of Otherness, an end that can be achieved only if the differences that set Others
apart are somehow naturalized, normalized, muted, consigned to another
time, or linked to a place and way of life the Others have left behind. The
Arab-American identity ACCESS fosters through its cultural programs
bears all the markings of this assimilative process, and the success of the
Cultural Arts Program depends on the following tendencies, all of which
buttress the interlocking (and largely unstated) agendas of the American
funding establishment.

(1) *Most of its programming is designed, carried out, or packaged in English.* As
with the monolingualism of Arabic TV in Detroit, the anglophone tendency
in ACCESS cultural arts programming is not as obvious as it seems. The
turnout for ACCESS events is heavily Arab-American, and many in the audience can speak (or at least understand) Arabic. Indeed, Arabic is spoken
by more Detroiters today than ever before. The growing reluctance to use it
(or Aramaic) at readings, workshops, festivals, art shows, and museum exhibits is attributable to the unquestioned link between English and the idea
of a "larger public." ACCESS cultural arts programs are meant to educate
and impress this public. To be effective, to improve the pervasively negative
image of Arabs in American society, these programs must be conducted in
English.

"The granting agencies put a big emphasis on education and developing new audiences for traditional art forms," Howell told me. "The new audience for Arab culture is the non-Arab audience, or the assimilated Arab-American audience, and both groups speak English. From my perspective as a grant writer, I'd say the whole multicultural arts movement is oriented toward English speakers. Basically, English is the language all the groups have to communicate in if they want to be heard."

The performance of Arabic song and the use of Arabic calligraphy in painting and other visual arts are important exceptions to this rule. But song lyrics need not be comprehensible to have emotional effect; and Arabic script need not be understood to have iconic power. When lyrics and letters are posed as "literature," and their aesthetic impact is based on what they *mean*, ACCESS programming quickly reverts to English. The Arab-American poets and novelists who read at ACCESS events do so in English. By contrast, the singers at ACCESS concerts perform only in Arabic, even though the introductions, the program book, the banter between songs, and the advance publicity for these concerts are in another language entirely. In both cases the same message is being sent: the audience ACCESS seeks to educate and impress speaks English, and the Arab-American identity it celebrates is constructed within (and as part of) an English-speaking discourse.

(2) *Although Arab culture is showcased, its American context is always dominant.* The idea of a "general audience," in whose presence Arabs must represent themselves, functions as a backdrop against which immigrants (and other marked groups) must consciously imagine America and attach themselves to it. This ideological exercise reveals itself clearly in the design for "Creating a New Arab World: A Century in the Life of the Arab Community in Detroit," an ACCESS lecture series and research project funded by the NEH. In accordance with NEH guidelines, the grant proposal for this project emphasized the need to make Arab immigrants part of the "American story," even though many Arabs and Americans would find their inclusion in that story coercive.

Many Arabs, especially Muslims, feel that their culture and religion distinguish them significantly from European immigrants, who came to America as members of the dominant Judaeo-Christian civilization. This latter view, though rooted in a sense of cultural exclusion that is real, ignores the extent to which local varieties of Islam and Arab identity have been shaped by life in America and are, for that reason, uniquely American. The difficulty many Arabs and non-Arabs face in making Arabs part of the American story is amply reflected in the local media. Every three years or so, the *Detroit Free Press* and *Detroit News* run multi-page articles on the Arab community, and in each bout of reporting—usually provoked by political troubles in the Middle

East—the Arab community is presented as if it were a novelty on the American landscape. The fact that Arabs have lived in Southeast Michigan, and elsewhere in North America, for the better part of a century has not yet been fully realized by most Americans. (ACCESS Cultural Arts 1994, 2)

Using the language of diversity and multiculturalism, ACCESS posed a solution to the problem that it hoped the NEH would fund.

The project we envision is committed to breaking down these well-established historical and cultural boundaries. It will address the challenge of identity and diversity by exposing Detroit's Arab-Americans (and members of the non-Arab community) to the unique society local Arabs have created through their experience as settlers in a new world. By focussing on a few central themes—family, faith, work, language, food, and the artistic heritage—we will attempt to tell the story of a living community that exists in a continual state of transformation. . . . On the basis of fieldwork done in Metro Detroit, twelve humanities scholars will present lectures designed to enable lay audiences (1) to situate the Arab-American experience in relation to larger world events; (2) to show the interaction between various American and Middle Eastern notions of family, morality, society, religion, and self; and (3) to point out how the outcomes of these cultural interactions have changed over the course of a century. (ACCESS Cultural Arts 1994, 2)

Despite the rhetoric of boundary breaking, the themes on which "Creating a New Arab World" fastens are located squarely within America's discourse about itself. The objective is to make Arabs an audible part of that discourse, a goal many Arab Detroiters enthusiastically support. The NEH was supportive as well. In 1994 it gave $85,000 to the project, making ACCESS the first Arab-American organization ever to receive NEH Public Project funds. One might argue that boundaries are falling down; one might as easily argue that Arabs are being encouraged (with generous government assistance) to imagine themselves in explicitly American terms.

(3) *The Arab artistic traditions presented are mostly folkloric or classical; the modern products of Arab popular culture, as they exist in Arabic mass media, are generally avoided.* When Howell approached the NEA in 1987 with ideas for cultural programming in Arab Detroit, she was immediately referred to the Folkarts Division. When she contacted the Michigan Council for the Arts, she was referred to specialists at Michigan State University's Folklife Museum. And so on.

"I learned from day one that Arab artistic traditions are categorized as folklore, at least for funding purposes," Howell told me.

A lot of funding agencies are interested in authenticity. They want proof the artists we present are part of a tradition. When it comes to Arabs, they don't support what we would think of as modern or Western-influenced art forms. We're much more likely to get money for the creation of a performance ensemble that uses ouds, *qanoons*, *nyes*, and *durbekkes* [Arab traditional instruments] than we are for one that plays the same music on electric guitars, synthesizers, and drum pads. There's actually a greater demand for modern instrumentation in the community, but folkarts panels only want the traditional stuff. You can fund a *dabki* [line dance] troupe, but you can't fund a theater group, because theater is not considered an authentic Arab tradition. It's funny. When we want to present modern music, like Asmahan or 'Abd al-Wahhab, we have to pitch it as Arab classical music—to prove it's authentic—which is exactly the way Arabs talk about it.

The same logic can be seen in the ACCESS Museum of Arab Culture—originally called the Arab Folk Heritage Museum—whose carefully prepared exhibits highlight traditional dress, weaving, jewelry, cuisine, coffee paraphernalia, embroidery, traditional housing (both urban and rural), oral tradition, and (at the classical end of the spectrum) Arab variants of Judaism, Christianity, and Islam, Muslim contributions to science, and the Arab-Muslim tradition of education. What the Arab world might look like in the modern, national era is only faintly sketched out in the museum, which is toured by more than six thousand visitors (mostly students) each year. The museum's newest exhibit, *A New Arab World*, focuses on life in Arab Detroit. Unlike the exhibits in the older wing, *A New Arab World* represents a community that is committed to tradition yet at the same time is historical, diverse, adaptive, and a natural part of the modern world. Given the close juxtaposition of these two very different representations of Arab culture, the visitor might be forgiven for concluding that Arab Detroit is historical, diverse, and adaptive because it is American and that the Arab world is traditional and slow to change because it is Arab. This view, be it said, is widely endorsed in both the Arabic- and English-speaking sectors of the Arab community.

(4) *Programming is concerned to position Arabs within American culture, not outside it, and this internal position is consistently marked as "ethnic."* Much of ACCESS cultural arts programming involves collaboration with other nonprofit arts groups, and with very few exceptions these groups are identified with Detroit's ethnic and minority communities. With Casa de Unidad, ACCESS put together *Andalusian Legacies*, a concert showcasing Spanish /Arabic musical and dance traditions. In tandem with New Detroit, a race-relations alliance dominated by big business and the African-American community, ACCESS organizes the annual *Concert of Colors*, a daylong world beat concert featuring Arab, African, Asian, Native American, jazz, and Latin performers. ACCESS poetry readings are often interethnic collaborations as well.

Blendings of this sort are based largely on programming expediency—they mirror political coalitions and can therefore be easily organized—but they also represent a way of marketing diversity that is supported by corporate, municipal, state, federal, and private funding agencies. The polite language, according to Howell, is one of "building audiences for ethnic and minority arts," but the rhetoric is easily translated into an idiom of "building markets" (for corporate sponsors) and "building constituencies" (for government sources). Diversity and multiculturalism are treated as means to these ends, and an organization's ability to expand programming beyond ethnically uniform audiences is always an important part of program evaluation. The following statement, which Howell inserts into a wide range of grant proposals, is addressed specifically to these themes.

> ACCESS has been successful at integrating Arab-American and non-Arab audiences. In recent years, the Cultural Arts Program has branched out from its earlier efforts to provide performances of traditional Arab dance in the community, or to teach traditional instruments and crafts to Arab-American youth. By assembling the Arab-American Arts Council in 1991, a volunteer advisory board made up of artists and arts patrons from all corners of the Arab-American community, ACCESS has been able to attract internationally known artists and writers such as Simon Shaheen, Jihad Racy, Foday Musa Suso, Bernie Warrell, Pedro Cortez, Anton Shammas, Naomi Shihab Nye, Mona Simpson, and Diane Abu-Jaber to perform for audiences that reflect Metro Detroit's true ethnic diversity. Our ability to collaborate with artists and arts organizations both within and beyond the Arab-American community has enabled us to transcend homogeneous crowds and attract new audiences. As we continue to serve the most traditional elements of the Arab community and to reach out to non-Arab Americans, we are forced to be flexible and responsive.

This image of vibrant heterogeneity is somewhat misleading. The programming policy Howell is trying to appease is one that attempts to locate "new audiences," label them, and turn them into manageable, mutually compatible units. In practice, ACCESS need not reach an audience that reflects the true ethnic diversity of Detroit—most of its events (like the events of other minority and ethnic arts groups) are effectively in-group affairs. Rather, ACCESS needs to build working relationships with the government agencies and corporate interests that, for reasons of their own, are trying to reach Arab Detroit.[10]

ARE WE TRANSNATIONAL YET?
(UN)PACKING OUR THEORETICAL BAGGAGE, AGAIN

> We need to think ourselves beyond the nation. This is not to suggest that thought alone will carry us beyond the nation or that the nation is largely a thought or an imagined thing. Rather, it is to suggest that the role of intellec-

tual practices is to identify the current crisis of the nation and, in identifying it, to provide part of the apparatus of recognition for postnational social forms. (Appadurai 1993, 411)

I began by suggesting that anthropology's move away from nationalism as a focus of inquiry and its avid pursuit of global perspectives are rooted in (1) the worldwide spread of modernity and modern social forms and (2) a resulting increase in the tactical mobility enjoyed by the metropolitan, managerial classes who imagine and administer human communities. This is why transnational approaches seem always to advertise themselves with appeals to (or critiques of) the transcendent, the cosmopolitan, the privilege of movement, and the collapse of space and time. We should expect as much. The people who produce, distribute, and consume the transnationalism rhetoric most devotedly belong to the academy, the corporate elite, and government—social bodies that, in their modern forms, are designed to exceed the limits of any human community they can imagine. Arjun Appadurai's call to "think beyond" the nation is standard fare in this brave new world of expansionist discourse. As a manifesto, its cutting-edge pretensions are overblown but essential: Appadurai is asking us to *invest*—intellectually, emotionally, politically—in postnational formations even he cannot yet pin down. Our investment will pay off, he tells us, because the idea of nation "is now itself diasporic. Carried in the repertoires of increasingly mobile refugees, tourists, guest workers, transnational intellectuals, scientists, and illegal aliens, it is increasingly unrestrained by ideas of spatial boundary and territorial sovereignty" (1993, 413).

When one looks closely at public culture in Arab Detroit, however, transnational forces are everywhere tied to the nation-state in obvious and ironic ways. Arabic TV impresarios like Ahmad Berry and Nabeel Hamoud flourish by copying material from media networks controlled and sponsored by Arab governments, and they can do so because they live beyond the reach (and attention) of those governments. They operate in a transnational domain, but contrary to Appadurai's vision, this domain depends for its survival on "spatial boundaries and territorial sovereignty." Moreover, the multicultural, hybridizing, diversity-based rhetoric so often associated with transnationalism is alien to the Arab impresarios and their political sensibilities. In its place one finds a jaliya-style nationalism that is conservative, inclined toward cultural authenticity, and unabashedly chauvinistic.

In Arab Detroit's English-speaking mainstream, one finds public arts programming that is avowedly multicultural, diversity celebrating, and transnational. Yet this programming functions, in practice, to make Lebanese, Palestinians, Yemenis, and Iraqis into Americans of a recognizably ethnic sort. The ACCESS Cultural Arts Program is part of a loosely coordinated *national* strategy addressed to a perennial American concern: how best to manufacture new citizens who can participate smoothly in America's public institutions, markets, and politics. Whereas the Arabic TV impresarios are nationalists making Arab identity in a transnational domain, there is nothing effectively transnational about ACCESS programs at all. They reflect, instead, the ability of Americans to imagine themselves as the world and to celebrate cultural diversity even as they work (often unwittingly) to streamline it in manageable forms.

If Arab Detroit tells us anything about local experience in a deterritorialized world, it is that the social imagination, even in a global age, cannot remain deterritorialized for long. Using a language (Arabic) that is strongly associated with another place, Arab immigrants try to attach themselves to Detroit by attaching Detroit to an original, ancestral homeland. Using a language (English) that is more local and more universal at once, Arab-Americans stake claim to an ethnic identity that, in many respects, is already mapped out for them. Both strategies rely on the imaginative and financial resources of the state, and this dependency, Michael Herzfeld suggests, is something most people are unwilling to relinquish:

> Whatever the specific historical reasons, the prima facie evidence of rampant nationalism at the very end of the twentieth century, just when everyone "logically" thought its time was past, suggests that nationalism is indeed the place to explore the question of how people—those embodiments of local interests—find their way around in a world still felt to be too large to call home. (1995, 124)

Before wandering into the open (and possibly empty) spaces along the postnational frontier, cosmopolitan ethnographers—whose agendas are shaped by borders as well as crossings—will have to confront the constant relocation of identity that even the most transient attachment to nation-states makes necessary. Limited though it may seem to us now, this way of building political boundaries and popular cultures shows little sign of fading away.

NOTES

1. There are notable exceptions to the transnationalizing trend. Lila Abu-Lughod's special issue of *Public Culture*, "Screening Politics in a World of Nations," explores the nationalist dimensions of television production in postcolonial states. Yet in 1993, when the issue appeared, theoretical trends were already headed elsewhere, and Abu-Lughod offered a mildly apologetic foreword to the issue. "It might seem surprising," she notes, "to privilege the national when the transnational character of television programming has been so frequently commented on" (1993a, 465). As I write this in 1996, Abu-Lughod's rather modest fallback position—that

"the nation-state remains crucial for the deployment of mass media" (1993a, 466)—can easily be read as a critique of "postnational" approaches to popular culture. For a sketch of recent trends in transnationalism and anthropological theory, see Blanc, Basch, and Glick-Schiller 1995.

2. The figure, which debuted in Abraham and Abraham 1983, is probably much too high. It is lower, however, than the 250,000 estimate commonly cited in the press, by social service agencies, and in academic circles. The latter figure has become a "social fact" of sorts, but its refusal to change (up or downward) during the last ten years of steady immigration suggests that 250,000 is a quantitative symbol of Arab Detroit's immense size.

3. This claim circulates widely in Detroit. It originated (I am often told) in the Michigan Department of Social Services. Hassan Jaber, assistant director of the Arab Community Center (ACCESS) in Dearborn, vouched for the claim's accuracy. Anyone familiar with the ethnic/racial demography of Detroit would find little reason to question his judgment.

4. This figure was provided by Ahmed Chebbani, owner of Omnex, an accounting firm that balances the books for almost all the Lebanese-owned businesses on Warren Avenue.

5. For critical takes on celebratory transnationalism, see Asad 1993, Harvey 1989, and Hannerz 1992, all carefully attuned to the oppressive potential of metropolitan cultural forms. For critiques that identify themselves more explicitly with the concerns and interests of the new transnationalism literature yet resist a "celebratory" tone, see Basch, Glick-Schiller, and Blanc 1994; Rouse 1995, 1996. For an extended consideration of ethnography's role in constructing global and local knowledge, the reader should consult the 1993 ASA Decennial Conference Series, especially the volumes edited by Strathern (1995), Fardon (1995), and Miller (1995b).

6. This figure was provided by Abe Osta, executive director of the American Arab Chamber of Commerce–Michigan.

7. The six networks are TV Orient, Arabic Time TV, Sada al-'Arab, United TV Network, Arab World TV, and Middle East TV. The sixteen public access programs are *Islamic Message, Islamic Center of America, Islamic Council, Islamic Speeches, Voice of Unity, Abundant Life, Islamic Teaching, The Secret Place, Lebanese-American Club Program, Lebanese Cultural Center Program, Islamic Mosque of America, Sundays Journal, Insights from the Holy Quran, Association of Islamic Charitable Projects, Education and Life,* and *Islamic Institute of Knowledge.*

8. I use the phrase "Arab culture" because people in the community use it. I do not think it describes a uniform, bounded object. Neither do most Arab-Americans. Instead, it is shorthand for "manners," "customs," "traditions," "heritage," "way of life," and any number of related concepts.

9. The predicament of the Arab-American Media Society was shared by many Arab-American organizations in the 1970s and 1980s, when the public space available for Arab self-representation in the United States was minuscule. Funding was hard to generate, and reliance on money from the Arab Gulf kept many Arab-American organizations from developing practical, grassroots coalitions that would enable them to engage effectively in domestic politics. For an intriguing discussion of marginality and its effects on Arab-American political culture during this period,

see Abraham 1989. Because it provided social services to America's largest popula-tion of Arab immigrants—a task of considerable benefit to the "host society"—ACCESS was brought into local (and national) political structures almost from its inception.

10. For detailed analyses of the corporate, political, and class interests underly-ing American multiculturalism, see Rouse 1995; Dresch 1995.

THREE

The 6/8 Beat Goes On

Persian Popular Music from *Bazm-e Qajariyyeh*
to Beverly Hills Garden Parties

Anthony Shay

Only recently has the study of popular and mass culture been deemed fit
for serious scholarly attention on a large scale. This seems peculiar in light
of the fact that popular culture in its various forms celebrates and eluci-
dates the "here and now" of every society, historical and modern, and reveals crucial discourses characteristic of particular societies. Popular culture, however, "still carries two older senses: inferior kinds of work cf.
popular literature (popular press as distinguished from quality press); and
work deliberately setting out to win favor (popular journalism as distinguished from democratic journalism, or popular entertainment); as well as
the more modern sense of well-liked by many people" (R. Williams, cited in
Strinati 1995, 3). The popular culture theorist Dominic Strinati considers
most important the extent to which "people's lives in western capitalist societies appear to be affected by the popular culture presented by the modern mass media." He continues, "It is important in other kinds of societies
as well, both historical and contemporary, but in these societies the sheer
volume of popular media culture which is made available gives it a specific
significance which needs to be looked at" (1995, xiii).

This avoidance of scholarly investigation into popular culture has been
particularly prominent in Middle East studies, in which, aside from definitively "premodern" folklore, popular culture is presumed relevant only to
the mass culture of the West. In contrast to nearly invisible popular traditions is what Edward Said (1978) terms the "timeless, frozen East" that possesses only what we would characterize as "high" culture. Our highbrow/
lowbrow distinctions do not necessarily work well as a description of the
state of Iranian culture, and yet they are relevant to some contexts.[1] Most
native Iranian music scholars, and their non-Iranian disciples, often eschew
the study of popular music forms because of their *amiyaneh* (popular) con-

notations and their often lower-class associations. I argue that popular music, especially the *mardomi* (people's music) genre, forms the Other, a negative space by which classical music is positively defined. No official canon for music exists in an Iranian context comparable to that which Martin Stokes (1992a) describes for government sponsorship in Turkey and Walter Armbrust (1996) discusses for Egyptian music in the context of icons such as Muhammad 'Abd al-Wahhab and Umm Kulthum. Nevertheless, the government radio under the Pahlavi regime sponsored a long-running series of classical music programs, called the *gol-ha* (flowers), which in fact provided a de facto imprimatur for classical music on a large scale. These programs were broadcast almost every evening and featured a large orchestra of Iranian and Western instruments and considerable use of harmony, counterpoint, and other Western techniques as well as Iranian ones. They typically opened with an extensive *pish-daramad* (overture), a *tasnif* (art song), an *avaz* (vocal and/or instrumental improvised section), and a restatement of the tasnif and sometimes concluded with a *reng*, or dance piece.[2] Thus a case can be made for the existence of a canon. Furthermore, the government never permitted broadcasts of songs by mardomi icons such as Mahvash, further emphasizing the difference between the genres.

I also argue in this chapter that unlike Westernized Persian popular music, which Iranian musical purists can, with justification, claim is "inauthentic" on a musical level, no such claim can be made for mardomi music, whose music and texts are extremely authentic and, in many cases, very old. Rather, in the manner in which Armbrust (1996) describes Egyptian reactions to the vocalist Ahmad 'Adawiya, many Iranian classical musicians and scholars dismiss the genre as vulgar "popular" entertainment, placing it beyond the pale of serious discussion.

In the modernist/nationalist discourse mardomi popular music also occupies a negative space: its cheerfully vulgar lyrics and music represent the old, the traditional, the backward; and its consumption was associated in the public mind with the urban proletariat and professions such as taxi driving and trucking. It presented to both educated classes and government officialdom a subversive genre in which sexuality, gender, and sly political references created varying degrees of discomfort. This contrasts with the manner in which Westernized Persian music represented, not modernity, but Westernization for a largely youthful population who aspired to live lives they imagined, through the media, to parallel the lives of their counterparts in New York, Paris, and London.

In contrast to Strinati, I argue here that the ubiquity of Persian popular music (or perhaps more accurately "musics," as I will discuss later) in the Iranian-American community represents, and formerly represented in urban Iran, in its own micro niche and environment, an imposing volume of production that holds relevant and diverse information for interested scholars in many fields of the humanities. In addition, I argue that Iranian popular music holds a unique position among music produced for exile, diaspora, and immigrant communities in the United States, because virtually all of its production and performance takes place outside of its homeland (see Naficy 1993, 54–59, and Zinder 1992 for details of the business of recording and distributing Persian popular music). Most of the major figures in all genres of the Persian popular music field—vocalists, composers, lyricists, and producers—reside in southern California. In contrast, although they are hosts to a few popular musical artists resident in southern California, virtually all of the other large immigrant communities, for example, Chinese, Japanese, Korean, Hispanic, Indian, Eastern European, and Arab, look to their homelands as the chief source of their popular, as well as classical and regional folk, music.

In this chapter I focus on one genre of popular music that I call "mardomi," or people's music (also known as *ru-howzi* or *motrebi* and *amiyaneh*, public or common), which has not been examined or analyzed in detail but rather reviled in the most strident tones, particularly by the self-appointed guardians of the sacred flame of "pure, authentic" classical music.[3] Although I appreciate and follow with interest the performance and development of Persian classical music, I must emphasize that the relevance of traditional popular music lies not only in its long history in the Iranian urban world, a position that it has occupied for well over two hundred years, and much longer in the view of some scholars (e.g., Ardavan Mofid, interview, December 14, 1996), but also in its continued presence and popularity in the Iranian immigrant community of Los Angeles in a variety of significant contexts that are often different from those in Iran.

Ardavan Mofid is a theater historian as well as an accomplished performer in *naqqali* and *shahnameh-khani*, two related traditional storytelling genres, and in *siyah-bazi* and *ru-howzi*, two improvisational comic theater genres. He asserts that ru-howzi–style performances can be traced not only to the Safavid coffeehouses (1501–1725), well documented by several European memoirs, but also to the Sasanian era (242–650), when professional poets hired popular entertainers, known as *qavval*, to perform their poetry to music in a professional manner at court. According to Mofid, such performers are also documented through the Timurid period (ca. thirteenth–fifteenth centuries).

There are many variations of this type of theater. Today the principal urban forms are siyah-bazi, or the black play, so called because the main character is a clown played in blackface, and ru-howzi, or above the pool, so called because, in the past, one of the most typical urban performance venues was a temporary stage created of planks constructed above the pool that is a fixture in most older Iranian homes. Both forms use the blackface clown and other stock cast members, improvisation, earthy, sometimes bawdy, language, double entendre jokes and puns, and sight gags, but according to Mofid and other informants, the siyah-bazi is a political theater that uses biting satire to expose political folly, whereas the ru-howzi is a social theater that satirizes domestic life. In other words, the content and the intent differ in the two variants. The term "ru-howzi" also refers to both dance and music styles that can be performed exclusively of any theatrical or dramatic performance. Parvaneh Azad stated that in her childhood (during the 1930s) "ru-howzi was performed in homes, but siyah-bazi, with its more political character, was more common in coffeehouses and other public areas which were commonly frequented by exclusively male audiences, who were more interested in political matters" (pers. com. February 4, 1994).

This chapter, then, is an analysis of the mardomi genre as popular culture, traditionally performed in a variety of social contexts such as coffeehouses, cabarets, traditional theaters, and, later, the Iranian cinema and of how these have altered in a transformed national setting. Its musical analysis awaits a thorough study. Although this project is not specifically a postmodern one, I do wish to use a postmodern strategy to decenter the prominence currently occupied by Persian classical music in both the scholarly and the popular literature and thereby reveal the complexity of this traditional urban genre. In this project I wish to follow the idea put forth by the culture theorist John Docker regarding the importance of popular culture forms:

> Modernist critical theory has demonized mass culture by apocalyptically condemning it as the chief danger to civilization. . . . Postmodernism—or at least the strands I like—does not ascribe to popular culture phenomena any single commanding meaning or purposes. . . . Rather it is interested in a plurality of forms and genres, a pluralizing of aesthetic criteria, where such forms and genres may have long and fascinating histories, not as static and separate but entwined, interacting, conflicting, contesting, playing off against each other, mixing in unpredictable combinations, protean in energy. . . . Postmodernism defends the "lower female genres" and their readers and audiences so excoriated by modernism this century. It sees popular culture as a frequent site of flamboyance, extravagance, excess, parody, self-parody, a self-parody that has philosophical implications for popular culture as a worldview, a cosmology, a poetics. (1994, xvii–xviii)

Docker's statement clearly reveals the predicament of studying Persian popular music, which has indeed been demonized. In addition, much of its corpus originated as a female genre. In analyzing and outlining the contents of the lyrics of traditional Persian popular music, and the theatrical forms in which they originated, I use Mikhail Bakhtin's (1984) notions of the "world upside down" and the carnivalesque, which constitute useful theoretical tools for the analysis of the role of this indigenous popular music in Iranian society.

BAKHTIN: CARNIVALESQUE AND GROTESQUE

Bakhtin's concept of carnival as a subversive, disruptive world-upside-down event in which the repressive views, lies, and hypocrisy of the officially run and dominated everyday world are unmasked provides a powerful theoretical concept for any study of Iranian popular theatrical and related musical forms. Bakhtin was concerned with polyvocality and the fact that from the onset of the European Renaissance the voices of the common people were increasingly not heard. The Islamic Republic's ban on the performance of improvisational comic theater would seem to support this theoretical stance with empirical evidence of official reaction. In the European context analyzed by Bakhtin, a writer, exemplified by Rabelais, enacts an important role because he or she reflects the voices of the low, the peasant, the outcast. In Bakhtin's view, the healthy voice of the low, which questions the high—the church and the state—is an important check on oppressive officials in a healthy society.

A full-fledged carnival—such as those in Rio de Janeiro and New Orleans—does not exist in the Iranian culture sphere. By carnival I mean a massive demonstration of excessive eating, drinking, and sexual and bodily exposure, popularly associated with Carnival in Rio de Janeiro, that does not occur within an Islamic/Iranian context. Threads and themes of carnivalesque and grotesque subversion, however, can be found woven through the fabric of the Iranian world. Here the needle that pricks the official religious, social, and political powers most is the traditional comic theater in its many guises.

In many ways siyah-bazi and ru-howzi embody Bakhtin's notions of the grotesque and the carnivalesque. *Gholam-siyah*, the blackface clown, the "low Other," always wins over his master: the world upside down. Gholam-siyah's extravagant clothing, movements, speech, and lower-class language demonstrate Bakhtin's dictum, "the grotesque . . . cannot be separated from folk humor and carnival spirit" (Stallybrass and White 1986, 43). Gholam's bright red costume and conical hat, for example, are probably the closest thing to carnival costume in the entire Middle East. William O. Beeman, a scholar of Iranian linguistics, discusses the blackface clown: "The clown distorts normal physical movement by jumping, running, flailing his arms, and twisting his body into odd shapes" (1981, 515). This is, of course, part of his repertoire, for sight gags make up much of the comedy of traditional comic theater. This grotesque twisting of the body is also part of the dancing that occurs in the comic theater, especially by the male characters.

One of the most important elements in all Iranian performance practices—music, theater, or dance—is improvisation. It is this crucial aesthetic element that allows for the creativity and unending freshness that
characterizes these performing arts and gives scope for their continued development. Mofid states that these theatrical forms are improvised to such
an extent that if the price of bread were raised by the government in the afternoon, that evening, ten minutes before going onstage, the players would
construct the play around that subject.

> The subject or topic that we choose for the performance is always the latest
> political event, preferably a scandal or outrage. Sometimes the event that we
> choose to make fun of, a ban on chewing gum from a certain country or an
> unpopular tax on bread, is only hours old. If bread is the topic, we do bread.
> Sometimes the person who hires us tells us to address a particular subject. We
> are steeped in these matters and always attuned to the latest political hap-
> penings as subjects of our plays. But because they were improvised, you would
> never see the same play twice. (Pers. com. January 24, 1994)

In all of these forms the lower and weaker characters triumph, at least
temporarily, in the theatrical context. Within the theater we can observe
Iranian life, but in reverse: the servant orders the master, the daughter
marries the suitor of her choice, the villager wins over the landlord—the
world upside down. Theater scholar Peter Chelkowski's incisive analysis
neatly sums up the social function of these theatrical forms: "Humour and
laughter have generally been the only outlet for grievances against the
harsh and autocratic governments, rulers and fathers. No other defense
was available or exempt from punishment. Rigid social codes and mores
were also softened by the antics of *Siyah* and the other comedians" (1991,
782).

In his analysis of Bakhtin, Robert Stam, a scholar of popular culture,
neatly pinpoints issues of the carnival theory that are pertinent to this
study. He observes that "artistic and narrative strategies associated with
carnival[:] parody and burlesque in the form of the 'low take-off on what
the high people were doing,'" are an exact depiction of Iranian improvisational comic theater in all of its forms (1989, 97). His characterization that
"marginal and subversive art with its adversary relationship to power and
to official culture . . . and the linguistic corollary of carnivalization [entail]
the liberation of language from the norms of good sense and etiquette"
(1989, 99) dovetails with both the literature and the personal interviews I
conducted.

Mofid stated that, because of its political satire, the Iranian government
is afraid of the siyah-bazi and that currently in Tehran it is being performed
underground (pers. com. March 4, 1994). Peter Stallybrass and Allon
White's observation of seventeenth- and eighteenth-century English the-

ater echoes Mofid's view of Iranian governmental reactions to Iranian the-ater: "Whilst the godly railed at the theatre for its idolatry and its impiety, the State, even as it patronized the actors, feared their potential for sedition and subversion" (1986, 61).

Stam points out that "carnivalesque art is uninterested in psychological verisimilitude or conventional audience identification with rounded per-sonalities" (1989, 109). His characterization is a valid description of two highly carnivalesque theatrical forms, the Italian/French commedia del-l'arte and Iranian siyah-bazi/ru-howzi. The latter genre resembles comme-dia dell'arte in the use of stock character types and thin plot lines for the improvisatory high jinks that are the soul of this type of theater perform-ance. In many ways the siyah-bazi, with its use of music and dance, epito-mizes Stam's analysis of the musical comedy as a "two-dimensional carnival in which the oppressive structures of everyday life are not so much over-turned (as in Bakhtin's conception) as they are stylized, choreographed, and mythically transcended" (1989, 92).

I suggest that Iranian traditional theater, in all its forms, embodies Bakhtin's notions of carnivalesque and grotesque, and this framework, cou-pled with the works of Stam (1989) and Stallybrass and White (1986), pro-vides the most useful theoretical approach for its understanding. It uses lower-body humor, depicts the world upside down in which the weak, at least temporarily, are on top, and satirizes the powerful. Improvisational comic theater is a mirror of Iranian culture, but a mirror that reflects the opposite of the political and social reality of everyday life and therefore might be said to operate as a safety valve for the expression of political and social discontent and frustration.

Mardomi music, which is enjoyed, even if not openly, by many individu-als of the upper classes, reveals the light side of Iranian life; it also exposes the underbelly of Iranian urban society that existed in the sometimes vio-lent world of the former demimonde café, depicted in many Iranian films of the 1960s and 1970s, and red-light districts. In this manner, this musical genre begs for comparison with such genres as flamenco and jazz, but, un-like those genres, which developed relatively unmolested, the production of popular music was banned by the Islamic Republic.

I argue that in an Iranian context, of the two broadest popular musical types, traditional and Westernized, the latter form was often dismissed by Iranian and non-Iranian scholars and intellectuals on the grounds that it was admired and consumed only by those elements of the urban popula-tion, particularly the youth, who avidly sought to emulate the West. The presence of such Western-oriented music contributed to and fueled the discourse of nationalism, purity, authenticity, and nativism. Ruhollah Khaleqi claimed that one reason for writing his history of Iranian music was that, because of Westernization, "the people have sought European music.

But because sufficient knowledge of it does not exist in everyone, they have become satisfied with the simplest form of it, jazz, . . . and in this manner they have ruined and corrupted our music" (1974, 2). The lyrics of this Westernized genre rely on Persian literary and popular poetry as well as on Western poetic models. Generally its texts do not present carnivalesque threats to middle-class values. Because of their sanitized lyrics, these genres of Westernized music form a relatively "safe" or "innocuous" body of music and, unlike mardomi music, are often played on the radio.[4] The perceived threat for some Iranians lies in the Western musical elements.

Historically, however, traditional popular music—mardomi, ru-howzi, or motrebi music—was disparaged and excoriated because of the perceived low class of its performers and its contents, contexts, and consumers. The content and performance of this musical tradition, while sometimes featuring conventionally sentimental Persian lyrics, largely emphasize the politically and socially irreverent, sexually playful, and satirical, witty, and frivolous broadsides. Many of the best-known songs come from the ru-howzi/siyah-bazi professional theater as well as the *bazi-ha-ye namayeshi*, or women's domestic theater, and thus these songs embody Bakhtin's (1984) notions of the carnivalesque and the world upside down. These theatrical forms, and the songs used in them, are deeply revealing of aspects of gender, ethnicity, and Iranian hierarchical society, all of which the songs lampoon and expose. They are also performed and created by both men and women equally, in contrast to the heavily male-dominated classical music world (see Khaleqi 1974, 465–66).[5]

WHAT IS PERSIAN POPULAR MUSIC?

It is important to specify what is meant by the term "popular music," because, like much popular culture, Persian popular music is not only ill defined but also often carries a pejorative connotation among classical musicians, ethnomusicologists, and other scholars as the Other in a high/ low artistic continuum. Although certain Iranian classical musicians attempt to create rigid categories to distinguish what constitutes classical and popular music, the ethnomusicologist Bruno Nettl more accurately states that "the distinction between classical and popular music in the framework of Persian musical culture is not always easy to grasp" (1992, 157). He adds that the Persian terms for and categories of classical and popular music "seemed . . . to be used mainly by musicians of the classical tradition in order to denigrate the rest" (1992, 157). Nettl stands as the only ethnomusicologist to attempt a serious investigation of the topic of popular music, as an adjunct to his larger study of aspects of the classical music system (*radif*). He suggests, "[Classical music] is a system with an internal definition and is thus self-limiting. Perhaps we may then be justified in considering and labeling what is left, if we also subtract music in a definitely Western style as well as certain religious musical phenomena such as Koran chanting, as Persian popular music" (1972, 219).

Although Persian popular music does constitute to some extent a blurred genre, Nettl's characterization falls short of adequately defining the phenomenon. For one thing, there is more than one genre of Persian popular music. One might look, for example, to Iranian contexts in which as long as the language of the particular musical production is Persian, the majority of Iranians will identify it as Persian popular music. In an Iranian context poetry and lyrics overshadow music and occupy a position unimaginable in Western society. This covers a wide range of musical output, including recent productions by young Iranian groups such as The Boys and The Black Cats whose rap music is clearly imitative of American productions and contains both Persian and English words, as well as the more classically oriented tasnif sung by vocalists such as Marzieh and Ellaheh, two well-known singers of the older generation. Both Marzieh and Ellaheh perform classical tasnif as well as newer classical songs that have become popular and other types of music that can be considered popular. This latter tradition of singing, to the accompaniment of a variety of traditional and Western instruments, is being carried out in southern California by a newer generation of vocalists such as Shakila, Mo'in, Sattar, Shahla Sarshar, Fayezeh, and Ahmad Azad. The economic dynamics of survival requires many of the performers of classical music in southern California to also perform popular music, known as *shad* (happy), as many of them make their principal incomes from personal appearances at weddings and nightclubs, where such music is requested. Interestingly, some of these newer singers and groups are performing older popular songs from the mardomi tradition in updated versions.[6]

As space does not allow for a purely musical analysis, I define Persian popular music, or musics, as (1) urban music, (2) primarily in the Persian language (although occasionally another major language found in Iran, such as Gilaki, Azeri Turkish, or Kurdish, is used), (3) that captures the imagination, attention, and devoted following of a large and diverse audience. Thus it is the consumer and the audience member, as well as the context, that define the meaning of "popular."[7] In contrast to classical music, vocal music dominates virtually all of the popular music genres, although an occasional reng from the mardomi tradition, such as *shateri,* may also be included. Further complicating the study of what may be considered classical or popular, certain classical artists, such as Golpayegani, became "popular" in the view of certain members of the classical establishment through radio, television, films, and nightclub and concert appearances.[8]

Two important genres of Persian popular music that will not be discussed fully here also deserve mention. In the 1940s and early 1950s frankly Western types of music with Persian lyrics appeared. Songs such as Jamshid Sheibani's renditions of Persian-language tangos and the Jolly Boys' 78 rpm Columbia recording of "Atal matal" (syllables used for nursery rhymes) to the tune of "Bell Bottom Trousers, Coats of Navy Blue" were representative of the genre.[9] A revolution in this style of Westernized music occurred in 1954 when the popular music icon Viguen sang "Mahtab" (Moonlight), inaugurating a new style of Persian and Western fusion, largely composed outside of the *dastgah* (modal) system and using only Western instruments. Viguen still performs widely in southern California, and among Iranians he is known as the "King of Jazz" (*soltan-e jaz*) (Zinder 1992). No history or analysis of popular music in Iran can afford to omit mention of the song "Mara bebus" (Kiss Me), which enjoyed phenomenal success and into which some segments of the public read political meaning beyond the overtly sentimental lyrics. Any historian describing and analyzing Persian popular music must also address the phenomenal career of Googoush, a vocalist and entertainer of true world-class talent. Googoush began singing in the 1960s and swept all before her. Her meteoric rise to fame in films, television, and her still-popular recordings recall the career of Frank Sinatra, and many Iranians reverently refer to her simply as "The Queen." Googoush is arguably the most popular entertainer in Iranian history.

Western music was not the only source of inspiration for popular music production in prerevolutionary Iran. The vocalists Jebbeli, Tajik, and, in the beginning of her career, Pouran sang many songs that were either direct copies of Arabic or, more rarely, Indian popular songs, or an attempt to emulate that style. This alarmed many Iranian nationalists. Compared to the Westernized production, this genre of popular music enjoyed limited popularity. The political scientist Mehrzad Boroujerdi wryly observes, "Today, in the closing years of this aging century, the West and modernity have replaced the Arabs and Islam as the favorite scapegoats of the Iranian intelligentsia" (1996, 179).

Many well-known vocalists of the older generation such as Ellaheh, Delkash, Pouran, and Iraj can be designated cross-over artists, performing with equal ease in classical and popular contexts. They often performed at large weddings and in fashionable nightclubs, and their recordings were top sellers. Therefore, in the Iranian case, there are several types of popular music, and they may be conceived along a continuum of musical content that ranges from that considered a legitimate portion of the classical dastgah system to that which contains increasing degrees of Western musical elements, such as instrumentation, harmony, counterpoint, vocal technique, and melodic and rhythmic patterns. The extreme is a style of music that is totally Western musically but with Persian lyrics. Musically, popular music exhibits some of the characteristics that Nettl identified, and which I would call a blurred genre. This is why, for purposes of this chapter, the consumer and the context of performance largely define what constitutes "popular" music. It is true, as Nettl points out, that most Iranians do not seem to make the clear-cut distinctions between popular and classical that, according to him, classical musicians make. Such distinctions by nonmusicians often take into account the literary quality of the lyrics, the context, and the particular vocalist. Most important, the "consumer" may patronize the live performances and purchase the recordings of a wide variety of music—Persian classical, popular, and folk music and various forms of Western classical and popular music. As the sociologist Bennet Berger sagely observes, "Everybody knows (or should know) that real life is usually more complex and subtle than the analytic categories and other abstractions that social scientists must use to make generalizations" (1995, 69). Nettl's sampling of musical tastes in Tehran in 1969 demonstrates that, along a continuum of educated to uneducated, and young to old, certain trends in musical preferences could be discerned. But by no means could he discern or predict any specific preference according to age or economic or educational group (Nettl 1970, 1972, 1992), demonstrating that it is analytically dangerous to essentialize audiences or musical categories. And, most important, most Iranian consumers of music happily listen to a wide variety of musical forms rather than confine their consumption to a single genre.

MARDOMI:
TRADITIONAL POPULAR MUSIC IN PREREVOLUTIONARY IRAN

The most "traditional" and oldest genre of popular music was, and is, that played by the *motreb*, a professional public entertainer who sings, acts, dances, and plays a musical instrument. The music is often referred to as mardomi, motrebi, or ru-howzi.[10] A singer of this genre is often called *khanandeh-ye mardomi* (people's singer), as in the twentieth century the term "motreb" constitutes an insult. This type of popular, urban music, or one similar to it, certainly dates at least to the nineteenth century, and according to travelers' accounts, such as those by Sir John Chardin (1987), Adam Olearius ([1662] 1977), and John Baptista Tavernier ([1678] 1961), probably centuries earlier. Thus when Nettl states that "before the introduction of broadcasting . . . whether there was a phenomenon which could be properly designated as urban popular music is certainly not clear" (1972, 218), I counter by suggesting that indeed the mardomi, ru-howzi/ motrebi musical tradition was present during the period investigated in Tehran, and still lives in the changed and different conditions of the southern California Iranian immigrant community. I argue that ru-howzi/mardomi constitutes a genre of definable historical urban popular music in Iran. Singers like Susan, Afat, Mahvash, Aghassi, Iraj, Ahdieh, and Parivash were highly popular performers of this tradition, with large segments of the urban working class, among others, forming their devoted followers.[11] This musical genre predated broadcasting. Broadcasting and, more important, film and recording media simply made this popular music more available, more often, to more people than before the advent of electronic media. Because the sincere and cheerfully open vulgarity of much of this performative genre emerged from the women's quarters, low-class cafés and music halls, and the red-light district, much of this music was not heard on government-sponsored radio, which primarily broadcast Westernized popular music and Persian classical music. The lyric content of these latter genres was a good deal less problematic for squeamish officials than the rough-and-tumble verses of the mardomi music, with their carnivalesque celebration and social critiques of sex and politics. Rather, the chief medium contributing to the popularity of this popular genre was the privately owned film industry. The mardomi musical tradition figured in the majority of films from the 1950s to the revolution, appealing largely to the working class. "To satisfy the not-so-critical Iranian audiences of such films, who expected to be entertained, Persian singing and dancing and often a comedy character were almost always included in Iranian feature films" (Issari 1989, 159). M. Ali Issari's encyclopedic history of the Iranian cinema demonstrates that the majority of moneymaking films in any given year during this period fell into this musical category.[12] I argue that in many ways the film industry carried on aspects of the traditional comic theater, ru-howzi, which used this style of music, dance, and comedy. The frenetic pace and haphazard style of the production of this type of musical film in Iran, well described by Issari, required the musicians and comedians to improvise, thus retaining one of the most important elements of traditional performance—improvisation. The musicians sometimes used trumpets and accordions, in place of *tar* and *kemancheh*, but in its essentials mardomi music has retained its traditional performative core: its essence lies in the transgressive and earthy wit, satire, and daring double entendre of its often improvised lyrics; its principal site of live, public performance, for exclusively male audiences, was the working-class entertainment center of the Lalezar, while women performed in the context of domestic women's improvisational comic theater, which, following Sayyid Abu al-Qasim Anjavi Shirazi (1973), I call *bazi-ha-ye namayeshi*—theatrical games or plays (Shay 1995a).

In contrast to the study of classical music, which constitutes an important vehicle for high-quality literary poetry and virtuosic vocal and instrumental technique, mardomi musical genres are perhaps of more interest to the sociologist or ethnographer than to the musicologist for the revealing content of its lyrics.[13] The rhythm of ru-howzi is always a driving or, alternatively, a highly sensual 6/8. The clever lyrics, often improvised and embroidered on well-known themes, are more prominent than the often simple melodic construction. The structure of the lyrics is repetitive: the singer refers to a series of body parts, men's professions, or family relatives, for example, in a serial manner. Audience participation is encouraged through the use of response choruses that call "yes" or "why not?" thus serving as a motor that moves the song. The most popular vocalists are appreciated for their earthy, raucous, often bawdy and daring style of delivery rather than for beautiful voices and classical vocal technique. The delivery sometimes takes on a patter style, containing many improvised elements relating to the specific context in which it is performed. Male vocalists of this genre often emerge from the ru-howzi theater, while women generally learned the songs and lyrics in a domestic context. Thus both men and women perform and are familiar with this genre.

As Docker (1994) aptly indicates, many of the lyrics and the content of the traditional music emerge from the "lower female strata"—from the women's quarters, which, in an Iranian/Islamic context, are off limits to males. Nevertheless, men imbibed these lyrics and tunes, created by anonymous female genius, from viewing them as children in the women's quarters and from seeing them performed by women in the professional locales of the red-light district and the Lalezar district.

In the traditional households that far and away make up the majority in urban Iran, where financially feasible, separate living quarters (*andarun*, female; *biruni*, male) are the rule. Most of the men, at least from the more traditional quarters of the city, spend the majority of their social lives among other men, at one another's homes, in teahouses and cafés or other social gathering places, and in religious activities. The majority of women do likewise, carrying out their lives in the parallel but private world of the andarun. This is the setting of the bazi-ha-ye namayeshi, and so here we find the voices of countless unnamed women who created, and continue to create, this genre. I say "continue" because the improvisational nature of this theatrical form lends itself to constant change and evolution. It is within the context of the *bazi-ha* (plays) that anonymous women's voices of Iran are most tellingly revealed, as it is here that women have used their creativity to develop and express their concerns and emotions in the context of traditional theater. In the next section I discuss ru-howzi, siyah-bazi, and women's theatrical forms as historical and contemporary sources for this musical genre.

WOMEN'S THEATER

A notable, but less well known, urban form of comic improvisational theater is women's theater, bazi-ha-ye namayeshi. In contrast to the ru-howzi and siyah-bazi, women's theater—although characterized by many of the same performative characteristics as the other forms—was created, developed, and primarily performed by and for women. Unlike the men's theatrical performances, these are strictly amateur, domestic productions. The contents of the sung and chanted verses, and the accompanying dancing and mimetic movements, deal with issues that are reflective of the lives and concerns of women. The political satire found in men's theater is absent in women's theater. Briefly, they principally differ from the men's comic performances in that they use more patter verse and dancing and less spoken dialogue. The clown figure does not exist in the women's plays.

Most important, in these games, women are allowed to behave outside the bounds of normal propriety. If the terms "grotesque" and "carnivalesque" indicate a distortion of the normal or natural to a degree of absurdity, then the women's games, like the siyah-bazi and ru-howzi, must also be included in the carnivalesque aspect of traditional Iranian life. As in Bakhtin's carnivalesque, the underdog always wins; this is one arena in which women always triumph.

The types of issues that interest traditional Iranian women form the topics of the lyrics of bazi-ha-ye namayeshi: keeping a husband's interest through being attractive and sexy; infidelity; children born out of wedlock; being forced to marry a man whom one does not like or know and who has been chosen by one's parents; problems with female in-laws (with whom a young bride traditionally lives); and proper and circumspect behavior. In these plays a woman may briefly escape the bonds of everyday behavior within the authoritarian, patriarchal system in which she often feels helpless and insecure and performatively act in a free manner denied her in everyday life. I maintain that these plays serve to mediate between what M. Reza Behnam characterizes as the "conflict between authoritarian and antiauthoritarian behavior," which he asserts pervades Iranian social and political life (1986, 9).

The theme of enumerating the qualities of men by profession (often using double entendre) is reiterated in a number of plays. In *Zari be Pari goft* (Zari Told Pari), *Mashti Sanam goft* (Mashti Told Sanam), and *Hodor-modor* (Nonsense Syllables), one of the girls tells another why she will not marry the butcher, the priest (*akhund*), the perfumer, the grocer, the shepherd, the colonel, the tailor, the dervish, or the day construction worker, among others, because the description of their work describes the worst part of their (often sexual) behavior. It is also a subplot in "Khaleh ro-ro," a popular game song in which the girl is "six months married and seven months gone" until she enacts the birth of her child whose father could be the butcher or the baker, among many others.

A more elaborate play featuring men of different professions, involving a mother and daughter, is acted out in *Kiye, kiye dar mizaneh?* (Who Is It, Who Is It Knocking at the Door?). A series of men of different professions and trades arrive at the door bearing gifts of their trade. In contravention of normative Iranian behavior, the mother urges the daughter to accept their offerings, and thus, implicitly, their sexual advances in return for the gifts, behavior that is never countenanced in real life.

Another major theme found in some of the bazi-ha is the tension between a young wife and her female in-laws, such as "Abji Gol Bahar." One such popular game, not included in the Anjavi Shirazi collection, recorded by Mahvash, is "In dast kajeh?" (Is This Hand Deformed?) The chorus responds, "Ki migeh kajeh?" (Who says it's crooked?). The young wife replies, "Madar shohar" (Mother-in-law); the chorus says, "Doshman-e te" (She's your enemy).

Sex is perhaps the most popular topic of these songs, especially in cafés catering to an all-male clientele. "Do ta limu daram, mikhari?" (I have two lemons, will you buy them?), to which the male response chorus answers, "Mikharam, areh, vallah" (Yes, I swear, I'll buy them), referring to the breasts. In another song with the same theme, "Jombun, jombun-e inja, menar-e jombun-e inja" (It's Shaking, Shaking Here, the Shaking Minaret [referring to a famous leaning tower of Pisa-like structure in Isfahan], Is Here), the vocalist also refers to her body.

Some of these games are seemingly performed for the sheer transgressive fun that they provide to the participants, who would never be permitted to act in such a manner outside of this group of confidantes. For example, one such game, "Murcheh dareh" (There Are Ants), is virtually a striptease (the very term used by Anjavi Shirazi [1973, 55–56]). During the dance-play, the main character points to various parts of her body asking, "Murcheh dareh che kar konam?" (There are ants [here], what shall I do?), to which the chorus responds, "Bekan o beriz, bekan o beriz" (Take it off and throw it away), referring to the various items of clothing until the performer is nude. In "'Amu sabzi forush" (Uncle Vegetable Seller), the woman approaches the vegetable seller: "Sabzit barikeh? Dalun tarikeh." "Is your vegetable slender?" she asks. "The hallway is dark," she affirms. "Man na'na mikham, to-ra tanha mikham" (I want mint, I want you alone), she continues, asking many questions about his "vegetable" in exchange for which she will give a kiss, shake her body, and so on (Anjavi Shirazi 1973, 117–18).

Sattareh Farman Farmaian relates how, during her childhood, one of the servants in the royal harem entertained the others and how these transgressive games were enjoyed by women of both high and low status:

> With Batul-Khanom there was someone with whom to sew, visit the baths, and enjoy the jokes, games, and clowning with which women entertained themselves in a big, fancy andarun like Ezzatdoleh's (daughter of the Shah and the first and former wife of Farman Farmaian's father). My mother was too strict a Moslem to clown, but she enjoyed watching the others' horseplay, especially one of Ezzatdoleh's maids, who could paint her naked buttocks to look like

two eyes and, dancing with them to the onlookers, would roll them so that the two eyes crossed. This made my mother, her little sisters, Batul and her daughters, and all the other women laugh until their sides ached. (1992, 37)

The value of such parody and satire should not be sold short. And yet this, in effect, is what scholars of Iranian music and theater have done by their failure to adequately analyze popular culture phenomena.[14]

CLASSICAL HIGH—POPULAR LOW

Earlier I alluded to the fear and loathing popular music and its accompanying performing style create among certain elements of the population, particularly strict Muslims and classical musicians, although perhaps for different reasons. Analytically it is important not to conflate and simplify such reactions and unproblematically refer to Islam's "well-known" repugnance to music, as many scholars have done (see And 1959, 1976; Farhat 1965), but rather to understand that these reactions are complex and that not all Muslims think alike. In many ways the phenomenon of popular music can be compared to jazz, tango, and flamenco (see, e.g., Savigliano 1995; Mitchell 1994). In a similar and parallel fashion, all of these genres have engendered similar reactions within their own societies. As the flamenco scholar Timothy J. Mitchell observes,

> Spaniards concerned about the moral tenor of their society came to look upon deep song with deep contempt.
>   There is much to be learned from people who find certain musical styles transgressive and threatening. As Roger Taylor argued in an important essay, the spread of American jazz is best understood by studying the reactions of those who were hostile toward it. Alarmed musicians, clergymen, journalists, and even philosophers heard the new music as sensuous and indecent, suitable only for houses of prostitution; its primitive rhythms aroused animal passions; jazz embodied a spirit of lawlessness and a general revolt against authority. . . . Like early flamenco, early jazz has been associated with despised ethnic groups, gangsters, free-spending bluebloods, and hedonism. Only by disguising its orgiastic origins was jazz able to become part of the musical mainstream. (1994, 45)

It was therefore neither unsurprising nor unprecedented that one of the first acts of the Islamic Republic was to ban dance and popular music: both the Westernized variety for its associations with the West and the traditional mardomi music and performance for its perceived sexual, social, and political sedition. In contrast, the Islamic regime supports performances of classical music of a serious nature and positively valorizes regional folk music. This means that, in practical terms, unlike jazz, tango, and flamenco, which largely resisted attempts at suppression and evolved into highly sought after, highly esteemed genres, mardomi music has had most of its creative roots and performing contexts destroyed. Its few professional performers in southern California, such as Susan and Aghassi, are often older and middle-aged and often perform songs from the prerevolutionary period that are familiar to their audiences. Younger performers enter the more socially acceptable classical music arena or the economically lucrative Westernized popular music field.

In Islam sexual segregation is a social response to the belief that, while sexuality is a powerful and legitimate force for both men and women, the force of uncontrolled sexuality is capable of tearing apart the fabric of society (for a full discussion of this issue, see Mernissi 1975; Haeri 1989). Uncontrolled sexuality can only be properly and effectively contained through segregation. It is therefore not merely the presumed vulgarity of popular entertainment that exercises the wrath of classical musicians, Muslim authorities, and sometimes establishment bureaucrats. Rather, it is the public performance of professional female dancers and singers in male space, performing before males who do not stand in a proper legal relationship to them, that incites the authorities to action. Throughout history, some, but by no means all, Islamic clergymen have inveighed against the use of dance and music. For example, in his famous *Kashf al-asrar* (Discovery of Secrets), Ruhollah Khomeini, later spiritual and temporal ruler of Iran, proclaimed that "music which encourages the spirit of passion and love among the youth is forbidden in the *shariat* and should be taken out of school programs" (1971, 313–14, quoted in Paidar 1995). Parvin Paidar, a scholar of Middle Eastern women's studies, observes, "Khomeini criticized Reza Shah [father of Mohammad Reza Pahlavi, the last ruler of the Pahlavi dynasty] and Ataturk as 'idiotic dictators' [for] spreading 'the means of pleasure,' and preoccupying people with unveiling, European clothes, cinema, theater, music and dance" (1995, 121). However, some clergy do not regard it negatively. In a recent broadcast on Radio Seda-ye Iran (August 27, 1996), Ayatollah Haeri, in a live interview from Germany, stated that he was not against dance or music. "Music is the food of the soul [*ghaza-ye ruh*]," he declared. Thus there is disagreement among the clergy over this issue. As we have seen, "attitudes have varied widely, from outright condemnation to advocacy of it as a means of spiritual growth and enlightenment" (Caton 1983, 61). A full discussion of the topic of Islam and music is beyond the scope of this chapter.[15]

Furthermore, in a nation in which Shi'i Islam is the state and majority religion, important elements, but by no means all, of the strictly religious population revile all music as sinful. This ambiguity of Islamic opinion may well be reflected in the emphasis on spirituality and Sufism into which musicians such as Safvat attempt to cast classical music.[16] Thus the dichotomy and barriers that scholars and performers of classical music attempted, and still attempt, to erect between those categories of music that they perceive as classical and popular enter the occasionally strident discourse of nationalism. Perhaps for some of the classical musicians, themes of authenticity and purity may be a matter of survival within an Islamic environment that Caton characterizes as "anti-musical" (1983, 61). Dariush Safvat, a conservative classical musician, expresses his opinions in an article entitled "Musiqi-ye pop faza ra masmum mikonad" (Pop Music Poisons the Atmosphere; cited in Miller 1995, 107). Lloyd Clifton Miller expresses some of these concerns:

> Finally under the constitution (1906) music became free after 13 centuries of being subdued by religious disfavor. Official freedom of music, however, opened Pandora's box and, according to master Safvat, it seems that every low class and uninitiated lout could and did become a "composer," a "singer" or "instrumentalist." Safvat says the more these charlatans were applauded, the more cocky they became and over the recent decades, authentic Iranian music was nearly totally destroyed by innovators and westernizers. (1995, 102)[17]

The term *asil* (authentic) is often applied to Persian classical and regional folk music by classical musicians and their followers (see During, Mirabdolbaghi, and Safvat 1991), thereby creating its dialectical Other, the "inauthentic." In fact, with the notable exception of Bruno Nettl, ethnomusicologists have consigned Persian popular music to the trash heap of whatever does not constitute "pure" (asil) classical music, on the one hand, and religious or regional folk music, on the other. Consequently, the existence of this "inauthentic" popular music, which still permeates the urban scene in southern California with its rhythmic and ubiquitous presence from every radio in every public café, wedding party, or private home, is both acknowledged and dispensed with in a paragraph or two by the more daring musicologists. This quest for a return to a "golden age of authentic" classical music of pre-Islamic origin is abetted by masters and instructors of this rarefied form who feel beleaguered by the vulgar sounds of Westernized popular music, or worse, the indigenous sounds of mardomi music. Such attitudes are often perpetuated and magnified by their non-Iranian admirers. Thus Miller, in his description of popular music, follows his mentor, Dariush Safvat:

> During the Pahlavi dynasty, the Ministry of Culture and Arts and the radio took the control of music away from the authorized masters. Because of this, people from the lower echelons of society with no spiritual conviction pushed their way into the limelight. According to Safvat, the *motreb* class of performers formerly involved with prostitution, procuring, alcohol and drugs suddenly became the purveyors of the tradition. Safvat explained that the modal system was eventually altered or discarded in favor of cheap *tarane* (pop

songs) fabricated by untrained amateurs who had the audacity to tamper with an art form perfected over thousands of years. (1995, 104)

What is not explained by Safvat and Miller is the fact that there is no possible way of knowing what music thousands of years ago sounded like, or who "authorized" the aforesaid masters.[18]

Jean During, Zia Mirabdolbaghi, and Safvat lay out a chart differentiating classical performance from motrebi (professional, nonclassical performances). In their scheme, among the attributes of classical performance is that it is creative, diversified, original, sober, balanced, and spiritual, whereas motrebi performances are imitative, repetitive, standard, ostentatious, diluted, and sensual. They acknowledge in their analysis that "this rather severe comparison does not attempt to discredit light music, which perfectly fulfills its function, but to clear up the current confusion between light and *asil* music" (1991, 21). In spite of such disclaimers, it should be noted that asil, or authentic, classical music is located at the top of the page next to "High Qualification" on their chart of the various genres of music found in Iran dividing the high from the low, the authentic from the inauthentic (1991, 25). To be sure, many ethnomusicologists and classical Iranian musicians vie to define classical music by its purity, spirituality, and noncontamination by Westernization and in so doing disagree among themselves on exactly which elements (such as harmony) are permissible, and under which conditions. This is done to categorize as "light" any music that they disapprove of or that they deem unworthy of scholarly attention. Some musicians, for example, would allow a recently composed tasnif to be considered to be classical (*sonnati*) if it meets certain qualifications, while others would deny it a place in the classical canon.

Thus Iranian music, classical and popular, in its performance and in its consumption, enters the discourse of nationalism and authenticity. Boroujerdi, while characterizing Iranian intellectuals in general, foregrounds the debate among music scholars as well: "They rejected the apish imitation of the West as fraudulent and the renaissance of the past as archaic. Nonetheless, the formidable ideological permeation of the West led many Iranian intellectuals, in search of indigenization and authenticity, to turn toward nativism and Islamicism" (1996, 176). While viewing Westernization with alarm and claiming that it is causing a lack of interest in authentic, classical music, particularly among youth, classical musicians often fail to mention that before 1906 this music was played only in the homes and courts of the Shah and aristocrats, who jealously guarded their musicians. As Beeman writes, "The disparate quality of Persian music is rooted in the social conditions under which performances took place previous to the constitutional revolution of 1908. Prior to that date there were no public performances of

Persian classical music. All music was performed in private, either for the wealthy or in the private ceremonies of certain dervish orders" (1976, 7). Classical music was never heard by and did not belong to the masses. The performances in the mardomi/motrebi style of professional and street musicians, however, were widely available, leading to this music being termed amiyaneh, or public, by many. According to Khaleqi (1974, 470–74), several bands of motrebs, both all-male and all-female, consisting of musicians, a singer, dancers, acrobats, and actors, of varying size and quality, plied their trade in Tehran, and many photographs and paintings of them are extant.

THE BEAT GOES ON:
POPULAR MUSIC IN THE IRANIAN-AMERICAN COMMUNITY

In Iran the Westernized genre of popular music represented modernity for its consumers. Its contexts, Westernized nightclubs and concerts, made the young people who patronized these performances feel modern and "up-to-date." After its almost total relocation among the Iranian immigrant community of southern California, Persian popular music began to take on subtle aspects of nationalistic identity and even defiance of the Islamic regime that had banned its performance and production. For decades the importance and impact of Persian popular music have loomed large in the Iranian community, both in Iran and, later, in southern California, home to the largest Iranian community outside of Tehran. Indeed, the chief consumers of the Westernized genre were many of those who fled the rigid Islamic order represented by Ayatollah Khomeini. Since popular music was banned in Iran by the Islamic Republic, this salience has not abated, and dancing and popular music can, in some contexts, be emblematic of resistance.[19] Although its primary consuming audience now resides outside of Iran, every individual who has returned to Iran remarks on the wide, underground availability of this music in Tehran. Iranian exile life is saturated with the sounds and images of this music and its star vocalists, musicians, composers, and lyricists. Through a barrage of front-page photographs in leading print media, MTV-style video images on the many Iranian television programs, posters advertising the newest recording or upcoming concert in every grocery store, and frequent interviews with well-known performers on television and radio, the Iranian community in southern California is filled with the sounds and images of popular music.[20]

Unlike Andrew Shyrock's (this volume) description of the Arab community in Detroit, which is made up of both urban and village and both highly educated and nearly illiterate populations, as well as several generations of now assimilated Arab-Americans, the Iranian community in southern California (and nationally) is overwhelmingly urban, highly educated, and only one generation deep. This Western-looking group constituted the chief consumers of Westernized popular music, a trend that continues. The generations are not divided by the genres of music that they consume, but contexts differ. The young attend discotheques where they can dance in large numbers, while the middle-aged and elderly are more frequently encountered at concerts of both classical and popular music. Recent concerts by the very popular Mortazavi were attended by thousands of people of all ages. Middle-aged patrons are encountered in cabarets and nightclubs where the few singers of mardomi music, such as Susan, Shahnaz Tehrani, Aghassi, Hemati, and Hojjati, perform, but these do not approach the numbers of people who attend Westernized popular music concerts.

As one might anticipate, certain changes occur in the musical production of Persian popular music in its new environment. First, in Iran music rarely carried references to Iran or patriotism, whereas in the United States many singers perform songs valorizing Iran, such as "Keshvar-e man" (My Country), which I heard performed in 1996 by Houshmand Aghili.[21] Songs and themes that cater to feelings of nostalgia are now staples of Iranian singers in southern California.[22] Second, many members of the younger generation have fewer linguistic skills in Persian than previous generations, and therefore the lyrics are of less importance than the driving 6/8 beat that animates the Westernized popular musical genre and to which they can dance. Abbas Chamanara, proprietor of the principal and most complete Persian music store in southern California, declared, "Instead of the sad and sentimental music that was produced in Iran, these kids want fast dance music.[23] They want *shad* [happy] music for dancing" (pers. com. December 10, 1996). Many older Iranians, who venerate fine poetry, vehemently decry the decline of literary quality in the music currently produced in Los Angeles. For these listeners, the poetry takes precedence over the music.

A small group of younger musicians, of Iranian parentage but born in the United States or brought here as young children and steeped in Western forms such jazz and New Age genres, are searching through Iranian classical and regional music for inspiration to create new types of fusion music.

RU-HOWZI/MOTREBI MUSIC
IN THE IRANIAN-AMERICAN COMMUNITY

Mardomi music currently enjoys some popularity in the Iranian immigrant community in Los Angeles. However, because its live performance contexts were severed by the authorities of the Islamic Republic, it was repudiated as vulgar and backward by many in the middle class who supported Westernized musical forms and who emigrated to the United States. In the United States it has nostalgic value. Several people told me that they now listen to more traditional music in the United States than they ever did in Iran, "because it takes me back." In their new environment Iranian-American youth have no cultural or linguistic skills for its apprehension, preferring instead the lively, driving dance rhythms of the synthesizer and flocking to discotheques and concerts where it is played at an incredibly high volume. For these reasons, for the young mardomi music is largely marginalized and eclipsed by the more popular Westernized forms.

Mardomi music now forms a nostalgic memory of Iran for the older and middle-aged public who experience it in some nightclubs, parties, and theatrical re-creations. Before the revolution of 1979, new output of this musical genre for the movies and entertainment district cafés was enormous, but in the United States, by contrast, its largely middle-aged and older performers often rely on songs they performed in Iran. A contemporary feeling is maintained by clever references to topical subjects, southern California landmarks, and American situations, as well as nostalgic references to Iran.

Mardomi music can also be experienced in siyah-bazi, a theatrical form that is still performed in the Iranian-American community in southern California. Siyah-bazi's emphasis on quick adaptation to new themes and topics currently enables a focus on subjects that revolve around political folly in the Islamic Republic and adjustment to life and customs in America. The highly nostalgic appearance of the blackface icon of ru-howzi and siyah-bazi theater, Hajji Firuz, who heralds the coming of No-ruz, the Persian New Year, appears on Iranian television networks both live and in animation performing mardomi-style music. The Persian New Year, with its patriotic and nostalgic character, is also the time when some of the well-known performers of this style, such as Bahman Mofid, Hojjati, Morteza Aghili, and Shahnaz Tehrani, can also be seen on television.[24] In addition, many of the advertisements for Iranian food products and services use mardomi-style 6/8 rhythm and its patter style of verse, which is somewhat different in structure and tempo from that found in the more Westernized popular music that dominates Iranian television and radio. Because of its domestic connections, mardomi-style performance is also sometimes used in children's songs. Most recently, with Ardavan Mofid and Bahman Mofid's successful new play, "Haft darvazeh" (The Seven Gates), it has begun to form a classicized and nostalgic look at Iranian performative genres, from the storytelling genres naqqali and shahnameh-khani to ru-howzi. In this review several references to the Lalezar district were made and short mardomi-style songs were performed. Shateri, one of the urban dances associated with the ru-howzi/motrebi musical genre, appears in a variety of music videos documented by Hamid Naficy (1993, 178–87), as well as in a recent classicized choreography featured in concert by the AVAZ International Dance Theatre.[25] Thus mardomi, like jazz and flamenco, may gain a new lease on performance life in new contexts and environments by those who appreciate the droll, satiric messages it conveys.

CONCLUSION

Mardomi/ru-howzi music constitutes a historical genre of popular music of Iran's urban centers, but because it is perceived as vulgar, Iranian musical scholars and their non-Iranian students and disciples have shunned it as an appropriate area of serious study. Some ethnomusicologists, such as Bruno Nettl (1970), questioned the very existence of popular genres before the advent of mass media. This avoidance, in favor of the study of highbrow music, has been unfortunate, as the texts of the mardomi/ru-howzi songs and the contexts of their performance contain vital information about many aspects of Iranian society, including attitudes toward gender, sexuality, and social relationships. Mardomi/ru-howzi music, through its satirical, earthy lyrics, represented a subversive genre discomfiting to the burgeoning middle classes of pre-1979 Iran and represented for many of them a backward expression of traditional life.

Persian classical music and Westernized popular music, by contrast, were regularly aired on the government radio, bestowing on the former the imprimatur and appearance of a semiofficial canon. Unlike Turkey as described by Stokes (1992a) and Egypt as characterized by Armbrust (1996), Iran before the Islamic Revolution did not use music as a symbol of modernization.

Whereas Armbrust (1996) shows a distinct generational split in patterns of musical consumption in Egypt, surprisingly, Iranian-Americans do not exhibit such sharp generational differences. Many people of all ages enjoy Westernized popular music and flock to concerts where it is performed. Concerts by Dariush, Ebi, Mortazavi, and Leila Foruhar draw thousands of people of all ages. The generational difference can be seen more in terms of the venues where the music is enjoyed: the younger generation flocks to discotheques and prefers music that is danceable; the older generation prefers concert and nightclub settings. For the older generation, the meaning and the quality of the lyrics form the most important element in their listening experience, whereas the younger generation, generally less fluent in Persian, seeks music with a driving, danceable beat.

Mardomi/ru-howzi lyrics are replete with many references to specific sites and customs unknown to the younger generation, with its limited experience of life in Iran. Because of this it provides nostalgic memories of the old country for those old enough to remember but remains largely meaningless for most younger people. Significantly, the singers of this genre are middle-aged and older: new performers in the United States enter the potentially lucrative Westernized popular music field or, more rarely, study classical music. Lyrics created for current popular songs have more patriotic and nostalgic content than was formerly the case in Iran. These are still not numerous compared to the sentimental and romantic lyrics of the vast majority of popular songs.

The entire popular music industry, banned by the Islamic Republic, relocated to southern California. It is unique in that it produces music not only for the millions of Iranians now resident in the United States and Europe but also for consumption in Iran. This music is made available in Iran through an elaborate system of illegal importation through the Gulf states where many Iranians work as well as through Iranians visiting home from abroad. Anecdotal evidence from every visitor to Iran attests to the widespread consumption and availability in Iran of popular music produced in southern California.

It is difficult to predict whether mardomi music will thrive in Iran, where reports of underground performances of siyah-bazi continue.[26] In the Iranian-American community, barring a revival, it will most likely fade with its aging performers.

NOTES

My sincere gratitude to the ethnomusicologist Danilo Lozano for his valuable comments and generous suggestions.

Bazm-e Qajariyyeh (parties from the Qajar era, 1795–1925) often took place in the extensive gardens of the rich and are documented in memoirs, paintings, and photographs of the period. As a vocal performer of music of both the classical and popular genres for more than forty years, I have personally experienced the powerful hold these 6/8 rhythms in all their manifestations have over their Iranian listeners. Early in the 1950s, when I began learning songs from both the *motrebi* and the classical traditions, I was struck by the unique 6/8 rhythms found throughout the Iranian world, including Azerbaijan, Armenia, Tajikistan, Afghanistan, and Uzbekistan, all of which are connected through important elements of dance, music, literature, and shared history, among others. In this vast region the 6/8 rhythm was or is performed in its many variations, including a nearly 7/8 rhythm in the eastern parts of this area. Iranian musicians told me that this rhythm ran in their veins and was called *shir-e madar* (mother's milk) because, like mother's milk, the rhythm was imbibed as young children. For a sampling of 6/8 rhythms found in Persian music, see Faramarz Tehrani's *Ritm-ha-ye varzeshi* (Exercise Rhythms 1991), a manual on how to play the *tonbak*, a goblet-shaped drum. Some scholars will perhaps argue that it is the poetry or music that excites the interest of an Iranian audience, but personal experience has shown that when the audience hears a 6/8 rhythmic introduction of a *reng* (dance piece) or song, even before any lyrics are sung or any melody is played, they begin to snap their fingers (*beshkan*) or clap in time to the rhythm in happy expectation of what is to follow.

1. For an excellent discussion of what constitutes highbrow and lowbrow, Lawrence W. Levine (1988) details not only how cultural canons are constructed but also how the cultural hierarchies of what constitutes "high" and "low" are dynamic categories that mutate under changing economic and social conditions.

2. The most detailed and important study of the tasnif is Margaret Caton's Ph.D. dissertation (1983). However, it should be noted that, like many ethnomusicologists, she limits her study to tasnifs, which belong to the classical canon in the opinion of most ethnomusicologists and Iranian classical musicians.

3. *Motreb*, a word of Arabic origin meaning "one who gladdens or makes happy," refers to public entertainers who variously and in combination acted, played musical instruments, sang, and danced. Historically such a category of performer dates back at least to the fourteenth century, where the term is found in the poetry of Hafez. These entertainers were linguistically and conceptually set apart from the serious musicians of the court. In the twentieth century, when public performances of all kinds of music became available, *motreb* came to refer, disparagingly, to those who play light music. It needs to be stressed that the designation "motreb" in the twentieth century constitutes a loaded insult, and those performers who consider themselves classical musicians are very sensitive to its negative connotations. I have personally heard numerous musicians disparage one another by using this term.

Truly low-class street musicians, as well as certain types of itinerant rural performers, were often called *luti*. The depiction of parties in Persian miniatures, accompanied by dancing and wine, and Europeans' shocked descriptions of wild drinking bouts, as well as the untimely deaths of several rulers of both the Timurid and Safavid dynasties (1501–1725) from overconsumption, graphically demonstrate that these gatherings were not contemplative philosophical affairs but revels calling for entertaining, rather than serious, music.

4. An exception to Westernized popular music containing "safe" lyrics were some songs performed by Dariyush that contained covert political criticism.

5. Ruhollah Khaleqi suggests that because women "went in search of decorating themselves to captivate hearts . . . they made little effort to acquire art and leave some traces of it and therefore the pages of history are filled with the names of male artists" (1974, 466). Khaleqi's portrayal of women as artistic lightweights extends through his chapter "Women and Art" (465–86), in which he characterizes women as more likely to inspire art than to create it.

6. As an example of this, I was recently interviewed on Radio Seda-ye Iran, the twenty-four-hour Persian-language station and asked by the host, Ali Reza Meibudi, to sing "Yek hamumi sita sazam, chehel sotun, chehel panjereh" (I Built a Bathhouse for You with Forty Pillars and Forty Windows), an old tasnif that hovers perilously between the classical and motrebi traditions and that has become associated with my performances. After I sang a verse, he segued into a new version, replete with synthesizers, by Shamaizadeh, an older popular music performer from Iran.

7. Regarding context, certain classical musicians insist that the setting for the performance of classical music must be intimate, contemplative, and spiritual, a setting where both performer and listener may concentrate. Thus songs performed at weddings and cafés cannot be considered classical. During, Mirabdolbaghi, and Safvat advise that classical music should be performed that "suggest[s] an element of

hal, contemplation, and concentration to younger generations by striking a balance between poetry and music, helping them liberate themselves from the ill effects of the age of the machine and the culture of money, violence and sex" (1991, 248).

8. In fact, one of the most successful attempts to "popularize" classical music was made by the immensely popular classical avaz singer, Golpayegani, of whom Lloyd Clifton Miller disparagingly writes: "Golpayegani was a promising vocal master who recorded on the UNESCO album entitled 'Iran' wherein he was accompanied by Borumand on *tar.* Sadly, he later fell victim to the applause of audiences and eventually decayed into a pop singer who crooned to audiences, milking them for cheers by exaggerated and contrived expressions of emotion" (1995, 229–30). While Golpayegani was reviled in some soi-disant elite classical circles, many Iranians praised him for saving classical music by performing it in new contexts for audiences who would otherwise never have listened to it. Reactions to Golpayegani's performances are not unlike those that criticize Luciano Pavarotti's "popular" appearances.

9. In an interview (December 23, 1996), Jamshid Sheibani told me that, in fact, he was the first singer to incorporate Western elements in his songs. He sang for the official opening of Radio Tehran in 1940 where he sang "Bi to" (Without You) and "Delbar-e tanaz" (Flirtatious Sweetheart). Sheibani insists that these songs and others he later recorded were "in the seven *dastgahs* [modal systems], but the rhythms, a slow rhumba and a tango, were Western."

10. An excellent sampler of four tapes dating back to the 1950s is available. It is titled *Shabi dar kafeh-ha-ye Tehran* (A Night in the Cafés of Tehran, 1987), published by Iranzamin Publishing Co. (P.O. Box 16234, Irvine, CA 92713), with the assistance of Morteza Varzi.

11. When Mahvash was killed in an automobile accident, thousands of bereaved fans attended her funeral.

12. Issari's work gives a year-by-year entry for every film made in Iran during the period, with complete credits, including all of the major actors, singers, and, occasionally, dancers involved.

13. For a more detailed discussion of the types of lyrics found in this genre, see Shay 1995a.

14. See also Pechey (1989, 51) on the importance of Bakhtin's concept of the carnivalesque in literature.

15. For a full discussion of the topic of Islam and music, see Choudhury 1957; Nelson 1985.

16. Some writers claim that this music is so spiritual that only Sufi poetry should be used for its performance: "But any traditional poetry with mystic and metaphysical meaning written in the metric system could be used. Yet one should choose Sufi or spiritual works such as those of Rumi, Hafez, Saidi and similar writers. Works of Omar Khayyam might not be suitable for song texts in the *radif*" (Miller 1995, 227–28).

17. Even with these changes, certain classical musicians disagree:

> The current tendency is to compensate for the disappearance of light music by arranging classical or popular airs in a pleasant and novel manner. Some traditional musicians completely disagree with this method, which, ironically, they call *pop-e-erfani,* "mystic

pop." What the purists criticize is not the music itself, which performs its function—to entertain—but the fact that it is presented as an expression of the learned tradition. (During, Mirabdolbaghi, and Safvat 1991, 54)

18. Morteza Neydavud, perhaps more wisely than those claiming pre-Islamic origins, states, "I don't know, and I don't think anybody else can. Even if you ask Darvish Khan, he would say that he got it from another master." He adds, "The origin, and originators of the *dastgah*s, modes, and the *gushe*s are actually unknown" (During, Mirabdolbaghi, and Safvat 1991, 202).

19. In Iran contexts for performing in secret, and even publicly, in defiance of the Islamic Republic's ban on this dance form, supply ample evidence that the performance of this dance creates a space for resistance to the regime. It is significant that Iranian women from throughout the diaspora chose to taunt the Islamic regime through the vehicle of dance at the International Women's Conference in Beijing in September 1995 (reported on Radio Seda-ye Iran, September 1995).

20. For an in-depth discussion of the Iranian recording industry and other issues of media in the Iranian diaspora of southern California, see Naficy 1993.

21. Music with patriotic themes, such as the well-known "Ey, Iran," constitute a single genre of music called *sorud* (hymn or anthem). Musically the sorud differs from all other forms of Iranian music: it is played in 2/4 and 4/4 rhythms and intended to be sung by groups, and it is often taught in school.

22. See Naficy 1993 for a full discussion of how nostalgia permeates Iranian music and television.

23. For a discussion of a similar intergenerational discourse on the topic of "sex, drugs, and rock and roll" in another Middle Eastern context, see Armbrust 1996.

24. A sampling of such performances of siyah-bazi and mardomi music and lyrics can be found on *Tanin Show, No-Ruz 1373* (1992), published by Caltex Records (9045A Eton Ave., Canoga Park, CA 91304).

25. The AVAZ International Dance Theatre is a repertory dance company that performs a large repertoire of dance and music from the Iranian culture sphere.

26. Ardavan Mofid, pers. com. January 27, 1994.

FOUR

Sa'ida Sultan/Danna International

Transgender Pop and the Polysemiotics of Sex, Nation, and Ethnicity on the Israeli-Egyptian Border

Ted Swedenburg

Disputes over sexual behavior often become the vehicles for displacing social anxieties, and discharging their attendant emotional intensity. Consequently, sexuality should be treated with special respect in times of great social stress.

GAYLE RUBIN, "THINKING SEX"

In fall 1994, when I was teaching at the American University in Cairo (AUC), one of my Egyptian graduate students handed me a music cassette that she was sure I would want to hear given that, as she explained, it was all the underground rage among Cairene youths. The tape contained two numbers, sung in English, Arabic, and (I thought) Hebrew, by an Israeli artist whose name my student did not know. It was poorly recorded and the lyrics were hard to make out, so I filed it away after listening to it a few times. Over the next months I occasionally heard the two songs from that tape blaring from cars and a cassette player at the AUC snack bar, and I eventually learned, through conversations and various lurid articles in the opposition press here and there, that the singer's name was Danna International; she was also known in Egypt as Sa'ida Sultan; she was Mizrahi, a Jew of Arab origin; and "she" was a transsexual.[1]

In August 1995 my interest was reignited by the discovery of a sensationalistic exposé—in Arabic—titled *A Scandal Whose Name Is Sa'ida Sultan: Danna the Israeli Sex Artist*, penned by Muhammad al-Ghayti and published by a press that was unknown to any of my friends.[2] The book's cover features a photo of the American pop star Madonna bending toward the camera in a metallic gold bustier and black net stockings, her cleavage and eyes blacked out, in the style of local scandal magazines. The upper left-hand corner announces "For Adults Only"; the back cover informs us that although the Zionists failed in their efforts to conquer Egypt politically, they have now succeeded, through the agency of Danna International's sexuality, in invading Egypt's bedrooms. The book elaborates on many of the is-

88

sues that both the Egyptian opposition and public-sector media started to raise about Danna/Sa'ida and her illicit cassette (known locally as *Busni ya Susu*, or *Kiss Me Susu*) in December 1994.[3] We find out that Danna International's given name is Yaron Cohen, that he was born to a Yemeni family that migrated to Israel after 1948, and that, while growing up, he learned traditional Arabic songs of Yemen and the Arabian Gulf from his mother (al-Ghayti 1995b, 18–20).[4] As a teenager, Yaron frequented the "perverts' clubs" (*nawadi al-shawadhdh*) of Tel Aviv, where his deviant tendencies were affirmed and developed. Eventually Yaron underwent hormone treatments and a sex-change operation and launched a singing career under the stage name Danna International, with the encouragement of the prominent Israeli-Yemeni singer Ofra Haza and devoted fans in the "perverts' clubs" of Tel Aviv (*F*, 21–22, 32–33, 35).[5] Although she aroused controversy among extremist rabbis who considered her sex change contrary to Jewish law, Danna nonetheless enjoyed the backing of the Israeli leadership. It was due to the support of Zionist power brokers, in fact, that her music was able to "penetrate" Egypt via the Sinai peninsula and "master" the ears of twenty million youths (*F*, 12–13).

Al-Ghayti goes on to inform us that Danna's inspirations in the world of show business are Elvis, James Dean, Michael Jackson, and, especially, Madonna, all of whom are major stars in Egypt.[6] He describes all of these international icons of popular culture as "deviants" (*F*, 38) and proceeds to rehearse some of their perverted adventures. We discover that Elvis, late in his career, spent hours indulging in "disgusting" sex at an S&M club, where he died; that James Dean used to bugger young black men in his dressing room; that the "disfigured black pig" Michael Jackson favors the company of children;[7] and that the biggest "deviant" of them all, Madonna, is a prominent supporter of civil rights for "perverts" (*F*, 40). Moreover, we learn that, according to her gynecologist, Madonna is not a 100 percent biological woman, because she is unable to bear children. "Can you imagine," the author asks, "Madonna, the global symbol of the naked woman, is not a complete female?" (*F*, 44).[8] We are informed as well that both Michael Jackson and Madonna are closely tied to and enjoy the strong backing of the Zionist lobby in the United States (*F*, 42, 46–47). Moving beyond vilification by association, al-Ghayti proceeds to illustrate Danna's depravity through an examination of her lyrics, sung in what he describes as a "devilish blend" of Arabic (in various regional dialects), English, and Hebrew (*F*, 58). The themes of her songs, he claims, are all sexual adventures, and their words are so scandalous that on occasion he feels compelled to leave blank spaces and simply describe what they mean. One of Danna's songs is an "unambiguous call for prostitution and immorality"; another features a sordid encounter bewee a woman and a dog; others are composed chiefly of "scandalous [read: orgasmic] groans" (*F*, 62). The final number on the cassette, sung in Hebrew and English, is said to exemplify how Danna's shameless voice and lyrics constitute a deviation from all morality and tradition as well as an attack on all the monotheistic Semitic religions and their principles and laws (*F*, 64).

According to al-Ghayti, Danna is merely one element of a larger Zionist cultural torrent that includes other Israeli female pop singers such as Ruthie, Nancy, and Suzanna Ma'ariv who have employed "sexual shouts" to win an Egyptian audience and to "penetrate . . . like a plague" the circles of innocent Arab youths. Several even used the devious tactic of making "corrupted" Hebrew recordings of tunes by revered neoclassicist Arab singers like Umm Kulthum, 'Abd al-Halim Hafiz, and Farid al-Atrash and punctuating them with orgasmic moans (*F*, 66). It should be emphasized that the latter are nationally revered, canonical figures in Egypt for whom there are no comparable examples in U.S. popular culture. (To get a sense of the cultural capital of such singers in Egypt, imagine that when Frank Sinatra passed away millions of weeping fans showed up at his funeral, that he is a central figure in U.S. nationalist mythology, that his music is constantly played on the radio, that his concerts and movies are endlessly aired on television, that video clips of Sinatra singing in concerts or movies are interspersed as fillers between TV programs on a daily basis, and, finally, that all popular music is measured in relation to Sinatra's standard of excellence. Then imagine that an artist from a vilified country, say, Iran, began to record "versions" of Sinatra's songs and that these were embraced by American youths.) Although Danna has in fact "stolen" only from the lesser Egyptian "pop" star Hasan al-Asmar, a figure whom the nationalist intelligentsia consider "vulgar," according to al-Ghayti, these corruptions of beloved Egyptian classics by Israeli singers manage at once to "penetrate" Arab youths and to destroy the Arabs' deep-rooted musical heritage (*F*, 66). This sort of theft and perversion of Arab heritage, we are informed, dates back to the days of Jewish presence in Egypt. The author tells, for instance, of Rachel Qattawi, scion of a poor branch of Egyptian Jewry's leading family, the Qattawi, known for its wealth and its collaboration with British colonialism. During World War II, Rachel worked as a barmaid at Cairo's Continental Hotel, where she befriended the great (and canonical) singer Asmahan as well as other Egyptian artists and mastered Asmahan's repertoire, all the while working undercover for Jewish and British intelligence.[9] When she emigrated to Israel, Rachel Qattawi "stole" Asmahan's legacy (Asmahan died in 1944), and she recorded an album of Asmahan's songs in 1967 (*F*, 92–94).[10]

Ultimately, for al-Ghayti, the entire Danna phenomenon boils down to a Masonic-Jewish conspiracy. Danna, who is accused of being a Freemason, advocates the individual's right to happiness and sensual delight, both of these being prototypical Masonic principles, invented by Zionist Jews, whose purpose was to destroy society (*F*, 50–52). This philosophy accords, as al-Ghayti argues with reference to such noted authorities as Wagner and Hitler, with the nature of the Jews, a parasitic and rootless people whose eternal aim is to destroy civilization (*F*, 106, 115–16). Therefore, Danna's influence must be resisted vigorously in order to defend and protect Egypt's young people from her poison. Although by the time we reach his conclusion al-Ghayti's argument has come to resemble the rantings of a neo-Nazi rather than cultural criticism, with the trope of the Jewish-Masonic conspiracy stemming from the notorious *Protocols of the Wise Men of Zion* and Hitler's anti-Semitic propaganda, the reader should be aware that the notion of a Masonic-Zionist plot is commonplace in Egypt, particularly in Islamist versions but also in Marxist and nationalist variants.[11] Several books have been published on the theme and can be purchased in "respectable" bookstores; Freemasonry, moreover, is banned in much of the Middle East.

ISRAELI "PENETRATION"

Running throughout al-Ghayti's arguments, in fact, are a number of ideological threads that are frequently articulated by members of Egypt's nationalist intelligentsia. One theme is the danger posed by Israel. Although the Egyptian government signed a peace treaty with Israel in 1977, most of the intelligentsia has vigorously opposed normalization (*tatbi'*) of Israeli-Egyptian relations. As Richard Jacquemond (1997) observes, "The only single issue capable of bringing together Islamists, liberals, Nasserists and Marxists is the rejection of 'cultural normalisation' with Israel. That is also the only terrain on which the young literary and artistic avant-garde—otherwise hostile to all ideologies—is willing to express an explicit political engagement." Egyptian universities, for instance, continue to boycott Israeli scholars, and although Israel established an academic center in Cairo in the early 1980s, it remains unthinkable for an Israeli scholar to deliver a public lecture at any Egyptian university. Indeed, numerous significant issues continue to animate anti-Israeli feelings and receive extensive coverage in the press.[12] However, although there is considerable apprehension regarding Israel's policies and its interest in dominating Egypt, there is not much coverage of Israel's considerable economic activities in Egypt. It is hardly known, for instance, that Israeli investors are leasing land and growing commercial agricultural produce in the Egyptian Delta, and it may well be that the government tries to prevent such activities from being publicized. Instead, anxieties about Israel's aims and power are displaced onto the linked domains of culture and morality, such that the press is constantly churning out inflammatory stories, many of them delusionary, about Is-rael's efforts to conquer Egypt and the Arab world culturally and to corrupt their morals.[13]

Typical of such incendiary sensationalism is the report that appeared in the Nasserite newspaper *al-'Arabi* in February 1996 discussing an Israeli cig-arette sold within the Palestine National Authority and said to be about to appear on the Egyptian market ("Waqaha Isra'iliyya").[14] The article, which reproduces the emblem on the cigarette package depicting two men driv-ing a chariot, tells us that the men are wearing distinctive American hats, that they are riding in an Egyptian chariot drawn by Arabian horses, and that one holds a whip whose lash hangs so as to form the Arabic word Misr (Egypt). In sum, Uncle Sam is deploying an Egyptian whip to control the Arabs, and the entire scenario is devised by the Israelis. One encounters the same Israeli arrogance and vision, the piece concludes, in the statements of (then) Israeli foreign minister Ehud Barak and in the trademark on an Is-raeli cigarette package. Although the notice is bizarre and its interpretation of the emblem fanciful, it is symptomatic of deep-seated Egyptian fears (es-pecially as articulated by many in the national intelligentsia) about Israeli official attitudes, policies, and designs. These must be kept in mind to un-derstand both the appeal of and the resistance to Danna International in Egypt.

In a similar vein, al-Ghayti elaborates quite obsessively on another aspect of Israeli aggression: the sexual threat it poses to the Egyptian bedroom. One of the means he uses to convey this "danger" is to misrepresent the sexiness of Danna's lyrics both through wild exaggeration and strategic mis-translation. The song that al-Ghayti calls an "unambiguous call for prosti-tution and immorality," for instance, is in fact a wedding song, sung from the position of the bride. This is made obvious not only by the lyrics—in Arabic Danna sings, "Ana al-'arusa" (I'm the bride), and in English, "Going to a honeymoon"—but also by the music (which features the ululations typ-ical of Arab wedding celebrations) and by the very name of the song, which—as I learned once I obtained the CD from Israel—is "'Arusa" (Bride). When Danna sings "Ana al-'arusa," al-Ghayti transcribes this as "Ana al-talmiza" (I'm the student), implying that the singer is asking for les-sons in sex. When Danna sings "giving me money" in English, referring to the money gifts traditionally offered at Arab wedding ceremonies, al-Ghayti translates this as "wa-taddini al-falus" (you give me money), implying pros-titution, or sexual services in return for money. If the song "'Arusa" is in any way "deviant," it is because the singer is not "really" a woman, a fact that al-Ghayti seems either to overlook or to ignore. Al-Ghayti's notion that an-other song concerns an encounter between a woman and a dog is the prod-uct of the fertile imagination of the antipornographer. As for the number that is supposed to represent an attack on all Semitic religions, it is simply a

remake of Queen's inoffensively campy "The Show Must Go On": the English lyrics Danna sings are "Show must go on / Inside my heart is breaking /
My makeup may be flaking / But my smile still stays on." All this is not to say
that Danna's tape is devoid of sexiness (al-Ghayti is correct to interpret
Danna's screams as orgasmic, but these are much less ubiquitous than he
claims) but to underscore the symptomatically hysterical and displaced
character of al-Ghayti's attack.

   Curiously, al-Ghayti's account of the classical homophobic topos of sexual penetration focuses on the aggressive and wanton Western-Israeli female who seduces the innocent young Egyptian male. The theme of the
Western male who sexually threatens the Egyptian woman (or man) is
mostly absent, in fact, from Egypt's journalistic, filmic, or literary discourse.[15] But the theme of the Egyptian man victimized by a predatory
Western woman is to be found in works of modern Egyptian fiction dating
back at least to the 1940s as well as to the first Egyptian film (*Layla*, 1927).[16]
Today's moral-sexual panic about the voracious and corrupting Western
(and now, Israeli) woman, however, is much more virulent and widespread
than in the past. AIDS, for instance, is widely represented by Egyptian agencies of public meaning as a disease that Egyptians contract when male nationals are ensnared by loose Western women. A 1992 film called *al-Hubb fi
Taba* (Love in Taba), which, despite its artistic wretchedness, airs frequently
on state television, is typical of this official story. It recounts the tale of three
naive Egyptian youths who are willingly seduced and entrapped by three
young libertine Western women while on holiday in Taba, a small resort in
the Sinai peninsula that sits right on the border with Israel. When the foreign women depart for home, each leaves a note informing her lover that
he is now infected with AIDS. It is significant that these events occur at
Taba, for the Egyptian media frequently depicts the Sinai peninsula as a
wild and dangerous frontier zone through which Israeli corruption enters
the Nile Valley, and al-Ghayti explicitly names it as the corridor through
which Danna's cassettes have "penetrated."[17] Meanwhile, the opposition
press and word of mouth assert that AIDS is being broadcast in Egypt by
prostitutes dispatched there for that purpose by the Israeli government
(see "Isra'il tuharib" 1995; AbuKhalil 1993, 34).[18] It is popularly believed
in Egypt that if a man has sex with a "foreign," that is, Western, woman, he
is in danger of contracting a sexually transmitted disease and so needs to
wear a condom. A public service announcement shown frequently on state
television manages simultaneously to provide accurate information about
HIV transmission and to suggest, through its visual imagery, that the main
danger of infection occurs when Egyptian males go abroad and are stalked
by prostitutes. The iconographic image is reinforced by an explicit statement that AIDS is a "foreign" phenomenon, that the Egyptian traveler
should beware, and that "abroad they use such things as condoms and

other methods to help prevent AIDS, but here there is no fear of such things because the principles which our youths believe in protect them from such evil." The spot concludes with a verse from the Qur'an.[19]

The announcement's anxious tone, however, undercuts the confident assertions about Egyptian youths and their deep-seated moral principles. And for al-Ghayti, the "evil" does not just lie in foreign lands or frontier regions but menaces the very heart of the nation. The focal point of the "danger," however, is strictly heterosexual cross-cultural encounters. Al-Ghayti does not suggest that "perverts" (homosexuals or transsexuals) constitute the true threat to Egypt, for he assumes that such people simply do not exist there.[20] What Danna's transsexuality and deviance serve to underscore instead is simply the repulsive character of her sexual success in Egypt. In this regard the transgendered Danna is like her hero the international sex symbol Madonna, who is also both very popular and very controversial in Egypt and, although more or less legal,[21] equally loathsome—not least, as al-Ghayti notes, because Madonna herself is not "really" biologically female. Transsexuality and queerness serve here to underscore the fact that the Western/Israeli sexual assault is not merely corrupting but that its very foundations are perverse and deviant. The challenge posed by Western mass culture, as exemplified by Elvis, Michael Jackson, James Dean, Madonna, and Danna, is essentially moral and sexual.

YOUTH AS "PROBLEM"

If al-Ghayti's diatribe can be read as a catalog of interlinked themes that run through the discourse of Egypt's nationalist intelligentsia concerning the threatening and corrupting influences posed by Israel, Westernization, sexuality, and Western mass culture, another important and related motif in this nationalist discourse concerns precisely who is at risk. Those said to be most threatened by these dangers are youths, the *shabab,* and particularly the young men. On August 21, 1995, *Ruz al-Yusuf,* Egypt's leading weekly magazine, a sensationalist but well-regarded nationalist public-sector vehicle, published an exposé about advertisements that had appeared in Egyptian magazines, promoting telephone numbers that promised to connect callers with "new friends." It turned out that such calls were quite expensive and that they connected the consumer to sex professionals in Israel ("Isra'il tuharib" 1995). Under the banner "Normalization by Sex with Israel" the issue's seductive cover photo of Tina Turner wearing a miniskirt and exposing considerable cleavage was intended to convey the dangers of "phone sex." In the predictably melodramatic account of the arrival of Israeli phone sex, we learn that once the peace treaty was signed with Egypt in 1978, Israeli intelligence agencies turned away from Egypt's military secrets and began to study Egypt's social ills with the aim of exploiting them.

What they discovered is that Egyptian youths are afflicted by sexual problems that are traceable to the country's economic difficulties and make it
difficult for them to marry and satisfy their sexual needs. Phone sex along
with AIDS, counterfeit money, and heroin are all Israeli exports designed to
take advantage of Egyptian youths' difficulties ("Isra'il tuharib" 1995, 21).

Despite its propagandistic exaggerations, the *Ruz al-Yusuf* article does
nevertheless point to some of the concrete causes of the "youth crisis."
Youths in Egypt do indeed face a crisis of opportunity, which particularly affects those from the lower and lower-middle classes who manage to get university degrees. An advanced degree is supposed to guarantee a government job, but today the waiting period for actually getting such a position is
about ten years. In any case, the pay for such sought-after jobs averages a
pitiful £E 100 (U.S.$30) per month, and legions of state employees must
moonlight to make ends meet. Opportunities for work in the private sector,
especially "respectable" jobs that educated youths will accept, are also limited.[22] Such economic obstacles in turn make getting married a laborious
and much-delayed process. Marriage, however, is a requirement for any
young person who wishes to become a social adult, to achieve independence within a nuclear family, to move out of his or her parental home, and
to gain sexual access.[23] Because marriage requires considerable outlays of
money and families of prospective brides demand the whole package (i.e.,
a furnished apartment, etc.) to ensure that their daughters are well settled,
unless a youth comes from a wealthy family, he will frequently not marry
until he reaches his early thirties. Many young men migrate to work in the
Gulf countries and toil there for as long as five to ten years to save up
enough money for marriage. The Central Agency for Statistics estimates
that four million Egyptians have "missed the train of marriage" because
they are well into their thirties, beyond the accepted marrying age; and
some have calculated that the number of marriages registered in the country has declined by nearly 1 percent (Alatraqchi 1996, 21), an astonishing
fact for a country with such a young population. As a result, the social category "youth" in Egypt includes large numbers of men (and some women)
in their late twenties and early thirties. It is widely recognized that the crisis
afflicting them is in part sexual, because sexual outlets outside of marriage
are limited, proscribed, and, usually, prohibitively expensive and because
"dating" is generally unacceptable unless one is already engaged.[24] Such
factors contribute to making "sex" a major topic of discussion and controversy in Egypt today.[25]

Young people are also considered a "problem" in the domain of culture.
Nationalist, especially oppositional, intellectuals commonly assert that
youths are the victims of a general moral decline in Egypt that is the by-
product of *infitah*, the economic liberalization launched in the 1970s by the
late President Anwar al-Sadat, and the consequent advance of materialism

and decline of traditional values.[26] The infitah is also regarded as indelibly linked to normalization with Israel and to the consequent Zionist penetration. Youths are seen as especially susceptible to the corruptions of both Western mass culture and "vulgar" indigenous culture (so called because it is regarded as rooted in "low" cultural values), both of which are said to be outcomes of the infitah and the attendant rise of a boorish and unsophisticated nouveau riche and the decline of noble cultural values. "Vulgar" or "fallen" Egyptian culture fails to meet the nationalist cultural ideal of a synthesis of the high, neoclassicist culture (which, in addition to elite Arab traditions, can also include elements of refined Western culture, such as ballet or Beethoven) and the best of folk cultural values (represented by the stereotypical "authentic Egyptian," the son of the people, or *ibn al-balad*). With regard to music, the canonical figures who serve to epitomize ideal national values and to represent the musical high points of Egyptian culture's "golden age" include the late Umm Kulthum, 'Abd al-Halim Hafiz, and Muhammad 'Abd al-Wahhab.[27] Cheap Egyptian culture is both "low" (because there is no synthesis with "elevated" culture) and, frequently, contaminated by "cheap" Western mass culture. In their ideological combat against the tidal waves of base culture, the nationalist intelligentsia's cultural mandarins therefore frequently condemn contemporary musicians who do not conform to canonical values, asserting that they represent the "fall" of Egyptian music from its glory days and describing them as *jil al-ghina' al-habit* (the generation of the vulgar song) (al-Najmi 1995). The frequent press attacks on "debased culture" and condemnations of "vulgar" musicians who threaten the authenticity of the Arabic song are responses to the fact that, although many Egyptian youths will publicly assert their admiration for Umm Kulthum and 'Abd al-Halim, they primarily listen to contemporary, so-called vulgar, Egyptian pop music. Thus the makers of public meaning invoke the shining example of a figure like Umm Kulthum to articulate a critique of the effects of privatization, structural adjustment, and normalization with Israel, and at the same time to put forward a blanket condemnation of contemporary youth culture, which can never equal but can only, at best, imitate past glories. As a result, many of the most popular musicians are consigned to the margins of public space, are never aired on television or radio, and are sometimes forced to resort to underground and illegal releases (see Khalifa 1995, 9; Armbrust 1996) that are marketed in the same cassette kiosks that deal in Danna's contraband cassettes.[28] This marginalization of a significant component of contemporary musical life in Egypt is yet another symptom of the general absence of autonomous public spaces (whether youth clubs, media, or dance halls) where young people might publicly articulate their desires or demands. The popularity of "vulgar" music, the object of so much thundering from nationalist intellectuals straining to shore up neoclassicist cultural values, can in turn be understood as a sign of a general disaffection on the part of Egyptian youths, of their skepticism concerning the economic and social possibilities awaiting them, and of their lack of interest in the great modernist projects of nationalism and development that were hegemonic until the mid-1970s.[29]

Many members of the nationalist intelligentsia, therefore, are prone to raise the alarm against Egypt's social fragmentation and the alienation of youths from the once-revered projects of national liberation and development and to cast themselves as youths' savior. Although intellectuals condemn young people for their cultural predilections, they are occasionally empathetic and assert that young people cannot really be blamed for their cynicism, as the government and the economy offer them so little (see Wahba 1995). Even such sympathetic analyses, however, deny Egyptian youths any agency and depict them as mere victims of government dereliction or dupes of foreign plots. Young people's own cultural concerns have no role to play in this rescue operation, for it is the national tradition and culture, as understood and articulated by the intelligentsia, that is to be their salvation.

ARAB JEWS

The final link between al-Ghayti and nationalist discourse has to do with the place of Arab Jews, whether in the Arab countries or inside Israel. In al-Ghayti's text, as in most nationalist discourse, this subject is essentially an absence. Although al-Ghayti notes Danna International's Yemeni origins, he pays minimal attention to the question of the Mizrahim in Israel and basically assumes that Arabs and Jews are diametrically opposed categories. He does mention in passing that Jews of Arab background occupy the lower rungs of Israeli society and that singer Ofra Haza faced many difficulties because of her Yemeni origins, but on the whole he manages to depict Israeli-Jewish society as homogeneous and monolithic. The author assumes that Danna sings in Arabic simply because her "target" is Arab youths outside Israel and so never takes account of other possible audiences such as the roughly 16 percent of Israel's five million citizens who are Palestinian Arabs, the 54 percent of the population who are of non-European and mostly Arabic-speaking origin like Danna herself, or the many Israeli Ashkenazis (Jews of European origin) who are familiar with Arabic and Arabic culture.

Al-Ghayti also treats the Egyptian Jews "within" as national traitors, collaborators with British colonialism, and agents of Zionism. He ignores the rich and varied nature of this now all-but-vanished community, which included rich and poor, communists and Zionists, and a majority of apolitical non-Zionists. Out of a population of 75,000 to 80,000, in fact, only about

14,000 emigrated to Israel between 1948 and 1951 after the new Jewish state was created (see Krämer 1989). It was only in the wake of the June 1967 war that this community was finally decimated, but even then only about one-third to one-half of Egyptian Jews emigrated to Israel.[30] (A recent study estimates that only about 70 Egyptian Jews remain in Egypt ["Egypt's Jewish Community" 1998].) Nor does al-Ghayti discuss any of Egypt's major cultural figures who were Jewish, such as the singer-actress Layla Murad, a still-revered icon of Egyptian film and music from the late 1930s to the early 1950s, who was raised as a Jew and converted to Islam in 1946 when she married the well-known actor Anwar Wajdi.[31] Also conveniently absent from al-Ghayti's account is any mention of other well-known Jewish cultural figures such as Layla Murad's famous musician father, Zaki Murad; the pioneering cinema director and producer Togo Mizrahi (responsible for some of the early landmarks of Egyptian film); the musician Da'ud Husni, remembered as one of the great artists who, along with Sayyid Darwish, revitalized Egyptian music in the early part of the century and who was responsible for Egypt's first full-length opera, *Cleopatra's Night*, in 1919.[32] In al-Ghayti's account, the Jews in Egypt (not *of* Egypt), as represented by Rachel Qattawi, are simply thieves of Arab culture and Zionist undercover agents.

DANNA'S EGYPTIAN FANS

Just who was actually listening to Danna in Egypt in 1994–96? How can one begin to characterize the massive and heterogeneous social category "youth" whom nationalist intellectuals like al-Ghayti want to "protect" from the dangers of Danna International? The difficulty of such a task is compounded by the fact that, because there is no public space for Egypt's young people to articulate their perceptions of "vulgar" pop music, there exists no real vocabulary in which to voice favorable views about controversial artifacts of pop culture.[33] There are no magazines or broadcasts that represent alternative views of or by Egyptian youths; youth- and pop culture–oriented magazines tend to be either of the gossip variety or public-sector vehicles through which "responsible" adults address young people. Very little of real concern to young people percolates up the cultural hierarchy from the bottom. Moreover, open discussion is severely constrained by official condemnations that create a sense that listening to Danna signifies immorality, an absence of patriotism, and a lack of respectability. Many thus simply repeat what the press says about Danna: asked if he had ever heard of Danna International, a taxi driver bringing a friend into town from the Cairo airport replied, "You mean the singer that brings AIDS from Israel?"

Although Danna's tape was sold strictly on the black market and for high prices (four to eight times that of a regular prerecorded cassette), she appeared to enjoy an extensive audience of young people, including students, from among the Westernized upper and upper-middle classes as well as the lower-middle and working classes.[34] One of Danna's chief appeals was that she was "forbidden," both as a "sex" artist and as an Israeli, and the press uproar simply served to drive up both the price and the desirability of her cassette.[35] High-priced versions of the cassette were sold under the counter in many of the numerous Cairo kiosks that specialize in prerecorded music tapes as well as contraband cassettes by "vulgar" Egyptian pop singers. In addition, enterprising kids made lesser-quality versions that they hawked in the streets for lower prices, sometimes disguising them, to avoid police harassment, as Qur'anic recitation cassettes. (Police raids on cassette shops increased after it was learned that Danna's tape had appeared on the market.) Although the buzz on the streets was that *Busni ya Susu* was a "sex" tape, the fact that Danna is a transsexual was less well known and did not appear to be part of Danna's attraction or to matter much to consumers. Most of the Egyptian audience is familiar with the Western pop musical sources—such as Whitney Houston, Gloria Estefan, Donna Summer, Queen, and the Gypsy Kings—that Danna draws on and does "versions" of, as these are international pop stars known and consumed both in Israel and in Egypt. Danna's practice of blending Western dance beats and textures with Oriental vocalisms and modes is equally familiar in Egypt and in fact is characteristic of a great deal of contemporary Egyptian pop music (as discussed below).[36] But many in this audience did not understand Danna's English lyrics.

My chief sources regarding Danna's reception in Egypt were Westernized upper-middle-class students at AUC who were quite familiar with the Egyptian and Western pop musical traditions Danna draws on, patronized the nightclubs where Danna's singles were being played (going to discos is almost exclusively an upper- and upper-middle-class practice), and—unlike most of Danna's audience—were fluent in English. These students dismissed the press attacks on Danna, saying that the nationalist opposition tends to describe everything as Israeli plots. But, reflecting the absence of public spaces for youths to assert positive views about sexuality and gender relations, they were rather defensive about claims that *Busni ya Susu* was a "sex tape"—it's not really "bad," at least most of the songs aren't, they would say. Their response also resembled the posture of youths interviewed in an exposé published in the public-sector magazine *al-Shabab* (Youth) about the popularity of Western "sex" pop (Danna, Madonna) and "satanic" (heavy metal) music. Most young people joined the chorus of condemnation; the few who defended their interest in such music claimed that they did not really pay attention to the lyrics and that it was ludicrous to suppose that merely listening to "satanic" rock would turn them into worshipers of Satan (Rahim 1995).

BUSI/PUSSY

My analysis assumes a listener who understands English, but someone with even a smidgen of English knowledge would "get" some of the lyrics and suggestions. Four of the nine songs on Danna's contraband cassette are sung mostly in Arabic, usually mixed with some English. "My Name Is Not Sa'ida" is a stunning remake of Whitney Houston's "My Name Is Not Susan";[37] "Samarmar" is a version of a song originally done by the Egyptian pop artist Hasan al-Asmar; and "'Arusa" is the "wedding" song discussed above. By far the most popular of the four was "Susu ya Susu" (Susu Oh Susu), a favorite in the dance clubs of Cairo and Sharm al-Shaykh as well as the street during 1995. As the song's Israeli title, "Danna International," was unknown in Egypt, the hit was known simply as "Susu," itself a pet name, a diminutive of Yusuf (Joseph), and a type of nickname employed mainly by the older, educated generation. An Egyptian friend of lower-class background insisted that "Susu" could not be a nickname for a male, but my AUC students said it could be a term of endearment for a man, one who was somewhat "fafi" (effeminate). A closer look at "Susu" will serve to suggest some of the pleasures Danna might offer a young Egyptian consumer.

"Susu ya Susu" opens with a male vocal chorus chanting a phrase with no apparent meaning, "Wa abiba ay wa abiba bomba bum baba." An Arab drumbeat from a tabla quickly backs up the chanting, which is then joined by a (Western) "house" bass dance beat until finally a "pure" house rhythm together with electronic keyboards override the "Oriental" rhythms, and the Arabic name Susu is chanted above the house beat. The entire song modulates between Arabic, house, and Arabic-house blended rhythms, modes, and textures.[38] The number is equally heterodox from the linguistic angle, constantly shifting between and combining English and Arabic, and occasionally using Mediterranean European languages—but contrary to al-Ghayti's claims, not Hebrew. Many phrases combine two or more languages, some are nonsensical (but fit the rhythm), some are articulated in such heavily accented English that I did not understand them until I procured the CD from Israel and read the lyric sheet,[39] and many words are ambiguous. In addition, there is considerable bilingual punning.[40]

The opening verse (to house backing) contains the following phrases (in Arabic and English):

Khudni lil Monaco	[Take me to Monaco]
Khudni lil Mexico	[Take me to Mexico]
Jubli bi taxi	[Bring me in a taxi]
I'm feelin' sexy	
Danna International.	

The subsequent verse goes

Khudni lil Baree	[Take me to Paris]
Kiss me, mon cheri	
Fih 'andi zumzum	[I have a zumzum]
Come see my zumzum	
Danna International.	

Although the word *zumzum* has no meaning in any of the relevant languages, one guesses from the context what the singer is inviting the addressee to "come see." The third verse also mixes English and Arabic:

Inta al-milyunayr	[You (masculine) are the millionaire]
And I have a golden hair	[the grammatical error here seems deliberate]
I'm feelin' / givin' bussy [busi]	
Come on and busi	

This set of phrases is extremely polysemic, for *busi* (long *u* and long *i*) means "kiss" in Egyptian Arabic—hence the origin of the name by which the song, and entire cassette, is known in Egypt, "Busni ya Susu" (Kiss Me Susu), even though the actual line appears nowhere in the song. In addition, *busi* is the form of command used to address a female, whereas the previous verse used the masculine form of address (*inta*). *Busi* also suggests "pussy," since the "p" sound is pronounced "b" in Arabic, as in Bibsi (Pepsi) Cola. Because the "English" here is not very clear, I thought Danna was singing "I'm feelin' busi." According to the lyric sheet accompanying the Israeli CD *Danna International* (not available in Egypt), she sings, "I'm giving busi." For the monolingual Arabic listener, the "pussy" reference will probably not be apparent. (Al-Ghayti, for instance, notices none of this lewd cross-linguistic and polysemic punning.)

The next verse goes

Shtaraytu bil duty free	[I bought it in duty free]
Shampoo Mal Givenchy	
And expensive pantaloni	[trousers, in Italian, here pronounced "bandaloonee"]
Compact disc and telefoni[41]	

Next, following the Arabic shout, "Ya lahwi!" (Oh disaster), the rhythm shifts, and the rapid beat of a solo tabla backs up Danna as she chants in near-perfect Egyptian Arabic and an enticing, charmingly feminine lilt punctuated by hiccups, a style that is stereotypical of the cute sexy female of Egyptian cinema: "Susu ya Susu" and "Albi ya Susu" (My heart Susu). The next line, interestingly, Egyptian non–English speakers hear as "Gismi ya Susu" (My body Susu) but English speakers hear as "Kiss me." The phrase therefore sounds "sexier" to the monolingual speaker of Arabic. The rest of the song more or less repeats these moments, but adds "Yalla [Come on] ya

Susu," "Khudni ya Susu" (Embrace me), and "Touch me ya Susu" during the "Susu" sequence.

SONIC INDIGENOUSNESS

Contrary to al-Ghayti's polemical claim that the Danna phenomenon is a case of foreign penetration and corruption, I want to argue that we should view Danna's Arabic songs as an intervention within the local culture. For it is her very indigenousness—operating on a number of levels—that accounts for much of her appeal in Egypt. This is already manifest in the tone of Danna's singing. Although the grain of the voice is clearly provocative, the seductiveness is not "foreign" but is recognizable on local terms, recalling as it does the prototypical coy, alluring, and usually blond starlet of the Egyptian movie screen. What is simultaneously shocking and appealing is that this coquettish and "forward" female tone of voice is asserted somewhat more publicly and openly by Danna than it is in the cinema. The "dirty" lyrics of Danna's songs are not foreign to contemporary Egyptian pop either; salaciousness, in fact, is one of the chief charges that cultural mandarins level against Egypt's so-called vulgar pop singers. At least in Arabic, Danna's lyrics suggest nothing more audacious than those of 'Adawiya's famous and extremely successful number, "Bint al-Sultan," or Sahar Hamdi's "Illi shartit 'aynuh bitghannin," or other songs by other "unrefined" singers who are massively popular with lower- and middle-class Egyptian youths.[42] Indeed, the "sexiness" of Danna's lyrics, I suggest, works mainly by implication: along with the crucial role played by the tone of voice, Danna's pronunciation and her use of multilingual combinations and nonsensical expressions render her meaning vague and open to multiple readings. In this regard "Susu ya Susu" recalls "Louie, Louie," the famous Kingsmen hit of 1963, which all adolescents at the time "knew" was a dirty song, even though, or perhaps because, its lyrics were virtually indecipherable. "Louie, Louie" too caused a "moral panic" in the United States.[43]

Although elements in the lyrics hint at Danna's transgendered status—"Susu ya Susu" vacillates between *busi* [kiss, feminine form] and *inta* [you, masculine]—as far as I can determine Susu's possibly "effeminate" character is not a significant issue for fans, or at least not one that is openly voiced. As in much of the Middle East, discussions of homosexuality are quite circumscribed in Egypt, but as a practice it is hardly rare.[44] Nor is it entirely absent from the public arena, as evidenced, for example, by Yusri Nasrallah's wacky 1994 film, *Mercedes*, which, directly inspired by the cinematic campiness of Pedro Almodovar, deals frankly and sympathetically (although not centrally) with homosexual characters.[45] Sex-change operations are not unthinkable in Egypt either. In fact, at the time there was an ongoing controversy regarding a man named Sayyid 'Abdallah who had a sex-change

operation in 1988 and applied as Sali (Sally) for admission to al-Azhar Islamic University. In November 1995 the Shaykh al-Azhar, Jad al-Haqq (the
country's leading religious authority), finally issued a *fatwa* (religious edict)
stating that sex-change operations were permissible,[46] thereby regularizing
the status of transgendered individuals in Egypt (Rizq 1995b; *Middle East
Times,* December 31, 1995).[47] The sad footnote to the "Sally" case, however,
was that after her sex-change operation was ruled permissible, she was denied admission to the women's section of al-Azhar for having performed as
a belly dancer. Just as with Danna, it was Sally's overt sexuality that was more
offensive to the powers that be than her transgendered status. Thus, for
Danna's Egyptian fans in any case, "Susu ya Susu" was principally a heterosexual "sex song" whose "transgressive" scenario is that of a cosmopolitan,
Western or Westernized Arab woman who is traveling, feels sexy, has "a
golden hair" (the quintessential sign of feminine beauty in Egypt), and
makes advances toward Susu in a mixture of Western languages and impeccable Arabic. Although the singer's forwardness was rather shocking in the
local context, it was appreciated by Egyptian youths, and this response no
doubt in part reflected changing gender relations and the increasing role
of women in Egyptian public life.

In terms of their musical style, Danna's Arabic numbers combine Western and Eastern rhythms, modes, and textures in a manner that is hardly
"foreign" to Egypt, as many of the country's most interesting pop musicians
engage in similarly innovative, syncretic, and hybridizing experiments and
in the indigenization of foreign pop styles (see Armbrust 1996, 173–84).
Two examples, chosen somewhat at random, of similar attempts to articulate an alternative vision of cultural modernity are the 1995 cassette, *Rab
musik li-al-shabab faqat* (Rap Music—For Young People Only), produced
by Ashra 'Abduh (Al-Sharq Records), and Muhammad Munir's 1995 hit
"al-Layla di" (Tonight), from his cassette *Mumkin?!* (Is It Possible?!, Digitec
Records). *Rap Music—For Young People Only* garnered negative reviews from
the mandarins, who saw it as another example of "vulgar" pop, but as usual
young people ignored the literati's admonitions, and the tape was a hit all
over Egypt in 1995, particularly in working-class neighborhoods. The
songs on the cassette are not really rap music at all but instead a shameless
and delightful blending of Egyptian pop vocalizations and melodies with
well-known recent U.S. and U.K. house and dance beats and samples. The
melody of one tune, "Sikkat al-salama" (The Road of Peace), for instance,
is from the 1971 song, "I'd Like to Teach the World to Sing," later used in
a well-known Coca-Cola advertisement. Muhammad Munir is an Egyptian
pop singer with a "respectable" reputation, whose music videos and concerts are routinely broadcast on television, and whose lyrics are often
penned by well-known national poets. Munir has been syncretizing Western and Eastern music for years and has recorded with the German rock

bands Embryo and Logic Animal. His hit, "al-Layla di," fetures funk beats, electronic keyboards and electric guitars, "Oriental" rhythms from a drum machine and a tabla, and an Oriental flute. The song's instrumental "hook" is played in a Western scale, while Munir sings the vocals in an Oriental mode. Because Munir has a reputation as a serious artist and because this song's lyrics are penned by one of Egypt's premier "folk" poets, 'Abd al-Rahman al-'Abnudi, this sort of musical syncretism is considered acceptable by the cultural establishment. Such hybridizing of Eastern and Western musics, which works through the "indigenization" of Western pop styles, is entirely typical of much popular music, whether it is considered "respectable" or "vulgar," heard throughout the Arab world. Stylistically, therefore, Danna's music is far from foreign but rather, like much contemporary Egyptian pop, falls into the category of what mainstream nationalist intellectuals label "vulgar" (habit) or "cheap" music. It combines lower-class or "popular" Egyptian and Arab musical traditions with Western pop motifs, without concern for neoclassicist conventions of synthesizing the "best" in high and low culture (see Armbrust 1996, 181–82). Indeed, some of Danna's tunes function in such an acoustically indigenous manner that they have even been employed in an advertisement for an Egyptian shampoo called Luna 2![48]

Just as issues of homosexuality do not seem to be a significant factor in the reception of Danna by Egyptian youths, the same can be said about another striking characteristic of her work and her cultural identity—her Arab-Jewishness. Danna is by no means the first and only Israeli Mizrahi artist to enjoy underground success in Egypt. An album recorded in 1984 by Ofra Haza entitled *Yemenite Songs*—later released in the United States to critical acclaim under the title *50 Gates of Wisdom* (Shanachie Records, 1987)—circulated widely in Egypt on contraband cassette in the late 1980s. Ofra Haza first established her reputation in Israel singing mainstream pop, and it was only after she was thoroughly confirmed as a respectable artist there that it was safe for her to return to her Mizrahi roots and record this set of traditional Arab-Jewish Yemeni music. Because the Ofra Haza cassette was understood in Egypt as "folk" music rather than "cheap" or "vulgar," and because it had no sexual overtones,[49] its underground circulation in Egypt did not provoke the controversies that Danna's cassette has ignited. The point is that Danna's music issues from a wider and extremely rich phenomenon of Mizrahi pop music in Israel that is Levantine and Middle Eastern (and as such is marginalized in Israel) and is therefore comprehensible and "local" to Arab audiences in the Eastern Arab world.[50] Mizrahi pop music, for instance, is heavily consumed and appreciated by Palestinian youths in the West Bank and Gaza, a phenomenon little appreciated or noted by observers of Palestinian culture. Moreover, Zehava Ben, an Israeli Jewish singer of Moroccan origin who sings the (canonical) repertoire of Umm Kulthum to the backing of a Palestinian Arab orchestra from Haifa, has played several concerts in the Palestine National Authority (Nablus, Bethlehem, and Jericho) and is massively popular among Palestinians (Tsur 1998; Agassi 1997). Ben's success among Palestinians suggests the existence of a lively but underground "Levantine" expressive culture that can be shared by Arabs and (Oriental) Jews. Moreover, Egyptian pop music has a tremendous influence on Mizrahi pop music, and the fact that Mizrahi singers like Danna International do "versions" of Egyptian pop songs should be interpreted not as Israeli "theft" of Egyptian music but as a kind of *tribute* to the tremendous importance and influence of Egypt's popular music on the "Levantine" music scene in Israel (see Regev 1995). Such a phenomenon of shared culture is incomprehensible if one thinks of the region as starkly divided into the polarities Arab (East) and Jew (West).

It is only when one has grasped the elements of Danna's sonic indigenousness that one can understand that what makes her cultural interventions in Egypt so effective is that she works within musical and cultural trends that are familiar to Egyptian youths. She pushes at the edges from inside a vibrant and innovating tradition, and this makes her music lively and exciting for many Egyptian young people. This is also precisely what makes her seem so dangerous to many nationalist intellectuals, much more threatening, in fact, than Madonna or Michael Jackson, as she is able to communicate with Egyptian youths in Arabic. Danna's liminality, the fact that she is at once Arab and Jew, is precisely what makes her dialogue with Egyptian youths possible and is also what is so offensive to mainstream nationalists of all stripes, whose ideology presupposes an essential difference between Arab and Jew. A nationalism that conceives of Egyptian society as homogeneous, unitary, and self-identical has no room for a border figure like Danna.

"THAT MUTANT"

Danna's significance and positioning in Israel during 1994–96 was quite different than in Egypt.[51] She was popular and highly successful, at least among certain, but mainly marginalized, segments of the population, but she was also highly controversial and looked on with disfavor by the cultural elite. One sense of the associated baggage attached to her name is conveyed by Yigal Amir who, just before he assassinated Israeli Prime Minister Yitzhak Rabin in November 1995, is said to have remarked to a nearby policeman, "Today, they give us the spectacle of Aviv Gefen; next time, they'll make us listen to that mutant, Diana [*sic*] International" (Schattner 1995). Amir was stalking Rabin at a Peace Now rally, at which Rabin spoke and during which he joined featured singer Aviv Gefen for a singalong on stage. Gefen, a major new Israeli rock singer whose long dyed-orange hair, heavy makeup, and androgynous clothing project a "radical" image, performs songs whose lyrics express "existential meaninglessness" and criticize the military establishment. But Gefen is also the offspring of elite circles, a close relative of Moshe Dayan, and his onstage gender ambiguity is entirely non-threatening. His "rebelliousness," in short, is firmly located within the national tradition and represents the "respectable" face of dissent.[52] It would have been simply unthinkable, however, for Yitzhak Rabin to have appeared onstage singing together with a "trashy" gender and culture subversive like Danna International. But Yigal Amir's remark does underscore one of the major issues in Israel with regard to Danna. When I asked an Israeli correspondent whether Danna's Arab-Jewish identity was of any concern in Israel, she replied that the mainstream media there focused almost exclusively on the issue of Danna's "sexuality, sexuality, and sexuality," and in particular, her *trans*sexuality. After Danna was chosen as a contestant in the competition to represent Israel in the 1995 Eurovision pop song contest, Ya'ir Nitsani, one of Israel's leading comedians, proclaimed that Danna should not represent Israel in this major international event because her transsexuality was a "shame." This sentiment appears to be widely shared, and to have played a role in Danna's failure to take first place in the competition (she placed second). When Danna appeared on one of Israel's major talk shows, hosted by Dudu Topaz (Israel's Phil Donahue cum Oprah Winfrey), Topaz interrogated her about her orgasms—"They're my orgasms," she replied—and asked (with a look of horror on his face) if she had really had "it" cut off during the sex change operation. The Israeli media has speculated that Danna did not really undergo a sex-change operation (although her breasts, an important part of her image, cannot be denied) and that rumors to this effect had inspired Danna to drop her lesbian girlfriend and take up with a boyfriend, an officer in the Israeli navy, to prove her femaleness. But, the story continued, this new relationship was a sham, really a gay relationship and not a heterosexual one (Yael Ben-zvi, pers. com.; Smadar Lavie, pers. com.).[53]

This sexual undecidability (does she have a lesbian girlfriend? a gay boyfriend? a heterosexual boyfriend? what kind of sex and what kind of anatomy does she have?) seems to have contributed to making Danna wildly popular among gay Ashkenazi men, who saw her as a "heroic" role model.[54] Danna started out in show business performing in drag shows in 1988. In the early 1990s, she participated in a Tel Aviv drag show version of "pre-Eurovision," the Israeli contest to pick the Eurovision entry. Her manager, Ofer Nissim, concocted a scenario in which Whitney Houston sang in Arabic in a concert in Saudi Arabia. Danna did an Arab-camp version of Whitney Houston's "My Name Is Not Susan," called "Sa'ida Sultan," in which she screams, "My name is not Sa'ida!" This was her first cult hit on the drag circuit (Ben n.d.; Ben-zvi 1998, 27). For Ashkenazi gay fans, however, Danna's Arab identity was merely "exotic" and did not, apparently, lead this audience very far in raising questions about Israel's Eurocentric racial hierarchies. However, Danna also enjoyed a substantial audience among the Mizrahim. According to correspondents, it was mainly the "disco youths" who were Danna's fans, and the majority of Israeli-Jewish youths are Mizrahim.[55] And in the youth press, Danna tends to be treated as a "normal" star rather than as a freak (Geir Skogseth, pers. com.). Dance music in Israel, however, occupied a rather low position in the Israeli cultural ranking system. As in Egypt, the Israeli cultural elite promotes "quality" music (in Hebrew, *eikhoot*), which is what the educated Ashkenazim (like the Egyptian elite) listen to.[56] That Danna sings in Arabic doubly disqualifies her from the category "quality," for Arabic music is severely ghettoized in Israel, consigned to the lowest rungs of the country's Eurocentric cultural hierarchy, much lower than dance music (see Regev 1995, 1996; Horowitz and Namdar 1997). This is compounded by Danna's Mizrahiness, which further positions her at the bottom of the prestige system.[57] It is precisely the fact that Mizrahi singers like Danna enjoy Egyptian pop and do versions of Egyptian songs that puts them at the bottom of the cultural hierarchy. Again, and contrary to al-Ghayti, such singers' relation to Arab music is one of tribute, not theft; a tribute, moreover, that leads the Ashkenazi elite to view their culture as "trash."

An otherwise favorable review of Danna's 1995 release, *E.P. Tampa*, in the daily *Ma'ariv* exemplifies the entirely commonplace stigma attached to Israeli Jews of Arab background (Assif 1995). The reviewer labeled Danna's music *frehiyoot-bivim*, from *frehiyoot*, a derogatory term that Ashkenazim frequently use to denote young Mizrahi women, meaning "slut," and *bivim*, meaning "gutter."[58] The Mizrahi community, however, is relatively unaffected by such Ashkenazi Eurosnobbism, and Danna has a more mainstream appeal among Mizrahim as a successful ethnic insider. For instance, a friend of mine took her son to see Danna perform a concert of children's songs for kids in Holon, a poor Mizrahi town near Tel Aviv.

With the exception of "My Name Is Not Sa'ida," it is her songs in Hebrew that are chiefly responsible for her fame in Israel. Among these are heterosexual love ballads that function as parodies in light of her sexuality, as well as covers that, from queer and Mizrahi positions, poke fun at canonical Israeli popular music from the fifties and sixties, including "songs of the beautiful Israel" and "military songs."[59] According to Smadar Lavie (pers. com.), when you hear a macho Israeli soldier song like "Yeshnan Banot" coming from the mouth of a "black" Mizrahi woman rather than from a muscular, blond, square-jawed Ashkenazi, the effect is hilarious. Moreover, that such songs emanate from a "trashy"-looking Mizrahi who appears hyperfeminine but whose very femininity is ambiguous adds another dimension to their uproariousness.

Danna's song, "Qu'est-ce que c'est" (on *Umpatamba*, 1994) is a hilarious riposte to racist Ashkenazi parodies of North African Jews' pronunciation of French. Such parodies were a constant theme of comedic radio and stage skits of the 1950s and 1960s, which exaggerated Mizrahi "mispronunciation" of "qu'est que c'est?" and made a play on words with "cous-cou-sou," referring to the North African food, couscous, as well as the similarity of "qu'est que c'est / cous-cou-sou" to the Arabic word *qus* (cunt). Modern Israeli Hebrew has borrowed most of its curse words and epithets from Arabic, so the word *qus* is, of course, widely used. "Qus ummak" (literally, the cunt of your mother; i.e., fuck your mother), is a curse shared by speakers of colloquial Hebrew and Arabic.

There is also an Israeli dimension to Danna's song "Susu ya Susu" that highlights the country's disavowed but complicated and intimate connections to Arab culture. When Israel started broadcast television in the early 1960s, it had more programming in Arabic than in Hebrew, and one of the programs developed in the Arabic section[60] was a children's show called "Sami and Susu," a kind of Arabic cross between "Mr. Rogers" and "Sesame Street." At the same time there were no good children's shows in Hebrew, so in the late 1960s "Sami and Susu" was given Hebrew subtitles, and it rapidly gained great favor with Israeli Jewish kids. According to Lavie (pers. com.), the name "Susu" therefore "evokes cuddly memories" among the generation of Israelis who grew up watching "Sami and Susu." The Sami character was played by the young actor George Ibrahim, a Palestinian leftist who eventually lost his job during the intifada when he started to express his political views openly. Sami used to tell Susu, "Khudni ya Susu" (Take me Susu), a phrase that reappears in the lyrics of Danna's song, and the two characters were then transported to a new site as an "airport/spaceship" sound track played, a musical theme that is also evoked in Danna's "Susu ya Susu."

LOCAL TRANSNATIONALISM

One typical Egyptian newspaper article described what was at stake in Danna's "sexual invasion" as follows: "Thus Israel tries to destroy us by any means. Will she succeed, or will our youths establish that they are really Egyptian?" ("al-Jins" 1995). Such alarmist rhetoric from the intellectual elite as well as the state's banning of her cassettes indicate the presence of resistance among Egyptian youths—resistance that is underground, inchoate, indirect, and mostly unselfconscious. Alberto Melucci (1985) suggests that in the realm of such submerged and everyday cultural practices, in the domain of what he calls "movement networks," alternative frameworks of meaning are produced. He claims that the hidden, quotidian practices characteristic of "movement networks" constitute the normal state of affairs for contemporary social movements and that overt social movements as such only emerge episodically and for limited durations. Perhaps, then, potential spaces for the emergence of movements and autonomous activity are being created through the consumption of Danna.

Danna's popularity is certainly indicative of widespread youth skepticism regarding the version of modernity being offered up by the Egyptian state and nationalist ideologues. Walter Armbrust (1996, 217–18), in his analysis of contemporary Egyptian popular culture, labels such attitudes antimodernist. But perhaps Danna's circulation in Egypt also suggests young people's desire for an alternative modernity (Appadurai 1991, 192), one that would offer greater possibilities regarding gender roles and the articulation of pleasure. Such desires do not seem especially focused on female or queer issues, but Danna's reception does suggest an openness in this regard on the part of Egyptian youths.

Danna-in-Egypt also indicates visions of a modernity that participates, without a sense of inferiority, in global popular cultural trends, a modernity that does not passively consume the likes of Madonna and Michael Jackson but actively reworks and rearticulates transnational cultural forms, assimilating or domesticating such forms within indigenous culture. But this case involves much more than transnational flows from West to East, the subject of most of the academic work on global culture. This is rather an instance of what I want to call local transnationalism. The cultural transactions here are not, in the main, vertical flows (North/South, dominant/subordinate) or the products of global capitalist forces but lateral flows, products of underground exchanges and affinities that traverse the borders of neighboring but hostile countries. Danna—at least in 1994–96—was not a "world music" or a "dance" artist with substantial audiences in the West, and unlike, say, Rai star Khaled or Madonna, she did not arrive in Egypt via established circuits of advanced capitalism. She was, rather, a local star, whose product was recorded and distributed by local Israeli companies (IMP Dance and Helicon/Big Foot) and not by the branch of a multinational firm and whose popularity was based chiefly on "local" tastes. Moreover, it was not Danna or her Israeli record company who reaped financial gain from the sale of a reported half million of her cassettes in Egypt; instead, the profits were shared among countless Egyptian bootleggers, black marketeers, and street peddlers.

It is this nonsanctioned commerce between Egypt and Israel that I find most hopeful, and most significant. What Egyptian journalists and the cultural mandarins cannot seem to comprehend is that Egyptian young people who consumed Danna's music were not identifying with "Israel," not "captured" by Zionist ideology. My elite AUC students who enjoyed Danna, in fact, were angered by ongoing repressive Israeli actions against the Palestinians in the Occupied Territories and Israel's ferocious bombing of

Lebanon in April 1996. They felt ashamed, moreover, at their government's kowtowing to the American and Israeli governments (what is known in the United States as "moderation"). Similarly, thousands of Egyptian youths are able to simultaneously consume the music of Madonna and Michael Jackson and to articulate strong criticism of the U.S. government's unwavering support for Israel and its harsh policies toward Iraq. If there is any "identification" with Israel on the part of Egyptian youths, it is an inchoate and mostly unwitting empathy with the culture of the Mizrahim, the Israeli Jews who originate from the Arab countries. Even in a context in which the Jewish strains of national culture have been so heavily suppressed and officially forgotten, connections continue to exist between Arab Jews inside Israel and Arabs across the border. Danna International's success, both in Israel and in the Arab world, is testament to the lively, vital, complex cultural reality of Israel's Mizrahi culture, which has been documented by scholars such as Ella Shohat, Smadar Lavie, Shlomo Swirski, and Ammiel Alcalay. Despite the Mizrahim's marginalization by Israel's Ashkenazi elite, their "Eastern" culture, fifty years after the founding of the state of Israel, continues to thrive and to produce sympathetic echoes in the Arab world. The phenomenon of Danna International in Egypt therefore should not be regarded a the pahological effect of Israeli and Western cultural imperialism or as the corruption of Arab culture but as potentially highly subversive. But this potential will remain merely latent, underground, and proscribed, in the absence of other political and social developments in Egypt and Israel that are congenial to the complicated but open national, ethnic, and sexual politics that Danna International portends.

UPDATE: DIVA!

A number of significant developments have occurred in the Danna story since I left Cairo in May 1996. First, the Egyptian press has continued to turn out discoveries of new Zionist plots against Egypt. In June 1997, for example, *al-'Arabi* ran Fatma al-Nimr's story about a plot to "Judaize the Arab eye" by plastering Egypt with the Star of David. Al-Nimr claimed to find the Star of David not only in the logos for the popular detergent Ariel and the sandwich chain Mu'min but also in food strainers, house decorations, and traditional lanterns used during Ramadan (Radi 1997; Engel 1997). That same summer, reports emerged that college girls in the city of Mansura were throwing themselves at boys, after chewing Israeli bubble gum spiked with progesterone, smuggled into Egypt through Gaza (Jehl 1996). Such accounts are frequently reported on by Western journalists, usually in such a manner as to render ridiculous virtually any Egyptian fears or criticism of

Israel and to divert attention away from real Egyptian grievances or problems.

Western journalists focused less attention on reports that about 7,500 Egyptian young people who entered Israel on tourist visas between 1993 and 1996 had stayed on to take illegal jobs. Twenty-five hundred of these were reportedly recruited for noncombatant jobs in the Israeli army, especially in Israel's "security zone" in South Lebanon, and were issued identity cards with Jewish names. At least one Egyptian has been convicted of spying for Israel who was reportedly recruited by Mossad when visiting Israel ("Egyptian Workers" 1996; "2500 Misri" 1996). Also, little notice was paid to the revelation that Israeli military officers were involved in smuggling tons of hashish from Lebanon via Israel into Egypt, for sale to dealers who supplied Egypt's conscript army. The scheme was hatched in response to security fears before the June 1967 war with Egypt, and the army-sponsored smuggling continued until the late 1980s. Egyptian military sources claimed that hashish consumption in the army rose by 50 percent in the late 1960s and early 1970s, when almost two out of three soldiers were regularly using it ("Egyptians Were Stoned" 1996).[61]

Danna's perceived threat to Egypt was also highlighted again in fall 1996, after she visited Egypt for a fashion shoot, to model a new line of dresses for Israel's biggest mainstream department store, Hamashbir. *Ruz al-Yusuf* ran a story describing the trip as a propaganda coup for Israel and reported that Israeli press accounts of Danna's visit depicted Egyptians as bribe takers (Danna's party reportedly paid off a policeman so that they could continue shooting at the Pyramids) and pervert-lovers (several Egyptian men professed that Danna is pretty and her music enjoyable). The magazine also reprinted several fashion photos of an alluring Danna, dressed in slinky outfits and posing variously with Egyptian policemen, inside the Khan al-Khalili, Cairo's tourist bazaar, and with a boatman beside the River Nile. The captions—such as "This Pervert Exploits Us"—attempted to ensure that the Egyptian reader was not enticed by what appeared to be a beautiful woman but was really an Israeli sexual deviant ("al-Misriyyun" 1996).

In summer 1996 Danna issued a new CD, entitled *Maganona*, whose title track (meaning "crazy" [*majnuna*] in Arabic) is a response to Danna's underground success in the Arab countries, a brilliantly wacky dance number that Danna sings aggressively in Egyptian dialect. Danna defends herself with lines like "Who do you think my husband is? / I'm a respectable woman [*sitt muhtarma*]," and, "You all think I'm crazy / I'm not crazy [*ana mish magnuna*]." The last line of the song goes, "ana mish magnuna / ana magnuna [I'm not crazy / I'm crazy]." Although the new CD was banned in Egypt, it was a black market best-seller (Bhatia 1997). Danna claims to appreciate her success with Arab youths, asserting, "I like to sing in Arabic. I like the language. I like the music. I like the instruments" (Grynberg 1996, 35).

But the most important development is Danna's Eurovision success. In November 1997 she was selected to represent Israel in the May 1998 Eurovision contest in Birmingham. Her selection raised a furor among ultra-Orthodox Jews. Typical of the reaction was the assertion of Rabbi Shlomo Ben Izri, health minister and Shas party representative: "Dana is an abomination. Even in Sodom there was nothing like it" (La Guardia 1997). Thanks to Danna's impassioned denunciations of the ultra-Orthodox, she has become a kind of heroine for secular Israelis (Sharrock 1997). But despite her embrace by the liberal Israeli establishment, she seems determined to continue her subtle mocking of Zionism, as evidenced by her statement to Sky News after she was selected to represent Israel at Eurovision: "As far as I'm concerned, I was elected to represent Israel's citizens, not the Jewish state. Which means that I'll go to the Eurovision as the representative of the Christians and Muslims who live in Israel as well."[62] In May 1998 Danna, at age twenty-six, took first place in the Eurovision contest, singing her song "Diva" before an estimated global television audience of 100 million. Thousands of fans celebrated her win by dancing all night in Tel Aviv's Rabin Square, chanting "Danna, Queen of Israel."

After her highly publicized Eurovision victory, Danna seems poised to become an international star. She is recording and making frequent appearances in Europe, her photo is featured in an Amnesty-U.K. poster with the caption, "Gay rights are human rights," and she is starting to be noticed by the U.S. media.[63] The danger is that, as she moves into a different political context, her multidimensional subversiveness will be reduced to the single issue of queerness and transsexuality and that it will be difficult for audiences in the West to sympathize, much less make sense, of her Arabness and her oblique lampooning of Eurocentric Zionism. An article on Danna in the November 1998 *Details* (Keeps 1998) suggests how the mainstreaming of Danna might proceed: it never once mentions Danna's Yemeni-Arab background.

NOTES

I would like to thank, first of all, Saba Mahmood for urging me to take up this project. Mona Mursi first alerted me to Danna International and gave me a tape with two of Danna's songs. Nirvana Said and Dina Girgis provided complete versions of the clandestine *Busni ya Susu* and information about Danna's reception in Egypt. Bob Vitalis brought me Danna's CDs from Israel, and has been a source of inspiration, timely anecdotes, and sources. I am grateful to Joel Beinin, Clarissa Bencomo, Sandra Campbell, Elliott Colla, Smadar Lavie, Don Moore, Martina Rieker,

Muhammad El-Roubi, and Geir Skogseth for their comments on earlier versions of the chapter; to Elliott Colla and Hosam Aboul-Ela for their help on the theme of the predatory Western woman in Egyptian literature; to David McMurray for calling my attention to the Yigal Amir connection; to Motti Regev for sending his articles; to Bruce Dunne for passing along AbuKhalil's and his own article; to Tom Levin for encouragement and sparkling editorial suggestions; and to Walter Armbrust, Joel Gordon, Geoff Hartmann, Joan Mandell, Samia Mehrez, Jeff Olson, Alan Sipress, and Salim Tamari for forwarding various news items. Yael Ben-zvi and Smadar Lavie served as invaluable resources on Danna's place in Israel. Special thanks are due to Clarissa Bencomo and Gamal 'Abd al-'Aziz for passing along relevant articles, assistance in transcribing and translating lyrics, and helping me to contextualize Danna in Egypt.

1. I have employed the spelling of her name that is used on her first four Israeli CDs. Her latest CD, *Diva*, uses the spelling "Dana." A wealth of information on Danna International—including pictures and links—is available at Geir Skogseth's webpage (http://w1.2225.telia.com/~u22260o821/Geir%2oSite/Geir_Danna_1.html). Danna's CD discography includes *Danna International* (IMP Dance, Tel Aviv, 1993), *Umpatamba* (IMP Music, Tel Aviv, 1994), *E.P. Tampa* (IMP Dance, Tel Aviv, 1995), *Maganona* (Helicon/Big Foot Records, Tel Aviv, 1996), and *Diva* (IMP Dance, 1998). Her recordings, difficult to find in the United States, are available from Hatiklit, an Israeli import company in Los Angeles (http://www.shalom3000.com).

2. I was never able to locate the publisher. Books with unknown or no publisher seem to be a commonplace in the street stalls of Cairo; see Abu-Lughod 1995a, 54.

3. The earliest report I was able to find was Majdi 1994. The campaign continued throughout 1995; see Rizq 1995a; *Ruz al-Yusuf*, October 16, 1995, p. 27; *al-Jumhur al-Misri*, February 18, 1995, p. 12; *al-Hayat al-Misri*, December 31, 1995. The *New York Times* even reported on the campaign in October 1995, (mis)identifying the Israeli singer on the banned tape as Sa'ida Sultan (Jehl 1995).

4. Hereafter, al-Ghayti's book is referred to in the text as *F*.

5. The author uses terms like "perversion" and "deviance" (*shudhudh*) throughout to describe gays and lesbians. According to AbuKhalil (1993, 34), this terminology is the product of the importation of Western homophobic ideologies and modern nation-states. He also argues that the term was not used in Arab/Islamic history, which demonstrated great openness with regard to homosexuality.

6. The upscale McDonald's in Ma'adi, the upscale Cairo neighborhood where I lived, featured posters of Madonna, James Dean, and Marilyn Monroe. According to al-Ghayti (*F*, 40), Marilyn Monroe was both an inspiration for Danna and a "deviant" (see below).

7. Ironically, since the publication of al-Ghayti's book, Michael Jackson has set up an entertainment company to promote "family values" with Saudi Arabian billionaire prince Alwaleed bin Talal al-Saud (Electronic Urban Report, March 20, 1996 [http://www.leebailey.com/EUR.html]).

8. Al-Ghayti's claim is that Madonna is not "complete" because she is unable to bear children. As the entire world knows, Madonna gave birth to a baby girl, Lourdes, in late 1996.

9. Although I have been able to find no information to corroborate this story,

apparently Asmahan was involved in intelligence operations. According to Nasser Eddin Nashashibi (1990, 82–83), in 1941 the British High Command paid Asmahan a tidy sum to convince her former husband, Shaykh Hasan al-Atrash, governor of Jabal Druze, to permit the Allies to enter Syria from Transjordan and "liberate" it from Vichy rule.

10. The year 1967 is clearly meant to resonate as the year of the Six-Day War and Israel's overwhelming defeat of the Syrian, Jordanian, and Egyptian armies. But given the very low status of Arabic music in Israel, especially as recorded by Mizrahim, Rachel Qattawi's recording must have been a very marginal phenomenon and not, as al-Ghayti implies, an Israeli "theft" of a valuable treasure. I have been unable to track down an Israeli who has heard of her.

11. It should be recalled that anti-Masonic/Semitic conspiracy theories also thrive in right-wing circles in the United States. Televangelist Pat Robertson, for instance, believes there is a Jewish-Marxist-Masonic plot to destroy the American way of life.

12. These issues included the nature of the Israeli-Palestinian "peace," which many regard as tantamount to Palestinian surrender and as a complete sham, Israel's refusal to dismantle its nuclear arsenal and make the Middle East a nuclear-free zone, and the Israeli government's failure to bring to trial the military officers responsible for carrying out the massacres of forty-nine Egyptian POWs near al-'Arish during the war of 1956 and of more than one thousand Egyptian POWs during the 1967 war. Public anger in Egypt was also aroused by Israel's April 1996 attacks on Lebanon, the Israeli army's targeting of the UN Qana base and the resulting death of more than one hundred civilians, and what was seen as the successful application of U.S. pressure to torpedo any censuring of Israeli actions. Needless to say, Israel's policies and actions appeared very different from the vantage point of Egypt than they do from inside the United States. A sense of that different perspective can be gained in the United States from the various writings of Edward Said and Noam Chomsky. On the Qana affair, see Robert Fisk's reporting in the *Independent*, for example, Fisk 1996; for my own views on the question of Palestine, see Swedenburg 1995, especially chapters 1 and 2.

13. For instance, see articles in *Ruz al-Yusuf* exposing Israeli efforts to steal and destroy Egyptian music (Abu Jalala 1995) and cinema (Khafaji 1994).

14. The claim, in fact, is rather ludicrous, as virtually no Israeli products are sold on the Egyptian market, and there are no compelling reasons why Egyptians might harbor desires for expensive Israeli cigarettes. As of this writing, I am unaware of any appearance of this item in Egypt.

15. The threat of sexual seduction posed to Egyptian women instead comes from Westernized and culturally hybridized Egyptian men (Walter Armbrust, pers. com. October 20, 1995). A good example would be the Ibrahim Faraj character in Naguib Mahfouz's famous novel *Midaq Alley*.

16. Novelistic examples include Yahya Haqqi's *The Saint's Lamp* (1973), Tawfiq al-Hakim's *Bird of the East* (1966), and Sulayman Fayyad's *Voices* (1993). The film *Layla* features a Brazilian woman who seduces Layla's love interest (see al-Bandari et al. 1994, 305). Thanks to Walter Armbrust for calling this film to my attention.

17. The press reports frequently on army campaigns against heroin and hashish

production in the Sinai. The peninsula's Aqaba Gulf beaches, moreover, are known as freewheeling resort areas: Sharm al-Shaykh (site of the 1995 antiterror summit) caters to upscale Western tourists and the Westernized Egyptian bourgeoisie; Dhahab and Nuwayba' are the meccas for scantily clad, drug-seeking Euro-hippies and Israelis. For descriptions of South Sinai's even wilder days under Israeli occupation, see Lavie 1990.

18. A report in the public-sector magazine *Ruz al-Yusuf* of August 24, 1998, titled "Senior Arab League Official Tells Us: The Story of the Israeli Blood Tainted with AIDS," claimed that blood units being sold to Arab states by an Austrian firm were being "treated" in Israel with "the AIDS virus, hepatitis B and bilharzia" before being shipped abroad ("Official Egyptian Newspaper" 1998).

19. One could read the closing scene of this TV announcement—the opening of the Pan-African Games held in Cairo in 1991—as an implication that the AIDS threat also emanates from sub-Saharan Africa.

20. It is significant that the "deviant" Western pop stars al-Ghayti discusses (Michael Jackson, Marilyn Monroe, James Dean, and Madonna) are depicted as sexual predators *on men*. Although al-Ghayti does not make a specific claim that Elvis preyed on males, the fact that he is said to have indulged in sadomasochism could be taken as implying this.

21. A number of books on Madonna in Arabic have appeared for sale at Cairo newsstands, such as *Madonna's Diet Book* and *Confessions of Madonna*.

22. Since the mid-1980s Egypt's most prestigious professional syndicates (doctors, engineers, lawyers) have been lobbying for the government to place limits on the numbers accepted into their professions' university programs in an effort to combat growing unemployment. The engineers' syndicate even attempted to block the government from opening new university programs and technical institutes. Thanks to Clarissa Bencomo for this point.

23. Before a young man can marry, he must, at the minimum, own an apartment, furnish it, purchase an acceptable amount of gold jewelry for his fiancée as an engagement gift (the *shabka*, which is the bride's property and serves as a form of insurance for her), and be able to finance a decent wedding party. A significant wedding party expense is the *firqa*, or music group, and wedding gigs constitute one of the major sources of income for Egyptian popular musicians and are often much more lucrative than recording. Thus, paradoxically, the same weddings that are a major source of support for the music that youths love also function—by virtue of their great expense—to oppress that same generation.

24. Still, young people's sexual adventures before marriage are more frequent than one would imagine from official representations. A survey of one hundred high school and college girls in Cairo reported that 8 percent had had full sexual intercourse, 20 percent had held their lovers' hands, 23 percent had kissed, and 37 percent had experienced sex without intercourse (Khalifa 1995, 7).

25. It is also often claimed that the youth crisis is a significant factor in the rise of Islamist movements. Government-style propaganda, such as the famous 1994 film *al-Irhabi* (The Terrorist), which stars Egypt's leading comedian, 'Adil Imam, asserts that innocent youths are attracted to Islamic militant groups because their perfidious leaders provide women to marry, at no cost (see Armbrust 1995). Although such propaganda is simplistic, it is indeed the case that youths, so heavily affected by

the crisis of opportunities, constitute the main adherents of Islamist movements. Whereas in the late 1970s and early 1980s the militant Islamist groups that employed violent means mainly attracted university-educated youths (Ibrahim 1982), by the 1990s such groups were also gaining lower-class youth adherents. The Muslim Brotherhood, Egypt's main Islamist organization and a mass movement that, although technically illegal, attempts to mobilize through legal channels and aboveground, successfully recruits university-educated youths. Although the Muslim Brotherhood has not "solved" the wedding crisis, the fact that it enjoins simple wedding ceremonies, where music groups and dancing are not permitted, ensures that what it calls "Islamic weddings" are much cheaper than wedding ceremonies that are the norm for the rest of the population.

26. This paragraph draws heavily on the arguments of Armbrust 1996.

27. On Umm Kulthum, see Danielson 1997.

28. The censorship and banning from radio of songs by "respectable" artists is also routine (see Hasan 1993).

29. Although class divisions within Egyptian society are gaping and getting wider, and although upper-class youths who are the direct beneficiaries of infitah do not face the same problems as lower-middle and lower-class ones regarding employment and marriage, the former are also alienated from the classical nationalist project and are negatively affected by the absence of public space for youths. One should, of course, make some distinctions. Some middle- and lower-class youths want to bring back the "golden age" of culture and politics represented by the Nasser era, while others would wish for the return of the public-sector safety net through halting or slowing down the pace of privatization and structural adjustment and for an expansion of the possibilities of working in the Gulf. Upper-class youths, meanwhile, are somewhat more focused on cultural liberalization. Thanks to Clarissa Bencomo for helping me to clarify this point.

30. The rest emigrated to Brazil, France, the United States, Argentina, England, and Canada (see Beinin 1998).

31. Murad's films are regularly aired on Egyptian television, her music is played on the radio and readily available on cassette, and her death in November 1995 brought forth a wave of laudatory obituaries and tributes in the Egyptian press. The exclusion of Egyptian Jews from nationalist discourse was also noticeable in the favorable tributes to Layla Murad that appeared, following her death, in the Egyptian press during November and December 1995: almost all of them failed to mention her Jewishness.

32. See Beinin 1998, chap. 3; Somekh 1987; *Bulletin of the Israeli Academic Center in Cairo*, no. 10, July 1988.

33. Ironically, much of the coverage of Danna in the press is written by poorly paid young stringers who have no real "voice" but merely ventriloquize official discourse.

34. Danna's claim, in an interview with *Jerusalem Report*, that a half million of her cassettes had been sold in Egypt is credible (Grynberg 1996, 35).

35. One of my students purchased *Busni ya Susu* on the black market for £E 8 (just slightly above the average price of a prerecorded cassette) before the media offensive was launched against Danna; her friends who bought the cassette after the onset of "moral panic" were forced to pay £E 50.

36. Algerian Rai star Cheb Khaled's 1992 hit, "Didi," also reached the top of the charts in both Israel and Egypt.

37. On Whitney's 1990 CD, *I'm Your Baby Tonight.*

38. Whereas house and "dance" music in the West normally uses major keys, Danna's dance music deploys Oriental modes; thanks to Smadar Lavie for observations on comparative musical modes.

39. According to Lavie, Danna is parodying the parodies of Mizrahi- and Palestinian-accented English by Israeli-Ashkenazi comedians such as Shaike Ofir.

40. Such polylingual wordplay is a long-standing tradition for Levantine Jews, going back at least to Andalusian Spain (see Alcalay 1993).

41. Telephone in Italian is *telefonare,* but *telefoni* rhymes nicely here with *pantaloni.*

42. Representative lines from 'Adawiya's "Bint al-Sultan" include "The water's in your hand / And 'Adawiya is thirsty . . . / Why don't you look at me / My little fruit, my pineapple / Water me, water me more / The water in your hand is sugar" (Armbrust 1996, 132); from Sahar Hamdi's "Illi shartit 'aynuh bitghannin": "The delicious ones / Because they're delicious play hard to get / Like this, like this, like this, like this . . . / May God forgive you, you who are on my mind" (Lorius 1996, 517). Both singers also frequently mix in English words with the Arabic.

43. The song's supposed lewd lyrics, in fact, got it banned from sales and airplay in Indiana and elsewhere and inaugurated an FBI investigation. Controversy only spurred greater sales, and the record hit number 2 on the *Billboard* chart and number 1 on the *Cashbox* chart (http://www.oz.net/~craigb/kingsmen.html).

44. On the peculiar contradictions of Egypt's homosexual community, see, e.g., Miller 1993, 68–69. Miller describes the complex situation of Egyptian gay life as follows:

> Making contact with a gay or lesbian community in Egypt was difficult. There was essentially no such thing. Egypt was the place I visited where there was the strongest social sanction against an openly gay or lesbian life, where a sense of homosexual identity was weakest, where there was the least degree of AIDS awareness. Paradoxically, in a society where the sexes remain strictly segregated, same-sex relations were commonplace, at least among men. But you didn't talk about the subject, except to your very closest friends, and perhaps not even then. In Egypt, sex had to be kept secret, and homosexual sex in particular was haram—taboo. Categories of sexual identity and orientation were slippery, elusive in Egypt and in the Arab world in general. Once you crossed the Mediterranean, the terms "gay" and "straight" revealed themselves to be Western cultural concepts that confused more than they elucidated. In modern-day Cairo, male homosexual sex was everywhere and nowhere. (1993, 68–69)

See also AbuKhalil 1993; Dunne 1990, 1998; Murray and Roscoe 1997.

45. This is also true of some of the work of Egypt's most celebrated director, Youssef Chahine. See, in particular, his film *Iskandariyya layh?* (Alexandria Why?). On "cross-dressing" and homosexuality in Egyptian cinema, see Menicucci 1998.

46. The Mufti of Egypt, Dr. Muhammad Sayyid Tantawi, opposed sex-change operations on the basis that what God has created should not be changed (Rizq 1995b). Tantawi replaced al-Haqq as Shaykh al-Azhar after the latter's death in March 1996.

47. Incidentally, sex-change operations are also performed in Saudi Arabia (the

cases I have read about are all female-to-male), again with fatwas from religious leaders.

48. I saw the ad in 1995 and 1996 on the video monitors that run a nonstop mix of music videos, ads, movie trailers, cartoons, snippets of soccer matches, and bits of "America's Favorite Home Videos" for passengers waiting to board the metro at downtown Cairo stations. The promotion of Luna 2 opens to the strains of Danna's song "Sa'ida Sultan" (the remake of Whitney Houston's "My Name Is Not Susan") and shows ordinary-looking (somewhat chubby by U.S. standards) Egyptian women dancing around and mouthing the opening words of "Sa'ida Sultan," "Wa-t'ulu eh, wa-t'ulu ah" (And you [pl.] say what, and you say yeah). Danna's tune rumbles in the background as the ad promotes the shampoo's virtues, and then the volume of the music comes up again as the spot closes with another chorus of "Wa-t'ulu eh, wa-t'ulu ah." I am unaware of any press attacks on Luna 2 for its exploitation of the music of Israeli sexual corruption to market its product.

49. Al-Ghayti, however, claims that Ofra Haza's tape was "licentious" (*F*, 34–35).

50. On Israeli "Oriental" music, see Regev 1995, 1996; Alcalay 1993, 253–55; Horowitz and Namdar 1997.

51. I depend in this section primarily on the Israeli correspondents Yael Ben-zvi and Smadar Lavie.

52. Regev 1996; Yael Ben-zvi, pers. com.; Smadar Lavie, pers. com.

53. Danna's gender and sexuality still resist pigeonholing. Although she is widely reported to be a transsexual, probably it is more correct to say that she is intersexual. In an interview in *Yediot Aharanot*'s weekly supplement, Danna revealed that she *does* indeed have a penis and has no plans to have it "cut" in an operation. She stated that she had had hormone injections for breast development and would soon have silicone implants. In response to the question of her sexual preference, Danna—who calls herself "a woman and a man"—divulged that she has a boyfriend and that she is not and has never been physically attracted to women (Birenberg 1996). Thanks to Smadar Lavie for translating this article for me.

54. But, according to Lavie, Ashkenazi gays' real role models are the same as those of straight Israelis, because they are so mainstream.

55. It should be noted that Mizrahi youths, because of their place in the economic-racial hierarchy in Israel, have not benefited from the Israeli economic boom in the wake of post-Oslo peace deals with Arab countries and that their hopelessness and alienation resembles that of lower- and lower-middle-class Egyptian youths. The Mizrahi position has worsened since the economic downturn that coincided with Netanyahu's accession to the prime ministership. The average salary of a Mizrahi, 79 percent of that of an Ashkenazi in 1975, was only 65 percent of that of an Ashkenazi in May 1997. Unemployment was two to three times higher among Mizrahim than among Ashkenazim. Mizrahim constitute more than half of the population, two-thirds of the working class, one-third of government workers and employees, and only one-fourth of university students (Rouleau 1998).

56. The extreme importance accorded to Western classical music in Israel, for instance, should be understood as part of Israeli Ashkenazis' unceasing efforts to project a "Western" identity. It is also noteworthy that the Israeli national leadership also occasionally warns against U.S. cultural imperialism, with reference to precisely the same icons of "trashy" cultural domination invoked by Egyptian nationalists. For

instance, Israeli President Ezer Weizman warned in August 1995: "The Israeli people are infected with Americanization. We must be wary of McDonald's; we must be wary of Michael Jackson; we must be wary of Madonnas" (Mid-East Realities, MIDDLEEAST@aol.com, August 11, 1995).

57. For an introduction to the position of the Mizrahim in Israel, see Alcalay 1993; Lavie 1996; Shohat 1988, 1989; Swirski 1989.

58. Although the word *freha* (pl., *frehiyoot*) literally means "chick" (the related word *farkha* has the same meaning in Arabic), it is more derogatory than "chick" (for young woman) in English. *Freha* can also be used to refer to an Ashkenazi woman, usually working class, but is mostly reserved for Mizrahim. Thanks to Yael Ben-zvi for translating Assif's article (1995) and for her gloss on *frehiyoot-bivim*.

59. For an analysis that highlights the critical edge of several of Danna's songs, see Ben-zvi 1998.

60. The administration of Palestinian-Arab citizens in Israel is essentially apartheid, with separate (and unequal) "Arab" sections in the Education Ministry, the Histadrut (Israeli Trade Union Federation), and other institutions.

61. Although the report of Israeli involvement in hashish smuggling is believable, its effects appear to have been mixed during the period in question, a fact not noted in the report. In the June 1967 war the Egyptian army failed miserably, but in the October 1973 war, it acquitted itself admirably.

62. Interview in Hebrew, at http://www.geocities.com/WestHollywood/4875/girls.html. Thanks to Yael Ben-zvi for the translation.

63. Until now, Danna has remained an underground phenomenon in the United States, largely in the dance-club scene. Dance mixes of her songs have circulated on the scene for several years (Henry Sutton, pers. com.), and Danna performed "My Name Is Not Sa'ida" in New York City, when it was on the dance hit list (Kerem n.d.). In December 1996 Danna did concerts at the Palladium in New York City and in Miami and Los Angeles.

FIVE

Playing It Both Ways

Local Egyptian Performers between
Regional Identity and International Markets

Katherine E. Zirbel

Egypt has been in the grip of an ongoing national debate in recent years over the nature of authentic Egyptian culture and identity. Pressures of economic decline, increasing moral conservatism, corruption in the government, and Islamic revivalism have intensified this debate. Underlying a national dialogue over authenticity and legitimacy is a much older cultural standoff between the rural south and the urban north. At the same time, new regional and international cultural markets have commoditized particular regional performance genres and performers who stand in specific relation to these debates. Here I discuss how two regionally distinct performance communities, who have recently come into international markets, have fared amid transformations in local idioms of gender, authenticity, nostalgia, geographic movement, and regional and national identities. I also trace the use of such idioms in the promotion and profile of transnational and world beat markets in which these two communities now perform and in the ways in which audiences conceptualize their interest in such products. The contrasts between these two performance communities' experiences in local and international markets provide insights into both Egypt's cultural debates and the global commoditization of culture.

It seems evident that, notwithstanding the desire by many Egyptians for access to communication technologies that signal the globalizing impulse, such technologies are not available to most. Likewise, in relation to the international commoditization of culture through tourist, folk art, and world-music markets, this gap recurs between those nations who are the procurers and those, such as Egypt, whose cultures are subject to this commoditization.

For, although some local groups have benefited more from these markets than others, they do not have access to the means of production and thus are not controlling these markets. These international cultural markets' obliviousness to their impact on local culture understates the mirage quality of the claims of globalization, especially in Egypt, where everyday life is inflected by the deepening struggle to reach a consensus over national identity and politics.

Local performers must be sensitive to changing morality and beliefs for their work to be well received, and this is particularly so in Egypt, where historically performers were socially marginal and their work was considered shameful according to religious and cultural beliefs.[1] Partly as a result of such cultural beliefs, both of the Egyptian performance communities I have been working with are accredited with notorious historical images. However, the currency of such images in new moral and economic climates is now being put to very different uses with the development of international markets. The performance community of Muhammad 'Ali Street is a nationally recognized historical site of popular culture in central Cairo, whose families have worked in the performing arts for many generations. Nightclubs are becoming their principal venues, and they perform before primarily Arab tourist audiences. They also contract work in the Gulf states. The community near the southern tourist town of Luxor is composed of hereditary musicians of alleged "Gypsy" ethnicity who provide popular entertainment in villages, performing vernacular epics and other genres that are now considered "folklore" within national culture. They have occasionally availed themselves to the tourist market by performing in hotels in Luxor. They also now perform in Europe as "world beat" musicians, and they have recorded several CDs that are distributed most widely in Europe and thus far not in Egypt.

I begin by exploring how these performers' experiences reflect the north-south split in the cultural authenticity debate whereby these competing regions view each other through pejorative constructions that are likewise characterized through each other's regional performance genres. Second, I examine how such regional characterizations of locale and populace are recapitulated to some degree in the relations between, on one hand, Cairene performers and their Gulf Arab audiences and, on the other hand, between the southern musicians and their Western European audiences. These emerging international markets feature gendered or ethnic-identified performance genres that gain contrastive meanings in two respects: (1) in relation to the changing gender expectations conditioned by Egypt's new moral conservatism; and (2) in relation to the shifting balance between the Cairene center, its southern periphery, and new geoeconomic realities.

CAIRO

My own avenue into the world of Egyptian performers began in the clamorous urban heart of Cairo, through my association with an old established family of popular musicians and circus performers who lived on Muhammad 'Ali Street. Through their indulgence I was able to acquire a degree of cultural competency and musical understanding necessary to the rest of my work in Egypt.

It was Monday evening, and Maha and I had been at the mosque of the Muslim saint Fatima Nebawiyya, to whom Maha is devoted.[2] Maha, the unmarried daughter of my primary teacher and benefactor in Cairo, Hajj Ahmad, was my best friend in Cairo. The mosque is in the ancient winding neighborhood of Darb al-Ahmar, where many of Maha's extended family still live among the minute local saints' shrines with their brightly painted doors and the medieval *madrasas* (religious schools) of massive stone. On Mondays the Sufis hold religious song-and-dance gatherings in the ancient walled commons across from the mosque. These gatherings formed a louder male counterpart to the intense fervor of women whispering supplications to their saint inside the mosque.

The long black *abayyas* and head scarves that most women wore to the mosque still constitute the normal daytime street attire for women from the popular classes.[3] These cover smocked housedresses that looked something like long nightgowns, complete with fake satin ribbons, little ruffles, and appliquéd characters. To Maha there seemed to be only two recognizable styles of public attire for women: the dour, veiled, and pious daytime look and the flashy, sequined, suggestive look that she metamorphosed into every evening.

Back at the family's flat, after dinner and the evening prayer, Maha began her nightly application of thick and many-hued makeup. She sat in the living room with a broken mirror in one hand and a big plastic shopping bag of makeup paraphernalia by the other, alternately concentrating on her makeup and on the blaring television soap opera. In this episode the evil Western-appearing daughter-in-law was again lying to her honorable husband as she plotted to swindle her dying father-in-law. The orchestra minibus was to pick up Maha, her sister, and her older brother early this evening, as they were performing at a wedding party (this only happened about once a month), so she had to hurry. Maha and her sister had been singing backup vocals for about half a year in the orchestra where their brother 'Abdellah had long played tenor sax for Jehan, a well-established belly dancer. Most often they performed at the midrange nightclubs in new suburban developments of eastern Cairo. Neither sister would have considered taking the job had not their brother or some other male member of the family also worked there. Maha was happy to be working. At twenty-

eight, still unmarried and with few prospects open to her, she was now helping to support herself and her aged parents whose sons had their own families to support.[4]

I sat with Maha's father, Hajj Ahmad, who dictated musical compositions
to me. Blind since the age of twelve, Hajj Ahmad could imagine complete
arrangements in his head. Apparently I could not, because when I wrote
down the notes of these melodies, I thought they sounded completely unlikely. Hajj Ahmad would become highly animated when he composed. He
had taught all of his eleven children and several grandchildren the ropes of
Egyptian popular music, and now he was teaching me. At seventy-five he
was mostly retired, but people still came to him for advice and hopeful talent occasionally appeared at his door asking for appraisal, sponsorship, and
blessings. He maintained a vast array of prominent connections, although
many were now dying. Community members considered him to be an ex-
ceptionally good and kind man. Blindness had not diminished his full life,
and he was perhaps the happiest person in his large family.

In the newly painted apartment below, we could hear Hajj Ahmad's son-
in-law Hosam giving a lesson on a failing electric piano to Samir, an op-
tometrist with musical aspirations. At 10:00 P.M. Hosam would go to *brofa*—
practice—with yet another belly dancer's orchestra that was currently
playing in a five-star hotel. Hosam met his wife, Amira, playing violin in the
Balloon Theater, the government-sponsored venue where Amira sang in
the chorus (along with most of her eight sisters at various times). Hosam
has a university accounting degree, in addition to his musical training. His
family opposed his marriage into a family of performers, but after almost
ten years Hosam got his way and married the woman of his choice. Amira,
now on maternity leave from the theater, collected her leave pay the first
Monday of every month, which, after inflation and union dues, was small
change. In this sense, she was in the same position as the thousands of other
Cairenes employed by the government.

Mahmoud, Hajj Ahmad's youngest son, was visiting Hosam. He still had
several hours before performing that night with the pop singer Muhammad
Fu'ad, whose new cassette had been number one on Cairo's pop charts the
previous season. Mahmoud was the only one of his generation in the family
to have gone to the conservatory. He dropped out before finishing and for
many years performed with a circus band in sub-Saharan Africa and in the
Gulf states. He seemed ill at ease around much of his family.

The community of Muhammad 'Ali Street is a part of Cairo's old performance district.[5] The street saw its heyday in the beginning of the century with the *hasabolla* brass bands and flourished through the 1970s as the
performance-networking center. The community has been famous for its
well-known women performers since the nineteenth century and has been
distinctive as a community where women have often been primary bread-

winners. As home to families of musicians, dancers, actors, singers, and circus performers, it was a neighborhood that gained quasi-bohemian associations with its intersection of working-class identification and popular arts, along with stories of licentious living, prostitution, and drugs. By the 1970s most of the neighborhood theaters and performance venues had closed. Newer nightclubs were flourishing across the Nile on the touristic Pyramids Road, playing increasingly to Gulf and Saudi Arab tourists. Many younger performers and their families subsequently moved to the Pyramids Road area, including some of Hajj Ahmad's family.

The community of Muhammad 'Ali Street identifies with the height of the nationalist period through historical, economic, and urban cultural links. The forty-odd years surrounding the 1952 revolution (from the 1930s to the early 1970s) was also the golden era of Egyptian song. Music and well-loved singers of the time such as Umm Kulthum, 'Abd al-Halim Hafiz, Ahmad Fawzi, and Layla Murad played a central role in the development of a national consciousness, unity, and pride. Furthermore, for performers, historically marginalized and morally compromised by their craft, the modern nation became their foundational and forgiving narrative. The secular liberalism advocated by the governments of this era accommodated the performance arts and reimagined this community as a colorful, nostalgic site in the mapping of national culture.[6]

In the apartment next door to Hosam and Amira, members of the national circus troupe were gathering at the home of Zuba, the trapeze artist, and her husband, Magid, a cousin of Amira and Maha. I was warned not to interact too much with them by Maha's mother, who felt that circus families were improper because of what girls and women wore and did in the course of their acts, not to mention other allegations.

Down the way, Maha's nephews waited on a balcony, watching for their uncle Sabr's minivan. Sabr was an impresario[7]—leader of a neofolkloric drum and bugle corps, one of many that in recent years have become "traditional" entertainment for the first half hour of virtually all wedding party festivities. The nephews were occasional members of the troupe. On Thursdays, dressed in bright green and gold satiny outfits, the troupe might perform at seven or eight weddings, zipping from one performance to another in the minivan with their drums piled on top.

From the balcony, one of the boys yelled that the orchestra bus had arrived down below. Maha was slowly clacking down the stairs in high-heeled clogs, hair whipped up, burning with bright makeup, and dressed in hot pink with a showy black blazer whose sequins were coming unsewn. At the bottom of the stairs, she giggled nervously over her nightly discomfort at being seen by people who had known her to veil and those who did not know her at all, which was potentially worse.[8] There were many overlapping communities on the street below, and in this era of growing moral conservatism, not everyone would recognize a difference between a vocalist from a pious family whose craft required exotic dress and a prostitute from the same neighborhood. Indeed, some might even intentionally refuse to recognize the difference. Being a pious woman meant that Maha should not know or reply to people on the street who were not directly associated with her family. This left her silently vulnerable to men's comments if she were so unlucky as to make the dash to the bus at the wrong moment.

Maha had begun veiling four years before, partly as a token of her piety, but also because the man to whom she was engaged at that time wanted her veiled so that other men would not think she was available. Generally once a woman commits to wearing a veil, whether for religious reasons or under social pressure, the decision is not considered reversible. In a time when many women performers in the community who could were quitting their work and putting on the veil, this job had forced Maha to make the unusual decision to take off the veil. There was no place for a veiled woman on stage.

Maha was thankful that she was only singing backup vocals and could sit behind the orchestra at nightclub engagements. For not only did lead singers and dancers have to parade in front of drinking, foreign Arab audiences, but they often had to play up to nightclub management to keep their jobs. Maha and her sister, contracted directly by Jehan, the belly dancer, had only to sing their vocals and hope to get home in time for *fagr*, the dawn prayer.

Two coinciding problems now face this community. The first is economic. With the legitimizing of performance through secularized nationalism, performers began to emerge from outside the craft and popular classes in the last generation. The Arabic Music Institute on Pyramids Road, nationalized after the revolution, promoted professionalism and created competition for jobs, which have come to override the old family and neighborhood networks. At the same time, audience tastes have changed. The community's primary historical market, performing for weddings and other ritual family celebrations, has diminished as live entertainment at local weddings has been replaced for the most part by cameo-appearance folkloric fanfare groups such as Sabr's, followed by a night of high-tech sound systems blaring recorded music.[9] This has eliminated a large market for conventional musicians, as have weddings that now feature singers or recordings of religious songs as entertainment. Furthermore, in the pop music scene, new music from outside Cairo, including Western pop, Nubian, and Bedouin music, has become influential. The musicians on Muhammad 'Ali Street say they do not like this music and suggest that the newcomers are inauthentic, whereas they, the old recognized performance families who helped create national popular culture, are the true heirs of Egyptian popular music. But their grasp on the market continues to slip.

The second problem is moral. It appears that elements of a long-standing debate over the status of music in Islam have come back to haunt this community. The economic depression resulting from market shifts and professionalization has coincided with the growing moral conservatism of the last twenty to twenty-five years in Egypt. The loss of their primary local market over the last ten years has had dramatic effects on the community's self-image.[10] The community members cannot escape their historical notoriety or their affiliation with secular liberalism, which is now under attack. Thus many have come to feel uneasy about the work remaining to them in nightclubs. With the economic decline and increasing moral conservatism, fewer Egyptians now frequent nightclubs. The audiences are made up mostly of Gulf and Saudi Arab tourists, whom performers generally do not like. These Gulf and Saudi Arabs often come to Cairo for the cosmopolitan life and entertainment it provides. Both my musician friends and nonperformer acquaintances in Cairo depicted these Arabs as rich, debauched men who try to lure young Egyptian women with their wealth. Nightclubs are one of the few public sites where such allegations concerning Arab men's pursuits gain substance.[11]

While these performers' old markets at weddings were famous for a kind of ribald, communally sanctified (and almost camp) gender play between men and women, the sense of shared community and fun does not exist at nightclubs. The gender "play" between performers and their Arab audiences has a serious, sultry, unsmiling aspect that seems to have more to do with seduction than art. Musicians feel that this cosmopolitan image of Cairo, which is responding to Arab audience predilections, is increasingly anachronistic in this time of increasing moral conservatism. While they feel bound to this work by economic need, they also feel compromised. As Mahmoud said once when he was working in a belly dancer's orchestra, "It is bad work, but I do not have a choice. If people wanted to listen to good music, real music, then we could all play as we liked. But they do not care about art now. They just want to see what women can do on stage."

Just as the Gulf comes to Cairo in search of a good time, so some Saudis and Gulf Arabs have sought to bring the good times back home. There is a quickly growing market for Cairene musicians, singers, and dancers in the Gulf, and many have responded to the local economic decline by contracting work there. Their work is part of the massive labor migration over the last two decades to the Gulf and Saudi Arabia. The primarily male Egyptian laborers work under denigrated conditions of reduced rights and liberties in Saudi and Gulf societies. For migrant performers the situation is worse, as there is no historical precedent for a liberal cosmopolitan nightlife in the Gulf. The brunt of the stigma falls on women performers, who are often equated with prostitutes there.

BEHIND THE UNVEILED

I had often wished aloud that my Cairene performer friends and I could form an all-woman band in Cairo and threatened to start one, which always got my friends roaring with laughter. It was inconceivable; there had been no such thing in the Egyptian music scene in any of their lifetimes. But as luck would have it, the day I got my ticket to go back for a visit to the United States, Maha called and told me to come over immediately. We had been offered a contract to sing in an all-woman band in the Emirates for three months. The Egyptian middleman, 'Abduh Fathi, who had contracted Hajj Ahmad's old orchestra to play at an Emirati wedding years before, had called to inquire about women musicians, knowing that Hajj Ahmad had many daughters who were in music. Maha wanted to go to the Gulf primarily because it sounded exciting, but she would not go unless I went also. The family would not let either of us go unless we went with 'Abdellah, Maha's brother, who could act as manager and guardian. We would make substantially more than she was making as a vocalist at the time in Jehan's orchestra. We negotiated with 'Abduh Fathi, but in the end we decided not to take the offer.

Several months later when I was back in Cairo interviewing some Bahraini and Emirati men about performances in Cairo, I mentioned that episode. Their reactions made me realize I had touched a live wire. So I began to ask about performances in the Gulf. Most Bahraini and Emirati male audience members I interviewed insisted that any woman who chose to work as a performer in the Gulf was either completely misled or, more likely, already morally adrift. Some said that even if these women were not already prostitutes in Egypt, they became prostitutes when they went to the Gulf. Two alternating narratives—both occasionally told by the same men—were given to support this assertion. According to the first one, women who came to the Gulf came only for the money. As performers, they would be continuously propositioned for large sums that would be unbelievable in Egyptian terms and difficult to pass up. These women would come to prostitute on the side, reasoning that no one at home would ever know. Second, there was the narrative about forced prostitution. Because of sociopolitical structures of power in some parts of the Gulf, if a prominent sheikh in the audience wanted a female performer for sexual relations, neither the performer nor the management could refuse, according to the men interviewed.

In either case, according to these men, the role of the women performers was to appear desirable and desirous on stage. Part of the pleasure men expressed finding in performance was the apparent availability suggested by the women. In most cases, these men readily acknowledged, there were no true feelings behind these performers' flirtations on stage, or relationships offstage. The women only desired money. However, several of these Gulf Arab men sheepishly claimed to have had feelings for, if not relations with, the female performers from Cairo (although none were from the community on Muhammad 'Ali Street). One man was hoping to contact a former dancer from Cairo during his stay there.

I had to wonder at, but not discount, the differences between these men's stories and the concerns with morality that made up so much of my female performer friends' lives on Muhammad 'Ali Street. While many of the men had worked in the Gulf, I never heard of any women from the community contracting work there except for some celebrations, when they had been specially flown in for a few days' work at weddings or special occasions. According to both audience and performers' accounts, the women who contracted work in Gulf nightclubs were from a different, and much lower, class. At least for those I knew well, the offstage reality behind the image played onstage by women most often involved a higher degree of moral constraint than that which I found among many nonperformer women from similar socioeconomic backgrounds.

Musicians' experiences in the Gulf, while economically rewarding, have further undermined their pride in craft. In response to such moral and economic inroads, members of this community legitimate their identity through nostalgic narratives that depict the community's past as both morally purer and economically more affluent.[12] In the nostalgic narratives of Cairene musicians, I was often told about a time of burgeoning resources and markets and a rich musical culture led by almost superhuman individuals who were able to move national and pan-Arab sentiment in the years surrounding the 1952 revolution.[13] The community of this earlier era is depicted as brimming with life, art, and friendship. In contrast, the circumstances today are described in terms of moribund possibilities, all morally impinged, where groveling for work and mistrust between community members is becoming the norm.

Nostalgia can be a comforting venue for dysphoria over, or resistance to, the present through displacement of desire onto an imagined past, often invoked via distinct places, individuals, practices, or acquisitions. Nostalgia can also become a habit and disposition. This seemed to be especially the case both for younger members of the community who were born as it began to slide and for those who were peripheral to actual performance activities. Even the most successful younger members of the community, who received formal training, remain deeply nostalgic for old times, old music, old "traditional" values, and old markets. Looking back is safer, especially in uncertain times, than looking ahead to the future. Susan Stewart (1993, 139–43) suggests that nostalgia can be a veiled critique of the present. In regimes in which oppositional politics are tolerated, or in which, as in preindependence Egypt, political sentiment was mobilized through per-

formers and performances, these performers perhaps could use their public forum to speak the minds of their local audiences. They could thereby
respond to, and perhaps partially resolve, the economic and moral pressures that now pull them in opposite directions. However, they are impli-
cated through their work in national troupes and their reliance on secular
principles that allow them to perform.

Intrusions from the remembered past constantly belie the completeness
of nostalgic assertions made by younger community members. Hajj Ahmad,
among other things, played in orchestras that performed both Egyptian
and Western pop in the 1940s for the British, and he continued to play
some big band and jazz through the 1960s, after which these genres essentially disappeared from Egypt. When happiest he still sings "In the Mood"
by Glen Miller and cackles gleefully if I harmonize with him. "Dadada—
dadada!—dadadadada—Da! Dadada—dadada—dadadadada—Da! . . . "
This is the heart of his own nostalgia, more cherished perhaps because this
music gets no airtime, unlike the late great Egyptian stars whose songs remain on television and the radio decades after their deaths. While most
musicians are passionate about old Egyptian hits from the 1940s, almost no
one recalls the once-popular big band music, historically associated with
the British, from before the revolution.[14]

Cairenes who know the community of Muhammad 'Ali Street best
through the frequently rerun mass-media portrayals of its past are quick to
forgive the morally skewed activities associated with the community precisely because these index an era that can be readily distinguished from the
present.[15] Cairenes share a nostalgic reminiscence for the glory years surrounding the revolution, forgetful that the libertine cosmopolitan image of
Cairo that Gulf Arabs now seek was nourished in that era. However, for
community members, this past is relived in their nightly work, the community's often-filmed public space, their own family histories, and the selective
tools of nostalgia that the media constantly employ. In the current moral
climate, the community's historic notoriety, while contributing to the distinct flavor of Cairene public life that provides work for performers, is becoming their albatross.[16]

The community's dilemma reflects an ongoing national dialogue on the
legitimacy of the state, which Islamists have extended beyond rhetoric in
the south of the country.[17] Cairenes in the north tend to be more closely
tied to the state than southerners, as most state apparatuses, jobs, and services are carried out within Cairo. While affected by the Islamist-influenced
religious conservatism, many Cairenes make a sharp distinction between
their religiosity and that of the Islamists. These Cairenes contend that their
values are more authentic and firmly rooted in Egyptianness. They stake
their moral and identifying claims within the nation's past, and sustain a
faith in the ideologies that have generated hopes in the past for the nation's

future. This mental leap hops over the present, shedding a nostalgic lime-light of the past into the future, and thus stabilizes the centrality and authenticity value of secular national culture. This remains the case for many Cairenes despite the fact that political liberalism has no currency with most present-day Egyptians and that many (including Cairenes) have lost faith in the current government. According to southern Islamists' religious interpretation, secular government is false a priori. Egypt's corrupt secular government provides them with the perfect example of the inadequacies of secularism.[18]

Again, it is important to consider the underlying regional debate that predates the Islamists, forming along an urban-north to rural-south axis. For many Cairenes, Cairo *is* the nation, the center to be emulated. Cairenes' allegiance to the city itself is often a fundamental orientation of Egyptian identity that undercuts other ideological affiliations. Cairene acquaintances who argued against the Islamists rejected their claims as misinterpretations of the Qur'an, but also because of their underlying rural southern identity. Southerners are often identified as Arabs by Cairenes, as well as by southerners themselves, based on some fairly ancient migrations. Cairenes describe southerners stereotypically as "hot-blooded" and crude, prone to violence—all pejoratively male images—and describe their lifestyle, customs, and music as "folkloric" throwbacks to an earlier, uncultured time.[19] As a result, many Cairenes I knew felt that southern Islamists had no claim in Egyptian discourses on whither the nation because, in their view, southern Islamic "fundamentalists" were neither historically or culturally Egyptian nor properly Muslim. The media, both newspapers and films, depict Islamists as terrorizing, relentless, and inhumane men. Islamists, in turn, describe the center through the already salient corrupt, feminized images of Cairo's nightclub performance genres, writ large. While many southerners might not agree with the ideologies of their fellow southern Islamists, they do concur on this image of Cairo.

TRAVELING SOUTH

I jumped on the 7:30 A.M. train to Luxor out of Ramses, Cairo's main station, without a ticket or a seat. It was my third attempt to obtain a ticket in as many days, and by now it was three days before the end of Ramadan. All the southerners living in Cairo were going home for the holidays. I had promised to spend the end of Ramadan and the holiday with my southern musician friends. I found myself crammed with half of Egypt in between two train cars. Squished next to me was Sawsan, who soon became my bosom travel partner. Sawsan was a twenty-year-old biology student at al-Azhar University who was on her way home to Nag' Hammadi to visit her family.[20] Without sleep and exhausted, I was not in the mood to talk, but

Sawsan held forth. I had sensed that she was not Cairene from her talkativeness and a kind of naive, open excitement in her approach.

Within an hour we were beyond the troubling rubble of jerry-rigged hovels that line the tracks in Cairo. The whole of Egypt rolled by along the train tracks—beautiful, flat, serene, a golden green glow of living wealth, ruled by luxuriant palm trees and dotted with occasional villages, spread out to the sandy brown bluffs and low mountains marking the lifeless desert on either side of the valley. Every time the train stopped, Sawsan and I, along with fifty others at the end of each car, hoped for a place to sit in one of the cars, but more people with tickets kept pouring on. Happy Holiday: "Kull sana wa-anti bi-khayr!" So we remained thoroughly uncomfortable as the midday heat rose, bumping ever less easily along in the crowded space between the train cars, along with *fellaha* (peasant) women, old men with huge cartons, and numerous *shabab* (young men) uncharacteristically not smoking because of Ramadan.

It was late afternoon before we got seats. By this time the surrounding seats were occupied entirely by southerners, mostly laborers or soldiers on leave, plus some assorted elderly men and women. Soon everyone began talking to each other. As each individual joined in, there was an exchange of village and family names and delight over discovering they knew people in common, or that they had heard of each other's families. Along with the fun of placing each other within known families and communities, each person was thereby bound to behave honorably according to their standing, so unlike the often-brusque anonymity of Cairo. The young men began joking together—ribald but harmless exchanges—and Sawsan joined in. The camaraderie was refreshing and felt very unnuanced by dubious innuendoes that might have interceded in a similar exchange in Cairo. (Cairenes consider themselves relatively relaxed in regard to gendered interactions when compared to southerners.) These southerners seemed relieved to be out of Cairo, and it was as if they had removed their masks together as they laughed away the tension of the city. The camaraderie was remarkable, and after most of the travelers disembarked in Nag' Hammadi and in Qena, the train felt very empty.

As it happened, in the hour before arriving in Luxor a fellow introduced himself as a nephew of Rayyis Ahmad, leader of one of the *mizmar* (Upper Egyptian oboe) bands whom I knew from the village of the mizmar players. He said he had seen me before at a village wedding and knew I was studying mizmar. He proceeded to entertain me with stories and conversation until he disembarked at Qus, the town before Luxor. Thus I too was treated to the peculiarly southern neighborly recognition and arrived feeling a happy surge of homecoming.

THE PERIPHERAL GAZE DOWNSTREAM

Southern villagers tend not to share the sense of national identity or unity found in Cairo, and, on the whole, have been made marginal to national history and lore. Earlier in the century a whole genre of Egyptian literature developed around the theme of poor, bright southerners overcoming the odds by migrating north to become successful in Cairo.[21] However, in the mid-1990s, national culture seemed to be cast in a kind of photo negative by southerners I knew whereby the national government and culture was believed to be corrupt and irrelevant to their lives. And for many of them, even those who attended school or work in Cairo, the center was losing its gravity because of labor migration outside the country and the appeal of the Islamist movement.

The rural southerners' lack of admiration for Cairo and the state often becomes a bastion for their own claims to authenticity and legitimacy. To them, Cairo is fraudulent, greedy, and capricious—a courtesan to surface whims of passing movements. It is both dangerous in its strengths over its subjects and weak in its moral composition. Southerners I knew would often point to differences between their ways and those of Cairo. They often identified their "traditional" dress as a signifier of the difference between the south and Cairo. Their modest dress had not changed over time, and many women in the south had always worn veils, while Cairenes had taken off the veil in the 1920s but now were putting it back on. My southern friends felt that Cairene women who now wore the veil and acted pious did so either out of fear of the Islamists or as a fashion.[22] The southerners I knew best lived in the area around Luxor, which, until 1997, was comfortably south of the area most severely affected by the conflict between the Islamists and the state. In stories about Cairo by Luxorite men who had worked there, Cairene women were made to stand for cultural corruption.[23] The only Cairene men ever mentioned came up in jokes about national political figures, where they were most frequently depicted pejoratively as having homosexual leanings. Southern men considered themselves to be masculinized by comparison, and both men and women felt they were more grounded, whole, and less compromised by dependency than were Cairenes. Southerners depicted their own culture as true, unswerving, and hospitable by comparison to Cairene culture, despite the jealousies and anxieties that attended being peripheral to power.

Likewise, in contrast to the sense of cultural demise expressed by Cairene musicians, things are going well for southern rural musicians who live in and around the town of Luxor. They are not subsidized by the state, unlike Cairenes such as the circus performers on Muhammad 'Ali Street, who work for government troupes in Cairo. They have been ignored for the most part by Islamists, at least for now. All the performers are men, so they experience none of the gender-related condemnation to which the Cairene performers are subject.[24] Their aspirations are in the international music market. While Cairo has long been the media production center of the Middle East, these southern rural musicians are now recording CDs that are not even marketed in the Arab-speaking world (see the discography). Paris has become their center.

For such musicians, the idea of touring abroad appears to become a geographic frame for contending ideologies about value and morality. Within this frame, the world outside Egypt is characterized by unlimited opportunity that increases with cultural distance, in juxtaposition to an increasing moral order and diminishing economic opportunities associated with Egypt.[25] Presenting themselves as "authentic" folklore artists, while using the most up-to-date recording and promotion technologies, these musicians have developed a strong following in Europe, as a part of the world beat music market, under the name Les Musiciens du Nil (The Musicians of the Nile). The image they present belies xenophobic beliefs about Middle Easterners that have prevailed in Europe. Rather, they evoke a timeless, nostalgic prenation past. Their identification as authentic "Gypsies" from Egypt—an identity that they agree on for foreign marketing purposes only—along with their un-European performance, becomes their prime selling point.[26]

As interest by Western Europeans in non-Western cultures has grown, along with the concomitant process of commoditizing them, international music festivals, shows, and a whole new recording industry and subculture have come to flourish around world beat music (Feld 1994). World beat music producers and audiences have focused most on ethnic minorities and peripheral groups to the exclusion of national popular culture, and this is also the case with regard to Egypt. The musical genres and performances of rural Egyptian "Gypsy" music—genres presumed nearly dead nationally—are marketable in the West for their authentic and traditional value. This authenticity is exhibited in promotional materials and CD covers featuring pictures of the musicians in "traditional" garb and dramatized ethnographic liner notes about their lives that, however, do not refer to the wider social context of Egyptian national culture. There are good ideological and economic reasons for promoting marginal groups. First, cultural difference, the world beat industry's product, is most plausibly found in marginal groups. Second, this marketing also feeds into well-founded concerns expressed in leftist and activist discourses about oppressed minorities and marginal groups. The implication is that as part of a marginal ethnic group, such musicians must therefore be oppressed. Thus buying their CDs will help to lift their oppression. Yet preference by foreign audiences for music from the peripheries of Egypt is a political and aesthetic choice that obliquely denies, or perhaps simply fails to recognize, the legitimacy of modern Egyptian national culture.

Beyond such exoticism and the investment in solidarity politics that patronizing culturally peripheral music often implies, there are aesthetic issues that are more specific to world-music listeners' comparative rejection of commercial Egyptian popular music. These listeners describe such music as a quirky kind of disco music that is consistently off kilter. Popular Egyptian music exhibits structural and percussive similarities to Western popular music while differing from Western "pop" by use of three-quarter tones, voice resonance, and embellishment in musical expression. Such differences are also present in the "folkloric" music of the southern musicians, but apparently listening to Egyptian popular music requires more of an aesthetic stretch for Western listeners than does the more complete unfamiliarity of the southern music.

I came to see these influences when Maha's father, Hajj Ahmad, made a demo tape for me to promote in the United States that included both older genres and new disco-sounding songs. He dictated a letter to me, introducing himself as a composer and arranger from Cairo who was able to work in all Egyptian and many Western genres. He was offering the tape as a gift to the recipient, a producer I was to seek out, in the hope that the producer would capture the U.S. market for Hajj Ahmad's modern Egyptian popular music. He knew about the success of southern musicians with whom I had been working. I did not think his music would work, even if I could get someone to listen to it. For all my struggling to understand the aesthetics of Egyptian music, it was only then that I consciously came to realize what kinds of music could be promoted in the new global markets, along with the agency allotted to such chosen musicians in making aesthetic and production decisions. Thinking about what might interest such audiences, I suggested that Hajj Ahmad might best market his music by noting his age and position in relation to the rich history of his community and Cairene popular culture in his letter. I also suggested that he explicitly feature his daughters, who sang on the demo, for the market that women's music might capture. He was not interested; it was not professional. He was interested in selling music and his skills. It was incomprehensible to him that these Western markets are interested in selling exotic cultural difference tinged with counterhegemonic politics. At least at this point, as an urban composer from the country's modern-affiliated culture, Hajj Ahmad had little chance of breaking into the world-music scene without a word of explanation that might show him to be either marginal to Egyptian society or oppositional in relation to political hegemony. He did not realize that while the world-music market produces an image of equalizing world relations, this is only how the market markets. Even in the case of the southern musicians, the agents controlled marketing and production, despite the implied politics that signaled a return to an imagined world moral economy, in which audiences, agents, and performers, along with the cultures that they represented, were equal players.[27]

In some real sense, the creation of such markets does hold a potential for mobilizing activism to promote economic justice and greater equality. It is a market that thrives on popular recognition and ratification of fissures in the idea of bounded territorial identities—such as in Senegalese fusion rock or Rai music (the Algerian diaspora music that became electrified in France)—through developing certain kinds of intercultural familiarity and appreciation. However, it is not clear that this political and cultural appreciation translates into action. With few exceptions (like rain forest and German antiracist activism), the market has arisen amid growing despondency in regard to grassroots local and global activism, suggesting a kind of faux politics or what Walter Benjamin called the "aestheticization of politics."[28]

Thus, instead of attaching to some kind of an authentic hook, Hajj Ahmad's professional earnestness—his authenticity—actually worked against him. Dutiful as I could be, back in the United States, I did try to get some folks interested in his music, but they just did not get it. I even had a segment recorded for a radio interview, but the producer cut it out and only used the southern musicians' music. As he said, the urban music was not exotic enough.

The image of Egyptian performance rendered for Europeans is a kind of pure rogue "Gypsy"-ness that is strikingly different from that conjured for Gulf Arabs in Cairene nightclubs that feature alluring and allegedly licentious women. Yet the sights and sounds that the southern musicians deliver in Europe are different enough to turn aside critical aesthetic assessments by audiences and turn on, instead, a kind of exoticism that, to European audiences who understand little about the local context of the musicians or the music, has a stamp of authenticity.[29]

KINDS OF AUTHENTICITY

The idioms of authenticity and nostalgia are central to both the identity of the Cairene and Luxor performance communities and the international commoditization of their performances, by way of either economic or moral reasoning. In Cairo performers identify with the glory of the national period. The southern musicians have benefited from being identified by the international music market as authentic Gypsies who appear to be isolated and unaffiliated with national identity and unimpeded by local morality.

There are several levels at which competing claims to authenticity operate. I have discussed links among regional, historical, and moral claims to authenticity. At the same time, in the tensions played out in performance and in audience expectations, we begin to see cultural, economic, and political relations that move well beyond performance. There are at least four dispositions of the "authentic." Here I clarify the term's uses to make sense of how the concept of authenticity is used by different constituencies in making claims to various kinds of legitimacy.

First, there is the kind of authentic artistic product by a known artist who produces his or her works self-consciously, for example, an "authentic" Rembrandt. Such works carry the pleasure of recognition for the viewer.[30] A second kind of authenticity, related to the first, is the philosophical notion that refers to inner truth of self, that which feels intuitively correct, ringing a bell of familiarity.[31] Third, there is authenticity of knowledge that is based on historically verifiable fact. This is the kind of authenticity on which the Cairene musicians base their claims through national cultural history—as do Islamists in the south, through their interpretation of Islam. This debate between religious and secular nationalism forms the central nexus in the current ideological battles over the nature of authentic Egyptian culture. Fourth, there is presumed authenticity regarding the complete unknown: artifacts or events whose aesthetics are so far outside of accepted criteria that their authenticity becomes the very unfamiliarity and inability of an audience to find a common ground in understood delivery, which therefore must indicate an authentically "other" worldview.[32]

This last kind of authenticity appears central to the southern Egyptian musicians' market in Western Europe. French and Swiss audience members with no previous contact with this music repeatedly said that they enjoyed the performances because the sounds and melodies were so different from music they had known. Some felt that, hearing the music, they could imagine Egyptian village life there. Within what I will call this exotic-authentica, Shelley Errington (1994, 213–15) has noted two opposing Western perspectives on the truth-value potential of non-Western art: it is perceived as signaling either the naive ignorant (which the West left behind) or the sublime (which somehow the West also left behind). This infinitely varied category just never seems to be on equal footing with the procuring West; that is to say, "ethnic" art is apparently either deep in pagan darkness or well beyond nirvana. But in either case, or at least in this case, it becomes excellent fodder for imaginative and wishful nostalgic projections by Europeans.

In the art world there is much anxiety and suspicion wrapped up in production practices and in the possibility of "fake" ethnic goods. But in the case of live ethnic performance, there is less doubt that these performers are who they are billed to be. However, fears of somehow being outwitted, attacked, or swindled offstage are present. Moreover, such fears are often bound up in the very construction of pleasure. In the West temporary exhibits and "celebrations" designated as foreign, exotic, or exciting, whether in the form of music festivals, circuses, or world fairs, contain elements that would be considered dangerous, frightening, and dubious, if allowed off-stage.[33] The stage here becomes a kind of double-bind holding tank, turning anxieties into pleasurable contemplation.[34]

The ambivalence that attends such exotic-authentica was demonstrated quite clearly in the media and community response surrounding the "Gypsy" music festival held as part of the classical festival in Lucerne to which the "Gypsy" Egyptians were invited in 1995. In response to community concerns, it was rumored that festival organizers had to sign an affidavit promising to reimburse all goods stolen or damaged by the visiting "Gypsies," before they were allowed to come. The festival itself was considered a popular and critical success.

In juxtaposition to such fears and pleasures that European audiences associate with "authentic Gypsy" Egyptians, it is instructive to note the inverse feminized image of inauthenticity in Cairene and Gulf nightclubs and in narratives by Gulf Arab audience members about Egyptian female performers. Male audience members acknowledge that especially female dancers are inherently duplicitous in their erotically suggestive dances that they perform for money before men for whom they have no true feelings. Nevertheless, these men describe their ultimate fantasy as the possibility of engaging in relationships with these women offstage. In this case, it is the acquisitive audiences against whom performers have to guard.[35] Figuratively speaking, here the foreign male audience comes to morally plunder haplessly weak Cairo, which is feminized discursively by both Egyptian and Arab audiences.

At the same time, southerners, masculinized by Cairenes and depicted as uncultured ethnic wild men (with musical leanings) by Europeans, are making inroads into Western European cultural markets. These two Egyptian musical migrations, especially that of Cairenes to the Gulf, where the investment is greater and more performers are involved, reflect the ongoing gendering of desire, region, labor, migration, and capital. Although very different visions of Egypt emerge in these international contexts, both are "Orientalizing." Changes particularly in the Cairene music scene have played into the hands of Islamists through the intensified characterization of morally charged difference between genders on nightclub stages. According to neoconservative religious views, the nightclubs should be shut down and more rigid forms of gender segregation reasserted. Below the surface of such discourses lies the imputation that both Cairo and its women, like Ibn Khaldun's center, are inherently inauthentic and corrupt and must be disciplined by masculine religious authority, austere and untainted by such women (or centers).[36]

It is difficult to avoid being caught in structuralist neatness when so many phenomena appear to line up, as they do here. If Cairo is debauched, there is an implicit expectation that the south, along with its cultural products, is pure. To provide a more balanced view, when southern musicians play locally in the vicinity of Luxor at weddings and *haflas* (parties), the tunes are not drawn just from local music and ancient epics to which Western audiences are attracted.[37] They play an eclectic mix "on request" that includes older Cairene music, transformed into these musicians' own rambunctious performance genre.[38] The music is supposed to set the tone for a bit of wild partying. At village weddings and haflas, some villagers are liable to bring out as much liquor as flows at the nightclubs in Cairo, along with hashish for men (most of these parties are gender segregated, with the women and children celebrating inside). This is their home culture, the apparently "authentic," and it stands in contrast to their performances before the sober and respectfully quiet Western audiences that have come for a "cultural event," to enjoy the unfamiliarity of their music. It is for such reasons that the musicians compare these Westerners favorably to local village audiences.

None of the southern musicians I know admitted feeling any direct pressures from Islamists, although they have lost some local audiences to religious singers and *dhikrs* (Sufi musical performances) that are becoming popular as wedding entertainment. While Islamists condemn Cairo's nightclubbing, Western-dressed urban tradition that is not theirs, perhaps they have a regionalist blind spot for these local, fellow southerners. It does appear from these interregional and international cases that exotica, and in other power arrangements, threat and danger, can only exist as clearly distinguishable from one's own identity. The kind of authentic culture on which the Islamists are focused is concerned with how morality ought to combine with power within the state. Although their staunchest support is found in the south, the political power they have directed their efforts to obtaining resides in Cairo. In the meantime, southern musicians playing for drunken villagers pass through the moral fire unscathed.

Viewed together, these performance communities dramatize the changing power relationships between peripheral "authentic" regional community, national center, and outside constituencies in the context of shifting market and moral economies. There is a definite split within Egypt and Egyptian culture, between national identity of the center, constantly in need of revival through nostalgia, and the burgeoning of regional identities, which, in the south, seem to be riding on the older regionalist biases between the urban north and the rural south. The interregional perceptions of performance reflect changing gender, political, and cultural relations within Egypt. At the same time, the historical power relations between Egypt and the Gulf states, on the one hand, and Egypt and Western Europe, on the other, resonates in the kind of performance genres audiences from these regions choose as representative of Egypt. These two very different

Egypts to which international audiences are responding—the folkloric, ethnic prenation wild men or the feminized cosmopolitan hot spot—reflect specific historical and economic relations between these regions and Egypt. While it would not seem to be in these countries' political interest to further destabilize Egypt, Arab and European audiences have become active participants in the current debate over authentic Egyptian culture and identity. They accomplish this through their selective patronage of performance genres that either contest Egypt's current moral climate or celebrate a marginal past that claims no national currency.

In Cairo there is now growing support for much of the Islamists' platform. Politically aspiring Islam provides a new model that is marketed as truly authentic living, backed by historical precedence, moral order, and God. This provides an alternative for a growing number of disenfranchised Egyptians, in a time when the government has often appeared morally unhinged and ineffective in domestic issues. Egyptians I knew considered government efforts toward reform and democratic rule as shallow impulses directed more toward maintaining foreign aid than signaling substantive change.

In this milieu the community of Muhammad 'Ali Street in the corrupt old center is feeling the chastening of bad times. Performers in the community have responded to the changing economic and moral circumstances as best they can. Many women, feeling morally pressured and wishing to express their own growing religiosity, have quit performing and donned the veil. Maha initially removed her veil to sing in response to her family's economic needs. When Maha became engaged to a bouncer from a nightclub, her fiancé forbade her to continue working, demanded that she wear the veil, and made her promise not to let his family know that she had been a nightclub singer. Although she relished the independence derived from her work, she agreed, anticipating that with marriage she would be able to distance herself from her family's demands on her time and that this would constitute a greater freedom. Even Jehan, the belly dancer in whose orchestra Maha sang, is rumored to be retiring soon, despite her success in the nightclub scene. Men are likewise responding by shifts in their work aspirations. Hosam, Maha's brother-in-law, is working on a Western "lite music" repertoire, hoping to get work in Western tourist hotels, where he no longer will have to back up belly dancers or play for Arab audiences. Maha's impresario brother-in-law, Sabr, gave up his folkloric troupe altogether to pursue unrelated work in Eastern Europe. Maha's brother Mahmoud got married to a woman from a family of nonmusicians and moved to Pyramids Road near most of Cairo's nightclubs. He works hard in nightclubs and recording but rarely plays for belly dancers. He is paying for his nephews' music institute tutors since their mother lost her singing job. Hajj Ahmad is still hopeful that I will find a producer for his compositions in the

United States, despite my insistence and the ample evidence that I am not the one to ask.

Meanwhile, the southern peripheral musicians are on the move, staking claims in European centers, and celebrated another musical CD release in 1996. The genres and images of these two communities of performers, in conjunction with the nostalgia and authenticity issues that surround them, reveal increasingly incommensurate notions about national identity and cultural history in Egypt. This, in turn, reflects a morally laden perception of cultural decay in the center, on one hand, and the recognition of flourishing opportunities by peripheries through international markets that appear to be morally exempt from local Islamist scrutiny, on the other.

I have demonstrated the value of closely examining the local and international components of these entertainment markets that have emerged at the interstices between cultures, to elucidate both the influences that create these markets and their local impact. This analysis reveals that such "global flows" flow only in certain directions, apparently specializing in the commoditization of festively rendered economic inequalities, aesthetic discontinuities, and orientalizing fantasies. Although such markets appear to be driven by international interests, the debates around which these two communities define themselves cannot be understood only, or even primarily, within a globalizing framework. Rather, they must be seen within the context of the moral and political processes that make up Egypt's intense and complex cultural disputes. At the intersections of such national disputes and international capital, the idioms of nostalgia and authenticity, movement, gender, and national identity become the trading cards of performers and audiences, producers and nations, that signal ambivalent yet ineluctable participation in local, national, and international transformations.

NOTES

1. There are long strings of edicts and laws from the Middle Ages to the end of the nineteenth century in Egypt circumscribing the lives of performers. See van Nieuwkerk 1995 for an excellent historical review of women performers' status and Racy 1977 and Danielson 1997 for a historical understanding of the changing status of performers in this century. See also Nelson 1985 on *sama'* (listening) for debates surrounding the propriety of musical performance in religious discourses.

2. For many Cairene women, visiting saints' tombs and mosques serves as both social outings and popular religious practice. Relations between devotees and their saints are often very intense.

3. By this I mean *sha'bi*, literally, "popular". This term carries connotations of both class status and adherence to practices understood to be traditional, patriarchal, and socially conservative. The term tends to include the urban working class, urban trade and craft classes, peasant immigrants to the city, and also those from

the petite bourgeoisie who work in offices by day but return to traditional home lives in the evenings. *Sha'bi* also has nationalist overtones, similar to those evoked by the term *awlad al-balad* (sons of the country), those who staunchly support the nation in opposition to the infiltration of the inauthentic and foreign cultural and political agendas (see El-Messiri 1978). Cairene musicians I knew felt that awlad al-balad were rarely found among younger generations today.

4. Historically sons were expected to help provide financially for aging parents. This practice is becoming attenuated, in part as a result of the increasing nucleation of families. Still, older people express both acquiescence and dismay that sons often do not make an effort to respect the older ways or their parents' needs. This is especially the case in this community, where extended families and occupational collaboration between generations endured until recently. Now modern practices and ideologies linked to professionalism, to which the younger generation aspires (as they must in music to be competitive), forms a rift between the elderly and their children.

5. The Muhammad 'Ali Street neighborhood is composed of a half kilometer of music stores, lute-crafting workshops, and musicians' cafés. Performers live in the six- to eight-story buildings above the stores and cafés with other crafts families and small workshops. The street begins at 'Ataba Square, a traffic-jammed transport and market nexus on the border between Islamic and downtown Cairo. It climbs two kilometers through famous old neighborhoods of Islamic Cairo to the paired mosques of Sultan Hasan and the Rifa'i Mosque, right below the Citadel that crowns the summit. Approximately a kilometer west of the community is Ezbekiyya, once the main theater district. Its private and state-sponsored venues once produced shows ranging from classical *taqasim* music to popular plays and opera. The street was named after Muhammad 'Ali, the Albanian-born ruler who governed Egypt from 1805 until 1848, whose plans for the street were part of his attempt to reshape Egypt based on modern principles and concerns about military access, sanitation, and leisure entertainment (see Abu-Lughod 1971; Behrens-Abouseif 1985; Mitchell 1988).

6. While the development of a pan-Arab press was crucial in Egypt to early nationalist thinking (as Benedict Anderson [1991] might suggest), wider public sentiment during this time of incomplete literacy was sparked by vernacular nonprint media such as film and live entertainment. Especially Umm Kulthum's concerts are remembered as having been imbued with nationalist sentiment. Even for those born after she died (in 1973), her voice has remained the voice of Egypt, or rather what was great about Egypt in the twentieth century (see Danielson 1997). Cairenes consider taxis to be the popular "venue" for the current recorded music scene, and until the early 1990s, Umm Kulthum prevailed "there." For a detailed discussion of the relationships among nationalism, language, and popular culture during the nationalist era, see Armbrust 1996.

7. Many performance-related terms like *impresario, brofa* (practice), and *theatro* (variety show), along with music composition terms found in Cairene Arabic, are derived from Italian.

8. Veiling means neo-Islamic veiling, which is composed of a longish triangular scarf that covers the hair and is pinned under the chin. For a thorough discussion of the cultural politics of veiling, see MacLeod 1991.

9. In the past, and occasionally still, for a small minority of people, a wedding typically lasted three days and included several live orchestras, dancers, and singers. In the 1990s, on any given Thursday night, the family I have partly described above would have been performing at these weddings, which were usually held outside in smaller streets (where many weddings are still held). The rented sound systems now used in wedding entertainment are notable for ever-increasing decibels, a trend that musicians and listeners attribute to Western "disco" influences. Most musicians I knew did not like these trends in popular music but believed this is what people expect. Many are aware of their own hearing loss caused by the high-powered sound systems.

10. Their uneasiness is not fully reflected in most nonperforming Cairenes' view of their community. Cairenes characterize the community as a remnant of a fading popular life and of entertainment that was family based and seem unaware that performers still live there or that they now perform in nightclubs. Karin van Nieuwkerk (1995) found that nonperformers considered members of this community to be good people, because of their historical work at weddings and ritual celebrations. However, the same interviewees felt that singers and dancers who lived and worked on Pyramids Road were little better than prostitutes and only interested in money.

11. There is a pattern of Saudi men marrying Egyptian women when on vacation in Cairo. Although some marriages are contracted in good faith, others allegedly only last for the period that the Saudi vacationer is in Egypt, after which time he repudiates his wife. (Divorce is relatively easy in Islamic law.) To the degree that such "summer marriages" do occur (no statistics are available), they are seen as proof of the immoral, predatory (and male) character of Arab tourists. There are also stories about wives of such Arab men who, unattended and with access to excessive money, are left to spend their time luring young Egyptian men into relationships. These stories mostly circulate among young Egyptian men, and their telling almost always contains an element of astonishment, whereas the "summer marriage" stories are considered common knowledge.

12. Does nostalgia have a center? As a narrative vehicle, nostalgia points to what is not there, making the past fan in and out of self-chosen points. Nostalgia works, for those who cannot afford to criticize, to separate oneself from a present, whether due to a sense of complicity or a sense of helplessness in the face of present problems. It also serves to derive legitimacy or show association or difference through emotive historical means, perhaps to substantiate or invalidate the present. Nostalgia is one of the few choices that subordinated people have: if there is no ascertainable future, one might thus at least choose one's conception of the past.

13. This is reflected in the postindependence ascendancy of Egyptian mass culture and political leadership across much of the Middle East, which dissolved in the wake of Sadat's signing of the Camp David Peace Accords with Israel, Egypt's subsequent expulsion from the Arab League, and recurrent economic uncertainty.

14. Even with all the recent nostalgic fascination with departed Egyptian royalty—who were essentially powerless under the British and were finally booted out by the revolution—there is no public nostalgia for any past cultural items brought in by the British.

15. While I was living in Cairo, one of the most popular long-running musicals was called *Shari' Muhammad 'Ali*. Perhaps the best-loved and longest-running Ra-

madan series, called "Layali al-Hilmiyya" (Hilmiyya Nights), is about the community on al-Hilmiyya Street that converges with Muhammad 'Ali Street. For an excellent discussion of such television serials, see Abu-Lughod 1995b. The many classic films set in the community include *Ahibbak ya Hasan* (I Love You, Hasan; 1958) about a young woman (played by Na'ima 'Akif) who comes to the community on Muhammad 'Ali Street and rises to fame; *Shari' al-hubb* (Street of Love; 1958), in which 'Abd al-Halim Hafiz plays a young man who exceeds his sha'bi Muhammad 'Ali Street background and becomes famous; and *Khalli balak min Zuzu* (Pay Attention to Zuzu; 1972), about a student at the university who, amid rampant classism, redeems her worth (and wins her sweetheart) after being revealed as a dancer from a sha'bi family of dancers on Muhammad 'Ali Street.

16. The problem is that there is still cachet in these images and their uses that together, in some contexts, form a kind of symbolic capital (à la Bourdieu 1977). Such images have served to reinforce the community's precedence in the—albeit diminishing—wedding market, although these antiquated images also typecast community members as throwbacks in a professionalizing market. The idea of symbolic capital gains special use in contexts that include mixed class, ethnicity, and special groups, especially in historical perspective. To the degree that symbolic capital is publicly identified with, or attributed to, a special group (in this case, a performance community), it can also become an ideological burden at different points in that group's history. Such contexts point to the potential double valence of symbolic capital.

17. Islamists are composed of several related groups, most based around the southern city of Assiut, that have worked to bring down the government through preaching against corruption, offering social services that the government has failed to provide in the south, and waging a guerrilla war with the government. They have gained most publicity through their campaign to terrorize Western tourists, on whose money the government relies heavily. Many Cairenes I knew felt that Islamists' violence was wrongly guided by misinterpretations of the Qur'an, which, they felt, provided proof that Islamists were not Muslims. Patrick Gaffney's (1994) work provides excellent insights into this movement.

18. The religious conservative movement touches a deep vein for many lower-class communities like that on Muhammad 'Ali Street, who have not fully shared in the benefits of educational and economic liberalism to the same degree as the aspiring middle classes.

19. Images of southerners come in two major forms. In films, from the 1930s to the present, southerners most often appear as clever but uncultured and ruthless men. These men either form excited roaring congeries in an outrage wrought of their own misunderstanding of some sequence of events (usually concerning honor) or are singular figures of treachery who attempt to kill, kidnap, or trick a hero or heroine. In the background small groups forever drink tea and *yansun* (southern anise tea). A more contemporary image comes from migrant male laborers to Cairo from the south. They are recognizable by their southern dress, and they dominate certain lower-class service and unskilled labor jobs. They are the frequent butt of Cairene jokes.

20. Nag' Hammadi was originally famous as a tourist destination both for the significant Pharaonic sites in the vicinity and for the discovery of the Gnostic man-

uscripts there. However, in early 1995, when gunmen attacked Italian tourists, it had become the southernmost site of Islamist-connected violence up until that time. The attack was widely publicized, but no one said anything about it on the train, which had been attacked numerous times and was heavily guarded. Later, southern friends of mine interpreted this incident as a case of innocents who got caught in blood-feud crossfire. They likewise interpreted much of the violence between Islamists and government forces as rooted in older feuds and vendettas.

21. This migration genre is most famously exemplified by Taha Husayn's autobiography (1932).

22. My Cairene friends were well aware of the changes in their habits, and women were often embarrassed to show me pictures of themselves from years past that showed them dressed "immodestly." Twice, when religious talk got serious, two of my Cairene friends asserted that they thought the world was likely coming to an end soon and they felt the need for repentance. When I was in Cairo, I could see their point, with the high level of environmental pollution, social pressures, illness, and lack of prospects. This feeling would melt away after a day in the south, despite the poverty that also existed there.

23. Southerners tell rumors of migrating female immorality from Cairo to the south. Some Coptic men friends of mine once got together to warn me of the impending peril I faced were I to return to Muhammad 'Ali Street. They claimed that though I thought I knew those women, I could not really know or trust them. They told me that unsupervised women from that neighborhood used to come down south in traveling shows and essentially act as prostitutes in the 1930s and 1940s, comparable only to the visiting nurses of the same period, who were also known for their alleged debauchery. Although none of these friends were born before 1950 or had ever been to Cairo, they assured me that they knew better than I did about the famous neighborhood in Cairo.

24. 'Afifi, a local man, was sometimes hired for his cross-dressing performances of singing and dancing for men at wedding parties. Men regarded him as a subject for hilarity rather than for serious moral scrutiny.

25. These ideations take up conceptual coordinates similar to early explorers' perspectives on travel as discussed in Johannes Fabian's (1983) discussion of time, space, and culture.

26. Their appearance in a recent French movie, *Latcho Drom* (1993), about Gypsy/Romany music from the Indian subcontinent to Spain gave precedence to this marketed identity, although their own identification with this ethnicity at home is much more ambiguous. Gypsies seem to call up romanticist nostalgia for many Europeans, resonating with an imagined prerationalized, preindustrial age (see Hoggart 1958; Williams 1973).

27. This rather optimistic view of commoditization as a practice in which everyone benefits finds its theoretical source in Simmel (1978), who focused on productive exchange to the neglect of productive labor. A similar spirit animates the popularized enthusiasm surrounding the issue of globalization.

28. See Benjamin 1969. I do not mean to somehow condemn the liberatory possibilities of listenership. It could be argued that willingness to listen, buy, and imagine the people behind world music in itself constitutes political engagement that

has subtle agency in the way we align our international politics and the degree to which we may be less willing to "otherize" particular groups.

29. Because of their proximity to Luxor, which is a major tourist center for Westerners, these musicians are used to being scrutinized for glimmers of an authentic past, the original Egyptian Pharaonic culture. Tour guides and guidebooks often depict residents as essentially unchanged since Pharaonic times. Luxorites working in the tourist markets make blatant use of such tendencies to sell their wares.

30. See Barthes 1975 for provocative commentary on the pleasure of recognition.

31. Charles Taylor (1992) discusses this in depth, noting that Rousseau first articulated this as an intuited moral evenness. Such self-awareness also has bearing on romanticist understandings of the artist's sensibilities that are present in narratives of Cairene musicians who have had conservatory training and southern musicians who have traveled abroad.

32. That is to say: "Look at the stems [stains, spittle] still hanging to the headpiece, it must be the real thing." Larry Shiner discusses criteria for authenticity in tourist art, remarking that "in the context of the 'primitive art' market, the art-versus-craft distinction undergoes a paradoxical reversal" (1994, 227). In the case of performance, there is yet more shifting about and aesthetic confrontation, both visually and aurally.

33. See Coco Fusco's *Couple in a Cage: A Guatinaui Odyssey* (1993). Robert Rydell's (1987) work on the world fairs provides historical instances of staging others. Mary Douglas's (1966) discussion of boundaries and danger is also helpful here, as is Ray Bradbury's fictional *Something Wicked This Way Comes* (1983), which explores the lurking fearful fantasies that have typically surrounded traveling circuses.

34. I am extending Gregory Bateson's (1972) use of the term in his discussion of schizophrenia here to indicate a kind of culturally shared schizophrenia.

35. These women rely on management and hired guards to protect them from audiences in Cairo, but apparently do not have such protection in nightclubs in the Gulf states.

36. Ibn Khaldun (1958), the great social historian of the fourteenth century, described the rise and fall of polities, believing that urbanity was inherently corrupting while rural tribal life was moral and politically strengthening. His model suggested that these two sociospatial entities provide foils for each other. As the urban center's defense is gradually weakened by increasing moral and political decay, it is easily attacked and conquered by disciplined peripheral groups. In turn, such conquering groups over time become urbanized, weakened, and corrupt and eventually fall to conquering peripheral groups.

37. Recognition by these musicians that their foreign audiences did not understand the words that they were singing would occasionally lead to mischief in the lyrics.

38. This resembles Redfield's (1956) great/little tradition. To refresh that concept, consider the American tradition of the synthesizer player at reunions, anniversaries, and some weddings, who performs everything from old rock (Beatles) and musical hits (the themes from *Dr. Zhivago* and *The Sound of Music*) to Ave Maria, all set to the same digital rumba beat.

SIX

Joujouka/Jajouka/Zahjoukah
Moroccan Music and Euro-American Imagination

Philip Schuyler

The Master Musicians of Jajouka enjoy a large and loyal following in North America. The musicians, who come from a small village in northwestern Morocco, completed two tours of the United States and Canada, in fall 1995 and summer 1996. There are currently eight available CDs of the group in different configurations and under different spellings, and two of these have done very well indeed. One, a reissue of the 1971 LP *Brian Jones Presents the Pipes of Pan at Joujouka*, produced by Philip Glass in 1995, was offered in both the regular "jewel box" and in a deluxe, velvet-bound, gold-tooled limited edition (with a bonus CD) for an initial list price of $75. Another, *Apocalypse Across the Sky*, was listed as one of the ten best records of 1992 by both Jon Pareles, chief popular music critic of the *New York Times*, and Steve McClure, Tokyo bureau chief of *Billboard* magazine. *Apocalypse* ended that year at number 10 on *Billboard*'s chart of best-selling world-music albums, behind Mickey Hart's *Planet Drum* and ahead of albums by Salif Keita and Bob Marley.

Jajouka CDs are a staple of a number of college and alternative radio stations, where they appear on the playlist along with music by John Cage, Maurice Ravel, Scissor Girls (a Chicago no-wave band), Harry Pussy ("Miami's supreme noise band"), and Meatmen (a Washington, D.C.-based, "old-school punk" band best known for the album *Pope on a Rope*). *Apocalypse* was recommended by the Vampire Server on the World Wide Web as a "Notable Gothic Work to provide mood music for MASQUERADE sessions, or even table top sessions." "For that international feel," the Vampire page advises. "Absolutely primal. You may not get it at first, but you will . . . " (http://www.vampireweb.com/vampire/moodmusic/index .html). Finally, the Brian Jones album has been a topic of favorable comment in *Didjeridu Digest*, a Usenet news group dedicated to the Australian

Aboriginal log trumpet, whose contributors discuss such issues as the effects of mouth jewelry (pierced tongues) on didjeridu resonance and the possibility of serenading dolphins and seals by playing underwater (http://redgiant.ee.nd.edu/digest/digest.252.html). These appearances on the Web are what the critic Terry Teachout recently called "an infallible index of Zeitgeistiness" (Teachout 1996).

The Jajoukans have performed on record with such musicians as Ornette Coleman (1973) and the Rolling Stones (1989), and they have been joined in concert by the Klezmatics (1996) and Donovan, the recently resurrected 1960s psychedelicist. Their music has been used in such films as Nicholas Roeg's *Bad Timing* (1980), Bernardo Bertolucci's *Sheltering Sky* (1988), and David Cronenberg's *Naked Lunch* (1991). They have been the subject of at least one journalistic "novel" (Davis 1993) and one ethnographic film (Mendizza 1983, on which I served as adviser, translator, and scriptwriter [Schuyler 1983a; 1983b]), and they also play a pivotal part in a performance piece by the poet Nancy du Plessis (1995).

The Master Musicians are, in short, a worldwide world-music phenomenon not unlike the late Nusrat Fateh Ali Khan and the Mystère des Voix Bulgares, but, as Peter Watrous pointed out in one of the few skeptical reviews of their 1995 tour, "The cult around the Master Musicians of Jajouka is unlike anything else in pop music." In this chapter I examine the history of this "cult," its guiding myths, and some of its effects on the village itself.

THE VILLAGE

Jajouka (or Zahjoukah, as some villagers pronounce it) is a village of about eight hundred people, located two hours south of Tangier in the Jbala region, an area of Arabic speakers in the foothills to the west of the Rif Mountains in Morocco. Like most villages in the region, Jajouka has special local industries to generate cash or trade goods, beyond the subsistence provided by its flocks of sheep and goats and its crops of grain, vegetables, and olives. In other villages the specialty might be pottery or weaving, basketry or pickpocketing, military service or marijuana smuggling. In Jajouka the specialties are music and, for want of a better word, mysticism. The musicians are best known for their performance on the *ghaita*, a short oboe, and the *tbel*, a double-headed side drum, which are played together for processions during weddings and circumcisions and for the weekly *hadra*, a healing ceremony. For more intimate occasions and, especially, for training and practice, the ghaita may be replaced by the *lira*, a small recorder-like flute. The musicians also perform secular entertainment music in a chamber ensemble consisting of a *kamanja* (viola), a *lotar* (plucked lute), and various drums.

The spiritual and geographic center of Jajouka is the tomb of Sidi Hmed

Shikh, who is credited by the villagers both with bringing Islam to the region and with providing them with their livelihood, music. The saint's name might be translated as "Lord Hmed the Leader," or "Mr. Hmed the Old Man." In Moroccan terms, that is roughly equivalent to calling him (with apologies to Jane Goodman [1995]) "Saint John the Unknown." His name offers no hint of his origin or his biological or spiritual lineage. According to the historian Hamid Triki (pers. com.), he appears in none of the major volumes of Moroccan hagiography. Indeed, his tomb may be empty, but that is not unusual: of the thousands of shrines in Morocco, hundreds are equally open to question. In sacred real estate the tenant is sometimes less important than the location. Thus many tombs are associated with some prominent natural feature, such as a grotto or a waterfall; in Sidi Hmed Shikh's case, there was apparently once an impressive fig tree in the courtyard of his shrine, but it has died and been replaced by a smaller successor. Nevertheless, a few pilgrims from the surrounding villages still visit the shrine in search of a cure for various ailments, principally infertility and insanity.

In the normal course of events, the descendants of the saint would care for the pilgrims, manage their treatment, and accept their donations. If necessary, the saintly family would also hire professional musicians to accompany certain rituals. But Sidi Hmed Shikh's descendants—if he had any—have died out, and the religious duties have fallen to the musicians. This is, as far as I can tell, the one feature of the village that is unique.

The musicians are of two lineages, named Rtobi and, most prominently, Attar, who together make up about half the population of the village. The musicians perform at weddings and other events in the surrounding region—or at least they used to—but it seems that the best and brightest have always exported themselves to the cities, where there was more consistent demand for their services. Many of them also enlisted in the sultan's army, as musicians or in other capacities. In either case, they returned whenever possible for holidays and, eventually, retirement.

This brief description, which differs somewhat from the Master Musicians' publicity, is what I have been able to deduce from the villagers' accounts and from my contacts with performers from other similar musical villages in the Jbala region. In any case, it seems that at the end of World War II, the village of Jajouka was in very straitened circumstances. Sidi Hmed Shikh was very much a local saint, who did not inspire great pilgrimages or generate great income (when compared, for example, to Sidi Mohammed ben Aissa in Meknes, Moulay Abdallah in El-Jadida, or Moulay Brahim in the High Atlas). The military option had been lost to the musicians during the Protectorate period (1912–56), when Morocco was split between the Spanish and the French, along a line just to the south of Jajouka.[1] Even as entertainers the musicians were not widely known. Unlike, say, the village of Mtiwa, farther to the north and east, which is famous for many kilometers around, Jajouka was virtually unknown to Moroccans outside the immediate area. As recently as fifteen years ago, one could mention the name to musically knowledgeable people in Rabat and they would understand—and repeat—"jaqjuqa," that is, "the shaking of a rattle" or, by extension, "meaningless noise" or "unruly behavior." Mention the name in Qsar el-Kbir, a large market town thirty kilometers from the village, and people would say, "Which one?" There are, I was told, three villages of that name in the region.

Paradoxically, the musicians' local obscurity may have facilitated their rise to international stardom (without the concomitant acquisition of fabulous wealth), as they were willing to entertain ideas—and people—that more prosperous musicians might have rejected. In this respect (and, indeed, in their music) the Master Musicians resemble Les Musiciens du Nil, discussed by Katherine E. Zirbel in this volume. As Zirbel points out, "World beat music producers and audiences have focused most on ethnic minorities and peripheral groups to the exclusion of national popular culture." Marginal groups may appear more exotic to Western listeners and more malleable to producers. At the same time, musicians who are well established in their own culture may not want to take the time to deal with strangers.[2] Clearly, the Master Musicians of Jajouka did not arrive at American record stores, radio stations, and concert halls by magic—although the idea of magic is an important part of their promotional strategy. Their success in the West is the result of record producers' use of exoticism and difference as a marketing tool, and the trajectory of their career follows a path determined by, as Steven Feld puts it, "the workings of capitalism, control, and compromise." But Feld, an ethnomusicologist writing about his own experiences as a producer, also notes that such "transcultural record productions tell specific stories about accountability, authorship, and agency" (1994, 258). In the case of the Master Musicians of Jajouka, whatever impersonal forces may eventually have come into play, the initial promotion of their music was, at bottom, a labor of love, the work of one man, Brion Gysin, with the help of Mohamed Hamri.

BRION GYSIN

Brion Gysin, born in England in 1916 of a Swiss father and a Canadian mother, was a citizen of the world and, eventually, of the United States. He was a painter, a writer, and, for a time, a scholar. At the age of nineteen, he was personally purged from the surrealist movement by André Breton. By the time he was thirty, he had written two books, *A History of Slavery in Canada* and a biography of Josiah Henson (1789–1883), the model for Harriet Beecher Stowe's Uncle Tom.[3] According to Allen Ginsberg, it was

Gysin who provided Alice B. Toklas with her famous recipe for hashish brownies, and he is widely credited with inventing, some years later, the cut-up technique of writing made famous by William Burroughs. In the years after World War II, Gysin was in Paris, living on a Fulbright fellowship and the remains of his GI Bill. He first came to Tangier in July 1950, at the suggestion of Paul Bowles. In later years Gysin liked to say, "I meant to stay the summer, or a month or two, something like that, and because of the music that I heard and got wrapped up in, I stayed some 23 years" (Mendizza 1983).

That summer Bowles took him to a festival near Tangier where, as he recalled in 1982, he heard some music "out of the corner of [his] ear, out of some sixth other sense," and he went off to follow the sound. When he came back Bowles asked him what he had been doing, and he replied, "That's the music that I want to hear for the rest of my life" (Mendizza 1983).

Within a year of his arrival, Gysin had met Mohamed Hamri, an adventurer and reputed smuggler, who was hanging around the European community learning to paint. Gysin later wrote about his friendship with the Moroccan in his novel, *The Process*, where Hamri is identified as "Hamid" and the protagonist, Gysin's alter ego, is portrayed as an African-American.

> Hamid is, after all, my Baba, my Bab, my little back door into Islam through which the hue of my hide helps me slip in disguise when once I slough off my American cultural color.
>
> "I'm an accidental Occidental, Hamid," I assure him. "I'm an African: same-same, like you. You say so, yourself," I insist. . . . Naturally enough, I have never been able to pull my Occidental mind along inside Islam after me but Hamid knows that and makes all sorts of allowances. (Gysin 1973, 70)

Gysin may have cast himself as an African-American because of his interest in the history of slavery, or he may have meant to compare the situation of American blacks to his own marginalization as an openly gay man. Be that as it may, there is a play on words here between "Baba," a term of endearment, "bab," the Arabic word for door, and "my little back door into Islam." Even more important is Gysin's recognition that he could not pull his Occidental mind inside Islam, which is amply demonstrated by his interpretation of Moroccan practices.

Hamri knew of Gysin's interest in music, and he invited his new friend up to Jajouka, his mother's native village and the home of her first husband, one of the Master Musicians. After several visits, Gysin finally heard the musicians play what he thought was the music that he had encountered at the festival with Bowles. A year or more had passed since he had first heard this music—briefly and from a distance. Even after all that time, perhaps he did in fact recognize the musicians and the music; but it is equally possible that it was some generic Jbala tune, first played by some other group and then later reprised by the Jajoukans, or that he simply (unconsciously) decided that the music in the village he had come to love was the same as the music that he "wanted to hear for the rest of [his] life." In any event, Gysin now focused his fan's attention on the Master Musicians of Joujouka (as he and Hamri preferred to spell it).

Hamri provided Gysin entrée to the village and served as his interpreter of its history and its customs. Together they codified, in effect, the mythology of the Master Musicians. Hamri, with the help of Blanca Nyland, later published his version of the legends in *Tales from Joujouka* (1972). Gysin introduced bits and pieces of the story into *The Process* and other writings, but mainly he spread the myth through the pens of his many visitors, including Robert Palmer (1971, 1989), Timothy Leary (1970), and Stephen Davis, who liberally transposed Gysin's tales and Hamri's *Tales* into his novel, *Jajouka Rolling Stone* (1993). The scope of this chapter does not permit a full examination of the complexities and contradictions of the various myths of Jajouka—Gysin's, Hamri's, and those of the villagers themselves—but several elements stand out:

- *The musicians' family name.* Gysin took the name Attar as evidence of the musicians' descent from an ancient lineage reaching back to the Persian mystic poet Farid al-Din al-Attar, author of *The Conference of the Birds* (Mantiq al-tayr). This seems to have been pure speculation on Gysin's part. The villagers tell a variety of different stories about their origins, but when I spoke to them in 1982, none corresponded to Gysin's tale. For one thing, the musicians' estimate (admittedly very hazy) put their arrival in Jajouka about two hundred years before the time of Farid al-Din al-Attar. In any case, Attar is a fairly common surname in the Jbala, where it is the designation of a rather low class tradesman—not a producer of exotic essences but a gatherer of herbs and spices.
- *The saint's power of healing.* Gysin maintained that the saint's curative blessing was administered through the *music* performed by the musicians. The musicians do claim to be conduits for the saint's power, which they convey through the touch of their hands and instruments. Curiously, they also claim that their music does not generate a healing trance state but rather that it is meant merely to soothe troubled minds.[4] In any case, the music alone, outside of the shrine and the ritual context, is *not* the sole instrument of healing.
- *The royal patent.* Gysin likened the musicians' role in the sultan's army to the relationship between the Scottish pipers and the Stewart kings. According to Gysin, the Jajoukans possessed a "royal patent" entitling

them to wake the monarch in the morning, pipe him on his way to prayer, and play him to sleep at night. The musicians may well have been the sultan's "personal musicians," in much the same way that all his soldiers constituted his private (as well as state) armed forces. Presumably, they once had a written commission to that effect. At present, however, the musicians have no "sealed *dahir*" in their possession, only a certified copy (from the 1950s) of a lost form (from the 1930s) issued by a Spanish Protectorate clerk acknowledging receipt of some undetermined document.

- *The figure of Bou Jeloud.* Bou Jeloud, a dancer dressed in goatskins, is the central character in a masquerade produced annually in Jajouka (and other villages and towns elsewhere in Morocco) in the week following the feast of 'Aid el-Kabir. The other characters in the Jajouka festival include an old man, known as "al-Haj" (pilgrim), and 'Aisha Hamqa (Crazy Aisha), a local manifestation of 'Aisha Qandisha, the well-known Moroccan she-devil. 'Aisha is always danced by a boy in drag, and was once danced by a *dozen* transvestites, in tribute to her multiple identities and great powers. According to my observations in the 1970s, members of masquerade teams elsewhere in Morocco included other transvestites, pseudo-Jews, boys posing as old men, amateur musicians pretending to be professionals, and kids wearing Halloween masks imported from Taiwan.

Borrowing an interpretation from Edward Westermarck (1968), Gysin equated the Moroccan "goat god" with Pan and suggested that 'Aisha might be Astarte, the Phoenician goddess of love. The Pan thesis has proven to be irresistible to Western journalists and listeners, and served as a powerful fuel for William Burroughs's imagination.[5] The argument, however, has been convincingly contradicted by *The Victim and Its Masks* (1993), Abdellah Hammoudi's detailed study of Bou Jeloud, the surrounding team of masqueraders, and their relation to the feast (not to mention their interpretation by Westerners). Hammoudi stresses that, however tempting the parallels to Pan might be, the participants are all Muslims, the masquerade itself is closely tied to the most important feast on the Muslim calendar, and the actions of the dancers have serious implications for the welfare of the village. In other words, this is not, as one website called it, "pagan party music."

Gysin believed that the quality of the music somehow depended on the pristine—not to say primitive—quality of the village itself. As Hamid describes the place in *The Process*, "Up there in Jajouka, there is no wheeled traffic, no running water other than rills and no electricity. Electric light scares Bou Jeloud away and one day soon, when it gets to my village, it will" (Gysin 1973, 78).

The best way to protect the music, Gysin believed, was to find a way to allow all the musicians to remain permanently in the village. This idea, however, was probably misguided: although photographs from the early Protectorate period show a band with thirty ghaitas (and villagers tell of groups with more than one hundred), such grand ensembles would probably have come together only on holidays. The local music economy would not have supported such a large group, so, even in the best of times, many of the musicians would spend most of the year at their jobs in the city or the army. In fact, for a couple of years Gysin himself contributed to this pattern of employment. Though he was never able to achieve his dream, for a time he did find a way to contribute to the village economy in a more traditional manner, and to support himself as well.

In early 1954 Gysin opened a restaurant called the 1001 Nights in the Mnebhi Palace in the Casbah of Tangier. To entertain his guests—mostly wealthy expatriates, including Barbara Hutton and Cecil Beaton—he brought rotating groups of musicians down from the village. It seems not to have occurred to him that the flash of diamonds could be as dangerous to the musicians as any electric light, but he still tried to protect their innocence in the big city. He said of the musicians,

> I realized that what they had was so precious and so volatile that I refused to let them have a radio, because I had heard the disastrous influence of that sort of movie music that comes from Cairo that has drowned out all the local musics in practically all the Islamic world. So they were not allowed to hear that. If they wanted to hear that sort of . . . rubbish, they could go to some other place. (Mendizza 1983)

Judging from this quotation, Gysin suffered from acute schizophonophobia, that is, to embellish an expression coined by R. Murray Schaefer (see Feld 1994), a fear of sounds separated by the recording process from their original source. But in this case, the affliction was unilateral, for although Gysin was vehemently opposed to having the musicians listen to the mediated, disembodied sounds of other people's music, he seemed to have no objection to having their music recorded and heard by others.

Gysin continued to support the musicians of Jajouka even after 1001 Nights closed down in the uncertain period when the International Zone reverted to the newly independent government of Morocco. In the 1960s he helped to fund the building of the *madrasa*, a clubhouse for the musicians where they could spend time away from their families, house and entertain visitors to the village, and, in theory, train the next generation of musicians.

Thanks to the restaurant, his association with Burroughs, and his own considerable charisma, Gysin had a wide circle of admirers among the Beat elite, and when Morocco became a popular destination for members of the counterculture in the 1960s, he was often sought out for advice. In those years he was described by Timothy Leary as "the elegant orthodox bishop of this metropolitan see [Tangier], . . . one of the great hedonic mystic teachers" (1970, 133–34). Gysin tried to turn his connections into support for the musicians by encouraging small-scale culture tourism in the village. Not everyone was impressed with the musicians—Burroughs first described them as looking like "a bowling team from Newark" (Morgan 1988)—but sooner or later even the skeptics seemed to sing the praises of the village.

BRIAN JONES

The most famous of Jajouka's visitors, of course, was Brian Jones, one of the founders of the Rolling Stones, whom Gysin took to the village in 1968. Jones took along a girlfriend, Suki Potier, and a recording engineer, George Chkiantz, who recorded examples of a variety of musics—including performances by the village women.

Jones took the tapes back to Tangier and then to London, where he began playing with them in the studio, mixing different tracks, splicing different sections together, running some of them backward, and putting it all through various filters and phase shifters. He never completed the project—he died a year to the day after his night in Jajouka—but the record was eventually released in 1971 as *Brian Jones Presents the Pipes of Pan at Joujouka*.

The Brian Jones album has been called "the first world music recording." If so, it was well ahead of its time. The term "world music" first appeared as a commercial category in the late 1980s, although the expression (not to mention the music) had been around for some time before that. The World Music Institute (WMI), for example, was founded in New York in fall 1985 to present concerts of a wide range of different musics, from blues and avant-garde jazz to flamenco, Mauretanian popular song, and Central Asian art music. WMI's founder, Robert Browning, traces the expression back to Bob Brown, who is said to have coined the phrase in the 1970s at Wesleyan University as an alternative to "ethnomusicology," a term he regarded as stodgy. Nevertheless, according to the editors of *World Music: The Rough Guide*,

> The name was dreamed up in 1987 by the heads of a number of small London-based record labels . . . initially as a month-long marketing plan to impress music shops, the critics, and buyers that here were sounds worth listening to. The name stuck, however, and was swiftly adopted at records stores and festivals, in magazines and books, on both sides of the Atlantic. (Broughton et al. 1994, introduction).[6]

A look at the diverse offerings in the WMI calendar or the catalog of

Realworld, Rykodisk, or any similar record label suggests that the term "world music" is intentionally inclusive and amorphous, promising only that a given concert or recording will be different, different from what one is used to listening to, different even or especially, from other world-music items. Even so, Timothy Taylor (1997, 19–31) has discerned a number of common themes used in marketing recordings in this category, among them, claims of authenticity in style, primality in emotion, spirituality in content (and in packaging), and celebrity in production and promotion. Each of these elements was, in fact, embodied in the very title of the first "Joujouka" recording. First comes Brian Jones, the deceased rock star and producer, followed by Pan, the god of delirium who goes back to the roots of European civilization and the bowels of human emotion, followed, finally, by the name of the village. In contrast to most ethnographic recordings of the time,[7] the country of origin is not mentioned at all, but the group is treated as a starring act. In short, if it was not actually the first world-music recording, *Brian Jones Presents* was certainly a harbinger of later work by David Byrne, Peter Gabriel, Paul Simon, and others. It also proved to be a watershed in the West's approach to Jajouka.

Although Gysin himself was clearly attracted by the Gnostic mysteries of the village, his friends were more stimulated by, as Burroughs succinctly put it, "drugs and sex." Burroughs did not need to specify that, in the 1950s and early 1960s, the sex was homosexual. But that began to change with the Jones visit when, for the first time, a woman joined the entourage. Gysin (who later claimed that he couldn't even remember Suki Potier's last name) objected that Jajouka was "no place for a woman," and when Jones insisted that she come, Gysin made her cut her hair and wear trousers. Gysin was, perhaps, right to be worried. In the wake of the Brian Jones visit—and, above all, the subsequent recording and press coverage—the number of visitors to the village increased dramatically, and many were not the sort that Gysin approved of. As a group, the new visitors could be characterized as hippies rather than Beats. The most famous among them were musicians, not writers, and the writers practiced journalism, not literature. At the same time, the sex changed from homosexual to heterosexual, and the emblematic drug of the visitors changed from heroin to LSD, although, of course, marijuana remained a constant (and not all visitors were drug users).[8]

After Brian Jones, one could say that the rest is history, but the beginning of history is not necessarily the end of myth. Whereas Gysin was capable of tempering his enthusiastic exaggerations and acknowledging his ideas as speculations (complete with supporting sources), others have tended to dispense with the scholarly pedigree and caution, distill the story to its most spectacular essence, and present it all as fact. Thus, for example, Robert Palmer (1971), writing in *Rolling Stone*, elevated the musicians from their (possible) status as royal retainers: "The musicians have always been an aristocratic group—Arabic rather than Berber-speaking, and set apart from the majority of the villagers." Although many journalists have identified the Jajoukans as Berbers, Palmer is correct that they are, in fact, Arabic speakers, but so is the great majority of the population for a hundred kilometers around. He is also right that they are set apart from the rest of the villagers, but their profession would be more likely to make them outcasts than aristocrats.

Similarly, Ornette Coleman, who recorded in the village in 1973, proclaimed that the music was six thousand years old (not four thousand, as Burroughs [1973] suggested, or jested) and that it had the power to cure cancer. Coleman's cousin, James Jordan, told *People* magazine in 1986 that Coleman was "accepted by the tribe as a master musician. . . . Coleman was so comfortable with the music he found on that mountain, it was almost as if he had undergone some kind of reincarnation." Coleman himself told his biographer,

> See, when I went there and started performing with them, I was never informed on what they were going to play, how they were going to play it, when they were going to stop, when they were going to start, any form. . . . I wasn't prepared for anything at all. . . . Sounded as if I had rehearsed it with them. It wasn't true. Not at all. (Litweiler 1992, 161)

The musicians had a different impression. According to what they told me, they were very impressed by Coleman's musicianship but also confused by his performance practice: "He could write down anything that we played, exactly. But when he played what he had written, it didn't sound like us at all."

Perhaps the greatest transformation has occurred in the character of Bou Jeloud. Thanks to a slip of the pen on the part of Paul Bowles, the festival has been transposed (in some sources) from 'Aid el-Kabir to 'Aid as-Saghir, the feast at the end of Ramadan. In most accounts the other characters in the masquerade simply disappear from the story. The musicians themselves have helped to emphasize this change: when they tour they bring along only one extra dancer to play the part of Bou Jeloud, perhaps because they sense that the American and European public may be fascinated by the reincarnation of an ancient Greek god but are less interested in, for example, pseudo-Jews and transvestite boys. Finally, in the press and in their own publicity, Bou Jeloud is no longer "like" Pan, he *is* Pan, a figure previously unknown (by name at least) in the village. A press release, attributed to Bachir Attar, the current leader of the musicians, goes even further, identifying Bou Jeloud as "The Male Principle." This is the sort of idea that may have appealed to Gysin, but it goes against actual practice. As

Hammoudi (1993) points out, Bou Jeloud (under a variety of names) is, at the very least, of ambiguous sexuality. In certain places the character is known as "The Cow" (*tamugait*) and has a single, prominent teat. Although Bou Jeloud in Jajouka has a masculine name, he is a curious example of the Male Principle, since he wears a woman's belt and hat.

In recent years stories about Jajouka have shifted their emphasis away from drugs, sex, and even rock 'n' roll to focus instead on the New Age, curative properties of the music. According to *Glow Magazine* (Sherrard n.d.), for example, Bill Laswell's recordings (of Jajouka and other groups) are "different from ethno-musical adornment, which is what Paul Simon does, adding ethnic elements to his songs like so much MSG. It is entirely different from ethno-music packaging, which is what Peter Gabriel's Realworld Records is: the music industry's version of La Choy Foods." In short, Laswell's productions "are in no way ethnomusicological 'field recordings.' They are recordings of trance masters produced by a trance master." Similarly, promotional material for Sub Rosa Records stresses that its new recording of Joujouka is "not another world-music record, but a unique experience—what is proposed here is nothing but a new way to live." Even Bachir Attar, on a world-music fusion album (with the Senegalese percussionist Aiyb Dieng and Maceo Parker, a saxophonist from James Brown's band), is described as "the numinous vehicle," the embodiment of "the latest model of energy . . . , the heir apparent to the thousand year legacy of Dionysian rockingitis, of Apollonian ecstasies—the multi-generational orchestra of high healing." A few fans, at least, seem to take this seriously. When Bou Jeloud danced at the group's Cambridge performance on their 1995 tour, a young couple came up to the edge of the stage, hoping to be swatted by Bou Jeloud's switch of fertility.

Meanwhile, back in Jajouka, the Western accounts have folded back on themselves, reentering the mythology of the village itself. When I talked to the villagers in the early 1980s, they said that Brian Jones had not made much of an impression at the time of his visit. He was only there for a night, and, aside from his appearance, he was not much different from the other people whom Gysin and Hamri brought up. By the time the recording came out in 1971, they had forgotten about Jones, and it was only through their new crop of visitors that they learned about the album and their new fame. Over time the villagers realized that Jones had brought them a blessing, mixed though it might be. Today Jones's picture hangs on the wall of the madrasa, next to the obligatory photo of King Hassan II. And now Bachir Attar says, "I was almost five years old when Brian Jones came, and I remember it like yesterday."

Whatever the Jajoukans actually think of Western musicians like the Klezmatics, Donovan, or Ornette Coleman, the interest of outside performers has become a part of the villagers' stories about themselves. Thus Bachir never fails to mention these contacts in newspaper interviews, and he often opens their concerts by dedicating the performance to Stephen Tyler (lead singer of Aerosmith), Lee Ranaldo (guitarist with Sonic Youth), or other admirers who may be in the audience. It is as though he is invoking a new sacred lineage in the village, replacing the missing hagiography of Sidi Hmed Shikh.

This litany of glitterati—from Gysin, Bowles, and Burroughs to Guns 'n' Roses and Philip Glass—helps to draw audiences to Jajouka concerts and persuades them to buy their records. It is not clear what these arbiters of taste and avatars of hip actually find in following the Master Musicians— other than the company of their peers—but musicians and listeners alike pretend, and perhaps actually believe, that, despite all the exposure to the West, the music of Jajouka is ancient, authentic, and unique. Nevertheless, the mixing of the two saintly lineages, East and West, has produced some decidedly unusual offspring. When *Daily Variety* refers to the music's "glorious air of purity . . . [that] makes no concessions to the Western world," the writer conveniently ignores both Bachir Attar's world-music experiments and the disco mixes on the second CD of the rerelease of the Brian Jones album.

In a field once characterized by anonymity, the Master Musicians of Jajouka have achieved brand-name status, complete with trademark battles. When the Brian Jones album was rereleased in 1995, the spelling of the name was changed from Joujouka to Jajouka, all references to Hamri were excised from the notes, and Hamri's painting was replaced on the cover by a silhouette of Bachir Attar playing the ghaita. Hamri responded by picketing the group's performances in England and distributing a broadside called "The Truth about Joujouka," castigating Bachir for ripping off his family and creating a touring group of ringers from outside the village.

Hamri's pamphlet raises a number of troubling issues about the results of this entire process—most notably, the question of who really owns and profits from this music. Past experience suggests that the villagers themselves are the least likely to realize material gain from the products marketed in their name. And as for "the truth" about Joujouka, or Jajouka, or Zahjoukah, it seems to have been lost in the mists of hype from the press, the musicians' friends, and the musicians themselves. "In short," as Robert Christgau (1996) noted in the *Village Voice*, "this tiny local style comes to the international marketplace burdened with more bullshit than any music can bear."

What's in a name? In the case of this village in Morocco, a great deal. Brian Jones, under the tutelage of Brion Gysin, called it "Joujouka," which sounds like a diminutive term of endearment—an appropriate image of

Gysin's intimate connection to the village. In his battles with Bachir Attar, Hamri, Gysin's first guide to the village, continues to use this spelling as a way to invoke a special kind of legitimacy, his direct link to the heritage of the Beats and early hippies.[9] Bachir, however, seems to have won both the publicity contest and the economic war. In addition to being more accurate phonetically, Bachir's preferred spelling, "Jajouka," is stronger, more streamlined, and, perhaps, more corporate. The "Jajouka" faction has its own logo and has even transcended its brand to contribute a new generic term to the English language.[10] Finally, "Zahjoukah" is the closest representation of the old Jbala pronunciation of the name, but this is just one of the complexities of local knowledge that international consumers are not yet prepared to hear. Oddly enough, however, the first time I saw the name spelled out this way was in metal studs on the back of Bachir's blue-jean jacket, suggesting that, for better or worse, the prosperity of music in this village is now inextricably connected to fashions in Europe and America.

NOTES

Field research for this chapter was carried out in Jajouka and northern Morocco in the summers of 1982 and 1983, as part of the production and distribution of the film *The Master Musicians of Jahjouka*. Subsequent research was carried out during the group's 1995 tour of North America. This work developed from an excerpt of a larger presentation made at Harvard University in fall 1995. An earlier version of this chapter was delivered at the Colloquium on the Politics of Culture in Arab Societies in an Era of Globalization, held at Princeton University in spring 1997. I am grateful for the comments of many people who have heard and read this work, particularly Walter Armbrust, Virginia Danielson, Abdelhai Diouri, and Kay Shelemay.

1. When I was in Jajouka in 1982, however, several members of the older generation of musicians were living off their pensions from the post-independence Royal Armed Forces, or off remittances from their sons currently in the army.

2. Popular musicians who enter the world-music market, such as King Sunny Adé or Salif Keita, often have considerable prominence in their own countries. Thus the obscurity principle put forward here is not invariable—but it is strong. For instance, the most striking counterexample is, to all appearances, Nusrat Fateh Ali Khan, the late *qawwali* singer, who was much in demand for both sacred and secular performances in his native Pakistan and for concerts and recording dates abroad. Despite the mystical, religious origins of his repertory, Nusrat was willing to collaborate with Western popular musicians like Peter Gabriel, Ry Cooder, and Eddie Vedder of Pearl Jam, and also to allow his music to be used in such violent films as *Dead Man Walking* and *Natural Born Killers*. As Richard Murphy notes in this volume (chap. 9), Nusrat eventually became the highest-paid performer in Pakistan, but Hiromi Lorraine Sakata (pers. com.) points out that Nusrat was for many years the victim of the same *khandani* snobbery that Murphy discusses. Only later in his career, *after* his success in Europe and America, did he achieve recognition at home.

3. *To Master, A Long Goodnight: The Story of Uncle Tom, a Historical Narrative* (New

York: Creative Age Press, 1946). At this writing, I have been unable to find any information about *A History of Slavery in Canada.* It may never have been published, or it may be a joke.

4. According to Abdelhai Diouri (pers. com.), it is not uncommon for musicians in religious associations to deny that their music is used for trance.

5. As Burroughs's biographer, Ted Morgan, points out, *The Ticket That Exploded* uses autobiographical experiences (including visits to Jajouka) that were modified according to his readings in science fiction and "filtered through his various preoccupations, such as the Mayan civilization, scientology, and a Reichian view of sex" (Morgan 1988, 422). The view through these filters may be distorted, but at the same time the book provides testimony to Burroughs's acute powers of observation.

6. For a more extensive description of these events, see Taylor 1997, 2.

7. For example, my first set of field recordings was published during the same period under the title *Moroccan Folk Music,* a name that was neither informative nor accurate. That it was not of my own choosing does not make the title any less embarrassing.

8. Many villagers are themselves enthusiastic smokers of *kif*, a mixture of marijuana and strong tobacco, which is no more (and no less) of a drug for them than caffeine and nicotine are for Americans. Indeed, the kif pouch of Berdouz, the musicians' lead drummer and master of ceremonies, was used as the centerfold in *High Times* magazine in the early 1970s, and the village was written up again in the magazine in 1996. The Moroccan government takes a different view, however, thanks to pressure from the United Nations and the United States and to its own interest in maximizing revenue from the state tobacco monopoly. When I worked with Michael Mendizza on the film *The Master Musicians of Jahjouka,* we were obliged to avoid any reference to or image of kif-smoking. The musicians also adhere to this line for official external consumption: in November 1995 Bachir Attar told Reuters World Service, "We do a song about this. 'Brian Jones, in Joujouka, very stoned.' It not mean stoned with drugs. Stoned with music."

9. The name Joujouka has been borrowed by other performers with no direct connection to the village, including a Japanese Techno duo in Tokyo.

10. The *Straits Times* of Singapore used the term "jajouka" (lowercase) as a synonym for trance music. As it turns out, the article was plagiarized from the *New York Times,* but that only reinforces the generic use of the term, detached from its specific origin. Indeed, two writers for the *New York Times,* Jon Pareles and Neil Straus, and Paul D. Miller of the *Village Voice* have repeatedly used the word to describe the performances of jazz or hip-hop musicians with no apparent connection to the village. Meryl Peress, an American belly dancer in New York, has performed under the name "Jajouka" since the 1970s.

SEVEN

Nasser 56/Cairo 96

Reimaging Egypt's Lost Community

Joel Gordon

In fall 1996 Egyptians lined up in record numbers—at seventeen theaters in Cairo alone—to see not the latest 'Adil Imam comedy, Nadia al-Guindi potboiler, or foreign thriller but a meticulously researched and restaged treatment of the 1956 Suez crisis, the nationalization of the Suez Canal Company by the relatively young Nasser regime and the subsequent Tripartite Aggression that did so much to put Gamal Abdel Nasser and his comrades on the world map. *Nasser 56* has already earned a place in Egyptian cinema history; it has also rallied, unnerved, and astonished people on all sides of an ongoing debate over the legacy of Nasser's eighteen-year rule. Ultimately, it will play a major role in the shaping of public memory of the man who dominates contemporary Egyptian history, of a social revolution that is recalled with increasing fondness, and of an era of cultural production that even cynics concede was golden.

Public memory, as the American historian John Bodnar suggests, "is a body of beliefs and ideas about the past that help a public or society understand both its past and present, and by implication its future." "The major focus of this communicative and cognitive process," he continues, "is not the past, however, but serious matters in the present such as the nature of power and the question of loyalty to both official and vernacular cultures" (1992, 15). Memory, the oral historian Alessandro Portelli reminds us, "is not a passive depository of facts, but an active process of creation of meanings" (1991, 52). Similarly, Robert McGlone, writing about memories of John Brown's raid on Harper's Ferry, describes the process of recall as "rescripting . . . not a deliberate rewriting of the past, but a transformation in the controlling expectations and logic of life situations [that] refocuses an individual's self-schema. . . . Rescripting adds or takes away information to make a life story coherent and believable at a particular time" (1989,

1182–83). How might this apply to the scripting of a new text about Nasser and its imaging on celluloid? Historical films raise questions about "history as a mode of knowledge, of historical accuracy, of memory and desire. . . . More than other genres, the historical film evokes a sense of the 'grand,' the visually enthralling, the huge canvass to portray the sweep of events that the past as completed action allows" (Chakravarty 1993, 183). No less for the viewers than for the filmmakers, we might add. So why Nasser? Why this particular story? How have the filmmakers, in this case scenarist, star, and director, chosen to bring the script to life? And why has the enthusiastic popular response both pleased and caused disquiet in official circles, including those that backed and promoted the project?

"ONE HUNDRED DAYS THAT CHANGED THE WORLD"

Nasser 56 is the brainchild of the veteran scenarist Mahfuz 'Abd al-Rahman in collaboration with Egypt's leading dramatic film star, Ahmad Zaki, who plays Nasser, and the veteran television director Muhammad Fadil. Originally intended as one of a series of hour-long dramatic biographies of Egyptian luminaries for television, each figure to be played by Zaki, the project blossomed into a full-length feature film on a grand scale.[1] Produced by the state-owned Egyptian Radio and Television Union (ERTU), the film was three years in the making, from initial conception to preview release in July 1995. Key portions were shot on brand-new outdoor sets at the 6 October Media Production City, the $300 million project designed to reinvigorate the flagging Egyptian film industry and maintain Cairo's virtual monopoly on Arab television production (Khalil 1996a; Saad 1996). The film then sat another full year, "frozen" is the word used by its creators, before its release in early August 1996.

Nasser 56, trumpets its ad, covers "one hundred days that changed the world." The actual span is 106 days, from June 18, 1956, Evacuation Day, until November 2, several days after the outbreak of war. The film opens with Nasser taking down the Union Jack; it closes with a famous speech from the minbar of al-Azhar Mosque. As bombs fall around Cairo, Nasser proclaims that Egypt will fight on and never surrender. Much of the action focuses on political deliberation among Egypt's leadership, formulation and implementation of the secret plan to secure the canal as Nasser addressed the nation from Alexandria on the night of July 26, and the subsequent political maneuvering of Nasser and his colleagues to defuse a crisis they cannot believe is escalating. Other well-known historical faces appear in subsidiary roles, among them military comrades Anwar Sadat, 'Abd al-Hakim 'Amr, Salah Salim, Zakariya Muhyi al-Din, 'Abd al-Latif al-Baghdadi, and Sami Sharaf and civilian associates Fathi Radwan and Mahmud Fawzi. More prominent supporting figures, such as the chief canal engineer,

فيلم الأفتتاح

قطاع الإنتاج

أحمــد زكــى

ناصر ٥٦

Figure 1. Ahmad Zaki as Gamal Abdel Nasser; announcement for the official pre-view of *Nasser 56* at the opening of the 1995 Television Festival. Courtesy of Mah-fuz 'Abd al-Rahman.

Mahmud Yunis, and his colleagues, are less familiar to many Egyptian viewers. There are no Egyptian villains in the piece, save for a small, rather pa-
thetic group of old-regimistes who petition Nasser to resign in the wake of
the tripartite attack.

The film was shot in black and white to effect a newsreel feel. In the
opening scene the camera shoots Ahmad Zaki from a distance, a deliberate
strategy to draw the audience, especially elders, into accepting an actor—
and such a well-known face—as Nasser. Other characters are played by less
familiar, younger actors, closer in age to their characters, also a deliberate
move to keep the film from becoming a parade of stars.[2] Documentary
footage of world leaders and combat punctuate this and provide broader
context for the story line. The only world leaders to appear in the scenario
are Nehru and Australian Prime Minister Menzies, played by opera star and
character actor Hassan Kami, Egypt's master of foreign accents.[3] The black-
and-white film also touches directly on a national bias for the classics, a nostalgia for black and white, from the era before color became the norm in
the early seventies.[4]

Historical accuracy aside—and the debate was quickly engaged on levels
great and small—the film's success rests ultimately on popular reaction to
the characterization of Nasser. Ahmad Zaki has by all accounts, and with
only a minimum of makeup to fill out his jaws and recede his hairline,
turned in a bravura performance that captures Nasser's personality, de-
meanor, speech patterns, and, ultimately, charisma. This is important, because for the generations born after Nasser's death in September 1970,
Zaki will, for better or worse, come to personify his subject. The filmmakers,
well aware of the burden on their shoulders, paid meticulous attention to
detail, shooting on location whenever possible, attempting to re-create sets
based on photographic evidence, and endeavoring to balance conflicting
memories about the most prosaic specifics: the physical layout of the Nasser
household or the brand of cigarettes Nasser chain-smoked.

The casting of Ahmad Zaki was both a foregone conclusion, because of
his personal role in promoting the project, and a natural selection. Zaki has
been Egypt's premier dramatic actor since the late 1980s. Perhaps too often
typecast in recent years as the poor boy trying to infiltrate the upper strata
or as the social rebel, and recently reduced to plot-weak action films, he remains a powerful screen presence, a major box office draw, and occasionally a trendsetter.[5] He is also dark, rare for an Egyptian leading man (or
woman), probably the darkest ever. He can, and easily does, approximate
Nasser's *sa'idi* (Upper Egyptian) features. The rest is pure acting, and Zaki
reportedly threw himself into the project and character, taking on Nasser's
persona on and off camera.

Regardless of critical or popular reaction, the film will remain a mile-
stone in Egyptian and Arab cinema history. It is the first film to dramatize

Figure 2. A familiar guise: Ahmad Zaki as social rebel in 'Atif al-Tayyib's *Didd al-hukuma* (Against the Government, 1992). Photograph by Joel Gordon.

the role of any contemporary Arab leader—with apologies to Youssef Chahine's 1963 rewriting of the Crusades, *al-Nasir Salah al-Din* (Saladin the Victorious), which portrayed the Kurdish Saladin as a pan-Arab champion, clearly alluding to Nasser—and the first Egyptian film to treat such a significant historical period in anything but caricature. A handful of Egyptian feature films in the mid- to late 1950s dramatized the Suez conflict, some as backdrop, several directly. War stories, focused on steadfast soldiers and civilians, they depicted the struggle against traitors at home—a frequent invective in early Nasserist rhetoric—as well as imperialism (Ramzi 1984).[6] *Nasser 56* decidedly has a point of view. It is a nationalist film—one Egyptian writer has called it a "quiet nationalism" (Ken Cuno, pers. com. April 1997)—but not a propaganda film in the classic sense. The target is no longer imperialism and Egyptian traitors but rather a present that has become detached from the moving spirit of a bygone era. If not a clarion call to restore that spirit, *Nasser 56* is certainly a lens through which to reimage and reassess that which has been lost.

"A MAN OF SIMPLE DREAMS"

The most critically acclaimed scenes are those that depict Nasser interacting with common Egyptians, praying in public, or at home with his family, an overworked father trying to balance politics with his children's desire for a beach vacation. In an early scene Nasser converses with a canal worker who has been sacked by European overseers, and is moved by the injustice of his plight. Up late in his study, he answers the telephone three times after midnight, only to find on the other end a peasant woman newly arrived from the village, looking for her son. The third time, flustered by her unwillingness to accept that she has not reached Hagg Madbuli, Nasser identifies himself: "I am Gamal Abdel Nasser."[7] Silence, then: "God save you, my son [*Rabbina yansarak, ya ibni*]" ('Abd al-Rahman 1996, 32). Almost everyone's favorite scene is stolen by the veteran actress Amina Rizq, who has been playing tradition-bound matriarchs for the past forty years.[8] Here she plays a persistent peasant woman who demands and is allowed to meet the president. Once inside she relates the story of her grandfather, a peasant killed digging the canal, and presents Nasser with the man's robe, a family heirloom. "When I heard you on the radio," she asserts, "I said, by God, Umm Mustafa, this Gamal has avenged you and eased our hearts; so I am giving you this robe because you are most deserving of it" (1996, 119–20).

These scenes, products of the screenwriter's creative imagination, encapsulate persistent popular memories of Nasser as populist hero, the man of the people. Allen Douglas and Fadwa Malti-Douglas, analyzing a comic-strip biography of Nasser that appeared several years after his death, note:

Figure 3. Nasser (Ahmad Zaki) praying for the nation in *Nasser 56.* Courtesy of
Arab Film Distributors.

> Nasser's communion with his people is so close that he shares their tragedies
> as well as their triumphs. He does not stand above them as all-knowing or all-
> wise. The Egyptian leader's closeness to the people is further reflected in the
> frequent use of his first name without titles or appellatives, both by the nar-
> rator and by the people. (1994, 41)

They could easily be writing a contemporary script for formal and informal
discussions of Nasser's personality and legacy with Egyptians from all walks
of life.

Egyptians who lived the Nasser years, including many who spent time
out of favor and in prison (although less so those who suffered economic
dislocation), still speak with exceptional warmth about Nasser. Grand politics, successes and terrible failures aside, they recount seeing him walking
the streets or driving unguarded in his car. They rarely, if ever, stopped to
greet him, but, more important to their personal rescripting, feel they
could have. In much the same fashion, Mahfuz 'Abd al-Rahman has described Nasser as "a man of the utmost simplicity and modesty, . . . a man of
simple dreams," for whom "the pleasures of life consisted of olives and

cheese, going to the cinema, listening to Umm Kulthum" (1996, 6–7), a man who "could not comprehend a home with two bathrooms," let alone a private pool (pers. com.). In interviews Ahmad Zaki, whose career blossomed at the tail end of the 1960s, has spoken of Nasser as a father figure (Ramadan 1995).

The very depiction of Nasser, albeit imaged as Ahmad Zaki, startles. For nearly two decades his likeness was everywhere, and he remains the symbol of the iconized Arab ruler (Ossman 1994, 3). But those images came down in rapid succession following Sadat's ascension to power. Where they could not come down, as at the rarely visited monument to Soviet-Egyptian friendship at the Aswan High Dam, Nasser's profile was all but hidden by a superimposed image of the inheritor. Private establishments still display personal icons, and one bust remains in an arcade in downtown Cairo. Once the heart of the cosmopolitan city, the area is now primarily shopping turf for the lower middle class, and the arcade is particularly rich in its selection of conservative headwear for women. There is no designated monument to Egypt's most significant ruler of this century, no stadium, airport, public building, or major thoroughfare that bears his name (a Nile-side boulevard running through Imbaba officially does, but it is universally referred to as Nile Street). Nasser's tomb, unlike Sadat's, is not visited in any official commemorative capacity. There is a Nasser subway stop, but it is adjacent to a fading city center, one that is not heavily used.[9]

Nasser's name still evokes great passion, and approbation is by no means universal or unequivocal. Like any regime seeking to foment and sustain a revolution, the Nasserist state razed before building, disrupted lives and careers of opponents, and devoured some of its own. The legacies of Nasserism remain multiple and will be weighed differently by different generations, proponents of different political and social trends, sons and daughters of different social classes. Nasserism is held accountable by some for virtually every social ill facing the nation, from traffic snarls and pedestrian anarchy to the fall of social graces. Nasser has been accounted a traitor by Islamists, a prisoner of his class by leftists, a tinhorn tyrant by scions of the old parties and aristocracy. The Nasserist political experiment is widely accepted to have failed in its stated goal of restoring a "sound" democracy. Arab Socialism, the economic strategy that produced nationalization and the creation of a vast public sector, will continue to polarize Egyptians, although the debate may increasingly turn on intentions versus consequences.[10] Nasserist foreign policy, Arabism and nonalignment, the conflict with royalist neighbors and Israel, also polarizes, and the generation that lived the period will always live in the shadows of Yemen and June 1967.

As the era grows more distant, historical perspective may help to contextualize the logic of certain directions and policies. Greater historical focus

Figure 4. The iconic Nasser outside a corner shop in a popular district of Cairo. Photograph by Joel Gordon.

has already produced notable changes in the ways in which Nasserism has been envisioned—and debated—in the quarter century since Nasser's death. Yet, contrary to Bodnar's (1992, 13–19) thesis—which may well hold for his American context—in which vernacular traditions gradually become subsumed into an official text, in Egypt, and presumably in other countries where an official discourse quickly and effectively silenced all others, the process seems to be going in the opposite direction. Vernacular discourses, allowed a voice after two decades, quickly drowned out the official text, leaving public memory of Nasserism very much up for grabs.

Nostalgia in Egypt today is a complex phenomenon. The majority of the population was born after 1967, and many after Sadat's assassination in 1981. Less than Nasser's shadow, they have grown up in a society in which popular memory is dizzyingly multivocal. In the past two decades, during which Egyptians have been free to openly debate their history, vernacular antihistories related by representatives (some self-styled) of old-regime parties, royalists, leftist movements, and the Muslim Brothers have emerged from the underground to become standard counterorthodoxies to the official Nasserist account of the revolution. Those affiliated with the Sadat regime comprise another orthodoxy caught between competing prior legacies. The Nasserist response, official and not, has become just another vernacular tradition competing for public memory.

Ten-year anniversaries, by their very nature as discrete constructs to mark and evaluate the passage of time, provide a convenient referent. In July 1972 the country still grieved Nasser's passing yet applauded Sadat's dismantling of the state security apparatus, the release and welcome home of political prisoners and exiles, and the purging and incarceration of those who had dominated the "centers of power" (*marakiz al-quwwa*). Ten years later, when the revolution turned thirty, Egypt again faced a change in leadership, power having been transferred suddenly in a moment of national crisis. A new regime now curried favor by opening political prison doors, by prosecuting a new cohort of power abusers, and by lending freer rein to opposition voices to speak, write, and ultimately participate in government. One consequence was a frank and multivoiced discussion of the political origins of the Nasser revolution, before and particularly after the July coup. The focus remained political, the general assessment of Nasserism critical, intensified by recollections of a period, 1952–55, when the officers squandered much of the goodwill that greeted their takeover and imposed their revolution by coercion more than charisma (Gordon 1992).

As the revolution turned forty, a pronounced shift in emphasis was under way. The exploration ten years earlier into political failure had been fueled by hopes of a truly broadened liberalism. By the early 1990s much of that hope had turned cynical. To a society riven by malaise, and at times and in certain places by interconfessional strife, Nasserism has increasingly come to represent an era of hope, unity, national purpose, social stability, and achievement. This was reflected in sentiments voiced on the street as well as in the press, official and opposition, where a growing number of Egyptians recalled a society in which there was a shared sense of community in which common, enlightened aims predominated and in which religion did not create barriers (Gordon 1997b).

Underscoring this nostalgia, and recalled increasingly by Egyptians, are recollections of a golden age of popular culture. The Nasserist state promoted and subsidized cultural production on many levels: classical Western dance and music, folklore, history, cinema, theater, radio and television drama, fiction, poetry, comedy, the fine arts. In retrospect much of it may have been hackneyed, too ideologically grounded, too often in the hands of bureaucrats rather than creative artists, some of whom left the country. Yet such assessments beg the issue of nostalgia. The faces and voices of popular movie stars and singers from the 1950s and 1960s—Fatin Hamama, 'Abd al-Halim Hafiz, Rushdi Abaza, Shadiya—have become deified. Film classics by Salah Abu Sayf, Kamal al-Shaykh, or Barakat—before and after nationalization—and even the B-films of Niyazi Mustafa and Hilmi Rafla will never be equaled.[11] Nor will the lyrics of Salah Jahin, Ahmad Shafiq Kamil, and 'Abd al-Rahman al-'Abnudi, paired with tunes by Kamal al-Tawil, Muhammad al-Muji, and Baligh Hamdi. These sentiments are echoed even by many who are otherwise highly critical of Nasserism and work to undo its economic and political legacies.[12]

The author of *Nasser 56* is quick to assert that he never has been a Nasserist. A secondary-school student with leftist links in 1952, he mistrusted the officers' motives and demonstrated against the regime. He never joined the party in any of its guises, even though he worked for the state media, and remains critical of the political order Nasserism fostered. Yet, like most of his generation, 'Abd al-Rahman was consumed with a desire for social justice and a dream of Arab unity—and was captivated by Nasser's charisma. He admits to being dazzled by his subject in ways unfamiliar to him:

> I have written about dozens of historical figures from 'Amru al-Qays to Baybars, from Qutuz to al-Mutanabbi and Sulayman al-Halabi. In drawing close to each of these characters I have always entered into a dispute with them, primarily because we are bound by our own era and circumstances. . . . What is strange is that when I wrote about Gamal Abdel Nasser the opposite occurred. . . . [I]t was when I tried to come to know Gamal Abdel Nasser as a person that I became so moved. It was not the oft-told stories that affected me so much as the little tangibles. (1996, 6–7)

Implicit in the family scenes, the images of simplicity, Nasser's meals of cheese and olives or Mahmud Yunis sleeping on his office floor, the scenarist seeks to recapture and reimpart a sense of what Egypt was and has lost.

Mahfuz 'Abd al-Rahman, like others of his generation, those who came of age under Nasserism, is rescripting the period with a focus on an enlightened community rooted in twin notions of progress and independence. His other great project in recent years has been a major revision of Khedive Ismail (1865–79), through the vehicle of a television serial that has aired over three Ramadan seasons, the prime month of television viewing (Abu-Lughod 1993b; Gordon 1997a). *Bawwabat al-Halawani* (Halawani's Gate) spins a tale of court intrigue that revolves around the romance between the musician 'Abduh al-Hamuli and his protégée Almaz, a poor girl taken from her parents and brought up in royal circles. But the backdrop is Ismail's desire to modernize his country, the financial and political costs incurred, and, ultimately, the Suez Canal. Dismissed by much of Western scholarship and Nasser-era history as a foolish spendthrift who, entranced by Westernization, broke the state, Ismail emerges under 'Abd al-Rahman's pen as a Renaissance man, a prisoner not of false illusions but of an international power structure that will ultimately not permit an independent Egypt.[13] In many ways the two projects, Nasser and Ismail, go hand in hand. Whatever their failings and failures, both leaders promoted cultural enrichment as a means toward liberation, and both ultimately confronted forces larger than they or Egypt.

Both projects also promote a paradigm that the state, for slightly different reasons—and obviously with less comfort in the case of Nasser—finds acceptable and beneficial in its confrontation with its most powerful vernacular challenge, Islamism. Egyptian television has always served to "produce a national community" (Abu-Lughod 1993b, 494). Yet, as Lila Abu-Lughod and others have noted, in recent years television serials (and the cinema) have become rostrums in "the most pressing political contest in Egypt . . . the contest over the place of Islam in social and political life" (1993b, 494). Long ignored, strikingly absent from drama that purportedly depicted contemporary society, Islamist characters have become almost stock figures in television serials and the subject of one major motion picture, *Al-Irhabi* (The Terrorist; Jalal 1994; see Armbrust 1995). Always militant—and misguided—they generally meet unhappy ends at the hands of their "brothers" after recognizing the error of their ways.[14]

'Abd al-Rahman's reexamination of the past has always been a personal search for the drama inherent in the historical moment ('Abd al-Rahman 1991). His work has spanned time and place, from early Islamic Iraq to modern Egypt. For him the dramatist has freedom to explore questions the historian cannot, but the dramatist must be bound by the historian's reliance on evidence. He is an indefatigable researcher who has battled both stolid academics, wary of the writer's craft, and, at times, popular historical and literary wisdom, against which his scripts have rubbed. 'Abd al-Rahman's favorite anecdote involves a particularly obdurate actor who, protective of his good-guy popular image, refused to play a brother of the legendary Arab hero 'Antar ibn Shadad, even though the script, which he had not read, revised the role, portraying the brother in a much more sympathetic light.

At the same time, like others who maintain intellectual independence yet work in or for the state-run media, 'Abd al-Rahman participates in "a shared discourse about nationhood and citizenship" (Abu-Lughod 1993b, 494) and thus represents at once a personal and quasi-official voice. To champion Ismail is, in today's discourse, to counter the Islamist claim to authenticity, one that would view Ismail's Westernization as anathema. Likewise, to script Nasser at Suez, to depict such a powerful moment of national unity, serves, among other things, to counter social trends that are nationally divisive, even "un-Egyptian." It is notable that the original cast of characters out of which the Nasser film emerged included products and leading champions of Westernization: Rifa' al-Tahtawi, 'Ali Mubarak, and Taha Husayn.

This is not to suggest that state production officials who backed the project, or the creators, envisioned it consciously as a weapon in the battle against Islamism. At the same time, the green light to make a film about Nasser, and one of such scale, could not have been given without serious consideration. Support for the film clearly represented a gamble—that viewers would rally around the moment, rather than the figure, and that the moment, one of national unity in the face of specific historical foreign aggression, would not transcend historical time/place to mirror more recent national struggles with foreign creditors (World Bank, International Monetary Fund), struggles in which the government in its drive to privatize the economy is often portrayed as serving personal and foreign interests. What government officials obviously did not bank on was the degree to which the film, by so powerfully imaging the crisis, the personalities, the national moment, would underscore present-day malaise and popular perceptions of their own inadequacies—and, ultimately, the degree to which the film would resurrect the image of its hero.

"NASSER! NASSER!"

The spirit of the film, a labor of love for its creators, proved infectious to those who encountered its images, even in production. The author has recounted with impish delight how a staged workers' rally on a studio set turned real. A crowd of extras, all workers hired for the occasion—cynics will note the irony—caught sight of Ahmad Zaki and, unrehearsed, began chanting "Nasser! Nasser!" Zaki, who immersed himself in Nasser's character while on the set, spontaneously began orating in character, and the workers responded with greater vigor. Their ardor fueled Zaki's performance, and performance quickly melded into reality. The assistant director, unprepared for a sound take, shouted for a cut, but the director, Muhammad Fadil, intervened and ordered the cameras to keep rolling.

The response to the film's preview, before an invitation-only audience at the opening of the Cairo Television Festival in July 1995, provided another occasion for a spontaneous rally.[15] According to observers, people in the audience applauded, shouted encouragement, and wept openly. The inclusion of several anthems from the Suez crisis, some not heard in nearly a quarter century, punctuated the response. "The day before yesterday I saw *Nasser 56*, and my eyes filled with tears to see Ahmad Zaki embody the character of the late leader who made such great sacrifices for the sake of our national honor," wrote one attendee (Mustafa Bakri 1995).[16] Mahfuz 'Abd al-Rahman recalls how a young man embraced him and Zaki a day after the preview and announced that he had now fulfilled his dream of meeting Nasser.

Such demonstrations before and after the preview may have given the government cause to rethink its promotion of the film. Critics lavished praise on Information Minister Safwat al-Sharif and ERTU Production Sector chief Mamduh al-Laythi and encouraged them "to undertake similar nationalist projects that reflect shining moments in Egypt's history" (Mahmud Bakri 1995). Then, suddenly, the film was put on ice, its scheduled theater release delayed indefinitely. No one offered a definitive reason. Official circles noted that final sound and print work was under way abroad. Skeptics suggested the film had been received too well, that the outpouring of emotion was not appreciated in the state's upper echelons, especially with parliamentary elections upcoming. Questions of video recording (and pirating), foreign rights, and television and satellite access complicated the matter. The Arab world was abuzz with anticipation. Syria and Libya supposedly offered to buy rights to air the film; so, according to the rumor mill, had the Saudis, but with ulterior motives.

A stalling game ensued that effectively delayed release for a full year. Cynics offered the following scenario: the fall 1995 election season was deemed inappropriate, then came Ramadan, when theaters traditionally do poorest, then the postholiday season of popular comedy-adventure blockbusters. The film did not seem to fit the calendar. In seeming incongruity with official desires to deflate, if not suppress, the film, teasers remained. A marquee arch on Gezira Island constructed before the 1995 Television Festival and left in place until the following summer featured a prominent photograph of Zaki/Nasser among other favorite productions.

So did a display outside the Radio and Television Building. If those displays reached a limited audience, discerning eyes could not help but notice a final dramatic image of Zaki/Nasser on the promotional leader that identified 1995 ERTU television productions.

Ironically, the film's opening, days after the fortieth anniversary of the Suez Canal nationalization, proved far more potent than an earlier release might have been. For the great majority of adult Egyptians who lived it or were raised in its wake, the Suez crisis represents the ultimate moment of national pride, purpose, and unity. Two other historical moments in this century, pinnacles of contested political legacies, rank closely: the 1919 Revolution and the 1973 October War. Neither is as central to the historical experience or is embedded in the consciousness of Egyptians in quite the same way, in large part because the canal had been for nearly a century the key symbol of national humiliation at foreign hands. "To my generation the Suez Canal was the core of Egyptian politics," explains Mahfuz ʿAbd al-Rahman.[17] When he set out to dramatize the Nasser years, ʿAbd al-Rahman deliberately chose the Suez crisis because it was the one period about which there is little, if any, dispute and because it was with Suez that Nasser's star rose. Suez occurred after the disappointments of the liberal era, amid the confused early years of military rule. Nationalization and the subsequent Tripartite Aggression lodged Nasser in people's hearts and ushered in an era of regional dominance that, however flawed in retrospect, has never been recaptured. In unguarded moments even the sons and daughters of discarded pashas—no doubt Muslim Brothers as well—will admit that they stood in the streets weeping, cheering, and shouting acclaim for nationalization.

The Suez anniversary prompted a far broader retrospective for Nasser and Nasserism than any other anniversary in recent years, and certainly more than the fortieth anniversary of the revolution in 1992. Revolution Day has lost most of its meaning to the average Egyptian. It is a day off for government workers. The president addresses the nation with a text that changes little from year to year. One of the national television channels traditionally airs an afternoon matinee, one of several classic stories of evil pashas produced in the years after the revolution (*Rudd qalbi* [Return My Heart], Dhulfiqar 1957b, based on Yusuf al-Sibaʿi's epic novel, has been the favorite). Sadat, once he felt secure in power, attempted to camouflage the revolution's anniversary behind that of Egyptian television, aired first on Revolution Day in 1960. Under Hosni Mubarak the state still acknowledges its kinship to the broad goals of the July revolution (even as it continues to dismantle fundamental pillars of its social-reform legacy in a drive to privatize the economy). But forty years later the progenitor remained largely ignored.

In 1996, however, the combined July anniversaries of revolution and nationalization inspired far greater coverage. Opposition papers sympathetic to Nasser's memory, even the Liberal party's *al-Ahrar* (July 22), published larger-than-usual special editions. The July 22 issue of *al-Hilal*, the venerable journal of popular literature and philosophy, posed the question, "What has happened to Egyptians, 1956–1996?" *Ruz al-Yusuf*, the widely read weekly of politics and the arts, abandoned its traditional "Where Are They Now?" July 23 format and asked three leading scenarists, including 'Abd al-Rahman, to script "What If [the Free Officers coup had failed]?" Reflecting Egypt's current passion for historicals, the editors noted wryly that "writers' imaginings are worth far more than historians' truths."[18] Sawt al-'Arab (Voice of the Arabs), the radio station most associated with Nasserism, broadcast a two-hour special on the Suez Canal, "Hadduta Misriyya" (An Egyptian Tale), that included interviews and nationalist songs. Television aired old documentary footage with nationalist songs in the background.

In addition to the celebratory atmosphere surrounding the Suez anniversary, the state has also recently decided that the time has come to participate in the shaping of public memory of Nasserism. In 1992 the government sanctioned formation of the Nasserist Arab Democratic party. By its very presence, the party has restored quasi-official legitimacy to the use of Nasser's image as political icon.[19] But the state no longer seems to be willing to consign Nasser to the Nasserists. Long-range plans are under way for a museum to be housed in the offices of the Revolutionary Command Council, a former royal rest house on the southern tip of Gezira Island (Khalil 1996b; Abu al-Fath 1996). Music, too, has been appropriated: when Arab leaders gathered in Cairo in June 1996 to consider implications of a newly elected Israeli government, the theme song chosen by state-run media was "al-Watan al-Akbar" (The Greater Nation), a stirring anthem to Egyptian-Syrian unity composed by Muhammad 'Abd al-Wahhab and Ahmad Shafiq Kamil in 1958. For Revolution Day 1996, television stations aired five movies over two days, four during prime time. The proliferation of regional broadcast in recent years—households with a reasonably good antenna now receive nine terrestrially beamed channels—added to the scope of what was unprecedented coverage of this holiday.[20] The change of heart is rather sudden and seems to be prompted both by a desire to keep in step with and to play a hand in shaping the wave of resurgent nostalgia for the Nasser era (Sipress 1995).

CONCLUSION: "WHAT HAPPENED NEXT?"

Modern history has been in vogue in Egypt for the past few years, fueled in large part by Mahfuz 'Abd al-Rahman, Usama Anwar 'Ukasha, and other prominent scriptwriters who have penned historical dramas for television that attract wide audiences and have been extended over several seasons.

The nineteenth century and prerevolutionary era of pashas and nationalist struggle are particular favorites.[21] Their influence has recently rolled over from the little to the big screen, although with much less panache or success.[22] Consequently, the tarboosh, Farouk and Queen Farida, and Ismail, have become popular images on T-shirts, in window displays of upscale shops, in television commercials geared toward young professionals, even in traditional "fast-food" eateries. The popularity of such items and images reinforces notions of creative rather than passive consumption, and should give those of us who read these melodramas as text cause to reconsider how their audiences in fact imagine them (Ang 1985; Armbrust 1996). Still, *Nasser 56*, because its subject is so recent, in the living or at least public memory of so many Egyptians, and because of its immediate political subject, is more serious business.

Demographics, the passing of the old-regime generation, the rise to prominence of the generations that lived and were shaped by Nasserism, and "serious matters in the present" point Egyptians ever more in the direction of Nasser and his era. The foundations of a resurgent nostalgia are a complex construct of political cynicism, uneven development, glaring social inequities, unfulfilled material expectations, and the vise of radical Islamist and state violence. Amid all this Egyptians are confronted daily with an alternative vision. Radio and television remain dominated by the cultural production of what was by all accounts a golden age of artistry. The songs, concert and comedy stage clips, and movies that captivated a generation still work their charms amid all that is new. Young boys in the street still croon 'Abd al-Halim Hafiz songs (Gordon 1997a), and teenage girls still fall for Rushdi Abaza's Egyptian-Italian eyes. If their loyalties are divided and distracted by younger—and foreign—stars, they still recognize the genuine national-cultural articles for what they are.

Historical memory among Egyptian youths is short. When *Port Said* (Dhulfiqar 1957a), a propaganda film about the Suez War, aired in June 1996—on the anniversary of Evacuation Day—the newspaper movie listing explained the historical context as if describing an event much longer past. That was several months before *Nasser 56* hit the theaters. Now the Nasser generation is reliving the period, rediscovering nationalist anthems that stirred their youth. "We have waited forty years for this film," wrote one reviewer. "And because we waited so long, I found myself sitting in anticipation, my eyes, ears, and heart tuned in anticipation" (al-Ghayti 1995a). And a younger generation is asking their parents about the period. The filmmaker Yusuf Francis (who has recently directed a historical film about Howard Carter) sat near an eight-year-old boy at an evening screening who pressed his father for details, then turned to him after the film ended to ask, "What happened next?"[23] Egyptians in their twenties and early thirties are no less curious.[24]

The popular response to *Nasser 56* has taken all involved by surprise. State officials have been quick to reassert their positive role in its production, notwithstanding the obvious irony of a state-funded film glorifying nationalization in the age of privatization and championing a charismatic, idolized ruler in an era of political malaise.[25] The most cynical observers still fear the film may never make it to television, that "like many political films that the film industry has produced, it will be locked away in a can after ending its run in Egyptian theaters" (Khalil 1996). For the true believers, the Nasserist faithful, Ahmad Zaki has thrown a little water on the fire, reasserting his desire to now play his other hero, Anwar Sadat.[26] And Mahfuz 'Abd al-Rahman has provoked unease in various circles by evincing a willingness to accept the challenge, put forth by critics who accuse him of taking the easy road via Suez, to pen *Nasser 67* as a sequel (al-Hakim 1995).[27]

Other contemporary history projects are in the works. 'Abd al-Rahman has been scripting a serial about Umm Kulthum, and Zaki says he intends to film the life of 'Abd al-Halim Hafiz. With the silver anniversary of the October 1973 war approaching, the Egyptian defense ministry announced its willingness to support—with guns, manpower, technical expertise, and financial aid—a silver screening of "the crossing" (*al-'ubur*). However, a controversy over who should script the film has held up preproduction. In the Manichaean intellectual world of Nasserists and Sadatists, the leading candidate, Usama Anwar 'Ukasha, is considered to be the former, and this is deemed unacceptable by the latter. 'Ukasha retorts that his script will feature not the commander but the common soldier. This fails to appease his critics, who well sense the implicit barb. The Defense Ministry has announced its unhappiness with several draft scripts, implying a threat to withdraw support.[28]

For the time being Nasser and Suez serve as springboards for the rediscovery and rescripting of an era that so far defies official ossification. On the heels of its Egyptian success *Nasser 56* has played to audiences outside Egypt. The first screening scheduled was a single screening in Paris in June 1996 before the Egyptian opening. Shortly after its Egyptian premiere the film played to great acclaim in Gaza and the West Bank.[29] The film has since shown in several cities in the United States—"The Arab film event of the year"—and is currently available on video with English subtitles.[30] To non-Egyptian Arabs and to Arab diaspora communities the film undoubtedly conveys other particular meanings, addressing Nasser's legacy in a broader Arab context.[31] *Nasser 56* may be a flash in the pan; some certainly hope this will be the case. Conversely, it may become the Revolution Day television matinee, which, if it displaced the classics, would be a shame. Within Egypt the film clearly does speak to "serious matters of the present," and it may well inspire, or perhaps become—if it is allowed to be—the monument to Nasser that never was.

NOTES

Earlier drafts of this chapter were presented to the Colloquium on the Politics of Culture in Arab Societies in an Era of Globalization, held at Princeton University in May 1997, and to the culture studies group at the University of Illinois–Urbana. Participants' feedback was greatly appreciated. Special thanks to Walter Armbrust, Marilyn Booth, Ken Cuno, JoAnn D'Alisera, Sonallah Ibrahim, and Robert Vitalis. Funding for a broader project on Nasserist civic culture was provided by the J. William Fulbright Foreign Scholarship Board, the Joint Committee on the Near and Middle East of the Social Science Research Council, and the American Council of Learned Societies. I am, above all, deeply indebted to Mahfuz 'Abd al-Rahman and Samira 'Abd al-'Aziz for their hospitality, insight, and candor.

1. Mahfuz 'Abd al-Rahman pers. com.; all other references to 'Abd al-Rahman or *Nasser 56*, unless otherwise indicated, are from personal conversations that took place in Cairo between November 1995 and August 1996.

2. The filmmakers reportedly approached Su'ad Husni to play Nasser's wife, Tahiya, but she was unable to take part. Ahmad Zaki then suggested Firdaws 'Abd al-Hamid (al-Ghayti 1995a).

3. Kami has also played Suez Canal builder Ferdinand de Lesseps in 'Abd al-Rahman's other mammoth hit, the television series *Bawwabat al-Halawani* (Halawani's Gate), which ran three successive Ramadan seasons through 1996.

4. In a variant of this common wisdom, Mahfuz 'Abd al-Rahman told me that Egyptians will always favor an Egyptian over a foreign black-and-white film and a foreign over an Egyptian color film.

5. Zaki's filmography is long and distinguished. The great exception to the poor-boy roles is *Zawjat rajul muhimm* (Wife of an Important Man; Khan 1988), in which he plays an officer in the security police. A classic example of the poor-boy role, and a film that established a hairstyle fad for young men, is *Kaburya* (Crabs; Bishara 1990; see Armbrust 1996, 138–46). For a critique of recent disappointments, see el-Assiouty 1996.

6. Ramzi (1984) counts eight films made since that deal with the Tripartite Aggression in any way. Of these, he states, only three treated the war directly. The most noteworthy are *Bur Sa'id* (Port Said; Dhulfiqar 1957a), noted below, and *Sijin Abu Za'bal* (The Prisoner of Abu Za'bal; Mustafa 1957).

7. The simple statement may recall for some Egyptians Nasser's impromptu oration on October 26, 1954, when an assailant shot at him. Nasser repeated the phrase "I am Gamal Abdel Nasser" numerous times, invoking a willingness to die for Egypt. It was his first great public oration.

8. These characterizations have not always been positive. However, she has most often portrayed pious, doting mothers, and she is much loved. Her casting here is a master stroke, although a few people I have spoken to find the scene somewhat contrived.

9. It sits between the two main termini, at Tahrir (Liberation) and Ramsis squares, both major works projects undertaken by the Nasser regime. These subway stops are named for Presidents Sadat and Mubarak respectively.

10. The Nasserist project is increasingly recalled as noble, despite its obvious failings; see, for example, Sid-Ahmed 1995. Alan Sipress (1995) quotes Sid-Ahmed

urging Egyptians to keep Nasser's "most important legacy alive; namely his in-domitable will to overcome any challenge," and notes, "Ironically, it was Nasser's will that sent Sid-Ahmed to jail for more than five years as a political prisoner."

11. As Armbrust notes in this volume, when film students and critics refer to "se-rious" cinema they often restrict their gaze to the 1960s when the state, through partial nationalization of the industry, sought to promote a national cinema guided by artistic rather than commercial concerns. Armbrust (and I agree) does not dis-pute claims that under the lead of influential public-sector artists Egyptian cinema embarked in new directions that persisted well into the 1970s. Yet he challenges the elevation of public-sector cinema by positing a "golden age before the golden age," which encompasses all commercial films made before the 1960s. My own research into Nasser-era nostalgia leads me to conclude that when people who lived the era think in terms of cinema, they recognize, consciously or intuitively, that a new gen-eration of directors and film stars came into their own and put a distinctive stamp on Egyptian cinema in the 1950s that carried over into the following decade. Their work undoubtedly was shaped by the onset and course of the Nasser revolution and constitutes, I would argue, a new, revolutionary cinema well before the "serious" cinema of the 1960s.

12. Key pillars of the Nasserist state—agrarian reform, subsidization, and the public sector—have undergone sustained attack in the past decade. See Hinneb-usch 1993; Abdel-Moteleb 1993.

13. Prior to the serial the most common popular image of Ismail would have been in the film *Almaz wa-'Abduh al-Hamuli* (Almaz and 'Abduh al-Hamuli; Rafla 1962), in which the Khedive is a surrogate for Farouk, with all the familiar imagery of the debauched and deposed king.

14. The caricatures have become even bolder in the past few years. Two recent examples are *al-'A'ila* (The Family), written by Wahid Hamid, and *Lan a'ish fi galabib abi* (I Won't Live My Father's Way), based on a story by Ihsan 'Abd al-Quddus. In the former the mistrusted Islamist is gunned down; in the latter Islamists try to run down a failed recruit. In *al-Irhabi* the title character is also killed after rejecting his calling. The film has become an official text and was shown on the primary televi-sion channel on the last night of Ramadan in 1997.

15. The following year the festival was expanded to become the Radio and Tele-vision Festival.

16. Also see Salih 1995.

17. Comments made on *Sawt al-'Arab*, July 26, 1996.

18. The other two scriptwriters were Usama Anwar 'Ukasha, who is discussed be-low, and Sa'd al-Din Wahba, late president of the Cairo International Film Festival, who scripted a series of important—and popular—films in the 1960s.

19. For the past four years the Nasserist weekly, *al-'Arabi*, has featured Nasser on its masthead. During the fall 1995 election campaign, Nasser's image appeared on banners and posters, trumpeting the party—and the memories—more than the slated candidates.

20. The films were *Rudd qalbi, Allah ma'na* (God Is with Us; Badr Khan 1955), *Fi baytina rajul* (There Is a Man in Our House; Barakat 1961), *Ghurub wa-shuruq* (Sun-set, Sunrise; al-Shaykh 1970), and *Shay' min al-khawf* (A Bit of Fear; Kamal 1969).

21. The most successful, in addition to *Halwani's Gate* has undoubtedly been

Layali al-Hilmiyya (Hilmiyya Nights), written by 'Ukasha (for more on 'Ukasha, see Armbrust 1996, 16–17). But there are now scores, many rerun on regional stations.

22. The undisputed queen of historical kitsch is Nadia al-Guindi. See Hani 1995.

23. Francis was quoted in *al-Ahram*, August 12, 1996; a cartoon in this issue shows a man watching a television commercial for seventeen consecutive showings and wondering how he can divide himself to attend them all.

24. Salah Muntasir (1996) tried to play down the significance of audience turnout as curiosity. More telling, I think, is the reaction of a friend: "I was born after 1967 so I do not have any memories of the period. I was really impressed by what he did. They made him look like a savior; I do not know if that was true or not. Because my parents and husband are totally against him. . . . My mother told me that they had so much confidence in him and he was so impulsive and disappointed them. . . . I encouraged my parents to go. . . . I think it is more impressive to the younger generations."

25. See comments by Mamduh al-Laythi, chief of the ERTU production sector, in *al-Ahram*, August 10, 1996.

26. See *al-Ahram*, August 3, 1996; *Ruz al-Yusuf*, May 15, 1995; Adwy 1999. 'Ala' al-Sa'dani (1996) urged Zaki to reconsider, arguing that one actor should not play two such leaders.

27. Relatives of 'Abd al-Hakim 'Amr, Egypt's chief of staff, who engaged in a power struggle with Nasser in the aftermath of the defeat, was placed under house arrest, and, depending on one's take, was murdered or committed suicide, contacted 'Abd al-Rahman to express their concern over how the relationship would be treated ('Abd al-Rahman, pers. com.).

28. The war over scripting this war may well prove to be far more interesting than the final product. See Essam El-Din 1997.

29. The Gaza opening was reportedly held up when local promoters could not find proper 35mm screening equipment. A projector had to be brought in from Egypt.

30. In the United States the film and video are available from Arab Film Distributors, based in Seattle. In addition to Seattle, the film has shown commercially in Portland, Los Angeles, Minneapolis, Cleveland, Boston, New York, and Washington, D.C., and was screened at the 1997 annual meeting of the Middle East Studies Association in San Francisco. For advertisements heralding the film's importance, see *Anba' al-'Arab* (Glendale, Calif.), May 1, 1997, and *Arab Panorama* (La Verne, Calif.), May 10, 1997. I would like to thank Yasin al-Khalesi for these ads.

31. An Arab-American community weekly published in southern California, *Beirut Times*, May 8–15, 1997, headlined "a film all Arab-American youth should see." Thanks to Yasin al-Khalesi for this information.

EIGHT

Consuming Damascus
Public Culture and the Construction of Social Identity

Christa Salamandra

If you enter the Old City of Damascus at the Eastern Gate, walk a few yards along A Street Called Straight, and turn down the first narrow alley on your right, you will find, jutting out from among the inward-looking Arab-style houses of this quiet residential quarter, a sign advertising "Le Piano Bar." Enter through the carved wood door, walk along the tile-covered foyer, under the songbird's cage, past a display case strung with chunky silver necklaces, and step up a stone platform to the raised dining room. Here well-heeled Syrians sit at closely spaced tables, drinking *'araq* and Black Label whiskey, and eating grilled chicken or spaghetti. Each of the walls around them is decorated in a different style. One features a collection of Dutch porcelain plates set into plaster. On another, strips of colored marble hold a series of mosaic-lined, glass-covered cases displaying wind instruments. Another features two floral wrought iron–gated windows draped in a locally produced striped fabric. Wrought iron musical notes dance on another wall. At the front of the long, arch-divided room is a huge mother-of-pearl–framed mirror. Set into the top of the mirror is a digital billboard across which the Piano Bar's menu and opening hours float repeatedly. The proprietor sings "My Way" and other Frank Sinatra favorites to a karaoke backup tape. When he finishes, video screens tucked into corners feature Elton John sing-alongs. On some nights a pianist and clarinetist play Russian songs as patrons clank wooden castanets.

Public cultural forms such as the Piano Bar play a part in the construction of social identities in Damascus. In one sense the Piano Bar is merely in the Old City; in another sense, no matter how unlikely, it is of Old Damascus. The localization of transnational cultural forms such as restaurants and television programs involves an imagined idea of the city and its past. Some cultural forms, like television programs, are easily available to all.

Others, like the Piano Bar, are accessible to a far more limited set of people. Selective consumption of this commoditized past has become a primary mode of class and social distinction.

Links to and representations of Old Damascus become increasingly significant in a context of rapid and profound social and demographic change. Like many Middle Eastern cities, Damascus has experienced a steady and significant population increase throughout the twentieth century. During the post–World War II, postindependence period the city's population multiplied fourfold, rising to 1,347,000 in the early 1980s.[1] Unofficial estimates now place the number at three million to four million. To house large numbers of mostly rural migrants, dormitory suburbs were rapidly and cheaply built or expanded and older two-story buildings replaced with high-rise apartment blocks. Some sections of the Old City have been cleared, and those remaining are threatened. Damascenes now find their city transformed, and themselves outnumbered by those distinct from them in social class, regional background, and religious sect.

CONSUMING THE OLD CITY

In Syrian usage the term "Old Damascus" refers to a number of closely related phenomena. Most concretely, it connotes the physical space of the Old City itself, past and present. Parts of Old Damascus have been torn down to make way for concrete high-rises and modern boulevards, but many quarters remain standing, including those inside the Old City walls. Old Damascus also refers to a lifestyle associated with the city as it was—or supposedly was—before the major social, political, and economic transformations that began in the early 1960s. Last, Old Damascus is an imagined idea of the past commodified in the form of restaurants, cafés, books, television programs, advertisements, social events, art and photography exhibits, and boutiques.

Old Damascus now features in state-sponsored art and photography exhibits, lectures, and folklore festivals designed more for Syrians than for foreign tourists. There appears to be a link between the tourist industry and the resurgence of interest in Old Damascus. During the 1980s the Ministry of Tourism's primary interest shifted from ancient ruins to the more recent past, and the minister of tourism from 1981 to 1988, Nawris al-Daqar, prioritized the preservation and reconstruction of the Old City. Al-Daqar, from an Old Damascene family and proud of this affiliation, encouraged events that celebrate the city. In addition, the majority of Ministry of Tourism employees are said to be of Damascene origin. The minister of culture, Najah al-Attar, who has been in office since the late 1970s, is also from an Old Damascene family. Tourism links the local and the global in unmediated ways, presenting a commoditized and depthless Old Damascus,

Figure 5. The Piano Bar. Photograph by Christa Salamandra.

Figure 6. The Piano Bar. Photograph by Christa Salamandra.

but those representations most resonant for Old Damascus advocates are found elsewhere, in the mediated forms of expressive culture, such as books.

A primary medium for the promotion of a sense of Damasceneness is a series of memoirs written by Damascenes, mostly from notable families, about social life in the Old Damascus of their youth. The first, Siham Turjuman's *Ya mal al-Sham* (O Wealth of Damascus), was published in 1969. Others date from the middle 1980s onward. Part autobiography, part social history, these works represent a type not found in classical Arabic literature. Unlike the traditional biographical and autobiographical form, the *tarjama*, these books do not merely recount the details and events of an individual's—usually a religious scholar's—life and the connections that constitute learned tradition (Eickelman 1991). Rather, they construct fragmentary, imagistic, and highly emotive accounts of the past more broadly. These books of personal reminiscence, whether knowingly or otherwise, evoke shared experience. Most memoir authors are prominent professionals—doctors, lawyers, and journalists—who know each other well and form an amateur literary circle. For instance, the introduction to the third edition of Najat Qassab Hasan's *Hadith Dimashqi* (Damascene Talk) includes acknowledgments to and letters of praise from many of the other memoir authors. Old Damascus reminiscences contain vivid, seemingly timeless descriptions of the Damascene-style house, methods of preparing and eating traditional foods, and customs and traditions related to holidays, weddings, births, and funerals. All lament the passing of what is seen as a wholesome, integrated way of life. In *O Wealth of Damascus* Turjuman recounts lovingly the sounds, smells, and tastes of her youth spent in various quarters of the Old City. Weddings, funerals, trips to the public bath, songs, tales, and proverbs are described in a glow of nostalgic yearning:

> When I go back to the old quarters where our ancient house sleeps or to the *suqs* with their smell of old age, I find that my attachment to things that are old is stronger than to modern ones. I discover that the only pure reality in my soul is the reality of childhood, as if childhood is a being, aware of what goes on around it, clinging to what is most genuine in order to keep it from changing. This reverence for the past reassures me that my knowing, attentive, pure childhood will reject anything false that tomorrow has to offer. (1994, 9)

What distinguishes these recent publications from earlier literary expressions of pride in and love for Damascus, notably Ibn Kannan's eighteenth-century *Yawmiyyat Shamiyya* (Levantine Diary) and Muhammad Kurd 'Ali's 1944 *Dimashq: Madinat al-sihr wa-al-Shi'r* (Damascus: City of Enchantment and Poetry), is precisely this sense of loss.[2] A particularly poignant example is Nadiya Khust's *al-Hijra min al-janna* (Exodus from

Paradise), a eulogy for an Old City quarter torn in half with the construction of Revolution Street:

> Much of what I feel today is sorrow because my daughter does not know what it is like to wake up in an Arab house, opening her eyes to its decorations. She does not know the joy of looking out from the ornaments of the parapet and jasmine down to the courtyard, and she does not know the alternations of light on the Kabad tree. Generations of lovers of civilization will not know what fell under the rubble in Damascus. (1989, 10)

In his *Dimashq al-asrar* (Damascus of Secrets) the Damascene journalist and former People's Assembly member Nasr al-Din al-Bahra also bemoans this loss of authentic culture, as the concrete high-rises of the New City grow to engulf the Old:

> Your Damascus is becoming two. The first, the authentic, is shrinking and declining. The second, having come into being like a small child, has come to grow like cancer, a blind growth, base and without identity. (1992, 14)

Memoirs, as representations of national memory, are among the cultural forms most readily accessible to the world beyond Syria. They fit neatly into the glowing global interest in other worlds, past worlds, to which Khust alludes. Books recounting life in Old Damascus have begun to attract translators. In 1994 the University of Texas Press published an English translation of Turjuman's *Ya mal al-Sham*, under the title *Daughter of Damascus*. Authors like Turjuman sell well in a burgeoning global market for Third World and women's literature. Yet within Syria Turjuman is a highly controversial figure; large segments of Syrian society are hostile to what they perceive as the elitism and exclusivity of the experience she recounts. Taken out of context, *Ya mal al-Sham* loses its political force. *Daughter of Damascus* is far removed from the complex cultural conflicts within which *Ya mal al-Sham* was conceived, and which render it richly illustrative of its milieu. Western media market such elite representations of local culture as uncontested authenticity.

Old Damascenes like Turjuman, Khust, and al-Bahra now find themselves a minority in "their" own city. As David Lowenthal notes, minorities often "deploy heritage not to opt out of nation-states but to achieve gains within them" (1996, 81). These authors present Damascus and Damasceneness as a metonym for Syrian national culture. Once this was easier, as the more emotive term for Damascus, *Sham*, stood for both the city and the Ottoman province of Syria, in the way that *Misr* signified both Cairo and all of Egypt. As Richard Handler (1985, 207–8) argues, the construction of national identity involves the appropriation of detached cultural objects, which are then made to stand for national culture. In this case, Damascus itself and memories of it have become objects of Syrian nationhood. Turjuman writes, "Damascus is the Syrian people and my people" (1994, 6). Likewise, Khust maintains that the city's unique architectural style is "not just the attraction of visitors, not just the earth which brings together generations, or the house which wants next to it the rest . . . rather, it is national memory" (1989, 11). Because the Old City represents generations of civilization, Khust argues, its preservation is "a matter of major cultural and national significance" (1993, 5). Addressing a second-person Syrian reader, she links her concern for Old Damascus to the loss of other authenticities:

> The modernity around you leads you to believe the past is a disgrace, and that the historical Old City is an insult to you. Until you distinguish between the white and black thread in life, and the dryness and cement spreads around you.[3] You see others in the world, having left their paradises for illusion and cold; they too gather fragments of memory and broken pieces of their abandoned gardens of the past. Before you, they understood the value of what was demolished, of what they left behind. (1989, 26)

THE CONTEXT

The Old Damascus phenomenon is linked to transformations in Syrian society over the past thirty years. Until the Baath party takeover in the early 1960s, a number of elite "notable" families with long ties to the city dominated social, economic, and political life in Damascus (Hourani 1946, 1968; Khoury 1983, 1987; Hinnebusch 1991). The first blow to this monopoly came with the attempted unification with Egypt (1958–61). With the consolidation of the Baath party government in 1963, political power shifted to a largely non-Damascene and nonurban military elite that became even more powerful after the perceived successes of the 1973 war. Dominating this military elite are members of the 'Alawi religious sect, Syria's largest religious minority, considered heretical by the orthodox Sunni of Damascus. The nationalizations of the middle 1960s further undermined the dominance of the notables. Also, those non-Damascenes— often peasants—who made fortunes in the Gulf during the oil boom of the 1970s often returned not to their villages but to Damascus, forming a class of nouveaux riches whose fortunes often exceeded those of the old notable families. The Damascenes were forced to do business with and even obey the newly rich and powerful whom they considered social inferiors.

But which group actually dominates which sphere of life is far from clear. For certain Old Damascus supporters, it is the barbarians from the countryside, who destroyed the older, Damascene-controlled forms of commerce by applying socialist policies, yet have themselves made fortunes by licensing legal trade and controlling smuggling. They argue that the most high-ranking government positions are reserved for 'Alawis. They see the twenty-eight-year-old Asad regime as having succeeded in obliterating

Sunni economic, social, and religious life. "There used to be a lot more ceremonies like this one," said a Damascene television director, after a Sufi ceremony held in an Old City house on the Night of Power,[4] "but the government did away with them. They try to destroy everything Sunni." I asked why people have become so interested in Old Damascus recently.

> Not all the people, only the true Damascenes. Why, because they feel they are in a minority. Damascus is a town invaded by its own countryside. People are here because the social life in the countryside is awful. They run to Damascus to have a better way of life. More, as they think, civilized than in their own lands. . . . If you go to Beirut, you find New Jersey. Damascus resembles the first face of the Orient in front of Western civilization. You are in a town which turns its back on all aspects of Western civilization. [Then] suddenly events happen which break everything.

He proceeded to describe what he saw as a conspiracy on the part of the Baath party to destroy the Muslim sections of the Old City, pointing out that the quarters that have been spared are predominantly Christian and Jewish.

Yet for non-Damascenes, it is the "merchant princes of Damascus," as an 'Alawi professor put it, who still control commercial enterprise. According to an 'Alawi writer from Latakia, members of his sect are not automatically preferred for government and other positions:

> The most important jobs are for Damascenes and Christians. The high-salary positions in the international hotels go to Christians. Diplomats are mostly Damascene and Christian; the Christians are sent to the West, the Damascenes to Arab countries. Grants to study in the West go to Christians; the head of the office in charge of sending students abroad is a Christian. They say that this regime is 'Alawi, but I don't think so. Or, you can say that there is a coalition of 'Alawis who are benefiting, but not the rest. There are 'Alawi villages that still don't have electricity. If you ask a Damascene, he will answer in a way that reflects his prejudices. He will say that they [the 'Alawis] have come and dominated everything, stolen everything, and so on. But those who came in from other areas live in the suburbs, in illegal, substandard housing, while those in the center are Damascene and Christian.

The university too used to be a Damascene preserve; the 'Alawi professor remembered a Damascene colleague complaining that all the outsiders had ruined the university. "Do you mean me?" the professor asked. "No, not you, but all the others," the colleague replied. The professor's wife asked me, "What do the Damascenes say when you talk to them, do they hate us?" I replied that there was some resentment. The 'Alawi writer told a similar story:

> I asked one [a Damascene], "Why are you so interested in restoring an old city, rather than building a city of the future?" I felt that there was something ideological in his answer. He said that before the many projects that changed

the architectural character of Damascus, people lived calmer and more balanced lives. They think that what happened to people in Damascus is that they became dehumanized, lost openness, communication, and trust. Yet Damascenes are very closed, they don't visit non-Damascenes, they don't invite non-Damascenes to their houses. You can't make friendships with the women, and with the men you can only make friendships that are not friendships at the same time. There is something sectarian that motivates those who show interest in Old Damascus. They isolate themselves as a special group from Damascene bourgeois families, and they consider people who come to Damascus invaders who corrupted or changed the majesty of the Old City.

But just what is a Damascene, and more specifically, who are the old elite families? How long a family's roots in the city must be and how prominent a family must have been to be considered notable are unclear. The concept of notable, *bint* or *ibn 'ila* (literally, daughter or son of a family), is difficult to pin down. Certainly, a series of well-known names are always included in this category, but it is sometimes more loosely applied. Even more problematic is the matter of where the old elite families are now, and what their relationship is to what I call the Old Damascus movement. Many old elites have married into the new moneyed classes. Many others left Syria decades ago with the advent of Baath party rule. Michael Herzfeld (1991, 66) points to a similar situation in Crete, where virtually all of the families who formed the commercial elite of Rethemnos at the turn of the century have since left the town. Those who remain bemoan the loss of "aristocratic values" even though they themselves can rarely claim aristocratic status.

Although the question of who can legitimately claim Old Damascene status seems an obvious one, it is ultimately unhelpful. What is sociologically significant is not so much the validity of status claims but how these claims are used in urban identity contests. Ties to an elite Old Damascus, genuine or spurious, have become cultural capital, in Pierre Bourdieu's (1984) sense, in a context of rapid social transformation and an increasing emphasis on public image and display. The Old City itself, twenty years ago a nether region associated with the backwardness of the past, is now a source of rich authenticity for Damascenes at home and abroad. In a global context that places an increasingly high premium on local cultures, Old Damascus is once again a status marker. Damascenes boast of the Old City's glory to foreigners and other Syrians alike. For instance, Rana Kabbani, a Damascene author and media figure now living in London, promotes Old Damascus's wealth of traditional natural beauty products to the readers of British *Vogue* (1998, 134–35).

Many Old Damascus supporters are not among the city's wealthiest citizens and do not represent marriages of new money and old status. Many are intellectually oriented middle-class professionals—lawyers, doctors, and journalists—with comfortable but in no way extravagant lifestyles. Their families usually have deep roots in the city; their names are well known and often associated with Damascene exclusivity. Yet they are not always awlad 'ila, members of old notable families. Many feel no sense of identification with the businessmen—some of whom are of old notable origin—whom they blame for working along with the government to destroy the Old City. For them, Damasceneness is a form of resistance to dominant values that they see as materialistic and superficial. Interestingly, some of the most prominent are former leftists who once believed in the nationalist project, and have since become disillusioned. According to a young translator:

> I've noticed over the past five years that I have become proud of being Damascene. I see this also with my father, who was one of the founders of the Baath party. The Baathists used to think Syrians were all simply Syrian. Now many of them regret this. Now they feel that they are distinct from all the villagers, but especially from the 'Alawis. They think: the 'Alawis may have the money, they may have the power, but we have the tradition.

The prestige of this tradition sometimes attracts non-Damascenes with aristocratic pretensions. Non-Damascene, but nonetheless Sunni, Defense Minister Mustafa Talas is a well-known Old Damascus enthusiast whose publishing house, Dar Talas, has produced one of the most widely read Old Damascene memoirs. At the same time, it may be that wealthy Old Damascenes who have married their fortunes to new money do not need to promote their Old Damascus status. Whatever the reason, the very wealthy tend not to be at the forefront of the movement. Some serious aficionados are disenchanted former leftists, and their switch of political affiliation is often pointed to, by critics of the Old Damascus trend, as evidence of typically Damascene weakness of character. Supporters see heritage as an alternative to materialism.

The interest in Old Damascus is occurring as material wealth is becoming an increasingly important measure of status in Syria. Areas of the city are heavily marked in this way. The most incisive question to a potential bride or groom is no longer "Who is your father?" or "What do you do?" but "Where do you live?" People speak wistfully of a time when education and family background mattered. According to a young writer from Aleppo, "It used to matter, who you were and what you did, but now all that matters is consumption."

This privileging of economic capital above all else is, ironically, in part a result of the Baath party's socialist policies. The authority of the old elite families was linked to a combination of political and economic dominance, access to the West in the form of travel, education, and consumer goods, and an urbane, cultivated lifestyle of high education, refined manners, and attention to matters of taste. It was sometimes connected to religious learning. The demise of the old families' dominance over social, political, and economic life in Damascus marked a shift in the understanding of what is considered elite.

FRIENDS AND INTERLOPERS

Many Old City activists belong to an organization called the Society of Friends of Damascus (Jam'iyat Asdiqa' Dimashq). Established in 1977 by "people who were very keen to have the city as it should be," as President Burhan Qassab Hasan—brother of Najat—put it, the organization founded the Museum of the City of Damascus and sponsors lectures and exhibits. Here too the purpose appears to be the promotion of a distinctively Damascene identity. Qassab Hasan estimates that 30 percent of Friends of Damascus's members are Damascene. "We don't place restrictions [against non-Damascenes], but we prefer to have Damascenes because they like Damascus more." Yet in practice membership is restricted; a candidate must be nominated by two current members. Qassab Hasan argues that such regulations exist because "we need people who work, not who have fun." He boasts of the organization's preservation efforts: "We stopped the tearing down of houses. . . . We are doing our best. All the government officials cooperate with us. Many would like to see Damascus as it was before. Whether they like it or not, when we say this or that, they have to agree."

Yet Friends of Damascus is often associated with lavish dinner parties that used to be held in Old City houses but now tend to take place at posh New City hotels. Much like the Daughters of the American Revolution in the United States, the organization's primary goal seems to many to be not the preservation and restoration of the Old City but the maintenance and promotion of the old social elite. Ardent Old Damascus activists often express irritation and frustration at the organization's lack of success in getting laws passed to protect large areas of the Old City. Themselves Friends of Damascus members, they point to a tendency to prefer socializing to activism. "It should be called the Society of Friends rather than the Society of Friends of Damascus," said one. According to another member, an architectural historian:

> They do nothing, just waste time delivering lectures. Delivering lectures means nothing; we need to move! . . . In Ramadan they will break fast at the Cham Palace [Hotel] with a piano. This is ridiculous! They should act in a very different way, they should educate people about Damascus, about conserving and preserving. They should publish articles, they should change their ideas and the way they work, in order to be much better.

And another, an architect, said, "What do they want, these Friends of Damascus members? They want what you could call prestige. They want to form

Figure 7. Old Damascus: Café al-Nawfara. Photograph by Christa Salamandra.

and maintain relations among themselves, and with ministers and other prominent people." A former member, a professional woman in her mid-thirties, takes this criticism further, "I don't know why you are interested in Friends of Damascus. It's becoming more of a matchmaking company than a society. Most of the women there are old maids looking for husbands."

Many Syrians of non-Damascene origin living in Damascus see Friends of Damascus as a sinister organization whose bigoted and xenophobic members aim to rid the city of all "outsiders." According to an 'Alawi writer originally from the coastal region:[5] "Their idea, which is not directly expressed, is that Damascus was invaded by many migrants who deformed its old or inherited identity. They consider those who have come to Damascus to have corrupted the majesty of the Old City. They would like us to leave."

CONSTRUCTING THE LOCAL

All the connotations of Old Damascus converge in the current transformation of the Old City into a recreation center. Most old notable families left their Old City houses decades ago, in favor of modern-style apartments in the elite districts of New Damascus. Their children and grandchildren are returning to the Old City now not to live as their ancestors had, or to shop during the day, like the peasants and tourists, but to spend leisure hours in the evening, either at the Piano Bar or at one of several newly opened restaurants. Set in old merchant houses, these establishments abandon the Western restaurant model that had inspired the previous generation of Damascus restaurants. Instead, they aim to provide a restaurant experience that is deliberately "Eastern" and, beyond this, distinctively Damascene. The most elaborate of these is the Omayyad Palace Restaurant, in the vaulted basement of what is believed to be the long-destroyed Umayyad Palace. "Damascus generosity and hospitality invite you to the Omayyad Palace," reads the restaurant's glossy brochure, in Arabic and English. The diner is ushered down a carpet-lined staircase into a cavernous room lavishly decorated with numerous carpets, a bubbling fountain, plants hanging from skylights, patterned marble floor, mother-of-pearl–inlaid and brocade-upholstered chairs, low brass tables, locally blown glass, copper urns, and glass cases filled with pottery and old photographs. Waiters in baggy black *shar-wal*, black- and silver-striped shirts made from local cloth, fezzes, and imitation Docksider shoes serve drinks. The floor show begins with a "folklore" troupe, in shiny polyester black-and-green outfits, dancing to taped music. The dancing continues for half an hour, after which guests are asked to help themselves to an almost exclusively "Oriental" buffet. Tea, coffee, and water pipes are offered after the meal, as a "traditional" band, dressed in *jalabiya*s and fezzes, plays old songs. Whirling dervishes and Sufi music round off the evening.

Figure 8. The Omayyad Palace Restaurant. Photograph by Christa Salamandra.

Figure 9. The Sheraton Hotel: Café al-Nawafir. Photograph by Christa Salamandra.

Commoditized representations of Old Damascus are not limited to the Old City itself. Old Damascus theme restaurants and cafés have sprung up in the wealthier districts of the New City over the past decade. Noteworthy among these are recent additions to the Damascus Sheraton, the city's most elegant hotel and favorite haunt of the city's elites. Al-Narabayn, built on the hotel's back grounds, is an upscale version of al-Nawfara, the popular café behind the Umayyad Mosque in the Old City. This establishment serves families and groups of teenagers coffee and tea and simple foods long associated with the poor, such as *ful* (fava beans) and *fatta* (a chickpea, bread, and yogurt dish), all at exorbitant prices. During the summer al-Narabayn moves outdoors, becoming al-Nawafir (a name again reminiscent of the popular Café al-Nawfara). The Meridien Hotel followed suit with Café Tric Trac, a two-tiered patio eatery decorated in mosaics and greenery, popular for water-pipe smoking and backgammon and card playing on summer evenings. Patrons pass away long hours, buffed, coiffed, and glittering in gold, talking and playing backgammon, seeing and being seen. Restaurants are uniquely intense people-watching sites. Unlike other leisure activities, such as cinema or theater, in which participants are afforded passing glimpses of fellow audience members, restaurantgoing provides a prolonged gaze of the other (Finkelstein 1989, 17). Tables are filled with *al-mas'ulun*—"the responsible," the powerful and well connected.

The Sheraton has also replaced its elegant French restaurant with the "Oriental" Ishbilia (Seville). Here too the atmosphere is consciously "Eastern" right down to the waiters' long waxed mustaches. On the night I visited, most tables were filled with Syrian men, many entertaining what appeared to be business associates. One table was composed of Syrian media figures. In 1986 the Sheraton invented a local tradition with its weekly Layalina, an outdoor, summertime, "Oriental" food and entertainment extravaganza that replaced the smaller and more expensive events at which French or continental food was served. This new event takes place around the hotel's swimming pool, which, because of its long, grand staircase designed for bridal processions, is the most sought-after location for summer weddings.[6] Layalina is held on Monday nights because hairdressers in Damascus are closed on this day, thus limiting the likelihood that the Sheraton would lose wedding bookings.[7] In addition to a lavish "open buffet" of local specialties, a server in old-fashioned costume doles out falafel—a street food not habitually eaten in restaurants, let alone one of the Sheraton's caliber—from a carriage like those once used in the Old City. Another serves sweets like those that used to be sold outside schools. All of these innovations were sound business decisions, according to the assistant food and beverage manager and service manager, Sami Farah. "People are fed up with classical European food," he explains, "they want *mezza*, grills, and *'araq.*"

Yet the popularity of Old Damascus theme restaurants should not be seen as a rejection of the non-Damascene, the foreign and the Western. Instead, local culture is taking its place, self-consciously, among global cultures, with Café Tric Trac literally next to the Meridien's Mexican restaurant and al-Narabayn next to the Sheraton's pizzeria. Although the contrast between the eclecticism of the Piano Bar and the image of the Old City appears ironic, one of the markers of social differentiation in Syria is the ability to command both cosmopolitan and local idioms.

The increasing prevalence of Old Damascus simulacra also reflects the development of modernity through the growth of new leisure practices. Once an integral part of communal life, leisure activities are now separated from work, privatized, and commodified (Rojek 1995, 191). Restaurants are a case in point. Dining out has become the most popular pastime among the Damascene elite. Just two decades ago restaurantgoing was largely restricted to foreigners, travelers, and students.[8] Damascenes used to denigrate the quality and cleanliness of their eateries. Dining was a home-bound, family-centered activity. Now restaurants are central to the experience of past and present, near and far, seeing and being seen, being and becoming. They are the locus of a new local culture.

Restaurants and other cultural forms relatively new to the Middle East are sites at which tradition is reinvented. Here the concept of "public culture," as developed by the pioneering journal of the same name, provides a useful framework. Studies of public culture are concerned with the local production and reception of transnational cultural forms, often in urban non-Western contexts. As Carol Breckenridge and Arjun Appadurai note, "Much of the non-Western world has now adopted forms of technological representation, consumption and commodification which are harnessed to the idiosyncrasies of their own traditions, and to the ways in which indigenous elites reconstruct these traditions" (1988, 1). I would add that what is occurring in Damascus is not mere synthesis of local tradition to Western form but the very construction of the local. While identity construction involves consumption of cosmopolitan cultural forms, these are locally produced and locally transformed.

Television is the most easily available of these forms. During the first half of the fasting month of Ramadan in 1993, Syrian television aired a fifteen-episode serial drama entitled *Ayyam Shamiyya* (Damascene Days), directed by Bassam al-Mallah. This series, said to be inspired by Egypt's successful *Layali al-Hilmiyya* (Hilmiyya Nights), was the first to depict social life in Damascus in the late Ottoman period (1910).[9] It is also said to be the first such program without a strong plot, and with politics as a backdrop rather than the central focus. *Damascene Days* attempted to portray daily life in an unnamed Old City quarter, concentrating on family relations, problems between neighbors, and local administration. Customs and traditions associated with rites of passage were carefully depicted.

Damascene Days was clearly the media event of the year. It is difficult to overestimate the extent to which the series was watched and discussed. Most Damascus homes receive only two television channels: Channel 1, which aired the series, and Channel 2, which broadcasts foreign-language programs.[10] Syria produces many low-budget serial television dramas each year, but showpiece productions are aired during Ramadan.[11] *Damascene Days* was shown during what might be called Ramadan prime time, one hour after the beginning of *iftar*, the fast-breaking meal. It is a time when most people relax at home with their families, digesting the first food of the day. Television sets were tuned to the series even in the presence of large numbers of guests. *Damascene Days* sparked lively debate in the media and in conversation. Syrian Television also aired a two-hour discussion, filmed in an Old Damascene house, with all those involved in the production.

Assessments of the series were generally split along predictable lines: people with Damascene origins themselves were enthusiastic, whereas non-Damascenes' reactions ranged from mild disinterest to fervent opposition. Most debates centered on the issue of authenticity. Critics argued that the series sanitized and romanticized life in the Old City, glossing over or collapsing social and economic differences. In *Damascene Days* both merchant and hummos seller have mother-of-pearl–inlaid furniture, and all characters are positively drawn, save the brutal but buffoonish Turkish soldiers. It was even argued that the Turks, who appear only briefly to hunt down a fugitive and to rape the sandwich seller's daughter, should have been portrayed more harshly. Supporters stressed the authenticity of the dialogue, which was rich in archaic idiom; of the decor, which showcased inlaid furniture and other local products; and of social customs, such as those connected to marriage. As for the supposed neglect of class distinction, fans of the series argued that social differences at this time were in fact less accentuated than they are now.

Old Damascus once again occupied Syrian Television's post-iftar slot during Ramadan 1994, in 'Ala' al-Din Kawkash's thirty-episode series, *Abu Kamil, Part Two*. Set in an Old City quarter during the last days of the French Mandate, this unsuccessful sequel to the popular *Abu Kamil* was heavily criticized in many circles, but particularly among Damascenes. Most thought it drawn out, outlandish, and dull. Unlike *Damascene Days,* which presented an Old City quarter galvanized against the Turks, *Abu Kamil, Part Two* depicted Damascenes as traitors who collaborated with the French and fought among themselves. Another series broadcast in a later slot, Najdat Isma'il Anzur's *Nihayat rajul shuja'* (The End of a Brave Man), showed the people of Baniyas, a coastal city, struggling together against French forces. Based on a novel by the acclaimed Syrian author Hanna Mina, *The End of a Brave Man* won high praise in many circles for its tight plot and high production value but also for its depiction of a valiant and noble past, in which everyone was unified.

DISTINCTIONS

Many of the older modes of social distinction are fading, having been replaced by mere consumption. Higher education is no longer seen as an important mark of social distinction for the elite, or as a reliable means to upward mobility for the humble. The democratization of Syrian universities has spread meager resources very thin. The majority of students graduate virtually unskilled. At the same time, low tuition fees and less-than-rigorous entrance standards have increased access to higher education, undercutting the prestige once associated with a university degree. The same is becoming true for degrees from Western universities, as the children of the expanding new-money classes are able to attain these with ease. Some upper-middle-class families encourage their sons to eschew university altogether and to go directly into family businesses. The title "duktur" no longer has the same deep resonance.

The trappings of Western elite culture—familiarity with current movements in the performing and visual arts; theater, opera, and moviegoing; museum and gallery visiting, highbrow fiction reading—do not constitute cultural capital in the upper reaches of Damascene society, as they do in Bourdieu's (1984) France. Foreigners—diplomats and oil company employees—are virtually the only visual arts patrons. Often the more impoverished part of the artistic community itself makes up the audience and readership for local high-cultural production. The same faces can be seen at all highbrow art events: concerts, plays, films, and exhibit openings. Paradoxically, mass media such as television link the most general of audiences to a few producers, whose success elevates them to honorary membership in the social elite.

Wealth is displayed in elite hotels and expensive restaurants and at engagement parties, weddings, funerals, and other rite-of-passage events. Elite consumption practices often privilege representations of Old Damascus, or at least allusions to older forms of social life— Old Damascus theme cafés, old-fashioned horse-drawn wedding carriages, iftars and *suhu*rs (Ramadan meals) in posh restaurants. The most talked about wedding of the 1995 season, staged by Najdat Isma'il Anzur—director of *The End of a Brave Man*—featured the bride entering the Sheraton Hotel on camelback. Reconstructions of Old Damascus, as status markers or as metonyms of national culture, have become central to the experience of modernity in

Syria. As Daniel Miller (1995a, 4) points out in more general terms, many social groups around the world are now constituted not through traditional value systems but through appropriation or rejection of global forms. Production, consumption, and rejection of Old Damascus simulacra are for Syrians the basic materials of identity construction.

The authentic Old Damascus of *Damascene Days* represents true mass consumption, available to all, rejected by some. But those who produce authenticity for the masses may themselves frequent exclusive venues like the Piano Bar, where drinks cost $5 each and the decor is an ironic hodgepodge of past and present, local and foreign.[12] Discussions of local appropriations of global cultural forms often gloss over such distinctions. At the level of imagery, however, it is true that the search for the return of Old Damascene authenticity is a journey into the urban, Middle Eastern experience of modernity: from the Old City itself (whose mostly lower-middle-class inhabitants would leave it if they could), to intellectuals and media figures who claim to represent local tradition and complain of apathy and frustration, to exhibits and dinner parties, bookshops and television shows, to that favorite haunt of the Old Damascenes, the Sheraton Hotel; and finally to the ultimate decenteredness of the Piano Bar, which, in the words of a librarian, "has absolutely no identity."

> The one who did the decor has assimilated too many cultures. We have a saying that fits: "From every orchard one flower." Those dishes on the wall are Dutch, but they are not arranged in a Dutch way. It's for younger people. You can never place it anywhere. They offer a very limited menu—*shish tawuk*, which is Turkish, and spaghetti, which is Italian. They have an old piece behind the bar that was part of the Umayyad Palace. Such a combination is unbelievable. And the curtains! I have never seen this fabric, which used to be used for cushions, used for drapes. Yes, it is Damascene, but it is used in a totally different way. Next I'm afraid I'll find part of my mother's underwear hanging as a curtain! They are arranging old things in a rather modern art way. We have this desire to live in a modern way, because at least in furniture we can do it. In our thoughts we are often tied to old ideas.

The final paradox is that "old ideas" is itself an image distinctive of modernity, and the pursuit of Old Damascus is a contemporary phenomenon.

NOTES

Funding for fieldwork in Damascus, 1992–94 and February-March 1996, was provided by a Social Science Research Council International Doctoral Dissertation Fellowship and a Linacre House Trust Research Grant.

1. These are the most recently released figures. The results of the 1996 census were not yet available at the time of writing.

2. For a discussion of Ibn Kannan and other eighteenth-century literary celebrants of Damascus, see Tamari 1998.

3. A reference to a saying (*hadith*) of the Prophet Muhammad regarding the appropriate time to break fast during Ramadan, when it is so dark that a black thread can no longer be distinguished from a white thread, and, more generally, when to say the dawn prayer.

4. Laylat al-Qadr, the twenty-seventh of Ramadan, the night the Qur'an descended.

5. The 'Alawi, Syria's largest minority group, are a religious sect considered heretical by the Sunni Muslims of Damascus. Originating from the villages of coastal Syria, they are strongly associated with the peasantry.

6. The Sheraton was eclipsed in 1995 with the opening of the lavish Nobles' Palace.

7. Visiting a hairdresser on the day of a wedding party is crucial for Damascene elite women, as weddings are among the most important occasions for social display. For more on Damascene weddings, see Tapper 1988–89.

8. Historically most Middle Eastern cities lack strong restaurant traditions (Hattox 1985, 89).

9. For a discussion of *Hilmiyya Nights*, see Abu-Lughod 1995b.

10. This was very true in 1993, but by the end of the following year middle-class households were gaining access to satellite dishes.

11. For more on Syrian Ramadan television serials, see Salamandra 1997.

12. A university-educated government employee earns $80 to $100 per month.

NINE

The Hairbrush and the Dagger
Mediating Modernity in Lahore

Richard McGill Murphy

Our language can be seen as an ancient city: a maze of little streets and squares, of old and new houses, and of houses with additions from various periods; and this surrounded by a multitude of new boroughs with straight regular streets and uniform houses.

LUDWIG WITTGENSTEIN, *Philosophical Investigations*

He who has not seen Lahore is yet unborn.

PUNJABI PROVERB

THE ARGUMENT:
REPRESENTATION IN LAHORE AND IN ANTHROPOLOGY

Debates about the nature and value of modernity permeate daily life in Lahore. I argue, accordingly, that competing representations of modernity are in large part strategies through which Lahoris negotiate the business of everyday life. These strategies often involve the conscious or unconscious manipulation of class rhetoric—the words, arguments, and turns of phrase that mark membership in a range of situationally constructed social groupings.[1] I read local discourses of religion, class, gender, and politics contrapuntally, in Edward Said's (1993) sense of the term, to achieve a multiple perspective on the rhetorical construction of modernity in urban Pakistan. These constructions take the form of texts drawn from newspapers and television dramas, from the sermons of Muslim preachers, and from the conversation of my Lahori informants. The argument (and, where I use it, the ethnographic present tense) is based on fieldwork conducted in Lahore between 1992 and 1994.

It is argued that what I call a crisis of social representation in urban Pakistan is best analyzed as a debate whose rhetorical positions undercut the naturalistic representation of truth by a constant questioning of the moral authority conveyed by any particular perspective on the social world. Perspectival multiplicity, uncertainty, and moral ambiguity are fundamental to the rhetorical strategies through which Lahoris construct and act upon the world. My analysis distinguishes three broad, often clashing moral perspectives within urban Pakistani society today: nationalism, modernism, and Islam. Some frames of explanation, such as formal Islam, encompass a broader world than Pakistan yet are deployed in very local ways. Others, such as nationalism, are less easy to deploy in the Lahori setting but set moral limits to the development of local "meta-narratives." Indeed, certain obvious possibilities for totalizing explanation ("caste" not least) are ruled out by a need for contrast with neighboring India.

The term "representational crisis" also applies to contemporary anthropology, another world dominated by rhetorical contestation. Since the early 1970s our discipline has been preoccupied with epistemological debates: what is another culture, and how do you represent it? After a lengthy initial round of postcolonial self-flagellation (see Asad 1973; Clifford 1988; Clifford and Marcus 1986), the terms of the debate have shifted somewhat. Now the emphasis is on arguments that displace the traditional self/other, center/periphery binarisms of neo-Cartesian epistemology in favor of a rather weightless globalism. All now seems to be capital flows, space-time compression, ethnic diasporas, ethnoscapes: in anthropology as in contemporary political and media discourse, the emphasis is on cultural, political, and economic processes that transcend the local (see especially Appadurai 1990, 1991; Ghosh 1989; Glick, Basch, and Blanc-Szanton 1992; Harvey 1989; Kearney 1995). Judging from recent literature, urban anthropology has been strongly influenced by this globalizing trend (see Castells 1989; Hannerz 1992; Martin 1996; Susser 1996). In a review article, Setha M. Low remarks, "The shifting terrain of public culture is constantly redefining the local according to the global" (1996, 393). My own ethnography, however, suggests that Low's formula should be reversed. The terms of Lahori self-representation often transcend the city. As a result of emigration, overseas labor remittances, international marriages, satellite television, and a dozen other factors, Lahore is densely articulated with the global cultural economy. But moral debate in urban Pakistan displays an ethnographic specificity that is not adequately captured by the giddy transnationalism of much currently fashionable anthropological theory.

Anthropology's theoretical capital was originally based on the study of practically or heuristically isolated local communities whose links with broader social worlds were often effaced by the terms of ethnographic discourse (see Fabian 1983; Sperber 1985). Without endorsing a return to village ethnography, much less colonial ethnography, it seems to me that our discipline is best suited to generating global insight through the prism of a local world. I would also note a family resemblance between Lahori debates on the nature and value of their own modernity and what has by now become an institutionalized anthropological penchant for self-examination.[2] Modern Lahoris often express an ambivalent nostalgia about their city's colonial past. Modern anthropologists are often ambivalent about their theoretical patrimony, drawing on the rhetoric and insights of classic ethnography while deploring the colonial power relations that made most classic ethnographies possible. (Lahoris are comparably ambivalent about the rural Punjabi world in contrast to which urban Punjabi culture is defined: Lahori modernist discourse tends to classify the countryside as simultaneously "authentic" and "backward.")

Low points out that urban ethnography has historically been marginal both to urban studies and to mainstream theoretical debates within social anthropology. Even so, the metropolitan, middle-class ghetto of poststructuralist anthropology and literary studies is permeated by a curiously placeless imagery of cosmopolitan urbanism. In this textualized universe, privileged readers play in fields of free-floating signification while effacing the materiality of life in a world of socially, politically, and economically differentiated nation-states.[3] Reflexivity, in short, is not confined to anthropology. Nor is multiperspectival ambivalence unique to Lahore. By providing a nuanced ethnography of Lahori perspectives on modernity, I hope to contribute to our understanding of how modernity gets constructed in cities and in social anthropology today.

Lahori social rhetoric is permeated by hierarchical imagery from which it is sometimes possible to infer a communal ranking principle based on the opposition of pure and impure. Many, perhaps most, Lahoris, further, behave in a castelike way when it comes to marriage and choice of occupation. But the caste model as such is undercut by orthodox Islamic discourse, which argues that there should be no rank in Islam.[4] It is also undercut by the discourse of the so-called two nation theory, which argues that caste is not a morally adequate perspective from which to understand Pakistan because it belongs to the Hindu world, in contrast to which Pakistan is identified as a nation-state. Islamic discourse is equally undercut by modernism, according to which Muslim preachers represent retrograde forces in a society progressing toward a vaguely defined ideal of social and economic "development" thought to be most closely approximated by the secular democracies of northern Europe and America. From both nationalist and Islamist points of view, however, this very modernism is attacked as un-Pakistani and un-Islamic because it is identified with non-Muslim foreigners who once colonized the region and continue, according to locally ubiquitous conspiracy theories of history, to exert enormous covert influence over everyday social and political life.

These perspectives do not exclude one another. People commonly shift perspectives, often within the same argument. And although Pakistanis tend to gloss this multiplicity of moral standpoints as "hypocrisy"(*munafiqat*), it is not precisely a question of saying one thing while doing another. Instead the various perspectives all carry some weight but are all challenged by alternate moral interpretations. Our argument engages with a world dominated by rhetorical contestation. Hence we proceed from the premise that the social facts with which we have to deal are not real objects but rather arguments about reality. Lahore, in this view, is not a set of objective social facts connected according to some more or less transparent logic but a set of mediated debates about social, political, and historical registers of truth.

NOSTALGIA AND MODERNITY IN LAHORE

The collective memory of urban society tends to contrast today's Lahore with an idealized, pre-Partition paradise lost. Consider the tautological Punjabi phrase "Lahore is Lahore" (*Lahore Lahore ai*). Normally this is an expression of pride in the city's glorious heritage as the political, cultural, commercial, and gastronomic center of Punjab. Lahore is Lahore because it is unique, incomparable.[5] Yet the local journalist Imtiaz Sipra modified the cheerful chauvinism of Lahore Lahore ai by appropriating it as the title for a series of English-language columns on Lahore's cultural identity. These essays shed a nostalgically normative light on contemporary Lahore, often harping on the theme that the core values of local society had been destroyed by modernization and urban growth: "The real, original Lahorite . . . illustrated politeness, helpfulness, love for nature and beauty and importance given to friends and friendship. . . . It has all changed now, thanks to modern amenities and 'urbanization' [*sic*]" (Sipra 1993, 3). Given the moralistic tone of this argument, its explicitly materialist conclusion deserves comment. Effectively, Sipra argues that technological progress ("modern amenities") and demographic change ("urbanization") together determine the nature of moral relations in society. Because of technology and urbanization, Lahoris have apparently become rude, unhelpful, and indifferent to nature, beauty, friends, and friendship. This is a materialism devoid of class consciousness, however: the "real, original Lahorite" belongs to no particular class, although (s)he is anachronistically defined as a Muslim: "This more or less uniform character and identity of Lahorites allowed them to 'integrate' fully with migrants, conquering intruders and converts and followers of religions other than Islam" (Sipra 1994, 3).

Sipra's narrative interprets the past selectively, ignoring the communal bloodbath of Partition and the fact that Lahore was a Hindu city for the first thousand years of its history, not to mention the mythical tradition of Lahore's foundation by the sons of the Hindu hero Rama. But it does reflect material changes in the demography and political economy of the city, whose population has exploded from about 400,000 in 1931 to perhaps 5 million today, growing at an annual rate of more than 4 percent (PEPAC 1993, 6). This dramatic growth has stretched Lahore's police, sanitation, transport, and communication systems to the cracking point (see Lahore Development Authority 1980; Qadeer 1983). The city has become demonstrably dirtier, more crowded, and less safe since Partition. Independence drew a line also between Lahore's multicommunal past and its overwhelmingly Muslim present. The city's Hindu and Sikh heritage is preserved only in the names of certain streets, in sacred architecture,[6] and in hospitals and schools endowed by long-dead philanthropists whose families now live in India. According to the 1981 *District Census Report of Lahore*, 42.8 percent of Lahore's population was fifteen years old or younger. As a result, the collective memory of pre-Partition Lahore is fading into romantic nostalgia for an imagined time when, as one local politician put it in a newspaper interview, "the pace of life was slower, evenings were lit by the soft light of lanterns and people had time for one another."[7] This sort of elegiac materialism is the complement of a progressive theory of history inspired by Western models of social and economic development.

In modern Pakistan the language of development carries with it a concept of time lived forward in moral as well as strictly chronological terms. This is a global discourse based ultimately on popular Victorian notions of social evolution, according to which the "developed" societies of the industrialized West represent cultural and economic advancement ("modernity") relative to the "backward" societies of the developing world. The main local symbols of modernity—high technology, the English language, Western styles of clothing and architecture—continue to enjoy widespread prestige. The rhetoric of "advanced" versus "backward" modes of life is also very much in local use. Rich and poor Lahoris alike, however, are conscious of what economists like to call the "costs" of Pakistan's highly uneven economic growth: pollution, crime, unemployment, and salaries that stubbornly refuse to keep pace with inflation.[8] In an increasingly polarized political context shadowed by the breakup of the country in 1971 and marked by sharp ethnic and sectarian tension in many parts of the former West Pakistan, this ambivalent sense of having, perhaps, grasped the short end of the Faustian stick has all the more influence over the ways in which people structure their personal and familial relations with the past.

In interior decoration, music, and fashion, for example, there is a growing urban upper-class vogue for styles perceived as "ethnic" or "traditional": handcarved Swati doors and arches, print reproductions of Mughal miniature painting, the Sufi devotional music (*qawwali*) of Nusrat Fateh Ali Khan,[9] embroidered mirror-work textiles from Sindh. A typical issue of the Lahore and London-based Pakistani fashion magazine *Libas International* includes articles titled "Mughal Treasures on Bond Street" and "Jewelry: Ethnic Richness."[10] And throughout the society great value is placed on belonging to an established family. While this is neither unique to Pakistan nor new in Lahore, the contemporary context of nostalgic reaction against "modernity" determines that more established families are currently perceived as living links to a time when society as a whole was better off.

The Urdu/Punjabi term for this sort of background is *khandani*, literally, the adjective form of *family* (*khandan*) but connoting the kind of family that has long held a position of social prominence. There are no precise criteria for being khandani. At most, khandani people say they have been in their social position "since the time of our [paternal] grandfather's grandfather" (*dada ka dada*) or point to some notable ancestor. However, one of the more striking aspects of Pakistani English is its appropriation of quasi-Marxist class terminology to mark everyday social distinctions. Often shorn of their critical implications in Western political theory, terms such as "elite" and "feudal" denote, respectively, the upper classes in general and the landowning gentry in particular. The term "feudal" is similar to other Pakistani class terms in that it changes its moral valence according to the social context in which it is articulated. Members of the landowning notability describe themselves, with no apparent irony, as "feudals." In Gulberg, a Lahore residential suburb where property values are among the highest in Pakistan, there is a tailoring shop whose signboard reads "Ossian Tailors, Stitched and Stitching, For Elites and Feudals." Yet in other contexts Pakistani intellectuals often blame the country's political and economic problems on "feudalism," understood here as a social system in which land tenure and political power are, if not freely convertible, at least organically linked.[11] Not all khandani families deploy rural landowning claims to social prestige. Nor is the term associated exclusively with upper-class families. Khandani lineage, in the diffuse sense of kinship claimed with some more or less distant ancestor of glorious repute, can be constructed in many different ways. Among working-class musicians in the Old City of Lahor, glorous ancestry is associated with the transmission of musical competence. Some of the more khandani musical families claim descent from musicians at the court of Akbar and other Moghul emperors. For urban notables such as my Old City patron, Mian Yusuf Salahuddin, the virtue of descent was political and patriotic prestige. His maternal grandfather was Allama Mohammed Iqbal, the poet-philosopher generally credited with articulating the idea of Pakistan; his paternal grandfather was Mian Amiruddin, a former mayor of Lahore. Leaving his Old City residence in Barud Khana Bazaar, Mian Yusuf would sometimes point to an empty chair in the doorway and remark, "From that chair my grandfather [Mian Amiruddin] ran the politics of Punjab."

The local term for this sort of distinction is *'izzat*, often translated as "honor" but more accurately glossed as the respect of society. As such, the 'izzat of a khandani family is construed in nostalgic terms, suggesting a glorious past rather than present-day political or economic clout. However, khandani status is always open to contestation. Lahoris are quick to point out that many of the leading families in society are commercial clans who have been upper class for at most three generations. Some have marriage connections with khandani rural families who in many cases rose to social prominence in the nineteenth century when they received land grants in exchange for their loyalty to the British Raj. While historically accurate, this is often mentioned in contexts of social rivalry. Thus great landowning clans are often attacked on nationalistic grounds by people wishing to challenge their claims to social eminence.

This was the thrust of a series of articles in the Lahore *Friday Times* titled "The Hidden Face of History." Written between 1992 and 1996 by the local historian Ahmad Salim, most of these essays examine the historical relationship between Punjab's leading political families and the British Raj, with particular reference to the honors and financial rewards granted to historical notables in exchange for supporting the British at moments of crisis such as the sepoy rebellion of 1857. Pakistani history textbooks invariably describe this conflict as a South Asian "War of Independence." The fact of having ancestors who sided with the Raj in 1857 is thus politically loaded in the context of modern Pakistani nationalism. In a piece on the Tiwana family of Sargodha, for example, Salim notes that Malik Sahib Khan Tiwana fought on the British side in 1857 and was subsequently granted "the title of Khan Bahadur and a life jagir[12] of Rs. 1,200 in addition to his previous life pension of Rs. 480 per year. On his return to the Punjab . . . he obtained a large grant of land." Salim concludes by describing how Malik Sahib Khan Tiwana's modern descendants had deserted their former ally Nawaz Sharif after his government was dismissed in April 1993:[13] "The Tiwana brothers were staunch allies of Nawaz Sharif. . . . Then they joined [Sharif's Islami Jamhuri Ijtehad (IJI) rival Manzoor] Wattoo and have been his staunch supporters since. From advisors to Sharif to manipulators for Wattoo, the transition has been remarkably smooth" (1996, 134). The unveiled message of this and most of Salim's other articles is that Punjab's more khandani political families are and always have been cynical opportunists with dubious patriotic credentials.

Even families of such unimpeachably patriotic antecedents as the Mians of Barood Khana can be described, by social rivals, as unworthy of their glorious ancestry. At a private Nusrat Fateh Ali Khan concert sponsored by the Mians at their residence in the exclusive Lahore suburb of Gulberg, one of the guests was heard to remark, cattily, "So these are the grandsons of Iqbal?" Another popular line of social attack against the Mians was to suggest that they were an immoral family because of their traditional ties to the Taxali Gate area of the Old City, which contains Hira Mandi (the Diamond Market), Lahore's notorious red-light district. (In this context it is ironic that among the socially despised Kanjar, or dancing girl, community that dominates Hira Mandi, certain families describe themselves as khandani in order to make the point that they have been established in the dancing business for longer than their rivals.)

The Kanjar community as a whole is perceived, predictably, as being in a state of sad decline compared with the past, when dancing girls (*tavaayif*) were northern Indian high-culture virtuosos and the sons of *sharif* (noble)[14] families flocked to learn music, poetry, and polite conversation at their feet.[15] This romantic image is famously conveyed by the 1981 Hindi film *Umrao Jaan*, a sprawling nineteenth-century historical drama about a tragic love affair between a dancing girl and the son of an Uttar Pradeshi nawab. Invidious comparisons between the vulgarity of modern dancing girls and an imagined golden age of courtly nawabs and polished courtesans singing tasteful Urdu *ghazal*s (lyric poems) are reinforced by films such as *Umrao Jaan* (Dear Umrao) and by many Pakistan Television (PTV) serials. The influence of Bombay films and MTV music videos, meanwhile, is often cited as contributing to Hira Mandi's "decline." Once again the historical accuracy of this contrast is irrelevant to its nostalgic force.

It is at this aesthetic level that we can most clearly contrast Lahori representations of modernity and authenticity. On the one hand, the modernist perspective casts history as a developmental process tending toward a vaguely defined ideal of moral, economic, and political perfection. On the other hand, the rhetoric of nostalgia devalues the present in relation to the past. From a nostalgic point of view, aesthetic products are dismissed as inauthentic insofar as they betray the influence of modernity. From a modernist point of view, the same products are dismissed as "backward" insofar as they can be identified with local tradition as opposed to international style. Authenticity and modernity contest the same aesthetic ground. At stake is the relative moral status of the future and the past.

POLITICS AND POPULAR CULTURE

Pakistan Television is a partisan organ of the Pakistani state. Incoming prime ministers invariably appoint their own loyalists to senior positions within the PTV bureaucracy, and programming reflects the government's point of view on domestic politics as well as international affairs. Shortly after the Benazir Bhutto–led Pakistan People's party won the national election of October 1993, the state television network began screening a fourteen-part Urdu melodrama called *Zard Dopehr* (Yellow Afternoon). The main theme in the drama's complex plot is the rise to political power of a balding, middle-class Lahori businessman named Malik Mehrban 'Ali (played by Shujahat Hashmi), who was universally viewed as a thinly disguised alter ego of opposition leader and, at that time, former Prime Minister Nawaz Sharif.[16] The writer and director of the series, Shahid Nadeem, is a prominent Lahori playwright, screenwriter, and television producer. He developed *Yellow Afternoon* during spring 1993 but was unable to get permission to produce it until Nawaz Sharif's bitter opponent Benazir Bhutto returned to power. Because the drama presents Malik Mehrban as a corrupt, brutal, "uneducated" Old City thug who bribes and bullies his way to political power while pretending to be a pious Muslim, PTV could not have screened *Yellow Afternoon* while Sharif was still prime minister and thus in a position to influence hiring and transfers within the PTV bureaucracy.[17] *Yellow Afternoon* played on the common upper-class Pakistani perception that the industrialist Sharif family were vulgar, "uneducated" arrivistes.

In urban Pakistan today representations of literacy and education are often conflated with class. Thus the adjective for polite or refined Urdu, *nasta'liq*, also refers to the court style of Persian script in which Urdu is usually written. The metaphorical equation between literacy and social refinement parallels the equation between rationality and class. Upper-class Lahoris in particular often argue that "uneducated" (in this context, poor) people are incapable of "rational" behavior. As one young professional put it, "The poor are like animals. They know getting up, eating, and working. Nothing else." However, it seems that poor people are naturally good (albeit irrational), as long as they stay poor. Urban Pakistanis tend to blame all social problems, including poverty, on "lack of education." Because "education" is also a metaphor of class distinction, poor people are blamed for their poverty (they are poor because they are "uneducated") while upwardly mobile people are blamed for escaping poverty (they are vulgar and corrupt because they are "uneducated").

In discussions of political and bureaucratic corruption, members of the self-described "old elite" frequently argue that corruption results from upward mobility on the part of the "uneducated." This is based on the widely shared assumption that it is impossible to succeed in the Pakistani economy without either paying bribes (*rishwat*) or benefiting from high-level patronage (*sarparasti*). Among the old elite this identification of mobility and corruption tends to dominate political discussion.

Upper-class Lahoris from old-money backgrounds often refer to themselves collectively as "Lahore Society." The term denotes a clique defined less by rules of exclusion than by exclusion itself, whose practice is justified by reference to a fuzzy set of values supposed to have been clearer at some time in the past. Members of Society often contend, for example, that Lahore no longer has a clear class hierarchy. This can make for frustrating ethnography. Asked to comment on Lahore's class system, they tend to reply that there is none: "There are no classes anymore. Money is all that matters in this society." This statement expresses a clear stance on the relative merits of inherited versus achieved status, in effect drawing on the same set of class distinctions whose continued relevance it affects to deny. In other words, money is not all that matters in Society. Hence the disdain that members of Society express for nouveau riche Lahore industrialists such as the Sharif clan, who have dominated Punjab politics since the death of President Zia ul-Haq in 1988 and are reputedly the richest family in Pakistan. During my fieldwork (1992–94), Nawaz Sharif served successively as prime minister and opposition leader in the National Assembly, and his brother Shahbaz was a dominant figure in the Punjab Provincial Assembly. As one Society hostess put it, however: "It will be a thousand years before they are accepted in Lahore Society." One of her friends added, "But you must remember that we are a powerless class, hence bitter. We sit in our drawing rooms and complain about the government, but we can't really do anything about it."

This was the social context that gave *Yellow Afternoon* its satirical bite. The drama begins in a courtroom, where a poor village caretaker named 'Ali Mohammed is being sentenced to death for the murder of a police constable. Crusading investigative reporter Sanya 'Ali (Samiya Mumtaz) decides that 'Ali Mohammed has been framed to protect some shadowy higher-up. Meanwhile, we see Malik Mehrban at a family council in his crumbling Old City mansion.[18] He announces that since the Mehrban Group is now one of the country's leading business families, he as family leader must enter politics to safeguard the family's interests. An elderly relative objects: "Politics isn't our job: it's for landlords [*vadairon*] and feudals [*jagirdaron*]. We're businesspeople: our job is to get the politicians in our grasp so they'll look after our interests." Mehrban retorts: "You don't understand. We've reached a point in business where we can either go up or down. We can't stay level. If we don't get some political power we could end up going down. Completely down."

This scene establishes Mehrban's class position conclusively: he is materially rich but morally middle class, in Lahore Society terms an upwardly mobile *shehri* (with characteristically Lahori ambivalence, the Old City, or *purana shehr,* is viewed simultaneously as the heart of traditional urban culture and the epitome of lower-class vulgarity). Malik Mehrban and his flashy young wife inhabit a garishly decorated bungalow in affluent Gulberg. His sister Saira Begum (Madiha Gauhar),[19] a middle-aged school headmistress, has elected to stay in the Old City and run a girls' school. For reasons that remain opaque for the first several episodes, she is unmarried and harbors a deep hatred for her genial, politically ambitious brother. She has two dependents: a young girl in a wheelchair who spends much of her time talking to pigeons and a dumb madwoman named Zaytoun (played by the leading dramatic actress Samina Peerzada) who speaks to nobody but seems to be in the grip of a terrible fear. In a recurring theme, Saira Begum tells her wheelchair-bound young ward installments of a dark fable in which an evil king walls up a handsome young prince alive in his palace. We eventually learn that the story is autobiographical. Saira Begum hates her brother because she believes that, years before, Malik Mehrban had her fiancé killed and buried in the basement of the family *havaili* (mansion) where she lives to this day, despite its distressing personal associations. (Her brother had opposed the marriage, it seems, because he was unable to bear the idea of alienating any part of the family property in dowry.)

In subsequent episodes the beautiful young journalist Sanya 'Ali uncovers evidence that appears to link Malik Mehrban to the framing of 'Ali Mohammed and to the mysterious madness of Zaytoun. 'Ali Mohammed, it turns out, had been Malik Mehrban's gatekeeper at his country house. Zaytoun had been married to 'Ali Mohammed until he committed suicide under mysterious circumstances. Sanya and 'Ali Mohammed's defense lawyer (Salman Shahid) enlist the help of Tariq Hussain, the police officer who had investigated the case against 'Ali Mohammed. Tariq helps them build a damning case against Malik Mehrban; in the process he and Sanya fall in love.

Mehrban, meanwhile, is scaling the political heights. He starts modestly, by hiring a political coach named Sadiqi, a Pygmalion figure in charge of smoothing his rough edges so that he can become a proper ruling-class politician. This means wearing Western clothes, improving his English, and learning various tricks such as a hierarchy of different handshakes with which to greet different classes of people (ordinary voters, political workers, and important political personalities), depending on how much respect, or 'izzat, he wishes to convey.

The image makeover extends to Malik Mehrban's entourage. He places two employees named Jaida and Shida in charge of campaign administration. "Jaida" (from Javaid) and "Shida" (from Rashid) are common working-class Punjabi nicknames. In Lahore *shida* is also slang for an "uneducated," working-class city dweller; in urban contexts it corresponds to the equally condescending *pindu* (villager/hick). Jaida and Shida speak thick, Punjabi-accented Urdu and wear *dhotti kurta* (tunic and wraparound skirt), a style of local dress associated with peasants, petty shopkeepers, and other "uneducated" people. Sadiqi renames them Jerry and Sherry and dresses them in jeans, loud shirts, and sunglasses. When they break into Punjabi, he orders them to stop talking like shidas. In episode 3, Sadiqi explains that if Mehrban wants to be a successful politician, he too must differentiate himself from the mass of common people, in the first instance by wearing a Western suit:

SADIQI: . . . The people should see that you're different from them, stronger than them.
MEHRBAN: That I am, by the grace of God. [*pugnaciously*] Am I not?

SADIQI: Malik Sahib, being and appearance are not the same. Look at Jerry and Sherry. Underneath they're still Jaida and Shida, but now they look different. Now if you appear before the people in this getup [the suit], you'll look bigger, stronger.

The subtext of this image transformation, of course, is that like his employee Sherry, Mehrban remains a vulgar shida no matter how "educated" (i.e., Westernized) he tries to appear.[20] Mehrban's career takes off when he is sponsored by a rich, drug-dealing film producer with close links to the Lahore chief of police. The chief is in turn taking direction from a mysterious cabal of (intelligence) "agencies" whose representatives appear mainly as disembodied telephone voices. After they rig Mehrban's election to the city council, he sets his sights on a federal cabinet portfolio. He also drops his political coach Sadiqi, replacing him with his own son Mustapha, who has just returned from America with a college degree and speaks highly Anglicized Urdu, even calling his shehri father "Dad." Mustapha brings in another U.S.-educated friend named Rehan to act as a public relations consultant. Muscle and money by themselves, they argue, will not propel Mehrban to national political leadership. They must manipulate the media by setting up a task force to research and plant stories about his enemies, particularly the journalist Sanya 'Ali.

This media manipulation subplot is ironic in relation to the political agenda of the television drama in which it is embedded. For all its subtle and varied social commentary, *Yellow Afternoon* was most obviously a satirical attack on a recently defeated prime minister, sponsored by his successor.[21] Lahori viewers were highly sensitive to this irony, pointing out that Shahid Nadeem, the director, was a Bhutto family loyalist with a long history of opposition to the late military dictator General Zia ul-Haq. Benazir Bhutto's archrival Nawaz Sharif, meanwhile, started his political career in the early 1980s as a protégé of General Zia.

Leveraged by his powerful connections within Pakistan, Malik Mehrban's slick new political strategy yields rapid dividends. He joins the federal cabinet as minister for trade and commerce, a post that offers huge scope for corruption. Soon Jerry and Sherry are installed in his outer office, charging fees for access to the great man, who is busily arranging industrial development permits and interest-free loans for all his cronies. Ultimately, however, the forces of virtue triumph. Sanya and her friends manage to prove not only that Mehrban framed 'Ali Mohammed for the murder of the police officer but that years before he had raped his previous gatekeeper's wife, Zaytoun. Her husband committed suicide, and she went mad, but she also bore Mehrban's illegitimate daughter, who his sister, Saira Begum, adopted to avoid scandal. The only heinous crime in the drama of which he is not guilty, in fact, is the murder of Saira Begum's fiancé. After she finally accuses her brother of having ordered this murder, he produces the fiancé, who is now married with children and working as a manager in Mehrban Industries. Mehrban had bribed him, it seems, to disappear from Saira Begum's life. But the heroic, highly "educated" investigative team of journalist Sanya 'Ali, police officer Tariq Hussain, and lawyer Nabil Khalid manage to prove that Mehrban is responsible for every other iniquity in the story. In the final episode Mehrban is exposed and ruined; in the end he flees the country for an undisclosed location in Latin America. Sanya and Tariq remain in Pakistan, morally triumphant and in love.

The character of Malik Mehrban encapsulates most of what Pakistanis tend to argue is wrong with their politicians. He is violent, corrupt, and "uneducated," as well as hypocritical in that he pretends to religious piety, strewing his conversation with Qur'anic phrases while behaving in a brazenly immoral manner. Interestingly, his character seems to belong both to the urban middle classes and to the rural elite. His roots are in the Old City of Lahore, and although he describes himself repeatedly as a businessman who does not come from an old "feudal" political family and must therefore use his money to get ahead, he is also a rural landowner with all the trappings of "feudal" power: land, a big house, police connections, and gunmen who terrorize the local population on his behalf.

The rape that ultimately destroys Mehrban happens in a village outside Lahore. From an urban modernist point of view, rape is often projected onto the "feudal" countryside, where it stands as a metaphor of all that is bad and backward about traditional rural society.[22] Malik Mehrban is thus not simply an alter ego of the urban industrialist politician Nawaz Sharif. He represents the corruption of the imagined "feudal" tradition as well as the "uneducated" pretensions of the urban middle class. And because Mehrban is "uneducated," that is, morally subordinate, it is logical that the plot denies him agency by placing his political career under the control of shadowy figures said to rule Pakistan from behind the scenes.

MUHASIRA: TWO NATIONS ON TV

The normative oppositions that structure class relations in contemporary Lahore are reproduced at a higher level of social segmentation, that of the Pakistani nation-state. The defining principle of Pakistani nationalism is that South Asian Muslims and Hindus cannot peacefully share a single state. Since Partition this "two nation" theory has been focused through the lens of Indian (in Pakistani rhetoric, "Indian Occupied") Kashmir, where separatist Muslim militants have been fighting a guerrilla war against the Indian government with moral and, perhaps, financial and military support from neighboring Pakistan since 1990. In Pakistan the Kashmir revolt is conceived in religious terms, as an Islamic struggle (jihad). The militants are invariably referred to as *mujahidin* (the agent form of jihad) in Urdu and "freedom fighters" in English, whereas the Indian soldiers are often characterized by epithets that deny them rationality and even humanity. This headline from the Urdu press is not atypical of Pakistani discourse on Kashmir: "Kashmiri mujahidin exploded a bomb in an Indian army camp. In the clashes eleven savage beasts [*darandai*, i.e., Indian soldiers] went to the valley of death." As with the Lahori rhetoric of "education," this rhetorical contrast between Muslim mujahidin and their subhuman, non-Muslim Indian opponents subordinates the latter to the former in the very terms of its discourse. The two nations are not merely opposed to one another: they are also ranked.

In spring 1994 I played the role of an intrepid foreign correspondent in a PTV docudrama about the Islamic nationalist resistance movement in Indian-controlled Kashmir. Called *Muhasira* (Siege), the story was based on the monthlong Indian army siege of the Hazrat Baal Mosque in Srinigar during autumn 1993. The mosque scenes were shot near Mirpur in Pakistan-controlled Kashmir, referred to in Pakistan as "Free [*azad*] Kashmir." Mirpur is full of people who once worked in Britain. Lloyd's Bank has a branch there to handle the remittances that have brought prosperity to the area, many of whose inhabitants speak fluent English in the accents of Bradford and Manchester.

Hazrat Baal (The Holy Hair), so called because it houses a hair from the beard of the Prophet Mohammed, is the most sacred and politically the most important mosque in Kashmir. The Indian administration sealed off access to and from the mosque on October 15, claiming militants inside were planning to steal the sacred hair and then blame the theft on the Indian government. Forty to fifty militants and 170-odd civilians were trapped inside. The government argued that the siege was necessary in order to preserve civil order, given that in 1963 Kashmir was swept by riots after the hair mysteriously disappeared from the shrine for a week.

Despite its documentary patina, *Siege* took several liberties with the historical record. The besieged were not in fact denied food and medical attention.[23] Nor, so far as we know, did an Indian "Black Cat" commando break into the shrine to steal the sacred relic, only to be so overcome by its sanctity that he placed his mask and gun on the reliquary and left quietly after saying a prayer and pulling at his ears in a token of repentance. And the standoff was resolved peacefully, not with a daring night rescue by a squad of heroic Islamic militants.

Siege was the direct result of a PTV policy to publicize Kashmir in a manner favorable to the official Pakistani point of view, which is of course that as the Kashmir valley is a Muslim majority area it should have gone to Pakistan at Partition. According to the minutes of a PTV General Manager's Conference held in May 1994:

Efforts should be made to project Pakistan's stand and support to Kashmiris effectively in various programming formats including plays, music, *mushaira* [poetry readings], interviews, short documentaries etc. . . . PTV being a Corporation within the structure of the government should look after the interest of the government and government orders be carried out . . . ; the burning issue of Kashmir in the present situation should intelligently be handled and subtle approach adopted for effective projection [*sic*].

Finding this document, incidentally, was one of the minor epiphanies of my fieldwork. Toward the end of the filming we shot a press conference scene in PTV's Lahore studio. The director noticed that none of the journalist characters had paper in front of them, so for the sake of verisimilitude he had one of his assistants distribute some. The minutes landed at my place.

I was an ethnographer playing the part of a Western journalist in a Pakistani propaganda effort filmed on disputed territory. This was disorienting, the more so in that the director and many of the cast members were Kashmiri, hence connected to the story line in a rather immediate sense. One Mirpuri extra recited anti-Indian Urdu verses of his own composition whenever he was off camera. He wore a yellow polo shirt with, as I thought, a hairbrush and the words "Brush India" embroidered over his left breast. Climbing into the crew van to leave Mirpur, I saw that the hairbrush logo was in fact a dagger over the words "Crush India." The double image lingers, somehow, as a metaphor of ethnography in a world of nation-states.

We might compare the mirror effect by which the two nation theory constructs Pakistan in opposition to India to the mimesis through which the ethnographic present tense transforms social facts into sociology (see Fabian 1983; Sperber 1985). In both cases history collapses into a simplified, putatively timeless set of ideal social relations presented as "reality" or "truth." According to the empiricist conventions of social anthropology, ethnographers find a timeless logic "on the ground" rather than fit social facts into a logical framework supplied from outside. Yet, by definition, arguments include (or construct) certain facts while excluding others, like a realist painter who selects details from three-dimensional space in order to construct a mimetic illusion on two-dimensional canvas. Ethnographic realism constructs narrative patterns out of the noisy flux of life "on the ground" by a similar process of simplification and exclusion.[24] In Pakistan, meanwhile, the descriptive apparatus of official nationalist discourse constitutes Pakistan and India as polar opposites. Because nonpolarizing social facts (linguistic overlap, religious syncretism) are left out of the argument, the radical distinction between Hindus and Muslims acquires a certain naturalism: the proposition "we are that which they are not" appears to be true because the structure of the argument excludes contradictory evidence.

CONCLUSION

Lahori constructions of modernity deploy multiple moral perspectives whose ethnographic particularity lies in a complex series of relationships among hierarchy, agency, and nostalgia. The rhetorically constructed foreground of Lahore Society evokes the novels of Henry James or Edith Wharton in its elaboration of rank and precedence, tension of inherited versus achieved status, and elegiac stance toward social change.[25] Given all this, it was at first difficult to understand Society's contention that hierarchy is a thing of the past. Yet class relations in the city are rather fluid, an argument in (and about) progress rather than a fixed set of sociological categories an empiricist could measure on some tangible "ground." Expressions of the idea that society used, somehow, to make more sense are not confined to the drawing rooms of the upper classes.

Nor is class the only issue. Lahore is permeated by nostalgia for an imagined society preserved out of time. History textbooks evoke a precolonial golden age of Muslim rule on the subcontinent. In political discussions people commonly date Pakistan's own "decline" almost from its foundation, arguing that the country's volatile history of intermittent military dictatorship and secessionist violence would have been different had Mohammed 'Ali Jinnah not died shortly after Partition. The sermons of Sunni and, to an extent, Shi'a Muslim preachers in the city, attended mostly by middle- and working-class men, are also colored with nostalgia for an imagined past, in this case the idealized seventh-century Medinese community of the Prophet and his first four, "rightly guided" successors in the Caliphate.[26] At the nationalist level media rhetoric subordinates Hindus to Muslims by describing Indian soldiers in Kashmir as "irrational brutes." In Lahore the tendency to attribute social problems such as sectarian violence to "lack of education" while dismissing subordinates and rivals as "uneducated" are equally examples of a rhetoric that justifies a given relationship of subordination (state/nation, rich/poor, Society/nouveau riche) by linking subordination itself to the absence of historical agency. Given that moral behavior as such is predicated on an agent's ability to discriminate between good and bad actions, it is paradoxical that this imputed absence is used to subordinate people on moral grounds. The paradox is managed in that the distinctions are made in a context of moral rhetoric rather than moral philosophy. The rhetoric is used to rationalize, rather than guide, positions of social and political exclusion.

In modernist, Islamist, and nationalist contexts, the rhetoric of urban Pakistani social distinction tends to construct outworlds according to a rational/irrational, "educated"/"uneducated" binarism rooted equally in the European Enlightenment and in the Qur'anic doctrine that the advent of Islam constituted moral and intellectual progress in relation to the pre-

Islamic "age of ignorance" (*jahiliya*).[27] As in Descartes, Thomas Jefferson, and the Qur'an, these Pakistani category distinctions rest on the originally Greek assumption that man is a rational animal. Just as nineteenth-century British administrators justified their rule on the grounds that they had come to civilize a "backward" subcontinent,[28] modern urban Pakistanis justify the moral subordination of Indians, religious minorities, rural people, poor people, and nouveau riche industrialists by figuring them as irrational, hence less than fully human beings.

Yet there is no single point within contemporary urban society from which to represent reality as a coherent whole. My analysis stresses a multiplicity of moral perspectives because Lahoris constantly express this multiplicity in their everyday social and political rhetoric. Uncertainty and moral ambiguity are fundamental to the rhetorical strategies through which Lahoris construct and act upon the world. Ambiguity is only partially resolved by the sleight of mind through which different views do not clash because they are expressed in different social contexts.[29] It remains the case that urban Pakistanis in all walks of life, on television, in drawing rooms, and on the street, are constantly expressing the belief that society no longer adds up. Sleight of mind, in other words, can only partially resolve the moral contradictions that result from multiple perspectives on modernity in Lahore and, perhaps, complex urban societies elsewhere in the world today.

NOTES

Fieldwork for the dissertation on which this chapter is based was carried out in Pakistan between 1992 and 1994. My work was supported by a Fulbright Scholarship, a Social Science Research Council Dissertation Fellowship, and a Senior Scholarship from Wadham College, Oxford.

1. These include the Pakistani nation (*qaum*), defined as a Muslim community in contrast to Hindu-dominated India, and the Punjabi-speaking qaum, as a linguistic community opposed to the Sindhi, Baluch, and Pushtu speakers of Pakistan's other three provinces. Lahore itself is a highly self-conscious urban community, defined in contrast to the village culture of rural Punjab and as the cultural and political heart of Pakistan (see Aijazuddin 1991, 9–14; Weiss 1992, 1–6). Within Lahore there is a basic spatial and ideological contrast between the "traditional," working-class Old City and the "modern" city that has grown up around it since the beginning of the colonial era. In turn, this contrast subsumes a wide, overlapping range of sociologically and spatially local identities, including the state bureaucracy, urban representatives of the landowning political aristocracy, sects within Islam as well as religious minorities, the emerging business elite, and several occupational groups. In the situational foregrounding of particular identities, Lahoris use distinct styles of behavior and language to distinguish themselves from others and to get what they want, be it a marriage, a promotion, an election victory, or an industrial permit.

2. I borrow the term "family resemblance" from Wittgenstein's (1989, 31–32)

discussion of games. The contrast between Lahori and anthropological reflexivity is inspired by Michael Herzfeld's ([1987] 1992) Cretan ethnography. Stressing that anthropology is as much a historically generated system of meanings as the societies it studies, Herzfeld's argument opens space for a critical reappraisal of the complex, mutually determining relationships between anthropological theory and ethnographic practice.

3. See Ahmad 1992a for an illuminating Marxist critique of poststructuralist writing on class and nationalism.

4. Lahori Muslim preachers routinely denounce caste and other modes of social inequality. Preaching at the great Badshahi Mosque near the Old City, for example, the Sunni preacher (*khatib*) Maulana Azad said: "In his time, Hazrat Usman Ghani [third caliph of Islam] stressed that there should be Islamic equality [*Islami musawat*] between all Muslims. There should be no distinction between high and low" (recorded June 3, 1994). Implicit in such formulas are contrasts between Muslims and non-Muslims and, within the Muslim community, between ideal equality and practical inequality. Nonetheless, orthodox Islamic discourse stresses that all Muslims are equal in the sight of God.

5. As another Punjabi saying puts it: "He who hasn't seen Lahore is yet unborn" (*Jinai Lahore na'i vekhiya oo jaamiya i na'i*). Or, most explicitly: "There is no comparison with Lahore" (*Na'i raisan shehr Lahore diyan*).

6. That is, what remains of it in the wake of riots following the December 1992 destruction of the Babri Mosque in India, when Hindu, Sikh, and Jain temples were attacked throughout Lahore and the rest of Pakistan.

7. One urban population who seemed to view their lives in at least marginally optimistic terms were migrants from elsewhere in Punjab and Pakistan. In a 1981 study of one lower-income squatter community living in a central Lahore slum area (*kachi abadi*), for example, 74.67 percent felt that their lives had improved as a result of moving to Lahore (Qureishi 1981, 25).

8. According to UNDP's 1995 Human Development Report, in 1990, 20 percent of Pakistan's urban population lived in "poverty," defined as "the income or expenditure level below which a minimum, nutritionally adequate diet plus essential non-food requirements are not affordable." Between 1990 and 1993 the labor force was only 28 percent of the national population, fourth lowest among all developing countries. Between 1981 and 1992, meanwhile, the poorest 40 percent of the Pakistani population had an income share of 21.3 percent.

9. Reputedly the highest-paid performer in Pakistan during my fieldwork, Nusrat was much in demand at high-society weddings and musical evenings in Lahore. (He died in 1997.)

10. *Libas International* 8, no. 2 (1995).

11. Beyond relations of production and domination, "feudal" also denotes an attitude, a particular way of being in the world. In Lahore Society the phrase "X is a real feudal" often prefaces anecdotes of X beating his wife and/or servants, selling land to finance his lifestyle, or arranging for the public humiliation of a rival's household women. Not unlike the apocryphal "droit du seigneur" in Norman feudalism, the popular Pakistani image of the "feudal" humiliating men with whom he is in conflict by violating the modesty of their family women is an informal metaphor of domination, whose empirical instances have no legal basis and are not

restricted to the landowning notability. Cases such as the following appear frequently in the Pakistani press, and have been documented for all levels of society: "In a morbid show of power, six armed men stripped naked two women and forced them to dance naked in the streets at Jhugian Khudayar, Shahdara [Lahore]. The accused, led by a local tough, Khadim Hussain, indulged in this sadistic activity to avenge [*sic*] victims' brother-in-law, Amjad, when he stopped Khadim from eveteasing [harassing women] in the area" (*The News*, August 24, 1993, p. 3).

12. *Jagir*: "fief"—in other words, Tiwana was granted the rental and/or crop income from a village or group of villages.

13. Sharif was sacked by then President Ghulam Ishaq Khan under the controversial Eighth Amendment to the Constitution of 1973, a legacy of the Zia dictatorship that gives the president broad powers to dissolve the National Assembly in cases where he has subjectively determined that the present government can no longer function in accordance with the Constitution. Since Zia's death in 1988, the Eighth Amendment has been invoked in the presidential dismissal of three consecutive elected governments, most recently that of former Prime Minister Benazir Bhutto in November 1996.

14. In traditional North Indian Muslim class nomenclature, the gentry were collectively referred to as *ashraf*, the plural form of *sharif* (see Cole 1988, 69–85). In modern Lahore the term "sharif" is more commonly associated with generic moral virtue than with genteel social status.

15. The venerable Lahori diplomat Sayyid Amjad Ali once told me that in his youth it was almost de rigueur for young Punjabi men of good family to form liaisons with Hira Mandi singers. He recounted a long story about a "feudal" friend of his named Javed, who was "attached to a very famous singer back in the thirties." Asked whether he had himself been attached to a famous singer, and if so which one, Sayyid Amjad paused, stared reflectively into space, and finally replied: "Let me tell you another story about my friend Javed."

16. Nawaz Sharif's party, the Pakistan Muslim League, regained control of the National Assembly after the general elections of January 1997. "Yellow Afternoon" refers to Sharif's famous, or notorious, Yellow Cab Scheme, a hugely expensive plan to stimulate private entrepreneurship by subsidizing the import and sale of taxis. Many non-taxi drivers simply took advantage of the government's generous Yellow Cab finance package to acquire cheap cars for their private use.

17. In May 1994 Nadeem directed me in the role of a foreign correspondent in his production of *Muhasira* (see below). As a result of our professional relationship I was able to obtain copies of the shooting scripts for *Yellow Afternoon*, as well as background information about the politics behind the production. Parenthetically, Nadeem was forced out of his job as a PTV producer after Nawaz Sharif returned to power in 1997.

18. For the exterior shots of Malik Mehrban's traditional, courtyarded mansion (*havaili*), Shahid Nadeem used my patron Mian Yusuf Salahuddin's havaili in Barud Khana Bazaar, the Old City neighborhood (*mohalla*) where I lived during fieldwork. Several other PTV programs with traditional urban accents were filmed in and around Mian Yusuf's havaili during this period.

19. Shahid Nadeem's wife and a leading theater director in her own right. During the Zia regime she and Nadeem started the Ajoka Theater Group, a progressive

company dedicated to social and political agitation through theater. Strict press censorship prevailed throughout Zia's dictatorship; as a result small guerrilla theater groups such as Ajoka became important channels for the expression of political dissent during the 1980s.

20. In a later episode, Sadiqi teaches Mehrban the proper way to address a political rally. He tells him to give the crowd a "V" for victory (*fateh ka nishaan*, "the sign of victory") which is the Mehrban campaign's political symbol. At his first big rally, however, Mehrban inverts his "V," turning it into the familiar British gesture of vulgar dismissal. Both "V" signs are of course British imports. While the vulgar "V" is not widely understood in Pakistan, it serves to make the point that Mehrban is hopelessly unsophisticated from an upper-class Anglophone point of view.

21. There was no comparable anti–Benazir Bhutto melodrama during the Sharif administration, although a press rumor did circulate, toward the end of 1992, about PTV's alleged plan to produce a "documentary" on Benazir's alleged extramarital sex life. It never appeared, but in the conspiratorial world of Pakistani politics there was no reason to think this was anything other than a consequence of Nawaz Sharif's ouster.

22. See note 11.

23. The Indian army wanted to starve the militants into submission but were overruled by the Kashmiri civil administration.

24. Considered as an interpretation of social reality, the two nation theory falls into the same category as this thesis and any other critical reading, be it historical, ethnographic, or literary. In this sense, Paul de Man's (1983, 109–11) contention that every literary insight implies a degree of blindness in other places applies both to Pakistani nationalism and to the general practice of ethnography.

25. This sort of analogy was not lost on Lahoris. The Hollywood adaptation of Wharton's *The Age of Innocence*, starring Winona Ryder and Jeremy Irons, enjoyed a vogue among the Anglophone upper classes when it came out on videocassette in Lahore. Several acquaintances from Lahore Society noted a resemblance between their own, rather rarified corner of the city and the late-nineteenth-century New York "Society" evoked in Wharton's novel.

26. Shi'a Lahoris (perhaps 15 percent of the urban population) have a different, but in its own way equally nostalgic, understanding of early Islamic history. It centers around the battle of Karbala (A.D. 680), when the Prophet Mohammed's grandson Hussein was killed, along with relatives and associates, by soldiers of the Umayyad dynasty, which triumphed over the Prophet's family (the *Ahl-e-beit*, or People of the House) in the succession struggles that followed the assassination of the fourth Caliph, 'Ali, who was also the Prophet's cousin and son-in-law. This "Karbala paradigm," to use Michael Fischer's phrase, marks the point, for the world Shi'a community, at which history began to go wrong (Fischer 1980, 7–11).

27. Given the anticolonial rhetoric of Pakistani nationalism, it is ironic that the Enlightenment half of this intellectual genealogy reached South Asia via the educational apparatus of the British colonial state. See Viswanathan 1989 for a full discussion of the relationship between British rule in India and the British colonial education system.

28. See Pandey 1990, 23–65, and Metcalf 1994 for good discussions of British colonial ideology in nineteenth-century India.

29. I borrow this phrase from Nancy Tapper's finely patterned discussion of marriage strategies among Durrani Pushtun tribesmen in northern Afghanistan during the 1970s. Tapper argues that ambiguity in Durrani marriage discourse is related to a more general "sleight of mind" in the local discourse of honor, which like many other Middle Eastern and Mediterranean "honor and shame" systems, employs precisely the same terms to assert equality and inequality. Only social context allows the two contrasting meanings to be distinguished, facilitating the use of honor as an "ideology of control" (Tapper 1981, 392).

TEN

"Beloved Istanbul"
Realism and the Transnational Imaginary in Turkish Popular Culture

Martin Stokes

When Mustafa Kemal Atatürk, the founder of the Turkish nation, died in 1938, his body was moved from Dolmabahçe, the last palace of the Ottomans in Istanbul, to a vast and austere mausoleum in Ankara, the capital he created in the center of the new republic. When President Turgut Özal died in Ankara in 1989, his body moved in the opposite direction, ending up, after a funeral service in Fatih (a stronghold of Islamist politics), to the Süleymaniye Mosque, which dominates the historic "old city." He was interred in a family plot, in close proximity to the mausoleum of another religiously minded populist liberal prime minister, Adnan Menderes, who was ousted and executed after a military coup in 1961. Thus "the uniform and unified Kemalist holy cosmos has yielded to a type of symbolic ambiguity," remarked Günter Seufert and Petra Weyland (1994, 85), and the focus of this ambiguity is Istanbul. This chapter is concerned with popular cultural images of what one might call, following Seufert and Weyland, an "ambiguous Istanbul": images that mediate the way its inhabitants perceive and act in a dramatically changing urban environment. This exercise raises a more general set of questions, of resonance outside Turkey. Is nationalist modernism in the Middle East a spent force, and if so, what is replacing it?

Modernity, following Max Weber's somewhat pessimistic diagnosis, has often been imagined as a total transformation, of one cloth, as it were, and a predominantly European and North American experience at that. Anthropologists have more recently begun to argue that this is a more complex and fragmented experience, that "modernities" should be spoken of in the plural and examined ethnographically, and that the preeminence of the European experience (and the subordinate relation of other modernities to it) should be questioned (note, e.g., Armbrust 1996; Faubion 1993; Miller 1994). Turkish modernity has, since 1923, been framed by the state's nation-building project, which, like others, has struggled to reconcile national with global imperatives. The production of a distinctly national social and cultural reality, rational, secular, functional, gendered, and ethnicized, has throughout been uneasily aware of its Other, rendered in Turkey in pathologized terms as Oriental, "Islamic," irrational, and transgressive. The production of a spatial imaginary of place and territory has also been crucial to the state project as many commentators have pointed out, a task of representation that (like all others) is never complete and easily undone.[1]

No place has had a more complex and crucial role in mediating the place of Turkey in the world than Istanbul, and this chapter is concerned with contemporary struggles over the representation of a "global Istanbul." If modernist republican aspirations were clearly focused on Atatürk's capital, Ankara, Istanbul was condemned as an unpromising site for national regeneration; the labyrinthine complexity of the streets, its "mixed" population and schizophrenic placelessness ("between" Europe and Asia) serving as a telling foil for the nation builders' vision of a modern society. The city, and what it looks like, has always been a crucial issue for Turkey's modernizing elites. The ordering principle is, indeed, insistently visual, constituting distinctly new kinds of urban views and viewers. The foregrounding of this kind of visualized functionality is one of the first principles of architectural modernism and modern urban planning, a technique that works particularly well when this functionality can be juxtaposed with "traditional" or "historical" quarters preserved precisely to this end. The importation of this kind of modernist planning into the Middle East, and the way it mediated an emerging colonial order toward the end of the nineteenth century, has been discussed persuasively by a number of authors (see Çelik 1986; Fuller 1996; Gilsenan 1982; Mitchell 1988; Wright 1991).

The point extends to the subsequent nationalism of the modern Turkish republic, whose dependence on the Western powers, as Çağlar Keyder and others have argued, only deepened after the war of independence (see, in particular, Keyder 1987). The secular elites who founded the republic established principles of realism, legibility, clarity, and function, principles that carried, and in some respects continue to carry, an extremely heavy moral and political load and that continue to mediate an unequal relationship with the Western powers. These principles were epitomized by the design of the new capital city and the state-promoted celebration of its Anatolian hinterland. In Ankara architecture and urban planning were explicitly designed to connect "Turkish" (that is, Hittite and Sumerian) prehistory to wider currents of European modernism and to efface the Islamic and Ottoman past. Istanbul thus came to stand for the reverse: Ottoman/pan-Islamic "civilization" as opposed to a national "culture" (to use the terminology of one of the republic's most influential political theorists, Ziya Gökalp), "the past" as opposed to "the modern," secrecy as opposed to clarity, hybridity as opposed to purity, complexity as opposed to simplicity, hierarchy as opposed to egalitarianism, "fantasy" as opposed to "reality," and so on.[2]

The parallel processes of structural adjustment and accelerated integration into a global economy that Özal initiated in Turkey have been accompanied by the conspicuous growth of Istanbul, a growth that is simultaneously demographic, political, economic, and cultural. As Kevin Robins and Asu Aksoy (1995) aptly point out, this is a fragmented and uneven process. Two distinct Istanbuls are emerging. One is the product of the business elites who have thrived in the liberal economic environment created by Özal. This Istanbul is one that is currently celebrating its "global" status as a center of commerce and culture for the new Central Asian and Balkan states and that is currently being marketed in ways that are designed to attract global flows in its direction.

The other Istanbul, in Robins and Aksoy's view, is the focus of a process of intense rural-urban migration that began nearly half a century ago. Migration has been actively encouraged by the state during particular periods of industrial development (some would argue that the policy continues through the more or less enforced movement of the Kurdish population away from the southeast to an environment in which they can be more effectively supervised and integrated into the national economy), but it remains an overwhelmingly popular movement. The present government continues to pursue the chimera of an Istanbul of limited demographic expansion, while migrants continue to pour into the city's squatter towns at an unprecedented rate.

It is the former Istanbul that constitutes the focus of an insistent new language of globalization, mobilized in particular around the 1996 Habitat conference and a number of events and exhibitions evoking Istanbul's "global" status. This discourse of globalization has been an important strategy in the legitimization of liberal and Islamist city managers; for the former, "opening up" Turkey to the wider global traffic in commodities, ideas, and opportunities, and for the latter evoking the Golden Age in which Turks dominated Europe and the Middle East. In practice the two strategies have converged, as Özal's liberalism was marked by an attempt to co-opt increasingly oppositional Islamist politics, and, in power, the main Islamist party, the Refah Partisi, successfully made common cause with the city's major business elites.

The city's liberal mayor in the 1980s, Bedrettin Dalan (of Özal's ANAP), and his Islamist successor in the mid-1990s, Recep Tayyib Erdoğan, pursued similar planning objectives in Istanbul, characteristically modern in their appeal to the city's visual order. Vast funds have been devoted to cleaning the Golden Horn, bulldozing inner-city *gecekondu* (squatter) development to create parks, rezoning unsightly heavy industry, illuminating the old city's mosques, and pointing up the city's picture-postcard skyline of domes and slender minarets, revealing the city—and hence the nation's—Islamic and Ottoman historical infrastructure. This visualization is a point of constant rhetorical appeal. A city council *Buletin* from these years (August 1995) contains a cartoon showing a young man looking across at the old city, the piled-up mosque domes and minarets vastly exaggerated. "Why should anybody need alcohol when we live surrounded by this mind-spinning beauty!" the caption exclaims. The message is absolutely clear, the young man is positioned in one of the popular locations from which one views the sun setting over the old city (probably Salancak, between Üsküdar and Harem). The flowers that surround him evoke the Ottoman poetic trope of the "rose garden of love"; in fact, a huge road, constructed in 1990 as a link in the new coastal-road project, has now destroyed this once-beautiful spot. What makes the view beautiful, at least from the point of view of the *Buletin*'s (anonymous) cartoonist, is the Ottoman/Islamic profile of the city, the manifestation of a political heritage of which Refah claim to be the true guardians. While the cartoon overtly accompanied their ongoing antialcohol campaign, the picture's meanings operate more generally against the background of Refah's pursuit of a simultaneously modern and Islamic Istanbul. "Historical," business, residential, and industrial areas are neatly and rationally zoned by the planners, and the process is pleasurably confirmed by the viewing subject in the cartoon.

Away from the fantasies of those who have the power to mobilize their visions in stone, cement, and legislation, Istanbul has become the focus of less solid but no less significant imaginings. The popular cultural urban imaginary is complex. It is an imaginary that has roots, but also a more pressing and recent history, in the face of policies that have rendered everyday life in the city particularly difficult for many of its inhabitants. It is also an imaginary that operates against the background of the particularly intense involvement of the Turkish state in the production of exemplary forms of national culture. The complex nature of literary representations of Istanbul make sense when set against this.

The connections between models of literary realism and the narratives of nationalism have been elaborated by Benedict Anderson (1991) in a well-known analysis. "Realism" directed writers away from elite Ottoman codes to the vernacular (in the Turkish case, heavily constructed through an intense process of linguistic reform) and away from a subject matter generated from within and often about the city. The purpose of the republic's exemplary literature was the evocation of life in the "real" Turkey, that of the Anatolian countryside, portraying "something self-evidently there, recorded for the purposes of changing it" (Holbrook 1994, 24). The same principle extended beyond language and literature. "Ottoman" music was purged for analogous reasons and replaced, primarily through the agency of the radio, associated conservatories, professional cadres, and archival projects, by an invented folk culture that aspired to reflect the "real" life of the villages (see Markoff 1990; Stokes 1992a).

This realist imperative directed musicians and writers to the countryside, away from Istanbul; for those who resisted this imperative (for a variety of reasons), the city became the locus of a distinct and complex phantasmagoria, approached via dream, fantasy, reminiscence, and guilty and uncertain backward glances. In fact, the city has a long history of distinguished literary celebrants throughout the republican period, notably in the poetry of Yahya Kemal Bayatlı and Orhan Veli and the novels of Ahmet Hamdi Tanpınar. The literary evocation of a phantasmagoric Istanbul might be traced in the work of all of these writers, but it is in the more recent novels of Orhan Pamuk (to which I return) that one can detect an explicitly countermodern literary tradition, dark, melancholy, convoluted, which tacitly interrogates the canon of Anatolian-oriented literary realist texts constructed and promoted by the nationalist intelligentsia.

Popular music provides more overtly dissident expressions of this kind of countermodernity. The genre known as arabesk, connected in the 1970s and 1980s to the local film industry, and now to video clips promoted by the music industry on the new satellite channels, constitutes a different yet equally explicit fantasy of the city. For the ruralites in the big city who constitute the stereotypical heroes and heroines of the genre, Istanbul is an object of attraction and fear; indeed, fate itself. In *Ayrılamam* (I Will Not Separate; 1987) the singer Emrah (playing himself, as always) and his widowed mother are seduced by their wicked uncle into leaving their village with the clinching words "Başka Istanbul yok!" (There's only one Istanbul!). In Istanbul they meet their paradigmatic end, manipulation, humiliation, violence, and finally solitude and death. Istanbul itself becomes a remote object of desire, an analogue of those "modern" women who manipulate and humiliate the male protagonist in so many arabesk dramas, while embodying their deepest hopes and desires (Stokes 1992a, 138–42).

The popular repertoire is full of songs that express this ambiguous attitude. Taner Şener famously "hated Istanbul" ("Istanbul'u Hiç Sevmiyorum") in the 1960s; this sentiment was echoed three decades later in Burhan Çaçan's immensely popular hit, "Istanbul'a Niçin Geldim" (Why Did I Come to Istanbul?; 1995), and Yılmaz Morgül's "Elveda Istanbul" (Farewell Istanbul) a year later. A distinct register of fatalism and pessimism focusing on the city thus marks this musical repertoire, a fact that has led to its persistent condemnation by nationalist intellectual elites and cultural legislators (Stokes 1992b).

Opposing an "official" nationalist modernity with an "unofficial" popular countermodernity runs the risk of dichotomizing and simplifying a complex situation, and of endorsing some of the less productive binarisms of nationalist modernizers ("traditional" vs. "modern," "Ottoman" vs. "Republican" Turkey, "rationality" vs. "irrationality"). It is, in fact, the links and interdependencies between the two forms of modernist cultural production that are striking; the complex forms of dialogue that are set up between them provide grounds for evaluating the continued significance of the nationalist project in Turkey today. Two recent popular texts, Orhan Pamuk's *Kara Kitab* (The Black Book) and Bülent Ersoy's recording of "Aziz Istanbul" (Beloved Istanbul), that are crucially concerned with the ways in which Istanbul might be "seen" provide my point of departure.

KARA KITAB

Kara Kitab concerns the necessity of memory and the problematic search for identity among people who are obsessed with imitating others. As an allegory of the failure of the entire state project in Turkey, the book could hardly be more explicit. One character, a lawyer named Galip (victor), searches for his missing wife, Rüya (dream), who has disappeared with her half brother, an evasive journalist named Celal (divine wrath) who is also Galip's cousin. The parallels between Galip's quest and the spiritual quest for the beloved are revealed both to the reader and to Galip himself, with constant references to Jalal al-Din Rumi's *Masnavi*, Attar's *Conference of the Birds*, Sheikh Galip's *Beauty and Love*, and the doctrine of Hurufism (the mystical interpretation of the letters of the alphabet). Indeed, the sense of following in others' footsteps, being trapped in other people's stories, without at the same time being able to transcend them, lies very much at the heart of Galip's "nightmare," a nightmare that ends in disaster.

The characters in the book are obsessed with time in quite different ways. The protagonist, Galip, lives in the past. His missing wife, we learn, is only happy when immersed in the future-directed telos of detective stories (this book is also a detective story in reverse, with the death coming at the end). The evasive journalist has a particular fascination with places and spaces that have been forgotten but is losing his memory and takes medicine that he believes will remedy the problem. The book's plot hinges on missed or chanced-on telephone calls and coincidental meetings; the failure of people to intervene in the passing of time and shape their own destinies is stressed throughout (the parallels with arabesk films should be noted). Rüya reads detective novels apparently as a means of evading other responsibilities. The journalist, whose articles dwell on forgotten, murky corners of the city in a veiled apocalyptic idiom, sends concealed messages to former lovers and political accomplices through his daily column, and they in turn act in ways he is unable to control. The best Galip can do is ponder the past, but of the three, he, a melancholy and solitary wanderer (not dissimilar to the *gariban* protagonist of the arabesk film), emerges "victorious" precisely as a consequence of his intervention in and identification with the past.

This engagement with the past is a constant preoccupation in Orhan Pamuk's fiction, and it marks the clearest possible difference between his novels and the forms of realism promoted by nationalist intelligentsia. The paradigmatic idiom of expression of the republic's novelists was everyday speech; a style of writing known as *devrik cümle* (lit., inverted sentence)[3] was specifically designed to reflect this. Brevity was a key feature of this modernistic realism, also partly a result of the expense of printing books, which meant that most writers' work was serialized in newspapers or printed as short stories. By contrast, Pamuk's novels (themselves on the lengthy side) are full of speakers who reminisce at excessive length. Galip recognizes his own capacity to bore, and Celal's prose is described by a bitter critic of his in the book as "unrealistic and imitative" and his work as "nonpolitical nonsense concerning his own private obsessions which he penned in an outmoded manner and a prose style that was unreadable and much too long" (1996, 395). Pamuk's ironic and self-referential voice should be recognized here: these criticisms are sometimes directed at the writer himself, and even fans speak of the fact that the prose is "cold," "distanciating" (*mesefali*), and sometimes simply "difficult." But these are also the techniques by which he critically comments on the norms of realism fostered in the republic, which Pamuk implies have been precisely responsible for the nation losing its literary memory.

Pamuk's dense and somewhat convoluted prose style, now generating a secondary literature of explanatory textbooks, is a metaphor for the city itself, which might perhaps be considered the key figure in the book. This fact is undoubtedly one of the key causes of the novelist's immense popularity. He writes about an Istanbul that people can actually recognize— cold, wet, impossibly huge, easy to lose one's way in, and of constantly surprising three-dimensionality. Pamuk's city is impossible to "see," in a variety of ways, but at the same time (as if to emphasize this visually conceived powerlessness), it is a city in which it is very easy to be observed. A column by Celal in the book elaborates a "metaphysical experiment" in which he observes himself being observed by a large eye while he is wandering around the streets on a dark night. For Celal this is an externalization of his own habit of self-surveillance, but the image haunts Galip, who is tormented by the idea that he is being watched and followed. The resonance of this for readers in Turkey in their thirties today, who experienced the military coup of 1980 and its aftermath as high school or university students, should not be forgotten.

The three-dimensionality of this city is for Pamuk a telling metaphor of Turkey's unseen and unwanted past. Two of the most celebrated passages in the novel describe buried history. In the first, Pamuk imagines the water draining out of the Bosphorus, and the life that would emerge among two millennia of junk, thrown away in order to be forgotten or concealed. The second describes the maker of mannequins around the turn of the century who begins to perceive that Turks on the street are losing their gestures, looks, and bodily movements, their "innocence" destroyed by imported Western films. His workshop turns into a museum of gestures and movements that are disappearing from the streets. As this obsessive task of documentation continues, he is obliged to dig deeper and deeper under the streets of Beyoğlu to make space for his growing collection, which finally becomes a parallel labyrinthine underground city. This burying of the past is part of the city's "incomprehensible" nature; the past has to be excavated with an act of the imagination, and the present can only be redeemed through this kind of excavation. This not only requires imagination but a rejection of a certain notion of "reality"—on the surface, there for everybody to see (like Ankara). The novel problematizes the act of seeing in the city. It is in precisely this way that Pamuk invites his readers to engage critically with the state's tradition of realism.

"BELOVED ISTANBUL"

Bülent Ersoy's "Aziz Istanbul" involves a similarly reflexive view of the city. The song raises the question of imitation in a more bluntly provocative way. For Pamuk, imitation is simultaneously a means of damnation and salvation. In the quest for selfhood (or, one might say, viable cultural identity), one cannot avoid imitating, but the process requires imagination. For Pamuk, the act of imaginative imitation, of being somebody else, actually denies repetition and closure; to look back at the past is not necessarily to repeat the past's mistakes (as Turkey's republican ideologues have been asserting since the 1930s)—it is, in fact, the only way forward.[4]

"Aziz Istanbul" is a rerecording of a song whose text was written by Yahya Kemal Bayatlı (one of the foremost republican poets of the city), and whose music was composed and recorded for HMV by Münir Nureddin Selçuk in the late 1940s. Selçuk stood somewhat apart from the state's musical reforms, being associated with the urban art-music genre, which was, in comparison to Ottoman literature, rather halfheartedly and unsystematically opposed (see Stokes 1992a). Selçuk was, however, a reformist, a popular exponent of the view that the urban genre should not be condemned but modernized, a process that would allow the music to engage with the wider currents of the "modern" and simultaneously (this being the ideological sleight of hand of Turkish, and indeed many other nationalisms) reveal its essential Turkishness.[5] He was, according to his Turkish celebrants (see, in particular, Kulin 1996), the man who put Turkish music in Western dress ("Türk musikisine frak giydiren adam"). The allusions to Atatürk are really quite explicit: the founder of the republic, quite literally, put Turks into Western dress. The promotional photographs of the singer show him striking a dandified, Westernized stance; smartly dressed in a variety of suits and hats, often looking at some point above and beyond the photographer, as in many of the more famous portraits of Atatürk that are to be found in offices and cafés all over the country.

Selçuk was a member of a family whose position in the bureaucratic establishment straddled the Ottoman and early republican period. His father was a high-ranking religious official; he himself learned his art at the foremost musical institutions in Istanbul and went to France to further his musical studies in 1926. He worked extensively with the emerging Turkish film industry, making a name for himself singing some of the first imitations of the Egyptian musicals that were so quickly banned by the new republic. His recordings were the best-selling hits of the day. He was the first Turkish musical "star" in other senses. Most conspicuously, it was he who initiated the practice of standing apart from the seated musicians. Formerly the singer (a mere *hanende*, seated alongside the instrumental *sazende*) was part of an ensemble; Selçuk was thus directly responsible for introducing a "modern" and hierarchical division of labor into Turkish musical practice. A statue in Kadiköy commemorates his passing.

Bülent Ersoy is the direct descendant of this kind of musical stardom—fabulous, remote, and spectacular. She too was the recipient of an elite form of musical education. Her trip to Europe, however, had a very different motivation: she underwent surgery for a sex-change operation in London in 1981. Her exile in Germany was at least partially the result of an intense debate in Turkey over whether a transsexual was in fact a man or a woman (an argument that has only relatively recently been resolved in favor of transsexuals). If Bülent's identity card stated that Bülent was a man, there was no problem, but if her card was to be changed to reflect her new identity (as she wished), then she had to get a special police permit to perform live; this was never granted, on moral grounds. The sexual politics of Bülent's music have a longer pedigree. Her very distinctive vocal style is explicitly modeled not on the avuncular Münir Nureddin Selçuk but on her teacher Müzeyyen Senar, a well-known lesbian. The lofty and somewhat remote gaze of Selçuk is thus opposed, in Bülent's version of his song, by a different kind of glance (quite literally encapsulated in the pictures of the singer on her cassette covers); campily ambiguous, engaging and questioning, and invariably directed at the camera/viewer.

It is not just sexual politics but a matter of style, and more particularly an attitude to the sung word itself that distinguish the two singers. Whereas Selçuk's voice has always been famous for its light clarity of texture, Senar's passionate and dramatic voice, for Turkish listeners, lacks precisely this quality. The musical style favored by nationalist ideologues was to be as clear and legible as it was realistic. Still today singers connected with Turkish Radio and Television (TRT) criticize others for their lack of *diksiyon*, which might simply be glossed as "clear communication." Although Selçuk had no connection with the resuscitated rural style that was shaped by nationalist ideologues in the 1940s, his work exemplifies a concern with legibility. Each word can be heard clearly. The same cannot be said for arabesk singers. TRT musicians interpret this both as an intellectual failure and as a lack of proper schooling, and, indeed, the two are connected in their minds. Why should anybody bother to sing things clearly when the words are practically meaningless anyway?

Bülent Ersoy's music is often identified by singers connected with the world of cultural officialdom as the logical conclusion of this art of vocal obscurity. Their point is put in classic modernist terms: too much passion and not enough technique. These are of course quite explicit, aimed-for vocal techniques on the part of such paradigmatic arabesk singers as Bülent Ersoy (whose singing is a vocal drama in which words are played with and deliberately distorted), Ibrahim Tatlıses (who sings at such a high pitch that words are very difficult to pick out simply for physiological reasons), and Müslüm Gürses (who mumbles).[6] The text of Yahya Kemal's poetry in Bülent's "Aziz Istanbul" is thus particularly hard to follow. The piece is sung, if anything, a little slower than the original, meaning that the words are more drawn out and more easily interspersed with sighs and gasps that disrupt and even conceal the text. As I have often discovered, while trying to identify a lyric heard as background music, people who have not made a particular effort to learn or listen to the words (and word books can be purchased to this end) have great difficulty in hearing what Bülent, and indeed many other popular singers, are actually "saying." Bülent's distanciating and convoluted vocal art might therefore be usefully compared to Pamuk's prose style.

Much of what is alluded to, hinted at, or actually obscured by the voice revolves in musical performance around the opening poetically conventional "ah," with which Yahya Kemal's poem begins, and which Münir Nureddin Selçuk and Bülent Ersoy elaborate in quite different musical ways.[7] Yahya Kemal's poem has the poet looking out over the city, "I looked down on you yesterday from a hilltop beloved Istanbul / I could not see one place that I had not strolled through, did not love / Create happiness in my heart as long as I live / Even the love of one of your neighborhoods is worth an entire life."[8] Münir Nureddin Selçuk takes the stereotypical sigh and cleverly turns it into a representational reference to the hill from which the poet is looking out at the city, Çamlıca.

Çamlıca has a very distinct place in Turkish popular culture. It is not only the space and the relatively fresh air that have made this a popular excursion since it was opened as a municipal park in 1867 but the view. One cannot only look across the city and see its edges, but one can also look down on it. This, as Donatella Mazzoleni (1993, 297) suggests, is a rare privilege in the modern city. In particular, the viewer experiences the sound of the call to prayer coming from below, rather than from minarets towering above. The opening "ah" traces the sound of the call to prayer in the faintest outline; the singer is echoed by a ghostly female chorus. The view of Istanbul, and the distant sound of the mosques, establishes the viewer as a sovereign modern. He (the viewer is unambiguously gendered) looks down on a glorious Islamic/Ottoman past that has been built on and transcended, the mosques that represent it quietly evoking the old rhythms precisely to signify their transcendence by the new (see Augé 1995, 75).

In other ways too the viewpoint constructed by Yahya Kemal's words and Selçuk's vocal performance is the product of a decisively modern experience. The popular practice of excursions and enjoying a view in itself is modern. Çamlıca has been the focus of an emerging culture of excursions and pleasure trips that can be dated with some precision to the beginning of the Tanzimat reform process, which involved, among other things, the increased interest in the appearance of the urban fabric and the expansion of a planned transport system across and beyond the city (Belge 1983). In Yahya Kemal's poem this view also encodes a moral position. The relationship that the singer imagines with the city is a modern matrimonial relationship, clearly gendered and based on romantic, lifelong, individual attraction, the very image of the late Ottoman and early republican ideal of modern marriage (Duben and Behar 1991). As if to emphasize the modern marital order that the song evokes, the opening "ah" is clearly gendered in the vocal performance. The first time it is sung by Münir Nureddin Selçuk, and on repetition it is sung by a chorus of women: a neatly balanced sentimental hierarchy.

If there is a hint of ambiguity in Selçuk's recording, it springs from the simple fact that the beloved city in question is Istanbul and not Ankara. Things in the beloved city are not entirely under control. The beauties alluded to (keying the beautiful women associated with Istanbul's upmarket neighborhoods in this musical genre) are distant, remote. Once seen, they disappear.[9] What modern technologies of transport and surveillance provide, they also whisk away. The observer is left on his own, with nothing more than memories. Yahya Kemal's poem begins with reminiscence, "I looked down on you yesterday from a hilltop, beloved Istanbul." There is a wistful nostalgia to the song that is characteristic of many of the poetic and literary representations of the view of the city from Çamlıca (and Yahya Kemal's poetry in general) that springs precisely from the more general fact that, according to the dominant logic of Turkish modernity, no more than the most fleeting backward glance could be permitted in the resolute westward march.

If this might be interpreted as a sneaking nostalgic doubt in Münir Nureddin Selçuk's version, it fades into utter insignificance in comparison to Bülent Ersoy's. Bülent brings to the performance a dramatic play on gender and sexuality, which clearly undermines the gently "paired" (although hierarchically ordered) masculinity and femininity of Selçuk's performance. Bülent's voice is, for most Turkish listeners, one of passion and transgressive sexuality (*aşk*); it is the voice itself, not simply the words, that constitutes the "meaning" of the song. For those who know the original, the cool, legible balance of Selçuk's version is entirely subverted. This destabilization makes its most dramatic manifestation in the opening "ah." The gendered dual "ah" of Münir Nureddin Selçuk is replaced by a three-way split: Bülent's voice at its most breathily erotic; the simultaneous sound of a "real" muezzin reciting the call to prayer in the background; and finally a mixed chorus. The call to prayer was sung by Bülent herself. The performance of the *ezan* by a transsexual caused outrage among Islamists when the cassette was released, which Bülent had not apparently anticipated and seriously regretted. Indeed, Bülent has recently made great efforts to present a sober religious persona to the general public, through the (highly publicized) observation of Ramadan and so forth.

TEXTS ON THE STREET

The mild outrage generated by "Aziz Istanbul" contrasts markedly with the reception of Orhan Pamuk's high-concept novel. Linking the two, for those familiar with Turkish highbrow literature, may be considered a somewhat provocative move. There is, however, considerable justification for considering the book and the song together. For all of its experimentalism, its austere style, and the relative expense of the novel itself (costing around £7 [U.S.$10] in Turkey in 1996), Pamuk's *Kara Kitab* is a popular phenomenon in its own right, both drawing on and contributing to other mass-mediated popular narrative forms. Cartoonists such as Galip Tekin, Erder Özkahraman, Suat Gönülay, and Can Barslan in comic magazines such as *LeMan* have, over the last decade, produced long and rambling stories full of baroque violence inspired largely by American horror films and comics and set in a dark and decaying Istanbul. Conversely, the most widely screened film in Istanbul throughout 1996 was *Istanbul Kanatlarımın Altında* (Istanbul Beneath My Wings), a historical drama noted at the time mainly for its portrayal of a gay Murat IV, but which also drew heavily on a persistent theme in Pamuk's novels, the sultan/pasha in disguise.

It is not just the figures and tropes that one can find in Pamuk's book that locate it so firmly in "popular" practice; it is, literally, its place on the streets of the city. My first discussions with Turkish people who had visited the United Kingdom in the 1980s revealed their incredulity at what they considered to be the absurd habit of reading on buses and trains. Shortly after the publication of *Kara Kitab* in Turkey in 1990, however, the novel was to be seen in the hands of people on boats, on trains, and waiting at bus stops all over the city. The book is published by the main leftist/secularist publisher in Turkey, Iletişim, more generally known for its pioneering translations of contemporary European political and social theory. Following this unprecedented popular success, an advertisement for his next novel, *Yeni Hayat* (The New Life), which simply presented the opening sentence ("One day I read a book that changed my entire life"), appeared on billboards all over the city. The remarkable physical presence of the text itself on the streets of the city, and the simple but startling fact that a novel could be a mass-marketing phenomenon at all, marked a radical transformation of popular reading practices. This kind of secretive withdrawal from one's fellow travelers is perhaps otherwise seen only in the reading of newspapers on Turkish public transport, which tend to be shared if circumstances and time permit, or in the murmured recitation of Qur'anic verses, which are, although in a different sense, shared property as well. The book thus initiated, or coincided with, the conspicuous emergence of a distinct and culturally elaborated figure, the public-transport traveler immersed in a novel.[10] This fact alone gave it a place in popular consciousness, a rare literary feat in Turkey that has perhaps not been achieved since the serialized publication of Yaşar Kemal's *İnce Memed* (Memed, my Hawk) in Turkish newspapers in the 1960s.

An indication of this can be found in a cartoon by Bahadır Boysal that appeared on August 21, 1996, in the cartoon magazine *LeMan* (no. 245, p. 8)—that is to say, six years after the book was first published. In the cartoon, a young man finds himself in a train compartment with (one judges by the shape) a young woman covered in what would be recognized as the most extreme form of religious garb in Turkey, a black coverall similar to the Afghan *burqa* in which the eyes are covered by a cloth grille. They sit opposite one another. The woman takes a copy of Orhan Pamuk's novel out of her bag and begins to read it. The experimentalism of the novel, and its frequent and intellectually playful references to Muslim eschatology, means that this book could hardly be said to be a popular read in Islamist circles. The young man looks on in astonishment. Expecting, perhaps, an unlikely sexual adventure, he eventually strikes up a conversation and asks to look at the book. The woman turns the book around; the pages she is reading are pitch black (an explicit reference to the final chapter in Pamuk's novel). She then pulls off the hood of the burqa, revealing herself to be Death, and decapitates the boy with a swipe of his/her scythe.

The cartoon plays on the associations between an oppressive and puritanical religiosity and sex and violence that would readily be made by *LeMan*'s readership; in some senses the novel is perhaps little more than a pretext for the gory and flamboyant draftsmanship. It does, however, touch on a more general issue in relation to Pamuk's book. The cartoonist and editors assumed that the reference would need no explanation to the readers. They were also able to play on knowledge of the "modern" habit of reading on trains and the fact that *Kara Kitab* is indeed, as the publisher's blurb suggests, a book that draws complete strangers into conversation. Its circulation within a popular cultural economy relates not only the ideas and representations that are contained within the text, therefore, but its physical presence on the streets of Istanbul.

The arabesk singer Bülent Ersoy appears, on the face of it, to occupy a more obviously "popular" location. She produces a new cassette at least every year, which is promoted throughout the city with the formidable resources available to S-Müzik, Raks's elite arabesk division.[11] Like many arabesk singers, Bülent Ersoy is a curiously absent presence. She rarely appears on stage and very rarely gives interviews. In fact, the hostile attitude of the Turkish state toward arabesk throughout the 1970s and early 1980s meant that the singer lived a life of virtual exile in Germany, only returning to Turkey in 1989 by virtue of a kind of amnesty granted by Turgut Özal (it was no secret that his wife was a great fan). This "amnesty" was entirely consistent with Özal's liberal politics; it coincided with the return of a number of other cultural and political dissidents (notably the former leftist singer Cem Karaca), and it was undoubtedly a political coup for Özal's regime. As a calculated and considered gesture, this was not, however, simply a matter of populism. The urban musical repertoire in Turkey occupies a space that straddles the Western European distinction between "high" and "low" culture (Adorno and many post-Frankfurt cultural theorists have done much to absolutize this highly culture-specific notion). A great many singers of arabesk and Turkish popular music were trained in either the state-run conservatories or in the more prestigious private conservatories (notably at Eminönü, Üsküdar, and Kadıköy) that maintained the "Ottoman" urban genre during the years of republican reformism. Performance in the arabesk/light classical genre starts with serious items from the historical canon of the genre, in the more "difficult" modal structures (*makam*), and concludes with rural and urban popular songs in more familiar modal structures. Bülent Ersoy cannot therefore simply be described as a "popular singer."

Indeed, the two main mass-media representatives of the urban genre in recent years, Zeki Müren (who died in October 1996) and Bülent Ersoy, have impeccable musical pedigrees. Zeki Müren was born in Bursa but educated at the Boğazici lycée in Istanbul, took classes at the Istanbul Academy of Fine Arts, and studied with Refik Fersan and Şerif Içli. Bülent Ersoy took classes at the Kalamiş Musiki Cemiyeti and studied with Muzaffer Özpınar and Müzeyyen Senar. Both have produced recordings in an austere Turkish classical style but also, in Zeki Müren's case, reworkings of Egyptian film music and, in both cases, recordings of contemporary arabesk. These movements have often been strategic. Bülent Ersoy's *Konseri* (Concert) was released at a time when there was a great deal of speculation about the repeal of what was referred to, in 1987, as "the Bülent Ersoy ban" (*Bülent Ersoy yasağı*).[12] This recording consisted of a strict sequence of pieces in a particular makam (tailored for cassette release), including the opening instrumental *peşrev* introductions and instrumental *taksim* improvisations, all in a severe monophonic style. This was in stark contrast to arabesk recordings, which are in a variety of unconnected makam, have no (or few) instrumental numbers, and are accompanied by guitars, keyboards, and a variety of other Western instruments. This severely "classical" recording undoubtedly added weight to the claim that Bülent's exile was to the cultural detriment of the nation; for Bülent it was a timely piece of work.

At various points in her career, the singer has produced other recordings, popular in vocal style but austerely classical in content. "Aziz Istanbul," on a record entitled *Alaturka 1995,* is one example; its "Easternism" signaled by the title, it used a large and well-drilled orchestra somewhat reminiscent of the Turkish Radio and Television style and contained a self-consciously "classical" selection of songs from the late Tanzimat to the early republican period, including peşrevs, instrumental taksims, and a virtuoso demonstration of a style of vocal improvisation (*gazel*) that has been almost defunct in Turkey since the 1950s.[13] The cassette was conceived as a present to Bülent's teacher and mentor, Özpınar, a composer and *tanbur* (an extremely complex long-necked lute) player who had been trained under Mustafa Rona at the Eminönü conservatory. Özpınar's tastes are severely classical, in spite of the fact that he has penned some of Zeki Müren's and Bülent Ersoy's most enduring hits.[14] Bülent proposed recording the cassette by way of tribute to her teacher. Although it was not a huge commercial success in terms of the sales figures with which S-Müzik normally operate (it sold approximately half a million copies, as opposed to the two million the singer would normally expect to sell), it was nonetheless to be found on every cassette and CD stall in the city for at least a year after the release, and has, in spite of the row that accompanied its release, furthered the singer's claims to a more elevated status.

There are grounds, then, for considering the two texts together. Both are material objects circulating in a mass-mediated cultural economy, both are familiar landmarks in contemporary urban experience in Turkey (whether or not one could claim to have read or listened to either), both have a conspicuous material presence on the streets of the city, both have done something to blur the rather flexible Turkish distinctions between "high" and "low" culture, both take Istanbul as an object of reflection and contemplation, and both intervene in this environment in distinct and identifiable ways. Both, I would argue, are read in Turkey as a critical commentary on the legacy of modernist reformism.

These texts are, however, embedded in a wide range of discursive frameworks. For Bülent's mentor, Muzaffer Özpınar, the cassette was the product of a sense of duty: the musician must contribute to the cultural health of the nation as well as make money from it. For S-Müzik's manager, Sacit Suhabey, the cassette plugged into a pleasing market for nostalgia— pleasing because it did not take too much effort and finance to service, and the mild notoriety of the cassette was, in the end, good publicity. For some fans, Bülent's music is the passionate truth of the defiantly isolated individual; for others, it is a joke, high-camp humor. The out gay community is ambivalent: many feel that Bülent could do great things as a spokesperson for radical gay politics in Turkey and lament the fact that she is more concerned with maintaining some improbable model of bourgeois respectability.[15]

One of my music teachers, a former officer who had retired from the Turkish army on health grounds, apparently knew the singer quite well in (then) his youth. His response touches more closely on the issue with which this chapter is concerned, the way in which a problematic past is imagined in the context of a resolutely forward-looking nationalist modernism. My teacher, like many musicians, played the bars and clubs in Çamlıca, and even when he did not have an engagement he would join the crowds on the hill on weekends, strolling, sitting, and enjoying the view. The subject of Bülent sometimes came up in our discussions, but I was never sure when it would be brushed aside irritably or be the subject of fond reminiscence. When I brought up the subject of "Aziz Istanbul," he was brusque but inconclusive. I got the impression that he couldn't make up his mind whether to be outraged at the violation of a classic or pleased that it had been given a new lease on life. "She's a commercial artist. She can do what she wants," he said, evoking the idea of musicians as cultural prostitutes as opposed to responsible worthies committed (like him) to the aesthetic long haul, before abruptly changing the subject. This was a criticism that he, as a professional musician, knew was often, and increasingly, directed at people like himself, particularly in the Refah-dominated neighborhood in which he lived and worked.

In relation to my teacher's life, the question of Bülent and the view from Çamlıca were curiously related—a relationship that was almost coincidentally suggested to me by the fact that my teacher had started to play in a club on Çamlıca at precisely the time "Aziz Istanbul" had been released. The song, the place, and these two people (one the remote and fabulous star, the other my teacher of nearly ten years) thus came together for me as a consequence of my own movements about the city that summer. But it soon became clear to me that there was more to this connection than the idiosyncrasies of my own movements. Bülent was a distinct figure from my teacher's own past and the music club that he still attends. I gathered in a discussion with a group of his old friends that Bülent had been invited to sing at my teacher's son's circumcision party, some time before Bülent's disappearance to London. "We had some clues even then . . . ," my teacher once said, tailing off and laughing. Bülent's connection to his own past and the music he continued to play was one that, he was entirely aware, did not fit in with the decent, masculine duties and pleasures through which he understood himself. Bülent was then an acknowledgment of elements of his past that did not fit, that could not be easily explained, and whose relationship to the present, and his self, was anomalous.

Çamlıca is, in Pierre Nora's (1989) sense, a classic *lieu de mémoire*, a place of memories and reflection on the not always smooth passing of time. Çamlıca is, as "Aziz Istanbul" suggests, a place from which one is almost obliged to contemplate the presence of the past, the troubling failure of the state to contain it, and the equally troubling efforts of the state's new managers to turn this view to their own ends. The place of Çamlıca in Turkish popular and literary culture is so thoroughly related to memory that I would seldom make this trip with any Turkish friend without discussion turning to the question of the past, what would have happened if we had not met, who we had been when we had first met or first come up here, what we had become, and how things might have turned out differently. As a cultural trope, and a popular experience, one might say that Çamlıca is about troubled memory: memory of a past that does not lead smoothly to the present.

CONCLUSION

In a society in which the state of being modern is cast so insistently in terms of forgetting, and in which the modern is so organically connected to the institutions of the nation-state, remembering becomes both a problem and a matter of cultural elaboration. This is not because the state is incapable of making people forget but because the politics of forgetting paradoxically demands the preservation of a variety of things to demonstrate the necessity of their having been forgotten. When one of these objects in the repertoire of the "forgotten" is an entire city, and one that currently houses at least one-sixth of the nation's population, the city itself is likely to occupy a large and significant problem in the national imaginary—a problem that springs out of the experience of modern nationalism itself. This is why the questioning of this experience through the ways of looking at Istanbul discussed in this chapter should, in certain ways, and for all their apparent "postmodernism," draw heavily on cultural techniques established by nationalist modernists (i.e., novels and solo singers backed by large orchestras) in Turkey. Although transnational realities shape Turkish life with ever-increasing clarity, as indeed they have done since the establishment of the republic, Istanbul's cultural space is still shaped significantly by popular cultural forms, which look to the nation both as a source of inspiration and as the focus of critique.

NOTES

I would like to thank Ayfer Bartu, Asu Aksoy, Jay Dobis, Dane Kusic, Kevin Robins, Michael Gilsenan, and Anne Ellingsen for their comments on this chapter and support along the way. I availed myself of John Morgan O'Connell's generously provided expertise on Münir Nureddin Selçuk. A more general context for this chapter has been several years of musing on the subject of nationalism with Richard English at the Queen's University of Belfast. A version of this chapter was read at the American Anthropological Association meeting in Washington, D.C., in 1995; it benefited greatly from Walter Armbrust's and Lila Abu-Lughod's discussion of the panel as a whole. I am particularly grateful to the Department of Sociology, Boğaziçi University, for their hospitality in summer 1996. The problems that remain are mine and mine alone.

1. The spatially destabilizing effects of global capitalism have been repeatedly stressed by Anthony Giddens, Manuel Castells, and David Harvey (see, e.g., Giddens 1990; Castells 1996; Harvey 1989); anthropological implications are explored in Kearney 1995.

2. In the context of my own fieldwork, every one of these binary constructions appeared in a discussion with a friend working as a state-employed musician at the Ankara radio station (the TRT), evaluating the relative merits of TRT work in "the capital" and in Istanbul. The national folk music project was never going to work in Istanbul, he suggested, because of its distance from Anatolia and the distracting complexity of big-city life, tied to the dead and undemocratic weight of Islamic history, powerful minority populations, and big-business interests, forcing the expression of Anatolian "realities" to accommodate to the "fantasy" of Istanbul-based arabesk. Precisely these facts had turned Istanbul-based radio singers, his peers and rivals, into national media stars at the time; under these circumstances, the speaker was forced to put his case in rather extreme terms.

3. In fact, as Geoffrey Lewis (1967, 242) points out, the devrik cümle technique has a history that long predates the republican era. This is somewhat ironic given that it was, during the height of nationalist reformism, considered to be the height of literary modernism. The word *devrik* itself has revolutionary overtones, suggesting as well "overturned" or "overthrown."

4. Homi Bhabha's discussion of mimicry, in "Signs Taken for Wonders: Questions of Ambivalence and Authority under a Tree Outside Delhi, May 1817" (reprinted in Bhabha 1994), is highly relevant here, even though the "text" that is being repeated here is of a very different kind, in a situation in which masters and colonial servants are much less clearly delineated, if they are delineated at all.

5. The scholarly argument was articulated by Hüseyin Sadettin Arel. See Stokes 1996.

6. A discussion of the particularities of vocal drama and the dynamics of vocal "concealment" and "revelation" in relation to these three singers can be found in Stokes 1995–96.

7. For other examples relating to the music and poetry of the city, see Aksüt 1994.

8. (Ah) Sana dün bir tepeden baktım aziz Istanbul / Görmedim gezmediğim, sevmediğim hiç bir yer / Ömrüm oldukça gönül tahtıma keyfince kurul / Sade bir semtini sevmek bile bir ömre değer / Nice revnaklı şehirler görülür dünyada / Lakin efsunlu güzellikleri sensin yaratan / Yaşamışdır derim en hoş ve uzun rüyada/ Senda çok yıl yaşayan, sende ölen, sende yatan / Sana dün bir tepeden bakdım aziz Istanbul.

9. Benjamin's (1983, 45) characterization of the modern city as the domain of "love at last sight" is entirely apposite.

10. As a slow reader of Turkish, and as someone addicted to reading on public transport, I had plenty of opportunities to verify this assertion for myself. Non-Turkish readers should refer to Güneli Gün's translation of *The Black Book* (Pamuk 1994). The translation of this might be usefully compared with Victoria Holbrook's translation of an early Pamuk novel, *The White Castle.* Both are literary feats in their own right, and both have quite different views about how Pamuk's prose should be represented. For the benefit of non-Turkish readers, page references are taken from Güneli Gün's translation in the Faber edition.

11. Raks currently dominates about 75 percent of the music market and associated industries in Turkey today. This emerging monopoly is underpinned by its movement into broadcasting and its enthusiastic support of the newly formed performing rights society in Turkey (MESAM). S-Müzik handles Zeki Müren, Bülent Ersoy, Kayahan, and Ibrahim Tatlıses, among others—that is to say, the music industry's all-time biggest sellers. Sacit Suhabey, S-Müzik's manager, claims that Ibrahim Tatlıses's most recent recording sold over six million—one recording per household (interview with the author and Anne Ellingsen, July 23, 1996).

12. For a contemporary Turkish account of the debate, see Görmüş and Baştürk 1987.

13. The last popular representatives of this virtuoso genre were Hafız Burhan Sesyılmaz and Münir Nureddin Selçuk.

14. Notably Zeki Müren's "Kahir Mektubu" of 1976, an LP-length song in the style of Umm Kulthum's later collaborations with Muhammad 'Abd al-Wahhab.

15. Interview of Anne Ellingsen and the author with "Demet" and "Ece," July 25, 1996. Demet was the founder of the socialist transsexual collective, a group that had been formed to mobilize residents of the main center for transsexual prostitution, Ülker Sokağı, just off Taksim Square, against police harassment during the Habitat conference in June 1996.

ELEVEN

Badiʻa Masabni, Artiste and Modernist

The Egyptian Print Media's Carnival of National Identity

Roberta L. Dougherty

Familiarity is what popular culture has delivered since the printing press.
JAMES TWITCHELL, *Carnival Culture*

Either sing monologues or forget it.
BADIʻA MASABNI, *al-Ithnayn*, AUGUST 20, 1934

INTRODUCTION: MODERNITY AND CULTURAL HIERARCHY

"Great books" by "great men" have typically been the tools of study of a society's literary culture. In the case of Egypt, the twentieth-century canon includes the works of litterateurs such as Taha Husayn and Mahmud ʻAbbas al-ʻAqqad. A society's high-culture canon can also include figures from other areas of endeavor—journalists, artists, musicians, dramatists. For Egypt the cultural icons of this part of the canon would include figures such as editor Muhammad Husayn Haykal, singer Umm Kulthum, composer, singer, and musician Muhammad ʻAbd al-Wahhab, and actors George Abyad and Najib al-Rihani.

For those who study Egyptian society and for Egyptians themselves, the achievements of these persons represent the culmination of an unbroken line of development from established traditions—both classical and vernacular—to modernity with just the right amount of Western technique added. Music critics and musicians themselves may link contemporary performers to musical giants such as Muhammad ʻAbd al-Wahhab and Umm Kulthum, whose artistic roots could in turn be traced to such late-nineteenth-century figures as Salama Hijazi, ʻAbduh al-Hamuli, and Almaz.[1] Critics and historians of the cinema and theater look back to the pioneers George Abyad, Najib al-Rihani, and Yusuf Wahbi, among others. Literary critics also follow this convention. For example, contemporary Egyptian critics usually trace the origins of social criticism in modern Arabic narrative literature to Muhammad al-Muwaylihi's *Hadith ʻIsa ibn Hisham*.[2] This story, first published in serial form in the newspaper *Misbah al-Sharq* in 1898, itself derives from venerable roots in classical Arabic literature (Allen

1992, 34, 68, 96–97). Contemporary Egyptian nationalist discourse makes distinctions between these canonical heroes of modernity and more problematic types of expression denigrated as "vulgar" or "commercial." It also seeks to separate the authentically Egyptian from the foreign.[3]

Both James B. Twitchell (1992) and Lawrence W. Levine (1988) have argued that distinctions between "high" and "low" culture were not fossilized in America until well into the second half of the nineteenth century. Before that, popular entertainments such as Shakespeare plays and opera were attended by all social classes, and what we would now consider the untouchable classics were even altered to suit the demands of the public. But by the end of the century, opera, Elizabethan theater, and symphonic music became subject to standards of connoisseurship. In Egypt the development that took nearly a century in Europe and America was skipped. Western novels were translated into Arabic for authors to imitate and learn from, and Western-style music was inserted into the local culture with the establishment of academies for its study and with the construction of the Cairo Opera House. Developed aesthetic sensibilities already existed for "classical" Arabic music and literature, but these sensibilities did not touch the Egyptian common man in the way that ordinary Americans had a taste for Shakespeare even in the frontier. Around the turn of the century bold experiments in theater and publishing helped to create a new consumer of creative talent: the fan of popular singers and short, entertaining songs and the reader of magazines devoted to film and theater. Later decades might canonize some of these artists and place them next to other achievers in the areas of nationalist leadership, religious reform, science, and literature. But in the early twentieth century, popular Egyptian magazines show us a world where culture *was* a salad bar, to contradict Twitchell (1992, 24), and these figures are shoulder to shoulder with now-forgotten politicians and members of the artistic demimonde.

THE POPULAR PRESS: *AL-ITHNAYN*

Popular Egyptian magazines from the first half of the twentieth century provide a wealth of untapped information about a modern national identity defined through seemingly bizarre juxtapositions of elements. Such juxtapositions are common in nationalist ideologies, which often function through a tension between the need to authenticate through reference to "continuity-based sociocultural integration" and requirements of modernization (Fishman 1972, 20–21). The nationalist imperative to fulfill sometimes incompatible needs can easily result in combinations of images that appear, at first glance, to be strange bedfellows. In this case the pages of the periodical *al-Ithnayn* convey an almost carnival atmosphere. Advertisements for modern consumer goods, Cairo and Hollywood films, cabaret

Figure 10. Badi‘a Masabni entices an audience for her latest program at the casino (*al-Ithnayn,* no. 206, May 23, 1938, p. 40). Courtesy of Dar al-Hilal.

entertainments, alcoholic beverages, and railroad service to beach resorts mingle with stereotypical images of a more "traditional" society: fat, be-fezzed pashas, Azhari sheikhs, demurely veiled women from popular quarters, and rustically comic fellahin.[4] The boundary between high and low, modern and traditional, even Western and Egyptian is not firmly drawn, and the canonical figures are right in the middle of the hurly-burly. This would not necessarily be expected, given the usually hagiographic treatment of such figures by establishment versions of Egyptian modernity.

One of *al-Ithnayn*'s running features in its first year of publication was called "Majlis al-ta'dib" (Disciplinary Board), a mock court that sat in judgment on contemporary affairs. Its "judges" included those members of the Egyptian high-culture canon listed above. But the composition of the majlis also included a few women who were on the fringes of both traditional society and high culture because they were public performers. One of these is Badi'a Masabni, an impresaria responsible for promoting the careers of many Egyptian artists and an actress, singer, and dancer famous in her own right. Why is Masabni next to the cultural demigods, her conspicuous profile a familiar image on the pages of a magazine that, in other respects, seems to be shoving Westernization down Egypt's collective throat?

Al-Ithnayn magazine first saw the light of day on June 18, 1934, although in a sense it had already existed for several years. Its title means "both." Dar al-Hilal, the great publishing house that produced it, combined on its pages two older publications, *al-Fukaha* (which first appeared on December 1, 1926) and *al-Kawakib* (which first appeared on March 28, 1932). As indicated by the names of its predecessors, the new periodical would include both *fukaha* (comedy) and *kawakib* (stars), that is, stars of the stage and cinema. The title may have also had a double meaning, because its first day of issue was a Monday (*yawm al-ithnayn*)—the day on which *al-Kawakib* had normally appeared (Tamawi 1992, 210).

Husayn Shafiq al-Misri, editor in chief of *al-Ithnayn*, was "warmly attached to the vernacular dialects of his country" (al-Misri 1980, preface by Prasse, vi). In his magazine he favored the use of one- or two-page humorous pieces in which fictitious characters from *baladi*[5] quarters comment on current affairs and give their earthy advice. One regular feature was the "contest of the quarters," featuring "challenges" from famous Cairo neighborhoods such as Bulaq, Bab al-Khalq, and al-Husayn. Each quarter speaks for itself in the first person, describing its qualities, both good and bad. For example, Bab al-Khalq asserts:

> The Royal Library is in my square, to which hie scholars of the East and West, in all their types and languages . . . and behind it is the Arab Museum. . . . I have the house of the Sheikh al-Islam . . . and his grandson, Amin al-Mahdi,

the greatest oud player in the Arab world. . . . And the alley of *ʻawalim* [professional female performers], there is no *ʻawalim* alley like it in the whole city, women like ghouls, with yellow faces and blue teeth and red eyes and voices like the braying of donkeys, they are singers [*mughanniyat*], who claim to be chanteuses [*mutribat*]. (*Al-Ithnayn*, April 1, 1935)[6]

Another series parodies the social page in *al-Musawwar*, called "Hay layf" (High Life), which featured the activities of members of the aristocratic class. *Al-Musawwar* was, like *al-Ithnayn*, a weekly publication of the Dar al-Hilal printing house and, in the abstract, one of *al-Ithnayn*'s competitors.[7] Al-Misri's response to *al-Musawwar*'s hoity-toitiness was to print a regular series featuring the doings of the "gypsycrats" (*ghajartuqratiyah*), called "Rabish layf" (Rubbish Life). Sample topics include a description of the "Alley Club" and "baladi etiquette" (*al-Ithnayn*, March 25, 1935).

The lifestyle of the urbanized effendi aspiring to middle-class respectability, with whom al-Misri and his readers identify, is contrasted to social imagery of the popular classes. But in addition to promoting baladi culture as a valid point of view for commenting on the contemporary scene, al-Misri's satirical articles used the device of placing high-culture figures and well-known political personalities with personalities from the worlds of journalism, theater, cinema, and the religious establishment in comical situations that commented ironically on the foibles of all. Things that are authentically Egyptian are contrasted to others that are obviously foreign imports. For example, the humorous pieces about the baladi quarters of Cairo appear right next to articles about the private lives and interests of Hollywood film stars, illustrated by lavish studio photographs supplied by Hollywood publicity agents.

Perhaps one of the most important elements used for comic effect in the magazine is the language of the targets of its satire. Characters from different social backgrounds use Arabic that can be colloquial, or extremely high-flown and flowery, or broken and ungrammatical, or even liberally sprinkled with foreign words and mispronunciations. El-Said M. Badawi (1973) has described the use of Arabic by its native speakers in Egypt as a continuum reflective of educational level and social context. He divided this continuum into five more or less arbitrary levels, ranging from colloquial Arabic spoken by the uneducated to *fusha al-turath* (the language of the classical Arabic heritage). In actual practice much subtler gradations of language level are used by native speakers, although most are aware of the basic differences between spoken Arabic and the Arabic of the mass media, and even make strong distinctions between this latter form of Arabic and a level of language perceived by them as purer and truly fusha (Parkinson 1991). Contrasts between levels of language can be consciously exploited

for artistic purposes, and al-Misri, with his acknowledged love of the colloquial language, makes overt distinctions in the language used by the characters of his fictions in order to create humor. In al-Misri's satirical pieces,
contrasts in levels of language are made even at the level of individual word
choice. Linguistic elements are juxtaposed that would be recognizable to
al-Misri's educated effendi readers as being either high or low, native or foreign, grammatically correct or incorrect, simple or bombastic.

These elements were all well-established characteristics of journalistic
satire before al-Misri. As the Egyptian popular press began to flourish in the
late nineteenth century, political humor had begun to come into its own,
most notably in the work of Ya'qub Sannu', 'Abd Allah Nadim, and Muhammad al-Muwaylihi (Allen 1992, 23–25). Al-Misri's use of the colloquial dialect in his characters' speeches, inclusion of foreign words written out in
Arabic script, and use of recognizable people in fictional situations to criticize contemporary conditions had all formed part of the toolbox of the
satirical journalist long before *al-Ithnayn* began publication, in Sannu''s
and Nadim's work. The selection of al-Muwaylihi's *Hadith 'Isa ibn Hisham* as
a secondary-school textbook in 1927 (Allen 1992, 41) probably means that
at least some of *al-Ithnayn's* intended readers had been exposed to this kind
of writing as part of their education.

CARNIVAL COURT

All of these elements are brought together and interact in the main satirical feature of the magazine's first year, the "Majlis al-ta'dib." The majlis,
which appears in thirty out of *al-Ithnayn's* first fifty-two weeks, is usually
composed of three well-known figures, plus al-Misri acting as court
recorder. It sits in judgment on Egyptian cabinet ministers or British protectorate officials and is therefore muckraking in its tone. In addition to being composed of famous literary figures and stars of the stage and film, the
court sessions take place not in an official courthouse but on a theatrical
stage or in a music hall or cinema. Onlookers are portrayed as behaving in
a manner that is appropriate to these venues and not to an actual courtroom. This means that the proceedings are frequently interrupted by applause and whistling from the audience.

In fact, nothing happens the way it should. The court recorder, who is
identified as *al-Ithnayn's* editor in chief, Husayn Shafiq al-Misri, seems to be
barely literate. He often protests that he cannot read the docket. Sometimes he is portrayed as misunderstanding and misrecording what has been
said in the courtroom. He leaps into the interrogations from time to time
while everyone shouts at him to remember he is only the scribe. The panel
of judges heap abuse and insults on him for his faults, as for example in the
first majlis:

AL-RA'ISA (UMM KULTHUM): Iqra' jadwal al-qada'.
KATIB AL-JALSA: Istanna amma ad'ak 'ayni.
AL-ANISA UMM KULTHUM: Ma-la'aytush ghayr al-a'ma dah katib lig-galsah??

PRESIDENT: Read the docket.
RECORDER: Wait 'til I rub my eye.
MISS UMM KULTHUM: Couldn't you find anyone but this blind guy to be
court recorder?? (*Al-Ithnayn*, June 18, 1934)

In *al-Ithnayn*'s fifth issue al-Misri again puts himself down:

'Uqidat al-jalsa tahta ri'asat al-Sayyida Munira al-Mahdiyah, wa-'udwiyat al-us-
tadh Fikri Abaza al-muhami muharrir al-Musawwar, wa-al-ustadh Tawfiq Diyab
sahib al-Jihad, wa-hadara Husayn Shafiq al-Misri bita'al-Ithnayn katiban lil-jalsa.

The session was convened under the presidency of the lady Munira al-
Mahdiyah, and the membership of professor Fikri Abazah, the lawyer, editor
of *al-Musawwar*, and professor Tawfiq Diyab, owner of *al-Jihad*, and Husayn
Shafiq al-Misri of *al-Ithnayn* attended as court recorder. (*Al-Ithnayn*, July 16,
1934)

In this extract al-Misri has humbled himself by omitting the respectful
phrase *al-ustadh* from before his name and using the term *bita‘*, a purely
colloquial word that sticks out like a sore thumb in the midst of the more
formal written language that has preceded it, to indicate in a deprecating
way his relationship to his magazine.

For the court's first six months its president is a woman. This in itself is
probably enough for parody, but in addition this female judge is in real life
a famous singer, and in the "Majlis al-ta'dib" her every word is greeted by
the hysterical acclaim of her fans who shout, "Again! Sing it again!" Her
declaration, "Fatahna al-jalsah," is always followed by "sustained, enthusiastic applause" from her audience. Her judicial pronouncements often meta-
morphose into quotations from light strophic songs (*taqatiq*,[8] sing. *taq-
tuqah*) as the pandemonium increases. The court session is further
assimilated to a concert by the hour appointed for the session—usually late
at night, around 11 o'clock—and the venue—the Opera House stage, or
Badi‘a's cabaret, or another 'Imad al-Din Street theater. These locations
were are all within a short distance of a real courthouse, the Mixed
Courts—another favorite target of al-Misri's satire—near Opera Square
(Berque 1972, 88).

Badi‘a Masabni is not the most frequently seen famous personality on
the court (that distinction goes to Mahjub Thabit, champion of Egyptian-
Sudanese unity). In fact, she appears no more frequently than that other fa-
mous female singer of the period, whose star had already begun to eclipse
Badi‘a's—Umm Kulthum. Badi‘a is also on the court as frequently as Taha
Husayn, another member of Egypt's high-culture canon. What is striking,

Figure 11. Badi'a Masabni in an elaborate costume from the production of *Yasmina,* one of her greatest successes with Najib al-Rihani in the mid-1920s (*al-Ithnayn,* no. 166, August 16, 1937, p. 26). Courtesy of Dar al-Hilal.

however, is not so much how often she appears as the fact that she appears at all beside these people who have become icons of modern Egyptian culture. The Egyptian cultural pantheon seems to have been rather different in 1934 than it has become since being represented in 1990 in a poster produced by the Ministry of Culture, and it included many more characters now deemed "ephemeral" by the cultural establishment.[9]

At the time the series of *majalis* appeared in *al-Ithnayn,* Badi'a Masabni was a cabaret artist and impresaria, owner of her own successful music hall (*salah*) in 'Imad al-Din Street. A Syrian by birth, she had risen from a poverty-stricken and extremely painful childhood to fame as a singer and dancer in Syria and Lebanon. In the early 1920s she met Najib al-Rihani,

still loved in Egypt today. One of the pioneers of Egyptian comedy, he is often referred to as "the Oriental Molière" (Landau 1958, 87).[10] Masabni
joined al-Rihani's troupe and became famous in Egypt as a comic actress.
She and al-Rihani were married in September 1924 but were quickly estranged and separated in February 1926.[11] In that year she opened her *kaz-
inu* (casino—in Egypt a nightclub or outdoor café, not a gambling venue)
in 'Imad al-Din Street, where all the successful theaters and cafés of the day
were located. Her stage hosted both Oriental and Western acts. She herself
continued to perform, either dancing or singing the *munulugat* (monologues)[12] for which she was famous. She claimed to have introduced new
movements to the traditional *raqs Sharqi* (Oriental dance, the characteristic
female solo dance of Egypt) to make it more interesting to watch, "for the
Egyptian danseuses used to dance only by shimmying the belly and but-
tocks" (Basila 1960, 297). Her other innovations included frequent
changes of program (at first she boasted a new one every day) and, beginning in 1928, special shows for women only (Basila 1960, 296, 312). This
latter innovation demonstrated her canny business acumen: any show that
was decent enough for a wife to see would be unobjectionable for her husband. The press received her new productions with nothing less than abject
admiration for her inventiveness and originality. For example, in a review
appearing in *al-Ithnayn*, her summer show in Alexandria is described thus:

> Badi'a appeared to the guests in the most splendid costume and in the slen-
> derness that distinguishes her from everyone else. She sang, danced, and in-
> vented entertainments that caused the admiration of all, for she did not con-
> fine herself to the Egyptian monologue in which she excels but created new
> things she had learned from the far Maghreb, which she had recently visited.
> Thus we heard from her the pleasant Tunisian dialect to the sound of
> stringed instruments, and we were spellbound by the captivating entertain-
> ment that Badi'a brought to us in this performance. (June 3, 1935)

In 1935 she produced and starred in a feature film, *Malikat al-masarih*
(Queen of Theaters), which was a flop (Basila 1960, 329–31). This caused
her to suffer a severe financial setback and very nearly a nervous break-
down as well, but she was known for her ability to make and keep money
and soon recovered. Her 'Imad al-Din Street casino was sold by her feck-
less, lovestruck son to dancer and former Badi'a protegée Biba 'Izz al-Din
(Basila 1960, 334). In 1940, after recovering from this shock, Badi'a moved
to larger, more elaborate quarters on Cairo's Opera Square. During World
War II the new casino was so popular that its motto could have been "Everyone goes to Badi'a's," although rampaging British and Australian troops
constantly tore it up (Basila 1960, 339–42). In about 1950 Badi'a began to
have problems with local officials over unpaid back taxes, and she decided
to flee Egypt rather than stay and be ruined (Basila 1960, 364–68). She

Figure 12. An advertisement for a later Badi'a Masabni show, which took its inspiration from that wonderful new invention, television (*al-Ithnayn*, no. 625, June 3, 1946, p. 21). Courtesy of Dar al-Hilal.

Figure 13. Badi'a Masabni, chairing her first majlis ta'dib along with Taha Husayn and Husayn Haykal, tries to discover why Prince Shakib Arslan was recently forbidden to visit Egypt. Husayn Shafiq al-Misri, the editor in chief of *al-Ithnayn*, acts as the incompetent "court recorder" (*al-Ithnayn*, no. 6, July 23, 1934, p. 13). Courtesy of Dar al-Hilal.

negotiated the sale of her casino, once again at what she claimed was a terrible loss, once again to Biba 'Izz al-Din, who seemed always ready to profit from Badi'a's impulses (Basila 1960, 364). Her escape from the country was a cloak-and-dagger affair in which she met an airplane in the middle of the night in the desert outside of Heliopolis, but she managed to escape her creditors and settled down to retirement on a chicken farm outside of Beirut (Basila 1960, 377). When the Opera Casino was burned in the Cairo fire of January 1952, therefore, it was no longer Badi'a's place. Her autobiography is filled with bitterness at betrayal and poisoned with a desire for revenge on those who had mocked and hurt her in her life.

Badi'a is one of forty-two figures from up and down the classes and occupations who appear as members of *al-Ithnayn*'s majlis al-ta'dib. In its first three months its president is always a woman: the diva Umm Kulthum (3 times), Badi'a Masabni (3 times), the diva Munira al-Mahdiya (2 times), the singer Fathiya Ahmad (2 times), the pioneer of women's higher education Nabawiya Musa (once), and the actress and musician Bahija Hafiz (once). Then there is a six-week hiatus while the editor experiments with a "conference of hashish addicts" theme (*mu'tamar al-hashshashin*), after which the majlis returns. The format continues to vary, with more abstract

courts composed of animals, students, and ancient Egyptians. For a while
the hashish smokers take over again, and finally by week fifty-two, after
some of the magazine's favorite subjects have taken the majlis for a trip to
the beach and in time for *al-Ithnayn*'s first anniversary, the "court" returns
again—apparently for its swan song, for it never reappears in the materials
I have been able to examine—with Badi'a at its head for the last time.

In her first appearance on the court (July 23, 1934), Badi'a, along with
Taha Husayn and the journalist Husayn Haykal, sits in judgment on the
hapless minister of the interior, Mahmud Fahmi Pasha al-Qaysi. In a round-
about way the judges try to get the minister to tell them why he refused to
allow Prince Shakib Arslan to disembark when he recently visited Egypt, or
to allow his friends to visit him on his boat.[13] Taha Husayn nearly derails the
proceedings when he recapitulates the prosecution's entire argument for
the minister in what readers must have understood was a parody of the famous litterateur's style:

> You say that Prince Shakib does not forge money, nor does he smuggle
> hashish, nor distill alcohol, and Prince Shakib does not distill alcohol or
> smuggle hashish or forge money, and one like Prince Shakib does not forge
> money or smuggle hashish or distill alcohol, and this is known and known
> well and well known, for Prince Shakib is a good man and it is not strange that
> he should be a good man, and why should he not be a good man as he is a
> good man, good because he is a good writer, because he is a good poet, be-
> cause he is prominent and a scholar too, and also a scholar, therefore why did
> you forbid him to come ashore and how could he be forbidden to come
> ashore and what is there in his coming ashore?

Then Badi'a interrupts the proceedings to exclaim that the "monologue"
Taha Husayn has just recited is just the thing for her next broadcast and
makes sure the court recorder has copied it all down:

> AL-SAYYIDA BADI'A: *Ya ruhi 'ala di 'l-munulug, iw'a tinsah ya katib il-galsah!*
> KATIB AL-JALSA: *Aruh andah lil-ustaz Muhammad 'Abd al-Wahhab yilahhinuh?*
> AL-SAYYIDA BADI'A: *Ba'dima nkhallas min ig-galsa 'ashan biddi aghannih fi
> rradiyu.*

> LADY BADI'A: Oh wow, what a monologue, don't forget it, recorder!
> COURT RECORDER: Shall I go get Muhammad 'Abd al-Wahhab to set it to
> music?
> LADY BADI'A: After we've finished the session, because I want to sing it on
> the radio.[14]

The minister finally admits that the reason the prince was forbidden entry into the country is that he is persona non grata because of having written an article critical of the government. Witnesses for the prosecution are
called who are incapable of sticking to the subject at hand, and finally

Figure 14. In the second of Badi'a's majlis ta'dibs, she chairs the session with Mahjub Thabit, champion of Nile Valley unity, and 'Abd al-Hamid Bey Sa'id, as they sit to judge Badawi Bey Khalifa, minister of public security (*al-Ithnayn*, no. 7, July 30, 1934, p. 17). Courtesy of Dar al-Hilal.

Badi'a adjourns the court "until after the band has played." When the court is reconvened she then reads the verdict to a tune by "professor al-Qasabgi."[15] The playful text of the lines she sings suggests that it consists almost entirely of quotes from taqatiq, with changes in the musical mode indicated in the manner of stage directions, juxtaposed with the formal phraseology of the courtroom:

> *Haythu innahu: Ya mahla-d-dalma ya mahla-d-dalmah,*
> *Wa-haythu: Yuh min ir-rigal,*
> *Wa-haythu (naghamat turki): Ana Bida'da*[16] *ya wad inta,*
> *Wa-haythu (min naghamat al-sikah): Ya mahla shahr il-'asal bass in tawwal!*

> Whereas: How lovely is the dark, how lovely is the dark,
> And whereas: Oy, men!!
> And whereas (*turki* mode): I am Bida'da', you fellow, you,
> And whereas (*sikah* mode): How lovely is the honeymoon, if only it lasted![17]

The sentence? The minister's friends will not be permitted to visit him, and he is to pay the court costs and the fee for the band.

Badi'a's second turn as president of the majlis is in judgment of the minister of public security, Badawi Bey Khalifa (July 30, 1934). Badawi Bey has been called for having accused an innocent man of being a radical and

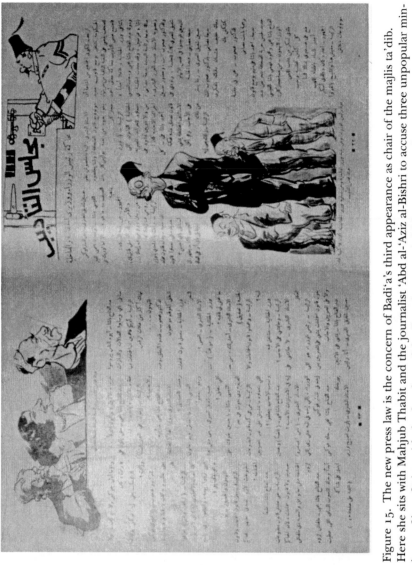

Figure 15. The new press law is the concern of Badiʿa's third appearance as chair of the majlis taʾdib. Here she sits with Mahjub Thabit and the journalist ʿAbd al-ʿAziz al-Bishri to accuse three unpopular ministers of interfering with the freedom of the Egyptian press (*al-Ithnayn*, no. 10, August 20, 1934, pp. 22–23). Courtesy of Dar al-Hilal.

imprisoning him for seventy days without any trial. Badawi Bey's defense: "Well, he did cause a riot when he sued us in court and won damages!" But the minister cannot hide from Badi'a's relentless pursuit of justice: "Well then, who paid the damages? You who imprisoned him wrongfully or the national treasury, whose money belongs to the nation? . . . Better you should arrest real criminals, like quack doctors and the women who wander in Fu'ad al-Awwal Street and 'Imad al-Din Street and flirt with people."[18] She adjourns the court "until after the entr'acte."

As she begins reading the verdict she cannot help herself from breaking into phrases from famous songs, as the audience applauds and cries, "Again, sing that one again!" She concludes with this line, a parody of a line from one of her own well-known songs:

> Wa-haythu innahu (naghamat hijaz kar): Ya mumallah ya Sudani, haga hilwa wa-'agbani . . . [19]

> Whereas (hijaz kar mode): Oh salty, oh peanuts, something sweet and makes me nuts . . .

This brings fellow judge Mahjub Thabit to his feet with applause, shouting, "Long live Egypt and the Sudan!" Badi'a's verdict puns on the word Sudani, meaning both "Sudanese" and "peanut," and Thabit is presented as being so enthusiastic about the concept of Nile Valley unity that he unreasoningly responds to the issue's merest suggestion. The verdict is "that the accused was unable to defend himself and he deserves everything he's going to get, he must pay the court costs and the cost of the buffet." The report is "signed" with Husayn Shafiq al-Misri's seal and Badi'a's thumbprint.[20]

In Badi'a's third appearance as president of the majlis she is teamed up with 'Abd al-'Aziz al-Bishri—the journalist who in 1939 would define the characteristics of the Egyptian effendi[21] in his column for al-Thaqafa magazine (El-Messiri 1978, 5)—and Mahjub Thabit once again (al-Ithnayn, August 20, 1934). This time they are sitting in judgment on some big fish: Ahmad Pasha 'Ali, minister of justice, 'Abd al-Fattah Pasha Yahya, the extremely unpopular prime minister, and Mahmud Fahmi Pasha al-Qaysi, minister of the interior (his second appearance as defendant).[22] The court has been called on by "the public" to pass judgment on the three for threatening to institute a new press law that will deprive the press of "what remains" of its rights.[23] Of course, because of the Capitulations, the new law will muzzle only the Egyptian-owned press and not those periodicals owned by foreigners, and this is the main thrust of the prosecution's argument.

The court comes to "order," if that term can be used, in Badi'a's own music hall in 'Imad al-Din Street, and once again Husayn Shafiq al-Misri reluctantly takes pen in hand to struggle through recording the proceedings. Badi'a declares, "The court is now in session," and al-Misri responds by muttering, "God preserve us!" She begins by flirting with Thabit, telling him his beard reminds her of Kishkish Bey (the famous vaudeville character created by her estranged husband, Najib al-Rihani), then turns to business. When she confronts the three cabinet members with her accusation, they break into song in the hijaz kar mode and the audience shouts its approval. She reproves them for singing *tawashih*,[24] and cries, "Ya-t'ulu munu-lugat ya balash!" (Either sing monologues or forget it!).

Then she continues, "Instead of a new press law, wouldn't it be better to make a law for Stanley Bay?" This Alexandria beach often crops up in the summertime issues of *al-Ithnayn* because of the scandalous goings-on that allegedly took place there. Badi'a observes, "Well, everyone knows that more is exposed at Stanley Bay than in the cabarets."[25] The ministers hedge, claiming they are working on a new law for the beaches. Badi'a presses them on whether it would be applicable to foreigners as well as to Egyptians and, in a dazzling legal argument that would boggle the mind of Perry Mason himself, declares, after singing, dancing, and getting the audience to sing along with her "I love you" (rendered in transliteration as *Ay luf yu*), that the Mixed Courts will never endorse any law the prime minister tries to apply to foreigners, whether the new press law or the bogus beach law she has connived him into agreeing to. The verdict is a confusing pastiche of references to popular songs and obscure incidents mixed with doggerel verse, like the following statement:

> *Wa-haythu anna al-wizarah: "Hazzaru ya gama'a is-sa'a kam w-ihna kida huh, rayhin gayin yadub id-dik yi'ul 'ku-ku-ku-ku,' tibuss til'ana sahyin."*

> Whereas the Ministry: "Guess everyone what time it is, and here we are, going and coming, as soon as the cock says 'cock-a-doodle-do,' you'll find us awake."

At the end of this Badi'a declares the ministers innocent of wrongdoing as her own argument has shown that there can be no justice for Egyptians in their own country. The majlis itself is to bear the legal expenses.

By Badi'a's fourth court appearance (December 24, 1934) its size has grown to five: Badi'a (an ordinary panelist this time), Muhammad 'Abd al-Wahhab, George Abyad, Umm Kulthum, and, at its head, Mahjub Thabit. Their victim is the English soldier who guards the High Commissioner's residence, and appointed to defend him is none other than Kishkish Bey himself. In language heavy with the letter *qaf* Mahjub Thabit threatens to hang the soldier in order to force him to speak the truth:

> *Wa-qarrarana qat'i qit'ati qumashin min qamisi l-maqbudi 'alayhi li-khanqihi bi-taqritiha 'ala 'unuqihi thumma taduqqu raqabatuhu idha taqalqulu fi al-nutqi bi-l-haqqi fa-qul ya qalila al-hidhqi ma ismuk?*

We have decided to cut a piece from the shirt of the accused in order to hang him with this snippet by his neck, so that his neck will thrum should he strum pronouncement of the truth, so speak, you unclever one, what is your name?

In language marked with Lebanese colloquialisms, George Abyad also demands that the soldier speak:

Yihraq 'umrak, shu sar fi lasinak? itkallim wa-lak!

May your life be burned, what's got your tongue? Talk or else!

Muhammad 'Abd al-Wahhab sensibly points out that since the accused does not speak Arabic he will need a translator. The soldier protests, in pointedly ungrammatical Arabic:

Ana Inglizi yi'raf 'Arabi lakin mish 'Arabi qa qa qa bita' ra'is galsa di zayy wahid farkha. Keman 'adi tani di ana mish yifham 'Arabi bita'uh "wa-lak lasinak shu?" Nu sir, di mush 'Arabi!

I am Englishman who knows Arabic but not qa qa qa Arabic like the president of this court like one chicken. Also the second judge, I do not understands his Arabic. No sir, she is not Arabic!

Although al-Misri (the author of the piece by virtue of being "court recorder") has accurately and humorously indicated the characteristic confused genders and misconjugations of the non-native speaker's broken Arabic, he has taken equal care in his representation of the language of the other two speakers. Thus not only is the soldier aware that the formal style of Thabit is incomprehensible to him in a way that is different from the colloquial Lebanese dialect used by Abyad, but the reader would be aware of this as well.

The soldier's crime was that he did not prevent Egyptian ministers from going to see High Commissioner Peterson (which, had he been a good nationalist, he would have done, to prevent Britain's meddling in Egypt's internal affairs). Even with his broken Arabic, however, he acquits himself well and captures the court's heart. Badi'a flirts with him, and 'Abd al-Wahhab sings him a snatch of song from the 1927 Sayyid Darwish opera *Antuniyu wa-Kliyubatra* (Anthony and Cleopatra).[26]

Kishkish Bey protests, "Have you come to judge my client or to flirt with him? If Husayn Shafiq al-Misri was the one in the dock you would all surely be putting your fingers in his eye!" After Umm Kulthum adds a line or two of song in tribute to the soldier, Kishkish Bey explodes, "What do you need me to defend you against, you son of sixty Manchesters rolled into one??" For his rebuttal he tells the court that his client was "just following orders . . . so pronounce him innocent, or sentence him to death, as you like. I don't care. I don't like this red race at all. Take him wherever you want." In its verdict, the court rules:

> Whereas: The accused could have prevented the ministers from entering the High Commissioner's residence in order to sow the seeds of difference between England and Egypt, and
>> Whereas: He deserves to be hung by the neck until dead, and
>> Whereas: He is English and his lawyer is Egyptian,
>> Therefore: The accused is declared innocent and his lawyer Kishkish Bey
> is to be hung. The condemned is also to bear all the legal expenses.

In response the soldier makes a daring escape: he leaps from the dock, boxes the judges' ears, and drags Kishkish Bey off under his arm, as the audience applauds and the Sha'b party falls.

Badi'a assumes the role of president of the majlis for the last time in her fifth appearance, also the last time the feature ever appears in the magazine (June 10, 1935). On this occasion she is joined by the actress Fatima Rushdi and the producer 'Aziz 'Id.[27] Music-hall comedian 'Ali al-Kassar, creator of the comic stage character "Egypt's unique barbarian,"[28] takes the role of prosecution against Sir Miles Lampson, the British High Commissioner. Britain had announced it had no intention of meddling in Egypt's internal affairs, and yet Lampson had refused to permit the application of the Egyptian constitution. When pressed by the members of the majlis he refuses to indicate why he will not permit its restoration, although he claims to have no objection to it. 'Aziz 'Id declares that Lampson is such a good actor, he should be a member of 'Id's performing troupe, and an argument ensues between him and Fatima Rushdi about the minimum requirements of art. Barriers between prosecution and defense break down as 'Aziz 'Id continues to express his admiration for Lampson's acting talent. Badi'a, dazed and confused by this point, asks the court recorder to reread a portion of the record. But he hasn't been writing anything down. Instead, he cocks his tarboosh forward in a fetching attitude and recites a comic monologue to the audience. "This court has become a dance hall," she groans. 'Aziz 'Id wants to declare a mistrial, but Badi'a savagely promises judgment after the judges' recess.

Her verdict: In view of the fact that Lampson has refused to tell the court anything and that the court recorder has neglected his duty, the tarboosh of the court recorder will be burned and Lampson will walk.

CONCLUSION: PURPOSEFUL LAUGHTER

Now, what is all this for? First and foremost, the function of these pieces was for fun. They read like sketches from "Saturday Night Live," with their many references to contemporary incidents I, as an outsider coming to the

محررو « الاثنين » ومصورروها كما يتخيلهم القراء

Figure 16. The editorial staff of *al-Ithnayn* struggles to put the publication together in an atmosphere of chaos. The editor in chief, al-Misri, is seated on the floor on the left, his cover artist Sintes is centered in the eye of the hurricane. The personal characteristics of the other members of the staff are revealed by the inclusion of telling details (*al-Ithnayn*, no. 32, January 31, 1935, p. 17). Courtesy of Dar al-Hilal.

material from considerable historical distance, may never be able to understand completely. They even look like scripts, with stage directions and the
names of players separated from their speech with dashes.

The dialogue of each character is at a level of language appropriate to
that character, with occasional surprises, such as Taha Husayn using a colloquial phrase or two, or camouflaged English and French words and
phrases sprinkled in among the Arabic. Language is often a barrier in the
court. When Bahija Hafiz is president of the majlis, she speaks almost entirely in French, and the other judges have to translate for her (*al-Ithnayn*,
August 6, 1934). Characters known for their high-flown speech in Arabic
likewise have to be translated for the benefit of speakers of the colloquial
language. Other times it is the accused who cannot communicate: either a
corrupt, fat, Turkified minister speaking broken Arabic or French or an
English official who stubbornly refuses to speak any language but his own or
the most basic Arabic. Police commandant Russell Pasha, on trial, answers
every question asked him with "Ana Inglizi!" (I am English!) as though
that's all he needs to say (*al-Ithnayn*, July 2, 1934). Certainly the confusion
in the language of the speakers and the puns and malapropisms that arose
from it was one of the main reasons readers found these pieces funny, along
with the juxtaposition of characters from different worlds.

Certain assumptions about the magazine's editorial policy and readership follow. For one, it is plain from the subject matter of the trials that the
magazine is pursuing a nationalist agenda, supported by the rest of the
magazine's contents. Everything from the choice of advertisements heavily
promoting local industry—for example, touting the advantages to the nation of wearing tarbooshes made in Egypt, not in a foreign land (*al-Ithnayn*,
March 11, 1935)—to the cover illustrations—Kishkish Bey on the inaugural issue, followed by lovely peasant women, familiar urban characters like
the licorice-juice seller, and so on—bears this out. Political columns sati-
rize the Sha'b party government then in power and level pointed accusations of meddling at the British.

The magazine refers to that which is local, and to a certain extent traditional, and at the same time makes a plug for modernity. A personified
"Egypt" first appears in the magazine as a comely, modern, modish young
woman, arriving at an international conference to finally take charge of her
own affairs (*al-Ithnayn*, October 1, 1934). Both colloquial Arabic and literate Arabic are used in the articles and features, suggesting that the readership was comfortable with reading an Arabic language that was expressed at
several different levels of Badawi's continuum simultaneously. In the debate
over whether modernity would be served in print through the use of a more
formal, pure Arabic derived from the classical language or through the introduction of a language referenced to the vernacular, Husayn Shafiq al-
Misri's editorial policy was clearly in favor of the latter.

Along with this modernity goes a certain amount of Westernization. The most obvious indication of this is the magazine's fascination with Western-style goods like wrinkle creams, Jantzen bathing suits, correspondence courses, and Phillips radios.[29] *Al-Ithnayn* also supplied its readers with materials to satisfy their fascination with the Hollywood cinema. Based on the trivia quizzes, the photographs of Hollywood stars distributed free with each copy, the readers' requests for mailing addresses of Buster Crabbe, Clark Gable, Mae West, and Ruby Keeler, and features like "If I were a man, by Joan Crawford" (June 25, 1934), it seems that the readership of *al-Ithnayn* was presumed to be familiar with the contemporary Hollywood scene.

Husayn Shafiq al-Misri not only promoted Egyptian and Western stars but also developed the cult of personality of his own editorial staff. A caricature titled "Editors and artists of *al-Ithnayn* as imagined by our readers" shows them all putting the magazine together in an atmosphere of total chaos and frantic activity (January 21, 1935). Al-Misri sits contentedly on the floor in the middle of the hubbub in his customary patched clothes, a bottle of ink spilled at his feet, scratching away with his pen. The caption describes the speculation of a loyal *al-Ithnayn* reader overheard in such a highbrow place as the tramway: "That Husayn Shafiq al-Misri must be a hashish addict, and Khayri Sa'id [another member of the staff] eats bread he dips in hashish instead of white cheese." Another adds, "All his editors are dope fiends." The head artist Juan Sintes, a Spaniard who had lived in Egypt for thirty years and was responsible for some of *al-Ithnayn's* most beautiful, and most "Egyptian," cover art, is declared to be an "impertinent foreigner, . . . and he too must be a hashish addict." The editor hastens to assure his public: "We swear by God Almighty that we are all drunkards, not hashish addicts, folks, for hashish is forbidden."

Al-Misri actively promoted the popular performing artists and literary figures of his day. The inaugural issue of his magazine had Kishkish Bey on the cover and a caricature by Sintes of Badi'a Masabni on the inside front cover. This dueling duo, along with al-Misri, Sintes, Umm Kulthum, 'Abd al-Wahhab, al-'Aqqad, Fikri Abaza, Husayn Haykal, and a constellation of similar "stars" of culture, were brought together, at least on the magazine's pages, to form an imaginary 1934 Egyptian version of the Algonquin Round Table. Their slightest doings were faithfully reported, and the editor in chief continued to represent himself in self-deprecating ways in his humorous pieces.

Although the magazine's thrust was nationalist, not a few foreigners are shown on its side. As mentioned above, the chief artist, Sintes, was a Spaniard by nationality, but one who was by all accounts extremely successful at capturing in his drawings and caricatures an essential, authentic "Egyptianness" (Rasim Bey 1941). George Abyad, a frequent member of the majlis, was Lebanese. One of the editorial staff caricatured in the cartoon described above is shown wearing an armband bearing the Star of David. Badi'a Masabni, a Syrian, was a foreigner, although her speech in the majlis is always rendered with characteristic markers of colloquial Egyptian Arabic (for example, addressing people with the typical baladi woman's salutation of "ya dil'adi"). Elsewhere in the magazine, however—such as in her autobiography serialized in 1939—she "speaks" in literary Arabic.[30]

To return to the court and its role in promoting Husayn Shafiq al-Misri's own political agenda: Its Marx Brothers–like anarchy shows al-Misri's own view that Egyptians would never succeed in their quest to control their destiny unless they could somehow rise above the chaos of their own existence. Although in every case the court is called on to pass judgment on a contemporary problem, sometimes large (such as the minister of public works' lack of planning for dealing with the record flood of 1934 in which hundreds of people died), sometimes small (some of the majalis described above fit this category), and although the president often makes a compelling case against the defendant, the court is never really successful in establishing the truth or in getting the culprits to confess their sins. Even allowing for the fact that this is a fictitious court created for a comic purpose, punishments are light, and the court ends up inflicting punishment on itself just as often as it does on the defendant.

The majlis al-ta'dib is a disciplinary board without discipline, and without any authority to enforce its judgments. Badi'a Masabni belongs on the court beside the high icons of culture partly because it was probably funny to place a famous popular entertainer next to someone like Taha Husayn, but also because she deserved to be there in spite of negative public perceptions about her profession, because of her obvious contribution to the social life of contemporary society and in recognition of her innovations. Although she is used for a nationalist agenda, however, she is ultimately a nationalist without a nation, who willingly abandoned the one that had made her rich when things got tough. Although the court's members are united, at least in the editor's imagination, on certain issues of importance to the nation, ultimately its members' self-interest and lack of ability to focus, added to its lack of legal standing, express an editorial point of view that action, even on the part of Egypt's "best and brightest," will be without fruit until Egypt has obtained real independence. In the meantime, subversive laughter is the best medicine.

NOTES

A shorter version of this chapter was presented at the 1995 conference of the Middle East Studies Association. I would like to acknowledge, with gratitude, the helpful comments and suggestions I received from Roger Allen and Walter Armbrust.

1. At a crucial point in his first film, *al-Warda al-bayda'* (The White Rose; 1933),

'Abd al-Wahhab is shown pacing his room as he makes his decision to pursue a career in music. He pauses to gaze, one by one, at photographs of al-Hamuli, Hijazi, and Sayyid Darwish hanging on his wall. This device is used both as a visual *isnad* (chain of transmission), indicating the passing of the baton of musical greatness to the deserving young musician by the masters of the past, and as the young artist's homage to them (Armbrust 1996, 110–11).

2. See, for example, for the *Hadith* as a precursor of the modern Egyptian novel, Badr 1984, 74; of the modern Egyptian short story, Nassaj 1984, 59–62. See also Berque 1972, 212.

3. Armbrust (1996, 7–10) notes that distinctions in Egyptian nationalism between local (vernacular) and nonlocal (classicist) cultural referents must also be balanced in some relation to the specifically "Western" and a more general sense of technological progress. The former (Westernism) was not an image with which many nationalists were eager to associate themselves, whereas the latter (science, technique) was of obvious benefit. Although the dynamics of this cultural calculus have changed over time (particularly since the 1970s), the outlines of a uniquely Egyptian nationalist and modernist discourse are still evident in discussions of topics such as music, visual representation, authenticity, and cultural heritage.

4. Many of these stereotypes were developed in earlier literature, such as *Hadith 'Isa ibn Hisham* (see Allen 1992).

5. *Baladi* is the adjective from the noun *balad*, which means both "country" and "town" but in certain contexts is used in phrases referring to a particular traditional urban class of people in Cairo, their characteristic behavior, and the quarters of Cairo where they live. *Abna' al-balad* (sing. *ibn al-balad;* lit., son of the town) are people who might sometimes be denigrated as "rustics" and at other times praised as "salt of the earth" or "diamonds in the rough." The feminine counterpart, *banat al-balad* (sing. *bint al-balad;* lit., daughter of the town), can be either naive and simple girls or streetwise, strong women who cannot be taken advantage of. The concept of ibn al-balad is usually contrasted to those of effendi (middle-class government bureaucrat, see below, n. 16), *ibn al-zawat* (son of nobility), and *khawaga* (foreigner). These terms are all part of a complex system of distinctions that social actors can use creatively but which often work, in specific situations, through an implied binarism. For a full discussion, see El-Messiri 1978; see also Armbrust 1996, 25–26.

6. Performers and critics alike made a qualitative distinction between a *mughanniya* and a *mutriba* (Danielson 1991, 47).

7. Dar al-Hilal was at this period producing many publications aimed at overlapping audiences. *Al-Hilal* was from the beginning a relatively highbrow periodical, whereas *al-Musawwar*, with its emphasis on illustrations, was more middlebrow. *Al-Ithnayn*, aimed at the struggling bureaucrat class, may be characterized as middle- to lowbrow, with an occasional tendency to go slumming.

8. The taqtuqa began as the female song par excellence (Racy 1977, 53) but after World War I was performed by both male and female singers. Its soaring popularity in the interwar period alarmed many Egyptian critics, who disapproved of the song's typically superficial and sometimes even obscene lyrics (Racy 1977, 54). Along with short nationalistic songs (*anashid*) and musical plays, the taqtuqa in the 1920s became one of "the most widely accepted tools of mass entertainment" (Racy 1977, 61).

9. "Mi'at 'am min al-tanwir" (A Hundred Years of Enlightenment), a painting by the contemporary artist Salah 'Inani depicting a constellation of Egyptian reformers, litterateurs, scientists, and fine and performing artists, was made into a poster by the Egyptian Ministry of Culture in 1990. For a detailed analysis of the iconography of this painting, see Armbrust 1996, chap. 7.

10. For more on the career and life of al-Rihani, see Abou Saif 1969.

11. Masabni's reason for the separation was al-Rihani's infidelity and greed for her money, al-Rihani's was Masabni's infidelity and miserliness (Abou Saif 1969, 127).

12. Monologues were a "theater-inspired" comic form often difficult to distinguish from other types of urban secular song (Racy 1977, 206, 211). Identical in content were the *diyalugat* (for two singers) and the *triyalugat* (for three; *al-Kawakib*, January 9, 1933, 6–7).

13. The elderly prince was a famous figure in the pan-Arab, pan-Islamic movement at this period, as well as a journalist and prolific author. He spent his life using his personal influence and presence to draw attention to his anti-imperialist cause. For this reason he was greatly distrusted by the British and French colonial authorities. His support of King Ibn Sa'ud was also viewed unkindly by the Egyptian royal house. These animosities caused him to be unwelcome almost anywhere he traveled. See Cleveland 1985.

14. Local broadcasting in Egypt had begun only two months before this issue of *al-Ithnayn* was published.

15. Muhammad al-Qasabgi was one of the most prolific composers for the diva Umm Kulthum, second only to Riyad al-Sunbati (Danielson 1991, 375–77). He was also one of Muhammad 'Abd al-Wahhab's music theory teachers ('Azzam 1990, 26).

16. Badi'a's nickname.

17. Fifty-two musical modes were documented by the Congress on Arab Music, held in Cairo in 1932 at the command of King Fu'ad. Most of these modes are no longer in use, and only four are widely used in popular music (Shawan 1981, 30, 62). The 1932 congress gathered a number of Egyptian and Western musicologists (including Bela Bartok) "in order to discuss all that was required to make the music civilized, and to teach it and rebuild it on acknowledged scientific principles." Its proceedings were published by the Egyptian Ministry of Information in 1933 (Racy 1991, 69). Does al-Misri's assiduous recording of the musical modes parody the conference's conclusions and Egyptians' sudden awareness of the multitude of modes and their exotic Persian and Turkish names? Did the conference's conclusions promote a sudden rush by performers to use as many modes as possible in their performances?

18. Badi'a's own theater was located in 'Imad al-Din Street, and some of those wandering women may have been performers from her own shows, taking a stroll in between numbers! The association of female performance with prostitution is a long-standing one, and the two professions were often practiced in the same part of town (van Nieuwkerk 1995, 46).

19. A parody of her song "Ya nawa'im ya tuffaha, haga hilwa w-kwayyisa" (What a Nice, Sweet Apple), which is represented in the 1975 film *Badi'a Masabni* as having been stolen from one of Najib al-Rihani's shows.

20. Masabni acknowledged to her biographer that she did not learn to read Ara-

bic until she was in her mid-teens (when she received instruction in the language from a member of George Abyad's theatrical troupe) and never learned to write Arabic well (Basila 1960, 91–92).

21. A Turkish word originally used to address a high-status individual, "effendi" was a term that in Egypt by the beginning of this century had come to refer particularly to "government employees who dress in suits and *tarboush*" (El-Messiri 1978, 5 n. 7). The caricaturist Sarukhan invented the character of "al-Misri Effendi" (Mr. Egyptian), the "regular guy" and "real Egyptian" of his age, in the mid- to late 1920s when he was working for *Akhir Sa'a* magazine (*al-Ithnayn*, February 3, 1941, 31). The caricaturist Rakha, interviewed by El-Messiri, stated that al-Misri Effendi was first introduced to the pages of *Ruz al-Yusuf* in 1929 (El-Messiri 1978, 48). In the pages of *al-Ithnayn* in 1934 the effendi is portrayed as an affected fop. But his fortunes changed rapidly, and by 1941, Rakha told El-Messiri, the editorial staff of *al-Ithnayn* decided that al-Misri Effendi had come to represent "the lowest class of government official, . . . petty bureaucrats" (El-Messiri 1978, 48). Al-Misri Effendi was no longer a suitable representative for the Egyptian common man. An editorial decision was made that "Ibn al-balad" (lit., son of the town; see above, n. 4), not the effendi, should represent the ordinary Egyptian, and Rakha invented a cartoon character by that name at that time.

22. It is not unusual for certain figures to make their appearance in the courtroom more than once, and, in keeping with the chaotic nature of the proceedings, some personalities show up on both sides of the bench, sometimes moving from prosecution to defense in the same session.

23. This was very little indeed. The 1881 press law had given the Egyptian government the power to summarily close down newspapers that criticized it. After 1894 High Commissioner Cromer was lax in enforcing the law, and the Egyptian press enjoyed a "golden age" of relative freedom of expression. But Gorst, his successor, reinstated the harsh 1881 law in 1909. The new constitution of 1923 superficially supported freedom of expression but only "within the limits of the law"— which meant that the press remained at the mercy of the government. In 1931 the government of Prime Minister Isma'il Sidqi issued a new press law that confirmed the subordination of the press to the government, including not only verbal criticism but also "drawings, paintings, photographs, emblems, and other means of representation." Husayn Shafiq al-Misri, *al-Ithnayn*'s editor in chief, had already been imprisoned once as a result of this law. With his new satirical magazine, he certainly seems to have been skating on very thin ice. The Capitulations, which excepted foreigners from the punishments of Egyptian law, protected the foreign-owned press as well. See Ayalon 1995 for more on Egypt's press laws.

24. Sing. *tawshih*, a term usually used to refer to Sufi religious music but commonly used in Egypt interchangeably with the term *muwashshah* (Racy 1977, 210). The muwashshah was a vocal musical genre with roots in the Andalusian tradition. Around the turn of the century it had been "a major interest for a handful of late nineteenth-century and early twentieth-century Egyptian composers," but it then fell out of favor and was barely recorded at all by the 1930s (Racy 1977, 60, 212). Badi'a's derisive reference to tawashih, whether she means the Sufi religious song or the ancient Andalusian one, is clearly to something old-fashioned, fuddy-duddy, and definitely not popular.

25. Between 1932 and 1934 several attempts had been made on moral grounds to suppress belly dancing in the nightclubs of 'Imad al-Din Street and the Ezbekiya Gardens area. Although Egyptians were forbidden to perform the dance, because of the Capitulations foreign female dancers were able to perform a dance that "would cause the forbidden dance to blush." Journalists and nightclub owners, "for once united in a nationalist spirit," took up the restoration of the dance as a nationalist cause (van Nieuwkerk 1995, 47).

26. *Anthony and Cleopatra* was one of 'Abd al-Wahhab's earliest theatrical successes. Left uncompleted on Sayyid Darwish's death in 1924, the opera was completed by the young 'Abd al-Wahhab at the invitation of the era's greatest female singing star, Munira al-Mahdiyah, who hoped the opera's success would boost her flagging career (Armbrust 1996, 74 n. 21).

27. Another famous theatrical couple. 'Id was one of the earliest pioneers of the modern Egyptian popular theater at the beginning of this century. Rushdi was at first his protégée, then his star, then his wife. Rushdi's scandalous infidelities to her husband were much talked about in the Egyptian popular press (Armbrust 1996, 201 n. 35) and readily confessed and shrugged off in her own memoirs (Rushdi 1971).

28. *Barbari Misr al-wahid* (Hakim 1990, 209), a Nubian character, played by Kassar in blackface, who makes fun of both Egyptian and non-Egyptian. See also Landau 1958, 90–91.

29. The juxtaposition of consumer goods to images of authenticity should not automatically be assumed to be a sign of cultural fragmentation, but rather it can be used to complete "autonomous ideological projects" (Miller 1994, 14). As will be mentioned again below, the editorial policy of the magazine is nationalist, and much of the advertising has nationalist overtones. Other advertising reflects the magazine's overtly modernist position (Armbrust 1996, 84).

The Egyptian state radio went on the air on May 29, 1934, barely three weeks before *al-Ithnayn* hit the streets, and *al-Ithnayn* began to publish critical reviews of the programming almost immediately. The very first installment of the majlis, in the inaugural issue, has Umm Kulthum as president of a court trying Prime Minister 'Abd al-Fattah Pasha Yahya over unfair allocations of airtime to local programming.

30. Her biographer, Nazik Basila, always represents her speech in the more formal written language, even when Badi'a describes an episode in which she broke a chair over Najib al-Rihani's head and hurled insults at him during their final painful breakup:

> *Innani lan ada'aka tadkhulu hadha al-manzil ba'da al-yawm, wa-idha haddathatka nafsuka bi-al-'awdati ila huna fa-lastu mas'ulatan 'amma qad yahduthu la-ka!*
>
> I will not allow you to enter this house after today, and if your soul tells you to return here then I am not responsible for what might happen to you! (1960, 278).

TWELVE

American Ambassador in Technicolor and Cinemascope

Hollywood and Revolution on the Nile

Robert Vitalis

COMING ATTRACTION

In May 1957 representatives of two of the largest American multinationals in Egypt called at the U.S. embassy. The visitors were by then a familiar sight at the tree-lined grounds of Qasr al-Dubbara, because companies such as Metro-Goldwyn-Mayer (MGM) and Twentieth Century-Fox, among other U.S. firms, were being saddled with new costs to doing business in their largest Middle East market.

The Egyptian economy had been on war footing since the Israeli attack on Port Said in November 1956. President Gamal Abdel Nasser had unleashed a punitive wave of expropriations against the French and British nationals who were the backbone of the foreign private sector. Controls on foreign-exchange remittances were tighter than at any time since World War II. Meanwhile, the populist policy currents associated with the March 1954 crisis and the Bandung conference in April 1955 grew stronger in the wake of the war. In the case of motion pictures, for the first time authorities passed specific legislation, in place of a long-standing informal or "gentlemen's agreement," requiring all theater owners to screen three locally produced films per year (Law No. 373, *Official Gazette* 88, November 3, 1956). The war, which led to a surge of arrests, internments, and deportations, also licensed the stepped-up stereotypes of Jewish control of the film industry and Hollywood's and the Egyptian-Jewish business community's financing of Israeli colonization.[1]

Though lobbying by the U.S. embassy and U.S. firms had gained American big business virtually complete exemption from the 1957 Egyptianization decrees, Hollywood on the Nile was anticipating a new wave of institutional and fiscal measures by the state aimed at reorienting Egypt's cultural horizon and rescuing its tottering filmmaking industry.[2] The local businessmen were savvy enough to know what played well with the State Department and, to shore up a main pillar of support, previewed the latest episode in the lurid drama of communist influence in Egyptian popular culture markets.

According to Oscar Lax, the American who oversaw Fox's Middle East market interests, back in October 1956 one of the revolutionary Free Officers, Wajih Abaza, was tendering huge sums of cash to rent a first-run theater in Cairo for screening Russian films. Theater managers again alerted the embassy early in 1957 that communists were in the market for movie houses and, in their latest visit, passed on the tip from the head of Egyptian customs. The Soviet Union had imported three hundred films into Egypt, in anticipation of a squeeze on American imports. Moreover, they warned that a new Arabic "publication is being prepared . . . for early release entitled, 'American Ambassador in Technicolor and Cinemascope,' . . . and is to describe the devices used in American films to gain a propagandistic effect for the United States."[3] The book, Safir Amrika, in fact was published later that year.[4]

In a post–cold war world the tales of intrigue at the customhouse, meetings between Russian agents and Alexandria businessmen, or a comrade of Nasser's with "suddenly a lot of money, to pay back old debts" that unfolds in the microfilm reels of declassified State Department files can feel like a revival of The Iron Curtain (Twentieth Century-Fox, 1948). Reconstructed in this way, a historical analysis of film and politics in Egypt promises little other than the pleasure of nostalgia. From another angle, though, the historical materials may shed some light on contemporary issues and debates.

Consider the evolution of the international market for sound films. Decades before the cold war, Hollywood had forged a coherent and generally successful foreign policy designed to preserve and extend its world market share, first in silent films and later in sound films, while excluding non-American imports from the home market, save when produced by its own subsidiaries (Jarvie 1988, 1992). The formal foreign policy apparatus of the United States aided this project, and, generally, policy makers and producers made similar arguments to each other about films effectively selling the American dream—whether in terms of values or valuable goods—abroad (Rosenberg 1982). Arguments that linked films to support of the American way of life were thus easily and readily adapted against not only the threat of new Russian empire but also against a renewed protectionist drive in the established European entertainment markets and the old empires' outposts in what came to be known as the Third World.

Hollywood's ability to maintain a dominant position in the international film trade remains a central feature of the global political economy long after the Russian empire began its collapse. In the 1940s the major studios were already dependent on their approximately 40 percent of gross revenues from overseas markets to sustain the industry (Guback 1985). In the 1990s, as Time-Warner co-chair J. Richard Munro reminded his audience in a speech, "Good-bye to Hollywood: Cultural Imperialism and the New Protectionism," the industry is America's second biggest net export earner after aerospace (Munro 1990). Both his talk's subtitle and its enumeration of screen quotas, import restrictions, investment barriers, and so on, across Europe, Latin America, and Asia remind us of some important continuities in the global motion picture regime for more than half a century.

Egypt's film industry, like those of other late industrializers (e.g., Mexico, Brazil, Argentina, India, Turkey), emerged in the shadow of Hollywood's global prominence, and one need look no further than Alexandria's pioneering Chilean-Palestinian producers, the Lama Brothers' *Qubla fi al-sahra'* (Kiss in the Desert; Condor Films, 1927), for evidence of Valentino-era America's aesthetic values influencing the first filmmaking experiments (al-Hadari 1989, 245–56; Malkmus and Armes 1991, 28–29). The outpouring of musicals in the 1940s, or, more recently, the steady flow of crime and karate films, serves as the foil in perennial arguments for finding and preserving an authentic national-cultural style in films, with Egyptians adopting the arguments invented by their own colonial overlords in the Foreign Office in the 1920s and 1930s.

Nonetheless, in this chapter I argue for resisting what Fred Halliday (1993, 145–63) calls "ideologies of the dominated" in studying the Egyptian industry's cold war (close) encounter (of the Third World kind) with Hollywood. The Egyptian case poses some critical problems for those who tend to see neocolonialism, cultural imperialism, and Third Worldism as the basic framework for organizing our understanding of the cultural economy of the "Global South." First, unlike other economic sectors, the local Egyptian film industry shared the same basic problem vis-à-vis the Americans as the British industry, the rest of Europe, and the emerging film industries of Latin America and colonial Asia. Second, the same European colonial system is not easily evoked as the cause of the lack of a film industry in most of sub-Saharan Africa and the Middle East *and* the development of an industry in Egypt. Third, by the 1940s, if not before, the Indian film industry, in the most deeply colonized country in Asia, was also far more successful than London in creating a domestic industry capable of competing "on equal terms with American imports" (Thompson 1985).

As I will show, Hollywood's export arm was not particularly successful in "dominating" the early postwar Egyptian feature film market in the way that it had become accustomed to in settings as diverse as Toronto, Mexico City, London, Paris, and Manila. According to the Americans' own market surveys, local production of Arabic-language sound films had proved popular, wresting the bigger share of an expanding moviegoing public's screen time. Though Egypt was not a large market, Cairo and Alexandria served the American firms as the distribution point for exports to Palestine, Lebanon, Syria, Iraq, Sudan, and elsewhere in the region. And these Middle East markets collectively grew more important as Europe, Latin America, and Asia pursued a new round of protectionism under the terms of the original General Agreement on Tariff and Trade (GATT). Egypt, by contrast, remained a relatively open market through the end of the 1950s, with Arabic providing an important degree of natural advantage for local producers.

At the same time, the Egyptian industry's increasingly insistent calls after the 1952 revolution for restricting screen times and raising levies on imports pointed to underlying problems in industrial organization. Similar to other sectors, the Egyptian motion picture industry could not make efficient use of its existing expensive plant (studios). In this case, however, demand for new films outstripped the available supply. The lack of capital markets and access to financing meant that the studios functioned as little more than rental facilities for speculative investors. After twenty years in business, the country's flagship firm, Studio Misr, still could not produce enough films to fill its one movie house in Cairo.

Though a concerted drive to attract investment from abroad, expand production, and exploit the potential of regionwide Arab film markets was, arguably, the only possible means to amortize costs and place a modest studio system on a sounder footing, the turn to import substitution industrialization (ISI) instead contributed to the studio system's demise. Ignoring the film sector entirely and the regional markets that were just beginning to be exploited by U.S. firms, American supporters of ISI in Egypt insisted that the country produced nothing that foreign consumers wanted to buy. The choices made by Egyptian authorities at this juncture compounded the problems of building a commercially viable motion picture industry.

Nasser appears to have resembled Ben-Gurion more than Lenin in his approach to film. Whereas "Lenin could insist that 'for us, cinema is the most important of all the arts,' . . . Ben-Gurion dismissed cinemas as 'subculture' and a 'waste of time'" (Shohat 1989). The industry was excluded from the ambitious development drive then being planned for Egypt and instead turned over to the propaganda czars to run. As the socialist phase of the revolution took shape and the studios came under state ownership, the output of the industry declined for the rest of the decade, leading to a new rise and new popularity for foreign imports.

This study of the political economy of the Egyptian motion picture industry in the 1940s and 1950s is necessarily speculative, not least because until now the entertainment sector (films, videos, recordings) is one that institutionally oriented economists and development analysts have seen fit to ignore. Instead the recent, often quite powerful wave of academic studies of "third cinema" and Third World film industries represents the turn to the study of popular culture in film history, anthropology, comparative literature, and so on (Armes 1987; Chakravarty 1993; King 1990; Mora 1982; Pines and Willemen 1989; Shohat 1989; Shohat and Stam 1994). Understandably, this wave is generally not oriented toward economic analysis of the industry. And the Egyptian case is not particularly well represented in the recent Anglo-American wave of national cinema studies.[5] Existing English and Arabic sources alike offer few reliable details about the industry's structure. Rather, the Third Worldism and often simple cultural imperialism presumptions and norms that inform much of this work make it imperative that an institutionally focused alternative be developed, minimally, to introduce a degree of empirical discipline to the ongoing debate about colonialism and culture.[6]

Although institutionalism may unduly privilege the economic and, especially, capitalist features of the motion picture industry, nonetheless there is a certain affinity between institutionalist political economy and the positions taken by theorists like Andrew Ross and other iconoclasts in the field of cultural studies (see Ross 1988). That is, we need not give in to the illusion that the market in global cultural production is free or, more important, fair. At the same time, intellectuals have long had an uneasy relationship with the consumption preferences of the millions of moviegoers in whose name they defend various versions of the national cultural interest, and we need to resist succumbing to the left auteur's dream that "any day the masses would opt for [so-called] quality films" (Stead 1981).

I resist any temptation to venture too deeply into the thorny debate on cultural imperialism, on the grounds that the approach taken here cannot be used to test the various claims about the psychological effects of American films and Western or capitalist values on which such debates typically turn. But the records of investors and policy-making elites in the 1940s and 1950s show that, whether they believed these ideas to be true or not, they often advanced similar claims about film's effects, for instance, in enhancing the sale of American goods and spreading American values. Hollywood in fact routinely premised its appeals for government support on such grounds. Similarly, Egyptians followed the practice of British governments in deploying these same ideas, with an opposite valence, as part of a "culturalist and patriotic" defense of a narrow sectoral interest group (Jarvie 1992, 152).

When I speak of Hollywood's dominance I am referring to market share in a particular territory, gauged in terms of screen time or what most consumers are buying.[7] An advantage of focusing on this dimension is that it was clearly the one in the 1950s with which local capitalists in Cairo's film studios, distribution offices, and movie houses were most concerned.

HOLLYWOOD IN THE INTERNATIONAL DIVISION
OF CULTURAL LABOR

There is now a substantial body of historical work on the U.S. film industry, its operations in its largest overseas markets and its strategies against its main competitors. The currently conventional view of the process by which the U.S. industry established its hegemony emphasizes the following points. World War I was a critical juncture. During the war years, 1914–19, American investors successfully cornered the domestic U.S. market (with some 20,000 theaters in 1931, this market was by far the world's largest) and began exporting on a previously unknown scale, at a time when capital was obviously scarce abroad, stealing audience share in England and virtually all other large, 1,000- to 5,000-theater markets.

Securing domestic market dominance and international market dominance were interrelated processes. That is, the scale of the domestic market allowed American producers to amortize their investment much more easily than British or Italian competitors. Vertical and horizontal integration of the industry, which in this case meant a small number of big studios that controlled distribution to their own large theater chains, served as an effective barrier against any meaningful foreign penetration of this market until the 1960s. To the extent that producers could recover their costs at home, they were able to undercut competitors' prices, and foreign revenues were plowed into the expensive production values, technical innovations, and marketing strategies of the "star system" that consumers commonly identified with Hollywood features and expressed powerful preferences for at the international box office.[8]

American market power at the dawn of the sound era in 1927 had already produced a wave of protectionist legislation across Europe that would result in boycotts by U.S. producers and the beginning of direct investment in production facilities abroad. Arguably, what secured the domestic industry in places such as Britain and Italy was the creation of American subsidiaries making "local" films to satisfy national quotas and sustain the dream of regaining U.S. market share. Thomas H. Guback argues that adoption of the sound film resulted in deepening the Americanization of this emerging mass medium. The cost increases associated with this conversion priced some erstwhile rivals out of the market, and as new sound theaters were built, the American industry shipped record amounts of celluloid to supply the world's moviegoers (Guback 1985, 468).

Because nationalists in places such as Mexico, England, Egypt, or Argentina often harbored the costly illusion that films are highly substitutable goods, it is worthwhile considering the institutions that came to shape demand for this particular commodity in the world market. Theaters needed reliable and scheduled deliveries of new films to show on their screens. But it was not sufficient simply to have a projector running. Their seats had to be filled to guarantee large enough receipts to keep theaters open and studios producing. The historical record suggests that this was a daunting task in virtually any country that attempted to build a sound-film industry, and, in comparison to other ISI sectors, one in which it was next to impossible to succeed.

As Ian Jarvie notes, investment in films or related mass-entertainment industries "is among the riskiest of large businesses, because it is a luxury, and because public taste is fickle" (1992, 430; see also Prindle 1993). Ahmad al-Aswani's exposé of the losses racked up by the Egyptian public sector productions in the late 1960s is a potent reminder of this problem.[9] The strategies Hollywood adopted to reduce this risk centered around the star system described above, the production of a wide variety of genres and styles, and the systematic marketing of movies and moviegoing, which won audience allegiance and constrained competitors to compete on Hollywood's terms for a share of the home market. But the rising costs of doing business, among other factors, also meant that export revenues played a direct role in supporting this production system.

The forces that shaped Hollywood's push into Egypt and other outposts on the periphery at the dawn of the cold war are equally well known to historians of the industry. Protectionist currents gained ground in its traditional export markets in Europe and Latin America, and because of the global shortage of dollars, profit remittances were subject to strict control. Epitomizing the postwar context, GATT, a global accord negotiated in Geneva in 1947, conceded the right of states to impose screen quotas on films (Film Daily 1960, 779; Jarvie 1990). The same year marks the beginning of a sharp, structural decline in U.S. movie attendance and box office revenues as new forms of leisure reshaped Americans' consumption patterns. Compounding the industry's troubles, one year later, in 1948, an antitrust decision forced the studios to divest themselves of their theater chains, which paved the way for the opening of the market to foreign-made films in the 1950s (Guback 1985, 475–77; Armes 1987, 36).

Expansion into Egypt followed the conventional pattern. As sales increased above a certain level, companies tended "to move from using an agent or licensing agreement to using a subsidiary company" (Thompson 1985, 3). Though American films had displaced French and Italian imports in the small Egyptian market by 1929, many were originally distributed by European suppliers. Drawing on this early history, Lizbeth Malkmus and Roy Armes concluded that "U.S. distribution companies did not become directly involved in the Egyptian market" (1991, 6). But the claim is incorrect.

Universal was distributing its own films as early as 1926, and its competitors all followed suit over the next decade.[10] The largest theater in Cairo in the 1940s, the Metro, was owned by MGM, which, together with Twentieth Century-Fox, also built theaters in Alexandria in the 1940s and 1950s. Thus American distributors represented the nascent Egyptian industry's main postwar competitors. They relied on permanent, locally based representatives and a long-standing information circuit that linked the embassy, the State Department, and the Motion Picture Association of America (MPAA) and required that their local subsidiaries establish or join a common association.[11] Supplementing these channels, as in other markets, Hollywood pursued collective interests in Egypt through the Motion Pictures Export Association (MPEA), which staffed an office in Rome. The emergence of a competing local feature-film industry in the 1930s provided the American firms a powerful stimulus to mobilizing.

IMPERIALISM AND REVOLUTION AT THE CAIRO PALACE

For most historians, the end of World War II marks the beginning of a new phase in Egypt's protracted struggle over decolonization, as students, workers, and others took to the streets in an escalating wave of strikes and demonstrations. One action on February 29, 1948, is not very well known, however. That morning, the Egyptian stage and screen star Yusuf Wahbi, one of the pioneers of the Egyptian film industry and head of its technicians' and artists' syndicate, led its members in a shutdown of the country's studios.[12] Their target was the local release of *Thief of Baghdad* (United Artists, 1940), which had been dubbed into Arabic and was drawing record numbers to Studio Misr's cinema on 'Imad al-Din street in downtown Cairo.[13]

Wahbi, who with resident Syrian investors was a part owner of Nahhas Studios, one of a rash of new local ventures that had attracted some of the fantastic profits earned in Egypt during the war, was artful in his weaving together of self and national interest story lines in his rallying cry that dubbing had hammered "the first nail in the coffin of the Egyptian film industry." Misr Studios, which had been opened in 1935 on Pyramids Road by the country's leading "national" capitalist coalition, the Bank Misr group, was the first of the country's eight modern sound-film studios.[14] But its capacity, like many of its other large-scale ventures, was underutilized, and the company began to distribute other films in the 1940s, minimally, to keep its single theater filled (Hasan 1986, 83).

The U.S. firms naturally backed the Misr group. To them Arabic was a type of trade barrier that producers like Wahbi used to extract monopoly rents from Egyptian consumers. Though local production of 35 mm feature films began to grow rapidly toward the end of World War II, from an average of 15 films per year in the late 1930s to 50 per year in the mid-

1940s, the U.S. distributors argued that the potential for the Arabic market was much larger. The major U.S. distributors alone imported about 250 films in 1945–46 to meet the demand of the small number of exclusive downtown theaters catering to the European residents and English-speaking Egyptians.[15] In 1945 local producers had used their political clout to force the owners of each of the seven largest Cairo theaters to screen one Arabic film per year.[16] Now the minister of social affairs arranged a similar voluntary, or "gentlemen's," agreement that restricted distributors to marketing no more than three dubbed films per year.[17]

Wahbi continued his attack on the American motion picture industry in the pages of *Dunya al-fann* (May 25, 1948), where he urged Egyptians on patriotic grounds to boycott American films, whose single purpose he said was to aid the cause of Zionism: "Every piaster paid for American films goes straight to the Jews."[18] Egypt was by that time in the midst of a war and American stars were highly visible in the campaign for Israel's defense. But the politics of the conflict and of post–World War II Egyptian society more generally had long since spilled into the lobbies of Cairo's movie palaces. During the student strikes in February and March 1946, exhibitors were pressured to stop showing English-language films and newsreels, and radicals tossed a hand grenade during the showing of a double bill at the Miami theater.[19] The MGM-owned Metro was bombed on May 6, 1947. Subsequently and prudently MGM and Twentieth Century-Fox, the other U.S. company represented among theater owners in Cairo, had agreed to allow the High Committee of the Nile Valley for the Liberation of Palestine to raise funds for the war inside their theaters, and the committee's activists papered over the likes of Danny Kaye and Mickey Rooney with posters of a "Jewish hand being forced by an Egyptian hand to drop a bloody knife."[20]

As significant new and canonical modern public spaces, it is hardly surprising to find political currents contesting in the theater lobbies as they might elsewhere in the city, for example, in the university, and to find theater owners and managers preferring to keep politics separate from the business of showing movies, however futilely in the case of the 1948 war. But, of course, same thing that American ambassadors in Cairo and elsewhere around the world recognized about these particular spaces when they celebrated films as "good propaganda for us" and the American way of life "here" meant that the Metro, the Diana, and the Royale were constituent elements in a landscape of power in Cairo.[21] And, clearly, it mattered not just what was shown on the screen and who could sell stamps in the lobby but also who sat in the seats. Egyptians understood that MGM's Cairo manager did not want to show Arabic films because he did not want working-class Arabic speakers in the house.[22]

In the early 1930s the fascist-styled Misr al-Fatat (Young Egypt) movement launched its famous boycott of foreign institutions with a campaign against the "Royal, Metropole, Triumph, Roxy, Olympia, and so forth" where "hundreds and thousands of young Egyptians" were "cooperating for the profit of a single foreigner . . . in spite of all the contempt which the latter shows them on all occasions."[23] And in comparing the films shown inside these places to "poisons," "drugs," and "alcoholic drinks," the party's ideologues ascribed to celluloid the same power over desire that American diplomats celebrated in their cables to Washington. In ensuing years cultural conservatives and authenticists of all stripes—from the Muslim Brothers to the Wafd's Vanguard—would blame Hollywood for the sexual obsessions of the young and the rising crime rate in the city streets. As an editorial put it: "We even would not be exaggerating if we say that such criminal ideas are deliberately directed to us and that those who supply this type of film intend to harm us. The West is trying to fight us with every weapon and harm us by any means."[24]

The early history of the Egyptian government's involvement with controlling the moving image makes clear that British officials saw lurking in the light and shadows the same subversive power that obsessed the shaykhs and other guardians of the moral and political order. The administrative machinery for reviewing domestic and foreign motion pictures in the 1920s and 1930s was located in the Ministry of Interior and was overseen by the infamous head of its European department, Alexander Keown-Boyd, to whom diplomats and representatives of Hollywood distributors routinely appealed when particular U.S. films were banned. Keown-Boyd had the power to overturn the decision of Egyptian censors, as he did in March 1936 in the case of *Mutiny on the Bounty* (MGM, 1935).[25] He would not budge, however, when the highly influential Motion Pictures Producers and Distributors Association (MPPDA) protested to Washington over the banning of another MGM product, *Rasputin and the Princess* (1932). He upheld the ban on the grounds that the film was "anti-monarchic, likely to cause anti-Christian feeling, and crude in its representation of the . . . execution of the Royal family by the mob."[26] Egyptians, "excitable and easily affected," had already shown themselves vulnerable in the past to "subversive communist activities." Although Keown-Boyd reported that he "thoroughly enjoyed the film" himself, he found "it impossible to sanction the showing of a *soidisant* priest using mesmerism, as this is a sight which will confirm in the eyes of the mob the worst allegations made against missionaries." He continued, "Moreover, I am sure that you will not think it proper that in a Moslem country, Christians, after constant recourse to prayer, signs of the Cross, etc., should be shown as being murdered by a brutal mob who have cast off all religious feeling."[27]

The vigilance of the censors survived Keown-Boyd's retirement from the government service and Egyptianization of the Interior Ministry, as American reports on the eve of the July 1952 revolution make clear. The list of film imports banned in 1951 is as good an indicator as any of institutional continuity, if not obsession: *Crisis* (MGM, 1950), depicting a revolution against an unjust ruler; *Sound of Fury* (Universal, 1950), an American film about student revolution; *I Was a Communist* (Warner Brothers, 1951); and *Quebec* (Paramount, 1951), which Americans described as being about organizing an internal revolution. Censorship extended to the ubiquitous newsreels when they depicted "riots, demonstrations or other scenes that touch royalty."[28]

The media policy of the ancien régime was not solely reactive, however, and in the wake of World War II government actors sought to harness this supposed power of the moving image in support of progressive reform. The support for local producers in their competition with Hollywood was in fact part of this process. The would-be Egyptian "imagineers" were housed in the newly established Ministry of Social Affairs, where modernist currents sought to design a way forward through, as they saw it, the fog of illiteracy, superstition, and reaction. The 1950 Wafd government's crusading social reformer, Ahmad Husayn, promoted the ministry's evolving mass-media propaganda department as critical to the promotion of people's welfare in the countryside, to include the use of mobile 16 mm film units in the ministry's showcase rural social centers.[29] Good propaganda is designed with particular audiences in mind, so when one of Husayn's protégés, 'Abbas 'Ammar, the head of the ministry's Fallah Department, lectured to the American University in Cairo in 1951, he carefully left the seventh, mass-propaganda department out of his sketch of the "six departments of the ministry."[30]

American sensibilities notwithstanding, in the wake of the Palestine war the U.S. government began to create similar kinds of propaganda films to publicize the new Point Four aid efforts and related projects, including those of the Social Affairs Ministry. A director of educational films was sent to Cairo to work with embassy officers on the project, and by July 1951 six short films were approved for production, though these were unlikely to draw many away from the latest Anwar Wajdi or Farid al-Atrash picture. The first four included *Leadership Training*, a twenty-minute documentary on the operation and purpose of the Fallah Department's recreation leader training program, which was designed to establish American 4-H–type clubs in Egyptian villages; *Point Four and Egypt* (30 min.); *NAMRU 3* (20 min.), on the navy's medical research unit; and *EAUF Egypt-American University Fellowship*, about the happy association of Egyptians and Americans in Egypt who have degrees from U.S. colleges.[31]

At the same time, both the American and the Egyptian governments devoted increasing attention to the presumed political effects of the newsreels that the exhibitors screened before each week's feature. The Americans had begun to develop newsreels on the Korean War, and MGM's representatives saw the opportunity for renewing the subsidies their firm received during World War II. The company's Cairo representative criticized the inadequate U.S. coverage in British-produced newsreels and argued that Egyptians and audiences throughout the region would welcome "material showing the industrial power of America, . . . the might of the U.S. Army, Navy and Air Forces, . . . facilities granted to all citizens without discrimination of race, color or class, . . . the daily life of the average Mr. Joe and ordinary worker, his family life, his house, comfort and car."[32] Two Egyptian government agencies were already subsidizing the Misr Studios newsreels, helping to invent that seemingly timeless genre of monarchs (then) and presidents (now) alternately enthroned in 'Abdin Palace with visiting dignitaries or cutting ribbons at some new public building.[33]

For Hollywood and its outpost on the Nile, films were first and foremost about making money, obviously. The Egyptian market had been profitable from the start of significant exports in the 1920s. Enduring features of the market were already in place by that time. There were only some 50 theaters operating in 1929, well below the Western world average when one controls for size of population (Landau 1958, 160; for background, see Sadoul 1966, 129–36). As the broadsides of Young Egypt ceaselessly reminded their readers, these were owned by members of the Greek, Italian, and Jewish colonies. This number grew to 315 by 1951, which included 239 covered and 76 open-air or seasonal theaters. Construction then stagnated through the 1950s and 1960s.[34] These approximately 255,000 seats were concentrated in Cairo and Alexandria. And early American reporting took note of the division between a European clientele in the cities' luxury movie palaces and "the lower class Egyptians patronizing the cheaper theaters."[35]

It also seems clear that by the end of the silent-film era American films had come to dominate screen time in Egypt. The American trade commissioner estimated that a minimum of 50 percent of all films shown were U.S. made. The manager of the Josey Film Agency, a subsidiary of the local Suarès group and the country's biggest distributor of American films at the time, argued that the numbers were much higher: "about 80 percent among the total films in Cairo. First rate cinemas run nearly 70 percent and popular cinemas about 90 percent of American films; French and other production are used on an average of 10 percent."[36] Thus, although Egypt's market was small in comparison to Europe and Latin America—there were, for example, one thousand screens in Argentina by 1930—the receipts were large enough to convince the big American producers to follow the pioneering efforts of Universal Pictures.

Twenty years later the industry's export arm, the MPEA, called Cairo the "center for the release of American motion pictures throughout the Middle

East," but at the same time its members recognized an important change in the nature of that market.[37] Egyptian films were playing on more screens and earning more revenues than American films. In fact, the vast majority of theaters—the so-called popular cinemas—were lost to U.S. distributors and showed only Arabic-language films in the 1940s and the 1950s. The American embassy guessed that at best only 10 to 15 percent of the country's theaters showed exclusively foreign films.

Data on the revenues derived from the Egyptian market are hard to come by, and the following must be considered at best as indicative of the general order of magnitude. Figures from the *Annuaire du Cinema,* 1951–52, sent back to Washington from the Cairo embassy, estimated that American films grossed £E 1 million (U.S. $2.88 million) in 1951 out of a total of £E 5.5 million (U.S. $15.84 million) for the industry as a whole. American films thus accounted for approximately 20 percent of total box office receipts and between 20 and 35 percent of total screen time. An average gross for a large theater exhibiting a "good" Arabic film was reported at £E 13,000 to 18,000 against £E 8,000 for an American film. We also have figures for the net revenues from the American exports in the form of remittances for the same year. At that time the government restricted firms to converting 35 percent (down from 50 percent) of total royalties for remittance abroad, which equaled $150,000. Thus total royalties were declared at the equivalent of some $429,000 in 1951, up from $400,000 in 1950.[38]

What was at the time a conventional understanding of the limited market reach of the American product has long since been forgotten, and today's third cinéastes draw questionable conclusions from the comparison of total films imported in any one year to those made by local producers. The top seven American distributors shipped 254 features in 1945–46 and local companies released 49 features, but many more of the more than one million estimated weekly moviegoers countrywide were likely to see Ahmad Badr Khan's *Shahr al-'asal* (Honeymoon) or Muhammad Karim's *Dunya* (World) than MGM's *A Guy Named Joe.*[39] And unlike virtually every other modern Egyptian industrial sector, local production emerged without resort to organized state intervention. Hollywood on the Nile was a virtually unregulated market when compared to the Italian, French, German, or British industries before and after World War II (Guback 1985).

The most obvious competitive advantage was the ability to make movies in the vernacular, or *'ammiyya,* at a time when relatively few Egyptians could understand English or read subtitles. But lost in the ritualistic dismissal of the styles, genres, and products of the era as vulgar, escapist, crassly imitative, vapid, and so on, is a serious consideration of the popularity of these films with their rapidly expanding audience. The war itself did not lead consumers to switch from imported to locally made goods, as was the case in textiles, food products, and virtually all other forms of consumer goods.

Western films continued to play in Cairo during the war years, and, need-less to say, the new flows of foreigners were not flocking to the latest Umm Kulthum musical. But, as is well known, the war drove Egyptians from the countryside to the cities, where work was plentiful and wages were rising. Licit and illicit gains—including the skyrocketing salaries commanded by the small pantheon of stars—are also widely believed to have been a main source of the capital behind the increased production of the postwar years.[40]

It is next to impossible to tease much more reliable information about the structure of the early post–World War II industry from the existing pub-lished sources and the primary materials exploited here for the first time.[41] Data on the industry are scarce and unreliable. Indeed, if the Egyptian in-dustry resembled the Indian case, then the systematic level of wheeling and dealing makes it unlikely that we will ever be able to determine the distri-bution of profits among stars, producers, and exhibitors, or the profitabil-ity of any particular filmmaking venture. The sector was small relative to other industries. Total capital invested in 1950 was approximately £E 10 million, some £E 1.5 million to 2 million in production and distribution fa-cilities and the remainder in theaters, projectors, and so on. And it em-ployed forty-five hundred men and women, numbers that were comparable to the petroleum sector.[42]

One conclusion I draw from these materials is that the local industry ap-pears to have had a viable—that is, competitive—product that consumers wanted to buy. This point is reinforced if the regional market is considered and, in particular, the fact that other Arabic-speaking countries had next to no filmmaking capacity. A second conclusion is that, its comparative advan-tage notwithstanding, the industry faced numerous obstacles to growth. Be-cause of the degree of risk involved, financing was difficult to arrange. De-mand may well have outstripped distributors' ability to supply the market, hence Studio Misr's attempt to dub American features into Arabic.[43] There is little doubt that individual maverick producers were finding it difficult to recoup their investments, despite the relatively low £E 20,000 that a typical Egyptian feature film reportedly cost. By contrast, however small the Amer-ican market share, it was eyed jealously because it was pure profit for Holly-wood, which dumped films already tested in numerous marketplaces for which costs had most likely been recovered long before reaching Cairo.

The third conclusion should be obvious. Clearly, there were distinct cur-rents at work in the pressures that the major American distributors faced in Cairo and Alexandria after World War II. But in the case of the local in-vestors represented by Wahbi, Hollywood was apparently a scapegoat to be used to rescue him and his comrades.

ON THE ROAD TO THE PERIPHERY

The nationalization of the production and exhibition segments of the Egyptian film industry in the early 1960s was by all accounts (save by those who looted this particular cash cow for a while) a mega-disaster. In the hands of bureaucrats, the studios racked up new enormous losses and production ground virtually to a standstill. Despite the rapid growth in population, the number of movie theaters in Egypt actually declined. This was clearly *not* the outcome that Yusuf Wahbi and the other studio owners had in mind when they began to lobby for government subsidies and protection in the late 1940s and more insistently after the July 1952 revolution. It is not clear, however, that these investors had much of a strategy in mind to solve the structural problems of the industry apart from some desultory rent seeking in the form of production subsidies and raised entry barriers for American film imports. When the state did finally step in, the film sector was not a priority of the economic planners—far from it. Instead, beginning in 1957 and culminating with the nationalizations in the early 1960s, the sector came under the authority of the revolution's new Ministry of National Guidance.

The remarkably efficient information arm of the MPAA drew the attention of Washington to the precocious signs of corporatist thinking within the Egyptian film sector in the months following the Free Officers coup in July 1952. An industry publicist floated a plan to create a National Film Center that would regulate entry into all sections of the movie industry and subsidize production—in the public interest, of course.[44] When such a center was finally created in 1957, its location within the propaganda apparatus clarified that politics would loom large in shaping the sector's future.

Hollywood's export cartel, the MPEA, again contacted the U.S. government early in 1954 when its member firms reported that Nasser's government was considering some form of protectionist legislation, similar to policies in France and Italy, on behalf of local producers and distributors who were suffering the effects of sharp declines in box office receipts in 1952 and 1953.[45] Although the local press reported continued trouble at the box office in 1954, the industry's representatives gained little from their continuing petitions to the propaganda czars as well as to the Ministry of Commerce and Industry where they were lobbying for new import taxes and mandatory screen time at all theaters.[46]

Local firms were finding it difficult to overcome entrenched prejudices that many elites harbored about the artistic, if not commercial, worthlessness of films and to gain recognition for the sector among emerging developmentalist currents. Take the case of the minister of commerce and industry, Hassan Mar'i. In 1955 he was busy implementing an ambitious, American-designed program of import substitution industrialization proj-

ects, precisely along the lines that film producers envisioned for their embattled sector (see Vitalis 1995, 202–6). But the minister instead struck a
classically liberal posture according to press accounts, urging the film producers to improve the quality of their films—that is, via the pressure of
competition—and, incredulously, given Hollywood's lock on the market,
promising to study ways to increase exports to cities with expatriate Arab
communities in the United States.[47]

Of course, the United States was also counseling Mar'i against the demands of the film producers syndicate. Unfortunately, the ministry's high-
priced American industrial consultants, handpicked and paid for by the
Eisenhower administration, argued wrongly (out of ignorance or worse)
that *no* Egyptian sector produced goods that could compete in wider regional Arab markets, and, quite unlike the views that are promoted today,
Egyptians were advised to concentrate on industry building behind tariff
walls (open, of course, to American capital). Then, as now, the film industry seems to have escaped consideration as an appropriate sector for capitalist development.

Political realities shifted in favor of the embattled Egyptian film producers in 1956. Populist currents were by then more solidly entrenched inside
the state, and the influence of key American allies such as Mar'i had waned.
Sectoral interests had built bridges to Nasser's circle (or perhaps the officers had imagined a cheap means to shape hearts and minds) through Wajih Abaza, who was the second-largest shareholder in a new distribution
company with Studio Misr and various actors and directors.[48] And the owners of Studio Misr must have been desperate to stem its mounting losses
(Hasan 1986, 77; al-Aswani 1983, 22). In October the head of Twentieth
Century-Fox in Cairo, Oscar Lax, was warning about the imminent imposi-
tion of new import restrictions and screen quotas in place of the informal
restrictions under which he and others were then laboring.[49] The text of
the new Law No. 373 was published on November 3, 1956, but the new
rules were far from stringent. Reflecting a more general pattern of prefer-
ential treatment of U.S. investment, exhibitors had to increase the screen
time reserved for local production to three weeks per year and to show
newsreels approved by the Propaganda Ministry.[50] These rules assumed
that there were twenty-five new features that could draw audiences to the
cavernous downtown showcases that the dwindling foreign communities
had patronized. More rigid quotas were unlikely to solve the industry's apparent woes.

The overarching reality is that the commercial cinema was far from central to those in Egypt who imagined an economy as a set of commanding
heights: dams, power plants, steel mills, skyscrapers, oil rigs, and so on. The
planners recognized that American imports represented a drain on hard
currency, but the domestic industry's modest size and the nature of its

product, labor, and export profiles fit poorly in the five-year plans. I would guess too that the lavish and libertine culture prevailing in the industry fit uneasily with emerging populist and revolutionary iconography, and not all its luminaries would be able to make the transition from *ibn al-balad* or *bint al-zawat* to *awlad al-thawra* (from son of the village or daughter of the elite to children of the revolution). After all, many of the industry's leading lights actually led the life that others, watching the films of the 1940s and 1950s, could only fantasize about or rebel against.[51] As I suggested in the introduction, the increasingly grave portraits painted by the local managers of MGM and the other American distributors in the wake of the 1956 war make it seem that Russian agents were more interested in the movie business than were Egyptian planners. But what is most obvious in the last frames of the State Department microfilm is the defensiveness of these particular businessmen as the regime pressed ahead in the direction of a command economy.

In summer 1957 the army officers in charge of the arts, culture, and propaganda divisions of the revolution announced the creation of the new National Organization for the Consolidation of the Cinema. At the time their civilian American counterparts in the United States Information Service (USIS) were busy in a futile campaign to get the Egyptian government to include more footage of atoms for peace and Point Four locomotives and less footage of the Red Army in its weekly newsreels.[52] Meanwhile, the representatives of MGM and some of the other U.S. distributors were looking into the costs of shifting their operations permanently to Beirut.[53]

The press leaks and rumors that surrounded the policy-making process hinted at a more formidable institution than the one that was finally unveiled, and of course foreign investors tried to ensure this outcome. The new organization, which followed the broad lines proposed by J. Pascal in 1952, was designed to regulate the domestic industry and subsidize its production.[54] When the new import taxes were finally unveiled, the shift from a tax rate based on weight to a flat charge per film meant that importers would be paying no more than before, though the new formula would keep out some of the marginal fare that was circulated.[55] The real problem for the American firms was the continuing obstacles put in the way of securing the necessary import licenses, which minimally suggested rent seeking on the part of customs agents, although some firms believed the impediments were more deliberate and systematic.[56]

Most stories about films during Egypt's revolutionary era start from this point (e.g., El Charkawi 1966, 92). That is, a public sector in some form is presumed to have been the correct counterweight to Hollywood's alleged dominance of local screen time, box office receipts, audience tastes, studio techniques, and filmmaking craft. The stories differ in explaining what went wrong, for instance, as when a young Raymond Baker bemoaned the failure to create a truly revolutionary cinema capable of mobilizing the masses, or when others blamed the regime for failing to legislate a commercially viable cinema (Baker 1974, 397).[57] And Hollywood's hold on the imagination is now stronger than ever.

A new story begs to be told, and it begins in 1957 on 'Imad al-Din Street. Late that year the sleekly modern Studio Misr cinema reopened under a new name, the Ritz, and under new management. The troubled studio had closed the theater in 1956, "for renovations" (Hasan 1986, 77). The precipitous decline of the firm and the faltering of the industry in the decade or so after 1950 have yet to be seriously described, let alone explained. What we can say at this point is only that the American Ambassador in Technicolor and Cinemascope had little if anything to do with it.

CONCLUSION

Iskandariyya layh? (Alexandria Why? 1978), the autobiographical film by Youssef Chahine, Egypt's most internationally renowned director, depicts himself and the theaters on Alexandria's Safiya Zaghlul Street as haunted by Hollywood (see Shohat and Stam 1994, 282–85). But Roy Armes does his readers an injustice in treating the same scenes as fact rather than metaphor on the printed page: "He [Chahine] has shown on several occasions that he feels the exclusion of Arab films from European screens very keenly, but he is understandably far more bitter about the 80 percent of screen time that foreign films traditionally enjoyed in Egypt" (1987, 245). Although other third cinéastes occasionally draw on aggregate import figures to support the idea of foreign market dominance, they forget what is most basic to the story: Cairo and Alexandria were colonial cities with a distinctive cultural landscape. Movie markets were—and there is nothing surprising here—segmented. It appears that a small set of theaters catered primarily to European residents. Many more venues drew many more Egyptians, or, more accurately, those who spoke only Arabic or preferred Arabic-language films. These were probably divided as well by class. In the provinces the markets were smaller (roughly 20 percent of all theater seats) but were probably preserves for the domestic producers.

The Cairo Palace and other showcases were every bit as much contested sites in the course of decolonization as 'Abdin, the barracks in Qasr al-Nil, and the embassy in Qasr al-Dubbara. Shirley Temple, not Fatin Hamama, made money for the exhibitors there in the 1940s, and quite reasonably some nationalists were committed to (and invested in) a project of liberating the marquee. But the reduction of the story of the industry as a whole to what was happening in 8 or 10 of Cairo's 120 theaters and to what a relatively privileged segment of the 500,000 or more weekly consumers desired is a mistake. The memories of those days and places are no less vulnerable to the effects of time and politics than are our stylized accounts to-day of the films of that "classic" era in the Egyptian cinema. Walter Arm-brust makes a case for looking at them afresh. The bit of archival footage I uncovered suggests we need to look just as carefully at the industry that produced them.

In *Unthinking Eurocentrism* Ella Shohat and Robert Stam criticize film his-torians and cultural theorists for their obsessions with Hollywood: "What we now call 'Third World cinema' did not begin in the 1960s, as is often as-sumed. . . . In the 1920s, India was producing more films than Great Britain. Countries like the Philippines were producing over fifty films a year by the 1930s, Hong Kong was making more than 200 films annually by the 1950s" (1994, 28–29).[58] Yet they fail to think through the implications of this decentering for the notions of "neocolonial dependency and domina-tion" that, contradictorily, they argue are fundamental to any "adequate ac-count" of the political economy of the Mexican, Indian, Egyptian, and so on, film industry (Shohat and Stam 1994, 17–18).

The reality is that the Indian case turns these ideologies of the domi-nated on their head; the "infiltration" of foreign capital that they disparage made possible many of the film industries that they want to celebrate. And the presumed benefits of trade barriers and quotas continue to go unex-amined just as long as they are opposed by the hegemon's agents in Univer-sal City, Geneva, and New York (Shohat and Stam 1994, 30). Abroad the audience for this stock tale of tragic heroes defending against an evil em-pire is dwindling (Vitalis 1996, 13–33; 1997, 15–21).

NOTES

I am indebted to Walter Armbrust and Vickie Langohr, who provided early, much-needed help on this project; to Zerxes Spencer, Danielle Yifrah, Chris Newsham, and Torsten Fetzer, students in the senior thesis workshop of Clark University's gov-ernment department, for early criticism of the first sections of the chapter; and to Ginny Danielson and Michael Suleiman, for encouraging counsel.

1. Many of the local managers of Hollywood's Big Eight (Columbia, MGM, RKO, Twentieth Century-Fox, United Artists, Universal Pictures, Warner Brothers, and Paramount) subsidiaries were Jews. For instance, Oscar Lax, who worked for Fox, sat out the crisis in Beirut. M. Sassa, who managed MGM's holdings, feared deportation (he carrried a Tunisian passport) and deposited copies of the company's files at the U.S. embassy. Jacques Kroub, an Italian national who managed the local Warner Brothers subsidiary, was barred from reentry into Egypt, until Egyptian business partners intervened (Cairo to State, December 20, 1956, No. 421, RG 59, 874.452/12–2056).

2. I use "Hollywood" to designate the Big Eight production-distribution multi-nationals and "Hollywood on the Nile," their Egyptian distribution business, as

shorthands of convenience. Hollywood was where motion pictures were made. New York was where these firms organized the global export of their product.

3. Cairo to State, May 10, 1957, No. 854; RG 59, 874.452/5–1057. For Lax's report on Abaza, see Cairo to State, October 20, 1956, No. 318, RG 59, 874.452/10–2056.

4. See al-Tilmisani 1957. I am indebted to Columbia University's Andrew Flibbert for locating the reference in the course of researching his dissertation-in-progress on the Egyptian and Mexican film industries.

5. In addition to the relevant sections of Armes 1987, Malkmus and Armes 1991, and Shohat and Stam 1994, see Baker 1974; Gaffney 1987; Thorval 1975. The Egyptian critic Samir Farid (e.g., 1977) is a powerful influence on much of this writing.

6. A critical exception is Armbrust 1996. Although the scope goes beyond films, it takes the discussion of this medium in a new direction. His work, together with Harris 1986 and Tomlinson 1991, shapes the perspective developed in this chapter.

7. Thompson uses import shares as a measure: "American film can be considered dominant in a market when it obtained a significantly larger share than its competitors—say, 40% of the footage available, with others supplying 20%, 15%, etc. In practice, the American share was often so large that the definition becomes automatic—achieving a 70–95% share is dominating a market by any standards" (1985, xi). But such an approach is misleading in the Egyptian case (and presumably others) because the market was segmented. A small number of theaters showed a large number of imported films, while a much larger number of theaters ran (and consumers saw) a smaller number of Arabic-language films each year. The Indian exhibition sector was structured in a similar way (see Shah [1950] 1981, 57–63).

8. Carroll (1985, 81) refers to "Hollywood International" or "popular mass-media films" in the "classical style," whether they be American, Italian or Chinese.

9. Al-Aswani (1983, 33) reports total receipts for 1967–70 of £E 404,000 on forty-four films that cost £E 1.2 million to produce. Some covered as little as 1.5 percent of their costs. He does not give box office data.

10. On Universal, see Cairo to State, April 15, 1926, No. 798, Enclosure, RG 559, 883.4061/10. RKO and Paramount were involved in a legal dispute over taxes in 1938 (see Cairo to State, January 31, 1949, No. 122, RG 59, 883.4061/MP/1–3149). Twentieth Century-Fox registered its Egyptian subsidiary, Twentieth Century-Fox Import Corporation, in New York in 1944 and in Cairo in 1945 (Alexandria to State, February 16, 1951, No. 105, RG 59, 74.452/2–1651).

11. See Cairo to State, March 5, 1945, RG 59, 883.4061/MP/3–545 CS/R.

12. On Wahbi, see Armbrust 1996, 329–37.

13. This account is drawn from the report in Cairo to State, March 2, 1948, No. A-161, RG 59, 883.4061/MP/3–248. The studio and movie house were outgrowths of the Misr Company for Theater and Cinema (Sharikat Misr lil-Tamthil wa-al-Sinima), founded in 1925, which despite its name was originally an advertising and publicity agency for Bank Misr and its other new ventures, using the medium of film, among others. The investors soon began planning for full-scale film production (see Hasan 1986). The artists' and technicians' syndicate was founded in 1943, according to Sa'd 1986.

14. The industry dates back to the silent era. For its early years, see al-Hadari 1989.

15. Figures from Sadoul 1966, pt. 6, Film Lists and Statistics; Cairo to State, April 1, 1948, No. 266, RG 59, 883.4061/MP/4–148; Cairo to State, April 12, 1952, No. 2084, RG 59, 874.452/4–1252.

16. These were the Metro, Diana, Royal, Metropole, Opera, Cairo Palace, and Miami theaters. They were apparently all foreign owned (e.g., Greek, American, Lebanese, etc.), with the exception of the Opera, which was part of a chain owned by Muhammad and Mustafa Ghaffar. A committee made up of theater owners and representatives of the Ministry of Social Affairs was formed to administer the quota system and select the films for exhibition. The length of the run was based on a minimum one week's earnings. See Cairo to State, March 23, 1945, Enclosure, No A-548, RG 59, 883.4061/MP/10–1545.

17. See Cairo to State, March 8, 1948, No. A-179, RG 59, 883.4061/MP/3–848.

18. See the account in Cairo to State, June 5, 1948, No. 470, RG 59, 883.4061/MP/6–548. For the roots of the stereotype, see Gabler 1988.

19. See telegram from George Goussy, Cairo to RKO Radio Pictures, Export Division, March 11, 1946, enclosed in Milliken [manager of the international department, MPAA] to George Canty, Assistant Chief, Telecommunications Division, State (Cairo to State, March 11, 1946, RG 59, 883.4061/MP/3–1346). On the student movement in 1946, see Abdalla 1985, 62–79; Erlich 1989, 154–68.

20. See the account and supporting documentation in Cairo to State, March 1, 1948, No. 171, RG 59, 883.4061/MP/3–148.

21. See Cairo to State, October 16, 1952, No. 701, The Film Diplomatic Courier, RG 59, 874.452/10–1652; Zukin 1991.

22. Cairo to State, October 15, 1945, No. A-548, RG 59, 883.4061/MP/10–1545.

23. Quotation from the handbill "To the Youth of Egypt, Egypt Appeals to You / Accede to Its Desire and Boycott Foreign Motion Picture Theaters," translation enclosed in Cairo to State, January 20, 1934, No. 33, RG 59, 883.4061/MP/1. For background, see Gershoni and Jankowski 1995, 18–19.

24. Translation of an editorial from *al-Misri* [date not given, but it appeared sometime during the first week of September 1953] enclosed in USIS Cairo to USIS Washington, September 4, 1953, No. 61, Crime and Western Movies, RG 59, 874.452/9–435; also "The Grand Mufti on Marriage, Divorce, the Cinema, Communism and Birth Control," *al-Musawwar*, March 12, 1954, translation enclosed in Cairo to State, March 17, 1954, No. 2209, RG 59, 874.40/3–1754.

25. Cairo to State, March 21, 1936, No. 563, RG 59, 883.4061-Mutiny on the Bounty/1. For background on the censorship apparatus, see Mumtaz 1985, 9–88.

26. See A. W. Keown-Boyd to Manager, MGM [no name], Cairo, May 2, 1934, enclosed in Cairo to State, May 31, 1934, No. 85, RG 59, 883.4061/MP/Rasputin and the Empress.

27. A. W. Keown-Boyd to Manager, MGM [no name], in Cairo to State, May 2, 1934, RG 59, 883.4061/MP/Rasputin and the Empress). Bert Fish, the Florida judge and Democratic party loyalist whom the Roosevelt administration rewarded with a posting to Cairo, was "inclined to agree with the conclusions [that it] is not

the kind of picture which should be shown to ignorant, and often fanatical, Mohamedan audiences."

28. Cairo to State, No. 2084, Entertainment Motion Pictures—35 MM, RG 59, 874.452/4–1252.

29. Designed to "to combat erroneous beliefs and superstitions through recreational methods." See Royal Government of Egypt, Ministry of Social Affairs (1950, 119). Nonetheless, officials at the Interior Ministry jealously guarded their prerogatives over the censorship administration. See Mumtaz 1985, 13–14.

30. See Cairo to State, March 29, 1951, RG 59, 874.40/3–2951. 'Ammar became minister of social affairs after the revolution.

31. See Cairo to State, June 9, 1951, No. 2927, Motion Picture Production in Egypt, RG 59, 874.452/6–951. For background on Point Four, see Godfried 1987.

32. See Cairo to State, July 19, 1950, No. 73, RG 59, 874.452/7–1950. For background on the cold war film policies of U.S. administrations, see Guback 1985, 473.

33. Cairo to State, April 12, 1952, No. 2084, Entertainment Motion Pictures—35 MM, RG 59, 874.452/4–1252.

34. Data in *Annuaire du Cinema 1951–52*, as reported in Cairo to State, April 12, 1952, No. 2084, RG 59, 874.452/4–1252; and Monaco 1966, 139.

35. J. Morton Howell, Minister, Cairo, to State, April 15, 1926, No. 798, RG 59, 883.4061/10.

36. See extract of a letter from Josey Film Agency enclosed in North Winship [American Consul, Cairo] to Howell, in Cairo to State, April 8, 1926, RG 59, 883.4061/10; on the Suarès group, see Vitalis 1995, 33–35.

37. See Cairo to State, March 5, 1945, Carl Milliken [manager, MPPDA] to Francis Cold de Wolf, Chief, Telecommunications Division, State, RG 59, 883.4061/MP/3–545 CS/R.

38. All figures in the last two paragraphs are reported in Cairo to State, April 12, 1952, No. 2084, RG 59, 874.452/4–1252. The higher figure on screen time, which attempts to account for Arabic-English double bills, is found in Cairo to State, June 23, 1954, No. 2943, RG 59, 874.452/6–2354.

39. The figure on attendance is merely for illustrative purposes, but based on government tax returns from ticket sales, the estimated annual attendance in 1950–51 was 92 million, or a weekly average of 1.84 million people. See Cairo to State, April 12, 1952, No. 2084, RG 59, 874.452/4–1252. For the 1945–46 film season, see Sadoul 1966, App. 6, Film Lists; and *Egyptian Gazette*, January 12, 1945, advertisement for the Metro.

40. See Armes 1987, 195–200. The better-studied and better-documented Indian case resembles the more anecdotal Egyptian account in key features. See Barnouw and Krishnaswamy 1963, 123–38; Oomen and Joseph 1991. But the claim by Armes (1987, 200), that after World War II films were the "easiest, quickest and surest" way of making a fortune, is not grounded in an adequate account of the market structure in which producers operated, nor can it account either for the rapid rise and fall of firms or the increasing demand for protection that I document below.

41. Two places for researchers to look in the future are the journals that U.S. embassy officers used. One is the *Annuaire du Cinema*, cited above. *Cine Film*, founded in 1947 by J. Pascal and housed at 27 'Adly Street, in the Cinema Metro building, is another. Both are presumably available at Dar al-Kutub. A third, per-

haps, is the Federation of Egyptian Industries, where an affiliated chamber of film industries was founded in 1947. See *al-Kitab al-dhahabi* 1972, 9. But the output of the sector is not even recorded in the aggregate statistical indexes of the federation.

42. Cairo to State, July 30, 1954, No. 173, RG 59, 874.452/7–3054. For employment figures in petroleum and other industrial sectors, see Abdel-Fadil 1980, 8.

43. See the discussion in J. M. Colton Hand [Commercial Policy Staff, Department of State] to John G. McCarthy [Vice President and Director, International Division, MPAA], Cairo to State, December 10, 1952, RG 59, 874.452/11–2852.

44. See McCarthy to Colton Hand, October 30, 1952, and Colton Hand to McCarthy, Cairo to State, December 10, 1952, RG 59, 874.452/11–2852.

45. Cairo to State, February 1, 1954, No. 1820, RG 59, 874.452/2–154.

46. See Cairo to State, January 24, 1955, No. 1434, RG 59, 874.452/1–2455; and Cairo to State, February 9, 1955, No. 1552, RG 59, 874.452/2–955, enclosing letter, Robert Carr [Counselor for Economic Affairs, U.S. embassy, Cairo] to Hassan Marei, February 8, 1955, and memorandum, E. Malek et al. [representatives of Hollywood distributors in Cairo] to Carr, February 7, 1955.

47. See Cairo to State, No. 1434, Motion Picture Industry–Egyptian Films Produced in 1954, RG 59, 874.452/1–2455.

48. See *al-Waqa'i' al-Misriyya*, February 17, 1955.

49. Cairo to State, October 20, 1956, No. 318, RG 59, 874.452/10–2056.

50. Cairo to State, December 13, 1956, No. 405, RG 59, 874.452/12–1355.

51. See the discussion of Yusuf Wahbi's memoirs in Armbrust 1996.

52. Cairo to State, June 10, 1957, No. 133, RG 59, 874.452/6–1057.

53. Cairo to State, December 20, 1956, No. 421, Egyptian Controls Affecting Certain Foreign Motion Pictures, RG 59, 874.452/12–2056.

54. Cairo to State, January 22, 1957, No. 504, RG 59, 874.452/1–2257; April 11, 1957, No. 766, RG 59, 874.452/4–1157; June 5, 1957, Telegram No. 3672, RG 59, 874.452/6–557; al-Aswani 1983, 21–22; Sharaf al-Din 1992, 23–24.

55. Rumored rates of £E 300 per film had been whittled down to £E 150 when the Ministry of Economy's new regulation was published in the *Official Journal* (No. 3, January 6, 1958). But the firms had estimated the average tariff per film under the old regime equaled £E 250. See Cairo to State, February 9, 1955, No. 1552, Proposed Increase in Import Duty on Motion Pictures and Requirement Regarding the Showing of Egyptian Pictures, RG 59, 874.452/2–955; Cairo to State, January 22, 1958, No. 719, Fees Imposed on the Importation of Motion Picture Film Into Egypt, RG 59, 874.452/1–2258.

56. Cairo to State, April 11, 1957, No. 766, RG 59, 874.452/4–1157; and Cairo to State, June 6, 1957, Telegram No. 3681, RG 59, 874.452/6–657.

57. He goes on, "The regime was content to continue the traditions of the ancien regime in regarding the cinema as merely a profitable business" (Baker 1974, 397). But this hardly explains its decline in the 1950s and 1960s. See also al-Aswani 1983; Gaffney 1987; Sharaf al-Din 1987.

58. They label this "Hollywoodcentrism" and argue for enhanced recognition and treatment of the global "filmic cornucopia."

THIRTEEN

The Golden Age before the Golden Age
Commercial Egyptian Cinema before the 1960s

Walter Armbrust

[In the 1940s] a type of film began which one could call a "collage"—a collage of songs and dances. But it wasn't cinema, or at least not what we know as cinema.
TAWFIQ SALIH, "AL-WAQIʿIYYAH"

One often encounters the opinion that "serious" Egyptian cinema dates from the 1960s, when the state partially nationalized the cinema, thereby allowing some directors to produce films according to criteria other than marketability. Although support for the public-sector cinema of the 1960s is not universal,[1] on one related issue intellectuals in both the pro– and anti–public-sector camps are substantially in agreement: there is little value in most of the films made in the three decades before the 1960s.

A small number of the nine hundred fifty Egyptian films made from 1927 to the early 1960s are excepted from axiomatic disparagement. These tend to be films interpreted as leading up to the 1960s, that is, works by directors who became prominent in the 1960s, and films that in retrospect are thematically similar to certain genres of the 1960s fare better than the rest. General audiences and fan magazines are more forgiving of the commercialism dominant in films made before the appearance of public-sector cinema. Critics attribute this enthusiasm to the misguided tastes of uneducated people suddenly thrust into the unfamiliar role of culture consumers. But is there really nothing more to be said of the hundreds of pre-1960s commercial genre films than that they are too vulgar to be worthy of attention?

Contrary to the conventional wisdom, I assume that early Egyptian films are important; that their ambiguous status as art should be a point of analysis rather than a reason to ignore them. Pierre Bourdieu suggests that the transcendence of art is "based on the power of the dominant to impose, by their very existence, a definition of excellence which . . . is bound to appear simultaneously as distinctive and different, and therefore both arbitrary . . . and perfectly necessary, absolute and natural" (1984, 255). Stuart Levine states the matter more directly: art forms, he says, are "not necessarily the product of 'cosmic truths, but are rather the result of certain peculiarities in the way in which our culture operates'" (quoted in Levine 1988, 2). Art is rooted ultimately in socially constructed systems of taste, and the converse is also true: lack of "good taste" is constructed through artistic expression, although it may not be recognized as such by arbiters of high culture. The social basis of artistic hierarchies—lowbrow to highbrow—seems obvious to anthropologists, but the idea has never taken root in the analysis of Egyptian (or more generally Arab) cinema.[2]

Early films are particularly important in the construction of Egyptian nationalism, as well as of Egypt's relationship with other Arabic-speaking societies. This is not to say that there is any simple congruence between nationalist ideology and the cinema. Many critics would simply dismiss commercial Egyptian films as a celebration of undesirable elements of Egyptian culture. Furthermore, even the degree to which the Egyptian cinema is truly Egyptian can be questioned from many different perspectives. Long before the tensions between globalism and localism became salient in academia, the Egyptian cinema was affected by both. The history of the uncomfortable position of commercial Egyptian cinema within local and nonlocal frames of reference was particularly relevant at an event recently held in New York—a large Arab film festival called the Centennial of Arab Cinema.[3]

Twenty-one of the forty films shown at the festival were Egyptian. Most of the twenty-one Egyptian films were either recent works or works in some way linked to the public sector.[4] Only two of the films shown had no link whatsoever—historically or thematically—to the public-sector cinema of the 1960s. Both were musicals, and it is one of these, *Ghazal al-banat* (The Flirtation of Girls; Wajdi 1949),[5] that interests me. In particular, the juxtaposition of *The Flirtation of Girls* with the film that followed it, a Tunisian production titled *Un été à la Goulette* (Summer in La Goulette; Boughedir 1995), shows how problematic the wholesale dismissal of commercial "genre films" can be, particularly in a cross-cultural context in which audiences may be ill-equipped to appreciate even the more rudimentary social and historical features of a film, let alone anything that could be described as a subtlety.

Film festivals are forced to juggle two not necessarily compatible objectives: "The desire to solve the problem of foreignness by overcoming difference or to communicate foreignness by revealing difference" (Schwartzman 1995, 90).[6] Reconciling the limitations of a metropolitan audience's perspectives with the imperative to present and interpret "difference"—a category that encompasses an obviously dizzying range of possibilities—is inevitably a part of any film festival. As a recent *Cineaste* editorial put it, "On the one hand, it seems foolish to discuss films Americans can't see, but if we

Figure 17. A collage of publicity stills in an advertisement for *The Flirtation of Girls* (*al-Ithnayn*, no. 761, January 10, 1949, p. 2). Courtesy of Dar al-Hilal.

don't promote *at least the best of them,* how will an audience for them ever be created?" ("Editorial" 1996, 1 [my emphasis]). The process of selecting "the best of them" often leads to a wholesale rejection of commercial films, which, in the context of "Arab cinema," means the bulk of Egyptian production.[7] The problem is that many commercial Egyptian films are excellent candidates for "revealing difference." Such films may exhibit a "density of local reference" (Crofts 1993, 59) lacking in films designed from the ground up to interpret one culture to another.

This is not to say that festival organizers have a great deal of leeway in their choices. They know that an audience can tolerate only so much "difference," and they are certainly not unaware that the fit between the films they exhibit and the audiences' ability to understand unfamiliar traditions is less than perfect. Festival curators are often intensely (even uncomfortably) aware of the difficulties inherent in selecting "a comprehensive group of films meant to introduce some . . . contemporary national cinema production to another country where there has been virtually no previous encounter with that cinema or culture in general" (Schwartzman 1995, 70).[8] I am not suggesting that the Centennial festival failed to achieve this objective but that the inclusion of *The Flirtation of Girls* was a factor in its success. Furthermore, this is not because the festival organizers were making a concession to commercial mass culture. *The Flirtation of Girls* belonged in the festival on its own merits as a film, which one would not expect given conventional opinions about the merits of Egyptian commercial films. Furthermore, as a means of "communicating foreignness by revealing difference," as Schwartzman put it, the film was probably without peer in the Centennial festival. It is ironic that expert specialist opinion generally encourages us to think just the opposite of such films—that they are simple, obvious, and culturally homogenizing.

The Flirtation of Girls played in New York to a rather small crowd of perhaps fifty people in the Walter Reade Theater, which can accommodate several hundred spectators. The film starred Layla Murad, a singer; Najib al-Rihani, a comedian; and Anwar Wajdi, an actor who played both comic and dramatic roles. The film also featured cameo appearances by two other prominent personalities, the actor and director Yusuf Wahbi and Muhammad 'Abd al-Wahhab, a singer and composer, considered to have been one of the greatest musicians of his day.

The Flirtation of Girls is nothing more or less than a showcase for stars— very much the "collage" mentioned so disparagingly by Tawfiq Salih in the epigraph to this chapter. It is primarily about media-constructed personalities, and even critics who are not favorably inclined to commercial films have conceded that it has a certain charm (e.g., Salih 1986, 200). Taken individually, each of the film's principals can be counted a national icon; the overall construction of the film, however, puts it in a category that gets very little critical respect. Scantily clad dancing girls were featured in quantity, alternating with slapstick comedy routines. Both were scattered through an implausible and barely coherent plot that showed complete indifference to the lives of "real" people. There was little effort to integrate the film's songs with the plot—they simply occurred at fairly regular, and no doubt commercially marketable, intervals.

But the dialogue, full of double entendres and in some places written in rhyming prose, is hilarious, even for a non-native speaker of Arabic like myself. Badi' Khayri, a colloquial playwright and the man who wrote the film's dialogue, might have been a minor figure compared to canonical authors who, by definition, wrote mainly in proper literary Arabic. But he knew how to connect with an audience, and he was one of the cleverest and most popular writers in Egypt.[9] The film ends with the cameos by Muhammad 'Abd al-Wahhab and Yusuf Wahbi, who play themselves. By the time they appear the principal members of the cast—Murad, Wajdi, and al-Rihani—are in Wahbi's mansion and 'Abd al-Wahhab is in another room rehearsing with his orchestra. Wahbi, known for melodrama, is hilarious in this scene—full of self-mockery, madly throwing out intertextual references to other works he and some of the other actors had appeared in. Then 'Abd al-Wahhab's orchestra starts to play and they all go to listen. 'Abd al-Wahhab, famous not only for his singing and composing but also for having expanded the traditional Arabic ensemble, appears directing an orchestra that includes balalaika and piccolo sections. The music brings everyone to an emotional crescendo; the plot is resolved through Wahbi's sage advice to the younger members of the cast; the various characters in the film see the folly of their ways; the right man marries the right woman; almost everybody lives happily ever after (more about that "almost" below).

When the film ended I went out to the lobby of the Walter Reade Theater and overheard an American man saying wearily and with heavy condescension, "Well, we have to see something that the unwashed masses watched." I was taken aback. He had just seen a film that tied together everything from low-down vernacular jokes to classical poetry; a film thoroughly embedded in what, in a context other than the much-maligned Egyptian cinema, might have been called a complex and sophisticated semiotic system. He had just seen an incredibly rich slice of Egyptian history—something that everybody in Egypt knows and many have practically memorized. Did he not come to the festival to get some insight into Egyptian society? What more could he want?

The experts brought to New York to comment on the phenomenon of Arab cinema had only encouraged him to think that he had just seen a bad film. All of them, including Tawfiq Salih, Egypt's sole official representative at the festival, sought to distance themselves from commercial Egyptian cinema.[10] Some did so politely on nationalist grounds ("It's not *our* nationalism being represented, but no doubt it's fine for Egypt"), and others were more vociferous in pointing out what they saw as the aesthetic shortcomings of Egyptian films. Salih, for his part, contended that the Egyptian cinema began with high ideals but degenerated due to the necessity of marketing to unsophisticated Arab audiences, followed by other economic and political upheavals.[11]

What the American man in the lobby wanted became clear from the next film, the Tunisian production that followed *The Flirtation of Girls*. This was *Summer in La Goulette*, and the crowd that turned up for it was many times larger than that for the previous film—probably a sold-out theater.[12] It was a nostalgic piece set just before the 1967 Arab-Israeli war, in a Tunisian beach town, La Goulette. La Goulette is portrayed as a place in which Christians, Muslims, and Jews lived in distinct communities that fit together in a blissful syncretism of polite equality. The only threats to this harmony come from the Arab East. The looming Arab-Israeli conflict poisons attitudes toward Jews among the weaker members of the community, but others in the Muslim community vigorously defend the honor and national commitment of their non-Muslim countrymen. Another incipient threat to local harmony comes in the form of a pious and greedy landlord who has spent too much time in the East, which has caused him to adopt a narrow and hypocritical interpretation of Islam. On a local level only benign traditional prohibitions against interfaith marriage cast a cloud on the perfection that was La Goulette, and even this does not prevent the younger generation from flirting with the idea of crossing that boundary.

It would not be stretching a point to say that the film was about no less a Western concern than multicultural pluralism, but of course set in Tunisia rather than in a Western country. At the same time there is no question that *Summer in La Goulette* contested prevailing American stereotypes about the "timelessness" of hostility between Muslims and Jews (although what proportion of the audience in the Lincoln Center held such stereotypes is an open question). The film revealed that the Italian actress Claudia Cardinale was born in Tunisia in this very town. In the course of the film she comes back to La Goulette, and no doubt many in the audience were inclined to see her cameo appearance as a sophisticated transnational representation that breaks down stereotypes and shows how borders are continually being crossed and blurred. In the end it was a pleasant film. A number of scenes featured bare-breasted women and nudity (not quite of the "full-frontal" variety), which will keep it from being shown in too many Arab countries.[13] The film also revealed Arab women as having a healthy libido, which may confound the expectations of metropolitan spectators inclined to see Middle Eastern women as repressed. It also suggested that pious religious prudery is not the "real Islam," and although academics have long cautioned against such essentialisms as "real Islam," an Arab film casting religious zealotry in a negative light will be enlightening for many a metropolitan spectator.[14]

Outside of a general awareness of the Arab-Israeli war of 1967 (the film's historical backdrop), very little specialist knowledge about Tunisia or North Africa was necessary to appreciate *Summer in La Goulette*. This was virtually mandated by the economics of the film; *Summer in La Goulette* began with a long list of corporate and governmental agencies that sponsored the film, all of them European. The film was made from the ground up as a production that *had* to be marketed to metropolitan audiences who knew little or nothing about Tunisia.

David Morley describes the postmodern world as subject to "simultaneous processes of homogenization and fragmentation, globalization and localization in contemporary culture" (1995, 15). His formulation is close kin to Schwartzman's curatorial dilemma of "solving the problem of foreignness by overcoming difference" or "communicating foreignness by revealing difference" (1995, 90).

Which film was the more "homogenizing," the unabashedly commercial *Flirtation of Girls* or the multiculturalist *Summer in La Goulette*? Considered purely as texts one could unhesitatingly say it was *The Flirtation of Girls*. In the context of a New York film festival audience more familiar with debates over multiculturalsm than with the conventions of Egyptian cinema, it is a much more difficult question.

One criticism constantly leveled at Egyptian cinema is that it did little more than plagiarize Hollywood. This was an accusation repeated often at the academic panels of the Centennial festival. But I would suggest that the reason *Summer in La Goulette* connects with an international audience so much more easily than *The Flirtation of Girls* is not so much because of its inherent sophistication or its refusal of Hollywood genres but because it understood film festival genres so well. It demands very little of its audience. One needs to bring very little to the theater to see this film. By contrast, *The Flirtation of Girls* was embedded in a thick web of local references; the jokes were far funnier for an audience that could appreciate shifts in linguistic register and the music much more interesting to people familiar—even just a little bit as non-native speakers like myself inevitably are—with the previous work of the actors.

An American-based festival of foreign films is about cultural diversity. But which film strikes audiences in unfamiliar ways? The one a Western audience can watch with no prior knowledge of the country represented in the film? Or the film that is actually quite inaccessible if one is not somewhat versed in the history and culture of the audience for whom the film was intended? Of course, *The Flirtation of Girls* could have been made more accessible with some program notes, and perhaps a brief lecture, but the people who organized the festival, and the critics and directors brought in to comment on the films, all subscribed to the stereotype that there is nothing worth saying about Egyptian cinema before the 1960s except for the rare flashes of interesting filmmaking that could be interpreted as leading to the golden age of the public sector.

But all this is only a prelude to the real irony in the juxtaposition of these two films. The Tunisian film was *about* history, and the actors in the film represented characters who were Muslim, Christian, and Jewish. But what nobody said was that the suave, sophisticated, and eminently multicultural *Summer in La Goulette* had been preceded by a 1949 Egyptian film that *starred* a Muslim (Anwar Wajdi), a Christian (Najib al-Rihani), and a former Jew (Layla Murad, who converted to Islam in the mid-1940s).

There was also an analogue to *Summer in La Goulette*'s having used a cameo appearance by Claudia Cardinale. Cardinale was certainly a nice touch, but the American audience of *The Flirtation of Girls* was never informed of the transregional character of its actors: both Layla Murad and Najib al-Rihani, like Cardinale, were born in one country to families that had emigrated from another. Murad's father was from the Levant, and al-Rihani's was from Iraq (Hasanayn 1993, 20, 158; Abou Saif 1969, 23). Many others of the film's personnel were marginal to Egyptian nationalism in various ways.[15]

Furthermore, it is likely that everyone in the Egyptian audience of 1949 knew that they were seeing a film starring a Muslim, a converted Jew, and a Christian. Religious affiliation was certainly not a prominent part of their public images,[16] but in 1948, shortly after the war in Palestine/Israel, the popular magazine *al-Ithnayn* (no. 737, July 26, 1948) did run a cover illustration showing Layla Murad wearing a Muslim prayer shawl and reading the Qur'an. The caption said "Layla the Muslim" and referred the reader to a two-page article showing Murad praying and receiving religious instruction from a sheikh. "Here is Layla's new film, in her private life, not on the screen. We know it by the name of 'Layla the Muslim'" ("Layla al-Muslima" 1948, 8). The article went on to explain that although Murad had been born "Israeli" (the word "Jewish" does not appear in the article), she had converted three years earlier but only recently declared her conversion publicly. The press, according to this article, was taken by surprise, with some papers believing the conversion to be sincere, while others speculated that it was done for publicity.

In terms of a metropolitan film festival this is obviously more along the lines of "the dialectics of presence/absence" (Shohat and Stam 1994, 223–30) than of the self-conscious celebration of identity featured in *Summer in La Goulette*. But the resonance of such a dialectic was surely very different in 1949 Egypt than it was in New York in 1996. Is an Egyptian film, in which the religious identities of the actors were subsumed by Egyptian national identity, less historically revealing than a Tunisian film in which the Muslim, Jewish, and Christian identities of the characters are foregrounded and made to look distinct? More important, more or less revealing to what sort of audience? *Summer in La Goulette* is a contemporary take on history tailored to the sensibilities of the Western audiences and agencies that fund it; *The Flirtation of Girls*, by contrast, *was* history. Where does *The Flirtation of Girls* fit in Schwartzman's balance between the need to solve the problem of foreignness by overcoming difference or to communicate foreignness by revealing difference? The conventional wisdom is that films like *The Flirtation of Girls* are not different enough to bother with because they are nothing more than commercial Hollywood clones.

I am suggesting that by emphasizing the explicitly multicultural Tunisian film and systematically downgrading the value of the Egyptian film we risk taking the path of least resistance. For an American audience the harder film to appreciate is *The Flirtation of Girls*. If we are really committed to the idea of interpreting cultural difference, this is a film that might repay greater efforts to understand it.

THE CINEMA AND ITS CRITICS

Americans can certainly be forgiven their unfamiliarity with the Egyptian cinema. Many are scarcely aware that there is such a thing, for over most of its history the Egyptian film industry has been systematically ignored in our literature on the Middle East. This is not the result of an oversight. Egyptian intellectuals themselves, who are the most influential interpreters of Egyptian culture in the West, do not for the most part patronize or praise their national film industry. It should be noted that the jaundiced eye cast by intellectuals toward the Egyptian cinema was not unlike the low regard American intellectuals had for their own national cinema, at least until relatively recently. James B. Twitchell (1992, 131–38) suggests that the transformation of "movies" into the more intellectually legitimate "cinema" dates, in America, only from the 1960s. He identifies Andrew Sarris's ([1962] 1994) adoption of "auteur theory" as a watershed in this transformation. Twitchell considers efforts to analyze films as art to be largely a waste of time and any artistic achievement in films to be incidental to the main objective of making money. For example, he quotes Charlie Chaplin as saying "I went into the business for money and the art grew out of it" (Twitchell 1992, 132) as evidence of the essential irrelevance of art in the film business. However, Chaplin's confession of commercial interest still leaves him some space for the artistic value many have seen in his work. By the same token the obviously commercial *Flirtation of Girls* should not blind us to the fact that the people who made it did take themselves very seriously as artists. And on an individual level, if not on the level of *Flirtation*'s generic conventions, so too do many Egyptian critics and nonspecialist spectators take the stars of the film seriously as artists.

But aside from a critical distaste for commercialism, which Egyptian in-

tellectuals shared with critics everywhere, one of the problems with Egyptian cinema in the eyes of its fiercest critics was the way it constructed Egyptian identity. In a nutshell, it was deemed too derivative to be truly Egyptian.
Samir Farid, a prominent Egyptian film critic, summed up the feelings of
many intellectuals in the following passage:

> Over the course of more than two thousand films produced in half a century,
> and then shown again on television and destined to continue being aired on
> the video, the image of the Egyptian prevalent in Egyptian films is Egyptian in
> his clothes, his accent and manner of speaking, his movements. But he is not
> Egyptian in his traditions and customs, behavior, thoughts, actions and reac-
> tions. The reason for this is the prevalence of the Western model in Egyptian
> filmmaking. The filmmakers are Egyptian, and the films are made in Egypt,
> but their content is Western. (1986, 209)

Farid wrote those lines in 1986. Possibly the only thing he would change if
he were to rewrite his article today is that now there are close to three thousand Egyptian films that have failed to deliver the goods.

But while intellectuals turned their backs on the Egyptian cinema early
on, there was still a broad audience for the product. Egyptian films were sal-
able, and Egyptian industrialists began investing in a film-production infrastructure by the mid-1930s.[17] Production began to rise: twelve films in
1935, twenty-two annually by 1942. What really put the film industry on
solid ground, though, was World War II, which brought together several
factors favorable to the Egyptian cinema. One was a sudden decrease in the
availability of foreign films to compete with the local product. The other
was an influx of capital into Egyptian hands. Egypt became a staging
ground for the British war effort, and much money was made, not all of it
legitimately. The cinema seems to have been regarded by Egyptian capitalists as an excellent investment, particularly, it is suspected, when the money
was earned on the black market. The period from 1945 to 1952 is therefore
known as the "cinema of war profiteers." In 1945 forty-two films were produced—almost double the total of any previous year in the history of
Egyptian cinema. Shortly thereafter production leveled off at around fifty
films per year, which is where it has been ever since. The latter date, 1952,
marks the accession to power of the Free Officers led ultimately by Gamal
Abdel Nasser, after which, one assumes, the laundering of ill-gotten gains
in the cinema subsided. At any rate, Egyptian film historians do not extend
the "cinema of war profiteers" label beyond 1952, when Egypt became independent. But then a new problem arose, which was that the financiers
were, for the most part, not Egyptian at all (mainly they were Lebanese)
from the mid-1940s until nationalization in the 1960s (Salih 1986,
195–96).

In particular, intellectuals censure the late 1940s—the period in which

The Flirtation of Girls was produced—as a period in which vulgarity was assumed to have predominated. In the 1940s, as Salih describes it,

> there were many people who had worked with the English army . . . who made a lot of money. . . . Because of this the cinema flourished, particularly since it was cheaper to see a dancer or a dance routine in a film than it was to go to a cabaret. The film gave you more details of the dancer than you could see in a cabaret. These economic and historical developments changed the character of the cinema. At the level of craft [*al-mustawa al-hirafi*] the effect was serious. (1986, 196)

Nasser did not take much interest in the cinema during the 1950s. A few directors were inspired by socialist ideals or by class consciousness, and some see their work as the foreshadowing of better things to come in the 1960s, once the state attempted to cut the association of cinema and commerce (Sharaf al-Din 1992, 16–21).[18] But aside from gradual concessions to overt nationalism and progressive social ideals in the few directors whose lineage led to the public sector, most Egyptian films remained derivations of genres developed in earlier films, and before that, the theater. Musicals, farces, belly-dance films, and melodramas predominated. At all periods of Egyptian cinema critics and intellectuals have denounced such films as grossly out of touch with the realities of Egyptian society, but at the same time locally made film narratives were rapidly becoming part of social reality whether intellectuals liked it or not. These generic conventions have created a horizon of expectations in the audience that later directors could copy but that they could also use creatively through unorthodox casting or unexpected twists in familiar stories.

CINEMA AS VERNACULAR CULTURE

Aside from the work of those directors who ended up becoming prominent in the public sector, the pre-1960s cinema was important in another way: it contributed to a de facto standardization of a national vernacular.[19] The modernity forced on Egypt partly by colonialism and partly by internal social dynamics would have made no sense in the absence of a means to authenticate it. In this respect nationalism is organically linked to modernity—a way to associate the presumed continuity of the past with the cultural ruptures that are inevitably part of modernity.

Joshua Fishman (1972) writes that language is a potent, if not necessarily inevitable, imagined link to a national past. Not surprisingly, one of the symbols of the continuity so important to Egyptian modernity is the Arabic language. But which Arabic? Nationalist ideology in an Arabic-speaking context formally recognizes only written Arabic, which must be conceptually (if not practically) linked with classical Arab society. Actual similarities between modern and medieval written Arabic are another matter, and linguists recognize that modern written Arabic is not identical to the medieval Arabic sometimes described as "classical." But at the same time, the scope of change permitted modern written Arabic has been sufficiently limited that the gap between it and the vernacular is described as "diglossic."[20]

Arab nationalism makes a link between territory and language, but the territory associated with Arabic encompasses all presumed speakers of *classical* Arabic (or its modern standard counterpart)—everyone and no one at the same time. No person speaks classical Arabic in daily life, and relatively few people read it easily (Parkinson 1991). And yet everywhere in the Arabic-speaking world, states have created an institutional apparatus to defend linguistic purity.

In doing so they construct a different relationship between nationalism and vernacular language than one often finds in Europe. The "official language," as Bourdieu calls it, "is the one which, within the territorial limits of that unit, imposes itself on the whole population as the only legitimate language, especially in situations that are characterized as more *officielle* (a very exact translation of the word 'formal' used by English-speaking linguists)" (1991, 45). Through a combination of official regulation and "normalization," the standard language is eventually "capable of functioning outside the constraints and without the assistance of the situation, and is suitable for transmitting and decoding by any sender and receiver, who may know nothing of one another" (Bourdieu 1991, 48).

In Arabic-speaking societies the official language was not abstracted from the vernacular of an elite but from a language that was not used in everyday life. Arabic-speaking societies saw a devaluation of nonstandard language similar to that of Europe (Bourdieu 1991, 47), and this devaluation was no doubt reinforced by the development of modern cultural hierarchies along the same lines as those in Europe and America (Levine 1988; Twitchell 1992). In relation to official language the vernacular had to be kept at arm's length, and was, by definition, not the proper medium for art or print media. But cinema and other nontraditional oral media (the gramophone, theater, and radio) were another matter. In these media the vernacular was never completely banished in constructions of Egyptian nationalism. To the extent that the nation was "imagined" (Anderson 1991) or "narrated" (Bhabha 1990), the medium of expression was *both* the official language and the vernacular. However, the importance of nontraditional media in constructing Egyptian and Arab nationalism has been substantially unacknowledged by the cultural establishment.

Despite its reputation as a Hollywood clone, Egyptian cinema from the 1920s through the 1950s tried to link itself to an imagery of social synthesis that defined bourgeois culture. This was a synthesis that used the vernacular but often made indirect references to constructs of heritage. In the end pre-1960s Egyptian cinema may have been extremely important in constructing the cultural synthesis of the bourgeoisie. And of course there was a linguistic analogue to bourgeois culture: modern language was also, to some degree, supposed to combine both the vernacular and traditional written Arabic. It is this modern "mixture" that is often identified as "modern standard Arabic." But written Arabic, the medium of literature, was "mixed" with the vernacular conservatively. The modern variant of written Arabic differs considerably from medieval written Arabic, but most of what counts as writing differs markedly from what people speak. By contrast, the medium of film, spoken Arabic, was the spoken Arabic of Cairene elites rather than written Arabic. And of course a national vernacular based on the dialect of the dominant city is typical of such European nations as England and France. In both cases, and also elsewhere in Europe, Latin was displaced as the language of writing by a synthetic vernacular. But in Egypt both vernacular and classical Arabic had to construct a sense of cultural synthesis without budging too far from the cultural hierarchies that kept each of them distinct.

Just as "modern standard Arabic" used by literate Egyptians differs significantly from the medieval Arabic on which it is based, the vernacular language used in audiovisual media is perhaps not identical to any specific vernacular. However, the vernacular identity constructed in films was frequently linked to both high tradition and to imported technique by visual means. It is not true, contrary to Samir Farid's claim, that bourgeois men and women depicted in Egyptian films were "Egyptian in their clothes, their accent and manner of speaking," but not in "traditions and customs, behavior, thoughts, actions and reactions." Rather, they were often pointedly *Western* in their appearance, and whatever they were doing in the hundreds of film narratives denounced as mindless or melodramatic, they possessed one immeasurably important avenue into the hearts and minds of mass audiences: they were easily understood by everyone from the illiterate to the most erudite.

At this point I want to return to *The Flirtation of Girls*, which I want to suggest was an excellent example of the power of commercial cinema to construct a national community. In a nutshell, *The Flirtation of Girls* connected with its audience by creating a common fund of images tied to a middle-class bourgeois nationalist identity—an image tied to vernacular authenticity, high tradition, and modern technique. Furthermore, the film uses that common fund of images as the preconditions for its production. Let me unpack the film a bit more.

The Flirtation of Girls was made in the late 1940s, just after the heady wartime rush to expand film production. As previously mentioned, critics refer

Figure 18. Layla Murad in an elegant publicity still from *The Flirtation of Girls* (*al-Kawakib*, September 9, 1958, p. 4). Courtesy of Dar al-Hilal.

derisively to the filmmaking of this period as "the cinema of war profiteers." Allegedly vast fortunes were made by hoarding scarce commodities and selling them on the black market, and then this illicit money was laundered during and just after the war through financing films. Allegations of money laundering went together with withering criticism of the aesthetic qualities of the films: they were made by people with no experience in cinema, people interested only in quick profit, people who had absolutely no regard for quality. With one or two exceptions films of the period are considered an affront to polite society—an outrageous triumph of the greedy nouveaux riches.

The ultimate source of finance for *The Flirtation of Girls* is unknown. This is, in many films (and not just Egyptian ones), a rather difficult question. But regardless of the film's source of finance, *The Flirtation of Girls* was anything but amateurish. Quick it was, industrial even. The film uses only four or five simple sets, a very brief outdoor scene shot in the garden of a mansion and some back-projected fake outdoor scenes. But everyone associated with the film was a seasoned professional. Indeed, despite its low-budget sets, the film was probably a rather expensive production. The quick postwar expansion of the cinema might have brought inexperienced directors and producers into the industry, but for a film to be marketable it had to have stars. There were a finite number of marketable names who were in demand for a suddenly much larger pool of pictures. Consquently stars could charge higher fees, and *The Flirtation of Girls* featured not just one but several stars.

The plot turns on education. A rich man hires a seedy and ineffective old schoolteacher (Najib al-Rihani) to tutor his daughter (Layla Murad), who is failing every subject, but most gallingly, she has flunked Arabic. Fortunately the Egyptian educational system allows a second chance for failing students to retake at least some exams during the summer, hence the need for a tutor.

The girl is a flirt, and the old teacher, despite the disparity in age between himself and the girl, falls in love with his student. Once he is hired the rich man buys new clothes for his new employee. Resplendent in a new suit, the formerly shabby Arabic teacher stands with his student and a bevy of "companions" (really Layla Murad's chorus). One of the companions tap-dances, the others sway suggestively, as Murad sings a saucy "alphabet song" that recapitulates the film's theme:

Abgad, hawaz, hutti, kalamun	ABCDEFG,[21]
Shakl-il-ustaz ba'a munsagimun	Now the professor looks good to me!
Ustaz Hamam, nahnu zaghalin	Professor Pigeon,[22] we're tricksters,
Min ghayr ginah binmil wi-ntir	We flip and fly without wings,
Wil-makri fina tab'i gamil	And in us, deceitfulness is a good thing,

Figure 19. The dashing pilot played by Anwar Wajdi (second from left) comes to rescue Layla Murad from her lounge-lizard lover. The lover, played by Mahmud al-Miliji (well on his way to becoming the most prolific screen villain in Egyptian cinema history), stands on the far left. The bumbling old teacher played by Najib al-Rihani appears on the far right (*al-Kawakib*, no. 9, October 1949, p. 60). Courtesy of Dar al-Hilal.

in 'ulna "la'i, la'i," ya'ni "na'amun"	If we say "no, no," it means "sure thing."
. . .	
In "ga'a Zaydun," aw "hadar 'Amrun,"	Even if "Zayd came," or "'Amr was present,"
W-ihna malna, inshallah ma hadarun!	What do we care? maybe he wasn't!
Lil-mubtada ha-ngiblak khabarun,	We'll get you the "predicate" to your "subject,"
Bi-nazrah wahda ha-yisbah 'adam.	With one glance the whole thing will mean nothing.[23]

The music, credited to Muhammad 'Abd al-Wahhab, is a delightful jazz adaptation with saxophones dominating the accompaniment. The girl's servant bangs gleefully on a grand piano. Her small white dog sits on the piano barking. Arabic grammar, the putative subject of the song, was never more enjoyable.

It transpires that the girl is distracted by a lover. She lures the old Arabic teacher out of the house by telling him she wants to run away with him.

They drive off, or rather she drives (he sits in the passenger seat) in, of all things, an army jeep. Unfortunately it turns out she is only using him to escort her to a shady nightclub where her lover waits. The old Arabic teacher is crestfallen, but when he overhears other denizens of the nightclub talking about how the girl's lover is only after her money—that she is merely the next in a long line of unfortunate victims of this nightclub Romeo—he tries to intervene. For his trouble he gets thrown out on the street. There he appeals desperately for help from a dashing young pilot who happens to be passing by. The pilot enters the nightclub claiming to be the girl's paternal cousin, and therefore her logical suitor according to Egyptian custom. Of course, she denies it, but he precipitates a fight anyway in order to "rescue" her. Then they jump into the jeep to deliver the recalcitrant girl back to her father. The pilot starts flirting with her. The old Arabic teacher is dismayed and tries to throw him off the track by stopping at someone else's house, which he chooses at random. He and the girl knock on the door, leaving the pilot outside.

The house turns out to be the residence of a famous actor (Yusuf Wahbi), who is entertaining a rehearsal by a famous singer (Muhammad 'Abd al-Wahhab). Solemnly the actor imparts words of wisdom to the youngster and to the old teacher who still accompanies her. "Just suppose," he says, "that a man falls in love with a girl who is too young for him and who is from a different social milieu." They start to fidget, recognizing immediately that the "just suppose" scenario spun out by the great man refers directly to themselves. By the time the actor is through with his "suppositions," the old Arabic teacher realizes his folly, and the young girl begins to understand that she has unintentionally hurt him. The crafty actor then ushers the two into an absurdly large auditorium, where his friend the musician is rehearsing a massive orchestra, which includes strings, trumpets, male and female choruses, and even a balalaika section. It is a supremely surreal scene.[24]

Finally the singer, holding a banjo, directs his balalaikas and piccolos, while singing a sad song about pure spiritual love:

Oh eye, why is my night so long
Oh eye, why did my tears pour forth
Oh my eyes, why did the lovers leave me
Why do all eyes sleep except you?
. . .
I sacrificed my joy for the lover
(Choir) ("Oh night witness him.")
I will live on his memory
(Choir) ("Oh night witness him.")[25]

The music makes the old man accept what his heart had known all

ﮐﺎﻧﺖ ﻫﺬﻩ ﺍﻟﻀﺤﮑﺎﺕ ﺗﻌﻂ ﺑﺎﻟﻌﻘﺪﻩ ﻓﻲ ﻓﻠﻢ   ﻏﺮﻝ ﺍﻟﺒﺎﺏ ٠٠ ﻭﺍﻟﮑﻬﺎ ﺍﻃﻠﺴﺪﻭﻣﺎ ﺍﻟﺤﺮﺍﻱ ﻋﺮﺽ ﺍﻟﻔﻠﻢ

Figure 20. Najib al-Rihani in *The Flirtation of Girls.* His countrified Kishkish Bey persona is obviously not part of this film, but his famous penchant for pretty (and Westernized) girls is on display (*al-Kawakib,* no. 6, July 1949, p. 6). Courtesy of Dar al-Hilal.

along—that a match between himself and his student makes no sense— and he gives his blessing to the romance that blossoms between the young girl and the pilot. In the final scene the three of them—the girl, the pilot, and the old man—drive off in the jeep, the camera lingering one final moment on Najib al-Rihani, who is grinning slyly. This was Najib al-Rihani's last instant on the screen, and the bittersweet look on his face is almost enough to make one think that he knew he wasn't going to be back. He died in May 1949 of typhoid (Abou Saif 1969, 273). In October the film was released.[26]

The Flirtation of Girls was hugely successful, but of course that hardly invalidates the criticisms made about films of the period: they were supposed to make money, at least enough to launder the ill-gotten gains of the shadowy investors. And the film is, in fact, still popular—a powerful engine of nostalgia that everyone has seen, one that brings smiles whenever it is mentioned. However, what is interesting about *The Flirtation of Girls* is not just that it sustains nostalgia but that it invoked nostalgia from the very first day it was exhibited to the public. The film is essentially an all-star revue. All of the principals were extremely well known, and many of the small roles were cameos by performers who were also known, or who, intriguingly, were about to become well known in the next decade. And almost all of them played themselves in the film, either in the sense that their characters bore the names by which they were known in public or in the sense that their roles in the film as actors or singers were identical to their roles in real life.

The film was a musical featuring Layla Murad, who played the young girl. She was in fact a bit long in the tooth for this role. Layla was the daughter of a well-known singer named Zaki Murad, and she began singing as a child in the early 1930s. One of her first public appearances was in the nightclub of Badi'a Masabni, an impresaria of Syrian origin who had been married at one point in her career to the comedian Najib al-Rihani. Al-Rihani was the actor who played the seedy old tutor in *The Flirtation of Girls*. Earlier in his career he was famous for a stage persona, which he performed live, on the radio, and in films, named Kishkish Bey. Al-Rihani's Kishkish character dressed in the rustic clothes of a provincial village headman (*'umda*) and was an old man with an eye for young, particularly foreign, women. The plays in which the character of Kishkish appeared were comedies known as "Franco-Arab revue," a genre inspired by French farce that was popular around the time of World War I (Abou Saif 1969, 33–60). Another of the ironies evoked by *The Flirtation of Girls* lay in al-Rihani *not* getting the girl at the end; in most of al-Rihani's Franco-Arab comedies the ending "celebrates his triumphant sexual union with a young beauty" (Abou Saif 1969, 56).

For a time the Franco-Arab comedy pioneered by al-Rihani played an important role in satirizing the social and political issues of the day, particularly during the heady days of the 1919 revolt against British rule. Abou Saif describes Franco-Arab comedy in largely sympathetic terms, but he also notes (1969, 76–77) that the genre was artistically limited by its tendency to string together unconnected "situations" with a series of song-and-dance spectacles.

Clearly the structure, if not the content, of *The Flirtation of Girls* owed a great deal to the earlier genre. The film, produced almost thirty years after the heyday of Franco-Arab comedy, is also a series of song-and-dance spectacles punctuated by the barest of plots. But the film contains few if any obvious references to politics, whereas Franco-Arab revue thrived on commentary about current events. Abou Saif quotes Badi' Khayri, author of *The Flirtation of Girls* and of many of al-Rihani's most successful Franco-Arab comedies, as saying that Franco-Arab revues were "cinema newsreels because, whenever possible, they were connected with an important crisis" (1969, 73). There was, then, no obvious satire of the sort that could get through to an American audience. But the significance of the actors and the structure of the film may well have been quite different for an Egyptian audience in 1949. The film is, in many ways, too "different" to communicate difference cross-culturally. To an American audience it looks like little more than a cross between 1930s screwball comedy and Parisian boulevard theater. But half of the film's fun comes from its implicit links to earlier works that were indelibly associated with specifically Egyptian meanings.

Layla Murad had appeared in a number of films—approximately twenty up to that point. Her first appearance was in *Long Live Love* (Karim 1938), and she was paired with none other than Muhammad 'Abd al-Wahhab, who was the foremost male vocalist from the 1920s through the mid-1940s. And 'Abd al-Wahhab, of course, was the singer in *The Flirtation of Girls* who was rehearsing in the actor's mansion that Najib al-Rihani used to try to escape from the young pilot. 'Abd al-Wahhab sang one song in *The Flirtation of Girls*, and it was his second-to-last significant appearance in a fiction film, although he lived another forty years.[27]

The owner of the mansion in *The Flirtation of Girls* was, in the story, a highly successful actor named Yusuf Wahbi. And he was playing himself: the real Yusuf Wahbi was, in fact, a highly successful actor, director, and playwright. Wahbi was the childhood friend of the man who directed all of the singer Muhammad 'Abd al-Wahhab's films. Wahbi's role in the film was to play matchmaker. He makes Najib al-Rihani see that an affair between him and this vivacious young girl is inappropriate and that she should really be encouraged to marry the dashing young pilot. At one point Wahbi scolds al-Rihani, telling him that if he really loved the girl he would step aside and let the pilot have her. But there are certain reverberations to Wahbi's admonition: when he says, "If you really loved her you'd step aside," he isn't just referring to Najib al-Rihani in *The Flirtation of Girls*. Wahbi is also referring slyly to himself. He had already "married" Layla Murad twice before in two of their films: *Layla bint al-rif* (Layla, Daughter of the Countryside; Mizrahi 1941) and *Layla bint madaris* (Layla, Daughter of Schools; Mizrahi 1941). This kind of intertextuality was very deliberate and calculated to play on the audience's knowledge of all of their previous work.

In the film Wahbi not only tied himself to Layla Murad, he also tied *The Flirtation of Girls* in to the history of Muhammad 'Abd al-Wahhab, the singer rehearsing his orchestra in Wahbi's mansion. This happens as Wahbi is playing matchmaker between Layla, his former celluloid lover, and the dashing young pilot. In the middle of the conversation between himself, Najib al-Rihani, and Layla Murad, he suddenly stops and says, "'Abd al-Wahhab is about to begin his new piece." They go to the auditorium in Wahbi's house and peek through the door. Layla asks him what the piece is about, and Wahbi replies, "It's a sad tale about a man who loves a woman more than anything, but he's forced to withdraw from her life for the sake of her happiness, and then watch them from afar, with his heart breaking." Of course, this is what *The Flirtation of Girls* is leading up to: the schoolteacher is going to have to give up his dream of marrying the girl so that she can be happy living with the dashing young pilot. Then 'Abd al-Wahhab sings his song, which once again reiterates the theme of a lover sacrificing his dreams for the sake of a woman's happiness.

What is not so evident on the surface here in America, but was not lost on an Egyptian audience of 1949, is that Wahbi is also describing the plot of Muhammad 'Abd al-Wahhab's first film, *al-Warda al-bayda'* (The White Rose), which was made in 1933 and directed by Wahbi's childhood friend Muhammad Karim. The man who plays Layla's father in *The Flirtation of Girls* was Sulayman Najib, who was the same actor who played the father of 'Abd al-Wahhab's lover in *The White Rose*.

At this point one should remember that one of the most common excuses given by scholars and critics for ignoring the Egyptian cinema is that the commercial Egyptian cinema is nothing but a Hollywood clone. It is true that *The Flirtation of Girls* looks very much like an American screwball comedy starring Cary Grant or Katherine Hepburn. But beneath the surface there is an intricate architecture of references designed to evoke not an alien film tradition but Egypt's own tradition. This was a carefully calculated effect.

No doubt it was also calculated to make money, but it is hard to see why this should exclude it and other films from consideration as a powerful force for constructing nationalism and, by extension, modernity. After all, Benedict Anderson's focus on print capitalism made "imagined communities" practically a household word, at least in academic households, and the books and articles his insight generated are practically a cottage industry. What we are seeing in the commercial Egyptian cinema is a kind of screen capitalism that is not greatly preceded by either the printing press or mass literacy.

Anderson suggests that the introduction of a new medium in a capitalist context results in new markets, which are inevitably exhausted. When Europeans began using the printing press, the market for writing was still primarily in Latin, a wide but thin market that was tapped out within a century and a half. However, "the logic of capitalism thus meant that once the elite Latin market was saturated, the potentially huge markets represented by the monoglot masses would beckon" (Anderson 1991, 38). In the case of Arabic-speaking societies, there are no precise estimates even for the size of the market for standard language. Ami Ayalon (1995, 142) notes that a 1937 Egyptian census reports a literacy rate of 18 percent. But he cautions against generalizing from such figures on a number of grounds. For one thing, literacy was localized: educated people were concentrated in cities. Furthermore, there is no qualitative measure of literacy: "The classification 'literate' did not necessarily imply the ability to read a newspaper; often it was merely a designation for someone who had memorized certain sections of the Qur'an" (Ayalon 1995, 142). However, there was also an unquantifiable "multiplier effect"—literates reading to others who were not able. Estimates of the circulation of printed materials are also imprecise, but in the case of newspapers (a critical medium both for Anderson and for Arab linguistic reformers), Ayalon writes that "it is safe to assume that at no time prior to the second half of the twentieth century were newspapers bought by more than . . . 3 to 4 percent of the population in Egypt" (1995, 153).

The standard language of mass print and the vernacular used in other media were introduced to the Egyptian public at very nearly the same time. In Europe the potential complications caused by the advent of new types of media not predicated on the written word come much later; print and the cinema are separated by centuries. In Egypt it might be stretching a point to say that print and the cinema are separated even by decades.

Let us return to Yusuf Wahbi and *The Flirtation of Girls*. As mentioned above, Wahbi's relationship to the other actors in the film was predicated on a rich intertextuality—but an intertextuality of film and theater texts. Wahbi's work was not exclusively in either literary Arabic or colloquial Arabic, although by the late 1920s he is alleged to have "descended to the level of the masses by doing plays in colloquial" (al-Yusuf [1953] 1976, 88). His characters were frequently at least aristocratic, and in this film he ties the aristocracy firmly to official language. In his cameo appearance he speaks a sonorous semiclassical Arabic that invokes—really almost caricatures—high culture, and in so doing he reiterates a point that had already been raised in the film's plot. Layla, we remember, was thrown together with Najib al-Rihani because she had flunked Arabic—proper written Arabic. Now we have Wahbi showing her just how sexy Arabic can be. She practically swoons in front of him. And in the larger scheme of things, Wahbi's classicism makes a nice contrast to al-Rihani's clever colloquialisms. At one point Wahbi explicitly juxtaposes the two. First he quotes classical Arabic, saying, "Wa-kullu muradi an takuna hani'atan wa-law annani dahaytu nura hayati" (All I want is that you be happy, even if I have to sacrifice the light of my life). Then Wahbi repeats the sentiment in colloquial Arabic, "Wilad al-balad biy'ulu, Iza kan habibak bi-khayr, tifrahluh" (Common people say, "If your loved one is well then you should be happy"). Furthermore, the juxtaposition of classical and vernacular elements in Wahbi's speech was rounded off by the presence of the dashing young pilot, who adds technological know-how to the other elements of national identity. The film is, in other words, an archetypal expression of

Figure 21. A publicity still from an advertisement for *The Flirtation of Girls*. The five stars are seated before the door of the theater in which Muhammad 'Abd al-Wahhab is shown rehearsing in the film. From left to right: Najib al-Rihani, Muhammad 'Abd al-Wahhab, Anwar Wajdi (standing), Yusuf Wahbi, Layla Murad. Courtesy of Dar al-Hilal.

nationalist and modernist ideology: one part authenticizing vernacular tradition; one part classical high culture; and one part technological innovation.

The history of Yusuf Wahbi leads to more intertextual connections between the film's actors and characters, not that the two can really be kept separate. In the 1920s Wahbi had founded a theatrical company called the Ramsis Troupe. The names of the actors who got their introduction to show business through the Ramsis Troupe would practically make a "who's who" list for the Egyptian theater and cinema. One of the most successful alumni of the Ramsis Troupe was an actor and film director named Anwar Wajdi. Wajdi, like his mentor Yusuf Wahbi, had also played the romantic lead in a couple of Layla Murad films, including *Layla bint al-aghniya'* (Layla, Daughter of the Rich; Wajdi 1946), which was an adaptation of *It Happened One Night*, and *Layla bint al-fuqara'* (Layla, Daughter of the Poor; Wajdi 1945). In real life Wajdi was Layla Murad's husband. And finally, Wajdi also played the dashing young pilot in *The Flirtation of Girls*. Not only that, he was the director. And the producer.

All these names and connections are important. If one added up all the songs, plays, films, and radio programs that featured Layla Murad, Najib al-Rihani, Anwar Wajdi, Yusuf Wahbi, and Muhammad 'Abd al-Wahhab, the total would number at least in the hundreds. Virtually all of this work was in the vernacular, and although films, songs, and radio programs are never extensively analyzed in discussions of Egyptian nationalism, they did constitute a common fund of images with which the audience was intimately familiar. The experience of this imagery was analogous to the mass rituals of reading novels and newspapers that Benedict Anderson (1991) identifies as an important means for knitting together "communities" of anonymous strangers. But more than the newspaper or novel, this film and others like it were intensely reflexive. *The Flirtation of Girls* was not really *about* anything other than itself. It was "about" primarily the popularity of the actors, and of course their popularity was built on the audience's informal experience with them. A very large proportion of the combined body of work of the actors and filmmakers who made *The Flirtation of Girls* was like the film itself in that their work had no direct connection to the imagery of vernacular culture normally emphasized in the implicit opposition between high literate culture and the "authentic" vernacular culture. *This* was Egyptian nationalism in the making. It was a completely synthetic system of communication that was instrumental in defining what Egypt was, and furthermore, a system of communication that lay partially outside the formal apparatus for teaching legitimate culture.

DOWN WITH VULGARITY

What happened to the Egyptian cinema after the 1940s? In terms of the political economy of filmmaking, the story of the decade following *The Flirtation of Girls* is the subject of the preceding chapter by Robert Vitalis in this volume. The state took over the industry by the 1960s, or more accurately, took over most of it. Proponents of the public sector see this as an inevitable result of film economics in Egypt and the Arabic-speaking world (Salih 1986, 205). Several years before the Free Officers revolution of 1952, the very success of the Egyptian film industry began to seriously affect production costs. As the product became more popular and the number of films increased, stars began to understand their market value. Even those less enamored of state intervention agree that profitability became a problem shortly after the first rush of expansion during and just after the war. For example, Samir Farid (1996, 8) writes that by the postwar period Layla Murad's fee jumped to £E12,000, almost half of an average film budget of £E25,000. A few other stars, including 'Abd al-Wahhab, could charge even more. Yusuf Wahbi accepted £E1,000 for his very brief appearance as himself in *The Flirtation of Girls*, but only on the condition that his part be filmed in one day (Hasanayn 1993, 72).

As production costs went up, the potential for making a profit on films went down. At the Centennial festival Tawfiq Salih claimed that before the 1940s a film covered its cost from the domestic market and made profits from foreign distribution. By the 1950s the foreign market had to cover part of the production costs as well. American and European films returned to the market. And to make things worse, as the Nasser regime consolidated power and began to broadcast revolutionary rhetoric (in a few films), some of the Arab states closed their markets to Egyptian product (Salih 1986, 205; Farid 1996, 9). In the view of Salih and other advocates of nationalization, these economic woes were largely responsible for what they saw as the poor aesthetic quality of Egyptian films. And it was particularly the hold of non-Egyptians (but as Vitalis reminds us, not necessarily Hollywood) over the vital profit margin that spoiled the cinema. In the 1940s foreigners dictated that most films would be musicals. Another source of indirect foreign meddling, according to Salih, was the effect of British money during the war. Abu Sayf described the problem bluntly:

> Nobody who has written about the "crisis of the Egyptian cinema" has investigated the causes of the crisis. The first reason is that the number of cinema production companies increased in Egypt during World War II because of the entry of war profiteers into the field of cinema production. They were eager to exploit the money they made without any of them knowing the slightest thing about filmmaking. This led to chaos that helped destroy the Egyptian

film, causing an increase in competition for artists, thereby raising their fees to unimaginable levels. It also increased the cost of studios, developing labs, and raw film, and led to a doubling in production costs. (1949, 17)

Tasteless producers catered to a low-class audience, which had also been enriched by the British war effort (Salih 1986, 196).[28] Lebanese producers, who Salih and others say were interested only in quick profits, put another nail in the coffin of "quality" Egyptian cinema. Lazy directors, who adapted foreign films rather than pay writers to produce scripts, then combined with the marketability of dancers, slapstick comedy, and melodrama, in what some see as a powerful alchemy of tastelessness. This provided an aesthetic argument for nationalization that paralleled the economic argument.[29]

Nationalization was already on the minds of many by the time *The Flirtation of Girls* was produced. Salah Abu Sayf, one of the most respected directors of the 1950s, was calling publicly by 1949 for extensive government intervention to alleviate the "crisis" in the film industry. He suggested a ten-point program, which is paraphrased below.

1. Stipulate a minimum capitalization of production companies at £E50,000. Companies will merge, and having fewer companies will reduce unfair competition.
2. Form a government committee that would include representatives of the artistic unions to limit the prices of the studios, labs, raw film, and actors' fees.
3. Create a cinema institute to prepare new talent for the screen.
4. Send film students on artistic study missions to Europe or America to study the cinema as a craft and an art so that when they return they can teach in the cinema institute.
5. The government should set aside a large sum of prize money for the best screenplay.
6. Lessen censorship. Many of the conditions of the current censorship were mandated during the period of colonial protectorship.
7. Allow the formation of unions organized by workers in the cinema industry.
8. Open new markets for Egyptian films, and lessen the hold of hard currency.
9. Exempt films from taxes.
10. Negotiate with the countries that show films in Egypt and demand that they open their markets to Egyptian films. (Abu Sayf 1949, 17)[30]

Abu Sayf got his wish, starting with the establishment of Mu'assasat da'm al-sinima (Organization of Cinema Subsidy), a cinema workers' union, and a cinema institute between 1959 and 1962 ('Ukasha 1990, 485–87).

But Abu Sayf perhaps got more than he bargained for (a point reiterated by Vitalis, chap. 12, this volume). In 1963 the Nasser regime ordered a large-scale nationalization of the film industry. Most crucially, the studios, development labs, theaters, and distribution facilities ended up in government hands, and Abu Sayf himself was appointed the first director of production in the new public sector. If the economics of filmmaking in Egypt had been in crisis in the late 1940s when Abu Sayf proposed government intervention, the intervention itself in the 1960s threw the industry into complete chaos.

The sudden decree to nationalize seems to have taken everyone by surprise. Sharaf al-Din (1992, 39) notes that the broad aim of nationalization in the early 1960s was to target industries in which a large portion of the necessary capital was in foreign hands but that the cinema did not fit in this category. Minister of Culture Tharwat 'Ukasha (1959–62)[31] said essentially the same:

> Up to September 1962 when I left the Ministry of Culture there was no thought of nationalizing the cinema, or of the state taking over film production because it would have slid into endless troubles [if it had been done] without prior preparation. Perhaps the subsequent unstudied haste to dominate the cinema is what led to the state's imprudent intrusion into the field of film production. Many factors contributed to this tendency and swept the Egyptian cinema into a new phase. (Quoted in Sharaf al-Din 1992, 40)

The result of what 'Ukasha characterizes as runaway nationalization was that prices for everything shot through the roof. Salih relates a story told to him by Salah Abu Sayf during the 1940s, when *The Flirtation of Girls* was made: "Abu Sayf went to a producer and asked for £E40 for a scenarist. The producer said, 'What do you mean "scenarist"? We produced such and such a film without paying anything for the scenario.' Abu Sayf said, 'For the story,' and the producer replied, 'I've never paid for a story'" (Salih 1986, 201). By the 1960s the pendulum had swung the other way:

> Any person working in the press as a critic could sell a story the following day. The public sector bought close to 500 stories that never saw production, and they were paid for, or at least partially paid for. We have an Egyptian proverb that says "Loose money teaches people sin." . . . Expenses for the cinema increased because the people making films were saying, "That's government money." (Salih 1986, 207–8)

But in terms of the content of films, nationalization opened the doors to directors who wanted to make films that were autonomous works of art. Many of these films deliberately cut their links to the traditions of commercial Egyptian cinema, and many of these films have been well received in foreign film festivals. Unfortunately, by 1970 the public sector collapsed, leaving a bankrupt industry.[32] The state withdrew from direct financing of film projects, although it has always maintained a grip on the facilities for producing films.

BACK TO THE FUTURE

Eventually Egyptian filmmakers reestablished their links with the earlier traditions of commercial cinema. The much-maligned star system returned, and so too did the potential for clever directors to exploit the intertextuality of actors and previous films.

Shortly after the Centennial festival I became involved in planning another film festival, this time for Egyptian films exclusively. I was fascinated to see that one of the films we chose for our festival was full of references to earlier films. The film is *Ya dunya ya gharami* (O Life, My Passion; Ahmad 1996), the debut film of Majdi 'Ali Ahmad.

The title comes from a song in Muhammad 'Abd al-Wahhab's third film, *Yahya al-hubb* (Long Live Love; Karim 1938). *Long Live Love,* as mentioned above, was also Layla Murad's first film. It is a cheery story in which 'Abd al-Wahhab plays an aristocrat who works as a bank clerk, hiding his true identity so that people will judge him on personal merit rather than by his social station. In the course of the film he marries an aristocratic woman (Murad), and of course when his true identity is revealed everybody lives happily ever after.[33]

O Life, My Passion, by contrast, is about three single women with no male guardians. In the film the three struggle to find mates in a social system that has allotted them few assets. Their potential husbands range from an exuberant con man to a prudish hypocrite. As in *Long Live Love,* hidden identities play a role in several characters, but in *O Life, My Passion,* secrets revealed always lead to a reality that is less than the appearance rather than more. The ending is neither happy nor sad; rather it is filled with ambiguity, as two of the three women are forced to marry men who are less than perfect.

O Life, My Passion has enough visual presence to do very well on the film festival circuit.[34] Furthermore, it sensitively and humanely portrays the lives of women in a Middle Eastern society, a topic that preoccupies Americans both in and outside of academia. The film is well acted and intelligently directed and was also extremely popular in Egypt. But what fascinated me most was the final scene. The story ends with one of the three women getting knifed by an angry fundamentalist. Fortunately she survives. We see her waking up in the hospital with her two friends by her side. Of course, they ask her, "How do you feel?" The stricken woman replies, "I feel like I'm headed for a disaster" (*Hasis bi-musiba gayya-li*). Then she says, "Oh God, oh God" (*Ya latif, ya latif*). The women in the scene express their concern for each other and their relief that the worst had not happened in "commercial filmese." The exchange is from a film, and the film happens to be none other than *The Flirtation of Girls*. In the original Layla Murad and Najib al-Rihani are in her jeep. Al-Rihani does not yet know it, but they are going to Layla's tryst with her nightclub lover. On the way they sing a delightful duet in which Layla asks al-Rihani, "How do you feel?" His reply: "I feel like I'm headed for a disaster." And Layla replies, "Ya latif, ya latif." From the title almost to the last line—these are just two of many examples, and there are doubtless many that I, as an outsider, missed—*O Life, My Passion* lives through other works, just as *The Flirtation of Girls* had in 1949. It portrays a social world that is also defined partly through works of popular culture.

Bourdieu describes the "autonomy of artistic production" as one of the conventional diacritica of pure taste. But the autonomy of art, he says, obscures its social embeddedness: "An art which ever increasingly contains reference to its own history demands to be perceived historically; it asks to be referred not to an external referent, the represented or designated 'reality', but to the universe of past and present works of art" (1984, 3). *The Flirtation of Girls* was born within just such a universe, but of course it was driven very much by the historically developed canons not of elite sensibilities but of popular taste. One of the hallmarks of a modern sensibility is that producers of art concede Bourdieu's point: they produce works that foreground the universe of past and present works of art rather than attempt to obscure it beneath the "pure intention of the artist . . . who aims to be autonomous" (Bourdieu 1984, 3). We tend to call this "postmodern," but perhaps the same dynamics are at work in other places and at other times.

What the director of *O Life, My Passion* has done is to find a way to make creative use of his own filmmaking tradition, and at the same time to make the film appealing to a foreign audience. It is an acknowledgment that there is, after all, some value in those three thousand films that came before. One hopes this is a sign that the Egyptian cinema will both survive and retain its unique character. Like all Third World film industries, Egypt will have to market its films in metropolitan markets in order to survive, because the economics of the local market will not sustain the industry. The omnipresence of the dreaded Hollywood global juggernaut is only one of the threats faced by the beleaguered Egyptian national film industry. The inability of the Egyptian government to exert any effective pressure on Arab governments to pay a fair price for Egyptian entertainment product is another. Furthermore, no Arab government, Egyptian or otherwise, has shown the slightest interest in policing video piracy. The American government too has turned a blind eye to piracy of Egyptian films on American soil, thereby rendering a potentially lucrative expatriate Arab market null and void as far as the film producers are concerned.[35]

Making films for exhibition in the United States, even if only in the limited circuit of universities and art houses, forces nonmetropolitan filmmakers to choose between making films with general appeal in their countries of origin and making films oriented primarily toward interpreting their culture to foreign audiences. Sometimes filmmakers can have their cake and eat it too. At the Centennial festival Ferid Boughedir emphasized that his films are shown in Tunisia and do quite well there. *Summer in La Goulette* will not, however, be shown widely in the Arabic-speaking world outside of Tunisia because it features a number of scenes with nudity. Ultimately the multicultural world elaborated in the film works better in New York than anywhere else.

More often the choice between specialist metropolitan and general national audiences is cast in terms favorable to the metropole—as between art and commerce. Films from other national film traditions shown here are shown because we think they are art. As the *Cineaste* editorial put it, they are "at least the best of them." By default the Egyptian cinema, as the only significant commercial film industry of the Arabic-speaking world, is given the role of the villain in this artistic economy. Egyptian and Arab intellectuals are full partners in casting this drama. Boughedir, Salih, and all the other filmmakers and critics at the festival were eager to proclaim their distance from the conventions of Egyptian cinema, but in doing so they perhaps inadvertently withheld the tools a metropolitan audience needed to appreciate one of the most strikingly different films shown in the festival.

Metropolitan film festivals sell themselves as glimpses into worlds of difference. And yet films like *The Flirtation of Girls* were dismissed as nothing more than Hollywood clones, leaving the audience to question, like the man in the lobby between *The Flirtation of Girls* and *Summer in La Goulette,* why it was subjected to what was essentially, by the standards of the festival's expert opinion, a bad film. The answer is that the organizers of the festival were wiser than their experts. *The Flirtation of Girls* is a great film, if not a film that a metropolitan audience can easily view without mediation.

NOTES

This chapter was initially conceived and written at Princeton University in the 1996–97 academic year, when I was a visiting fellow at the Institute for the Transregional Study of the Middle East, North Africa, and Central Asia. My initial impressions of the films were formed in the company of Ted Swedenburg, with whom I attended the Centennial festival in New York City. Versions of the chapter were presented at the Columbia Society of Fellows and at the Middle East Center of the

University of California at Los Angeles (UCLA); the manuscript benefited from comments by Anne Waters (at Columbia) and James Gelvin (at UCLA) and by the students and faculty who attended the lectures at both institutions. Thanks are also due to Robert Vitalis and Roberta Dougherty, both of whom read the manuscript and gave valuable suggestions for changes. And finally I wish to thank Susan Ossman and Gregory Starrett (the reviewers from the University of California Press, both of whom waived anonymity on their reports) for their comments.

1. For example, the film critic Samir Farid is less sanguine about the success of public-sector film production than many. He views many films of the period as "propaganda" (Farid 1996, 12). Farid is particularly harsh on films produced before 1968, although he dispenses relatively grudging praise even to the best public-sector films made between 1968 and 1970. It is the later public-sector films that are most often identified by proponents of the period as masterpieces. Even supporters of the public sector concede that the early years were at best chaotic (e.g., Salih 1986, 206–8). Farid's negative opinions on the public sector are likely to be seen by many as particularly controversial. In the editorial notes to Farid's article Alia Arasoughly (1996, 18) cites a number of articles that argue, contrary to Farid, in favor of the public sector. Informally one encounters such polarized feelings about the public sector very often. The issue serves very easily as a lightning rod on political stances toward the Nasser regime.

2. Nor is the social basis of artistic hierarchies universally accepted in the West. Richard Jenkins (1992, 137) describes Bourdieu's agenda in *Distinction* as "dissolving culture into culture"—in other words, refusing the absolute separation of high culture from society. Jenkins suggests that while the sociological basis of the judgment of taste may not be in question to social scientists, "some art historians and critics—and many more of their readers (not to mention those who do not read, but know what is art and what isn't)—certainly *do* [believe in an ahistorical and nonsociological aesthetic sense]" (1992, 137; italics in original). Levine (1988), for his part, approaches the problem of artistic canons through an examination of how Shakespeare was transformed in Victorian-era America from popular theater into an icon of "elevated" art that required the mediation of specialists. Their questioning of the "naturalness" of highbrow/lowbrow distinctions is certainly relevant to the analysis of Middle Eastern mediated popular culture, where even social scientists (let alone literary specialists and art historians) have barely begun to analyze contemporary Middle Eastern popular culture in a wider sociological context.

3. The festival took place from November 1 to December 5, 1996, at the Lincoln Center and was co-curated by Alia Arasoughly and Richard Peña.

4. It can be argued that all of the post–public-sector directors were, to some degree, products of the 1960s. Whether their work reacts favorably or unfavorably to what each director sees as the legacy of the period, none of them can afford not to have a position on the ideals of the period.

5. The other anomalous film shown at the Centennial festival was *Intisar al-shahab* (The Triumph of Youth; Badr Khan 1941). All the remaining early films are linked to the public sector. *Al-ʿAzima* (Resolution; Salim 1939) and *al-Suq al-sawda'* (Black Market; al-Tilmisani 1945) are seen as films that stood apart from the main-

stream of their times and contributed to a kind of social realism. Others were by directors who later became prominent in the public sector: *Darb al-mahabil* (Fools' Alley; Salih 1955), *Bab al-hadid* (Cairo Station; Chahine 1958), *Shabab imra'a* (A Woman's Youth; Abu Sayf 1956), and *Hayat aw mawt* (Life or Death; al-Shaykh 1954).

6. Andrew Shryock (1998) describes a similar dynamic in the process of making a film that addresses cultural boundaries. His terms are "mainstreaming" (what Schwartzman calls "the desire to solve the problem of foreignness by overcoming difference") and "othering" (Schwartzman: "the desire to communicate foreignness by revealing difference").

7. This is not to say that antagonism toward commercial cinema is unthinking or unreasonable in the context of contemporary mass media economics, where blockbusters (usually American) threaten to crowd out virtually everything else—even productions that are profitable, but on a less than gargantuan scale. This was a key assumption of the *Cineaste* editorial ("Editorial" 1996). Twitchell (1992) gives a more extensive account of the growing dominance of the blockbuster in several different media.

8. Schwartzman refers to the Venezualan cinema, which, on a smaller scale (some 250 films compared to approximately 3,000 in the case of Egypt alone), parallels the problems of presenting a film festival to an American audience with almost no prior knowledge of its history or conventions. The "national" aspect of the problem is also rather different in the case of the Centennial festival, as compared to Schwartzman's Venezuelan festival. "[Venezuelan cinema,] as any national cinema, is comprised of continuous and discontinuous narratives related by and for multiple communities" (Schwartzman 1995, 72). However, the diversity subsumed by the imaginary construct of a Venezuelan nation is analogous to that of Arabic-speaking societies; the status of an "Arab nation" is far more vexed. Some would argue passionately for its existence, whereas others would admit only to the existence of Arab nations in the plural.

9. Indeed, although Khayri is never put in the company of such "serious" playwrights as Tawfiq al-Hakim or Alfred Faraj, he became a semicanonical figure, largely by virtue of the satirical anti-British plays he wrote around the time of the 1919 revolt against British rule. Khayri enjoyed a long career as a poet, playwright, and film script writer. Most of his work was comic, and he was the main literary collaborator with Najib al-Rihani. For more on Khayri, see his memoirs (Khayri n.d.).

10. The Egyptian film critic 'Ali Abu Shadi would have added a second Egyptian voice to the panel of experts at the Centennial festival, but he was unable to attend. A number of academic papers were presented at the festival and later published in Arasoughly (1996; n.d.). Several directors also attended, including Burhane Allaouie (Lebanon), Barouk Beloufa (Algeria), Ferid Boughedir (Tunisia), Fashid Masharawi (Palestine), Usama Muhammad (Syria), Tawfiq Salih (Egypt), Khalid Siddiq (Kuwait), Abderrahmane Tazi (Morocco), and Moufida Tlatli (Tunisia). Abu Shadi's contribution to the festival literature left no doubt that the expressed attitude toward commercialism was conventional:

> The harshest criticism of genre cinema in general is that genres have usually affirmed the status quo and its existing values, and have resisted any innovation or change. More

often than not, these values express dominant mores and ideology. They provide easy formulaic answers to difficult questions in order to please their audiences. The exceptions are far and few in the history of cinema. (Abu Shadi 1996, 85)

11. Salih's Centennial festival presentation offered substantially the same view developed in Salih 1986.

12. *Summer in La Goulette* was produced in 1995 and was being shown in the United States for the first time at the Centennial festival. However, the disparity in the size of the crowds that attended the two films was not due to the greater scarcity of Tunisian films in the American film-festival circuit but rather to their prominence. The director already had a following, as a result of an earlier film he had made, *Halfaouine, Boy of the Terraces* (1990). *Halfaouine* was also shown at the Centennial festival and was one of a handful of films shown three times (most were shown twice).

13. In Egypt, for example, *Summer in La Goulette* will be a good candidate for the Cairo International Film Festival, where it cannot be censored without risking the festival's status as a recognized international event. However, films shown out of the competition at the International Film Festival play only once or twice, and ticket prices are inflated far beyond the normal rate, which effectively limits access. Films in the festival's competition are even more restricted. *Summer in La Goulette* will never show in a commercial Egyptian theater unless Boughedir submits the film to censorship, which, in the case of the nude scenes, would be quite severe. In other Arabic-speaking countries restrictions on the film would likely range from Egypt's limited tolerance to an outright ban (in, for example, the Gulf states).

14. However, within the conventions of Egyptian cinema polemics against religious extremism are possible, although until recently they were rare (see Armbrust 1998).

15. For example, Yusuf Wahbi, who made his cameo appearance near the surreal conclusion to the story, was from an aristocratic family with Turkish connections (Wahbi 1973).

16. Al-Rihani's autobiography (1959) says nothing about either his religious background or his Iraqi father. Abou Saif (1969, 23) dispenses with the issue in a single line in which she mentions that his full name was Najib Ilyas al-Rihani (Ilyas is a Christian name), that his mother was Coptic-Egyptian, and that his father was Iraqi. In the case of Murad, Hasanayn says nothing about her Jewishness and conversion to Islam except insofar as it became an issue in a public campaign started by a Syrian newspaper accusing her of having made donations to Israel in the early 1950s—a charge that Hasanayn rejects in the strongest possible terms (Hasanayn 1993, 85–98). I have never seen any evidence that the general public does not completely agree with Hasanayn. Murad's songs and films remain popular and are often broadcast on Egyptian television.

17. Studio Misr, a subsidiary of the Egyptian industrialist Tal'at Harb, was by far the most important effort to create an independent film industry in Egypt (see Davis 1983).

18. This is not to say that Sharaf al-Din, or most other critics and historians, gives even the nationalist films of the 1950s a full endorsement:

It must be noted that in the ten years after the July Revolution a not inconsiderable number of directors were able to make good films, despite the continued prevalence of commercial films. . . . But their works were still in the framework of traditional social circumstances that could be criticized without running afoul of the new regime which had begun to show its teeth, although it had not yet revealed its complete identity. (Sharaf al-Din 1992, 20–21)

19. It is ironic that a degree of vernacular standardization through the cinema may have taken place in some cases through the efforts of the many non-Egyptian or immigrant actors and filmmakers who worked in the industry. Farid (1994) discusses the cross-fertilization of Egyptian and Lebanese cinemas, as does al-Aris (1996) from a Lebanese perspective. More generally the issue of more broadly defined marginality (including groups not prominently featured in constructions of Egyptian nationalism as well as foreigners) in Egyptian film workers is yet to be explored.

20. A lengthier discussion of the relation between vernacular and written Arabic in a nationalist context appears in Armbrust 1996.

21. The first line is part of a rhyme for memorizing the Arabic alphabet. The full rhyme is "Abgad, hawaz, hutti, kalamun; safasa qarasht thakhathun dadhaghun."

22. "Professor Pigeon" (ustaz hamam) is the name of al-Rihani's character in the film. Throughout the story various characters make puns on or hilariously mispronounce his name.

23. The transcription and translation was done by Roberta Dougherty.

24. Indeed, to a contemporary American audience the scene, coming as it does on the heels of a succession of very effective comic scenes, is difficult to view as anything but camp. It is, however, unlikely that an Egyptian audience of 1949 (or, generally speaking, even today) would see it as such. 'Azzam describes the song, "Ashiq al-ruh" (Lover of the Spirit), as an important example of what he calls "the grand songs" of 'Abd al-Wahhab. The grand songs were produced from 1941 to 1949 and were characterized by "a) extended length, b) long freely rhythmic sections that left little, if any room for improvisation, c) themes that were elevated above the mundane, and d) texts written in classical, yet modern language that appealed to the general audience" ('Azzam 1990, 192). The scene is meant to be a visual and aural statement about the avant-garde character of the singer; some viewers of the film in 1949 might have found the song overly modern, and of course some intellectuals then and now might have found the juxtaposition of 'Abd al-Wahhab's high-art style to the film's often anarchic spirit to be absurd. But it is unlikely that a 1949 Egyptian audience would have found the scene humorous, as many in the Centennial festival audience did.

'Azzam (1990, 192–237) describes in detail how the songs of this period diverge from the conventions of traditional Arabic music. It should be noted that in an earlier work (Armbrust 1996, 89) I erroneously stated that such analyses had not yet been done.

25. The translation is 'Azzam's (1990, 385).

26. It is possible that the film editors deliberately chose what was, in effect, a fascinating study of al-Rihani's poignant facial expressions for the final instant of the film as a tribute to the beloved actor. The review of The Flirtation of Girls in the film magazine al-Kawakib also noted that in his performance al-Rihani spared no effort, "as if he sensed that he was writing his last line in the book of his unique acting life" ("Ghazal al-banat" 1949, 38).

27. 'Abd al-Wahhab's last appearance in a fiction film was in *Muntaha al-farah* (The Utmost Joy; Salim 1963), a state-funded film praising Egyptian soldiers returning from their intervention in the Yemeni civil war. In that case 'Abd al-Wahhab was one of several famous singers (again playing themselves) appearing in the film.

28. The phenomenon of the suddenly rich war profiteer was a popular issue in 1945. Magazines had a field day publishing caricatures of the alleged profiteers, who were portrayed as grotesquely obese and incredibly stupid (see, e.g., *al-Ithnayn*, nos. 550–600; virtually every issue contains at least one "war profiteer" cartoon). In terms of cinema, the recipe for tastelessness described by Abu Sayf and Salih depended on cash flowing into the hands of both producers and consumers—but predominantly uneducated consumers rather than the literate middle class. One film from the period portrays precisely this vision: *Black Market* (al-Tilmisani 1945). The film portrays the war as a time of great suffering for the masses while a few unscrupulous individuals hoarded scarce commodities and preyed on everyone else. The film begs the question of how the demand for new films could have risen if only a few individuals were prospering. *Black Market* was produced by Studio Misr, which earlier in the war had stopped producing its own films and leased its facilities to other companies (Salih 1986, 199). It is possible that with the end of the war other companies were able to break Studio Misr's hold on critical production facilities and that *Black Market*, with its frank protest of precisely the forces that expanded the film industry, contains an element of economic self-interest.

29. Of course, neither the economic nor the aesthetic rationales for the troubles of the pre-1960s Egyptian cinema need be taken at face value. This chapter questions the cultural devaluation of Egyptian films, suggesting that the aesthetic standard by which local products were judged as autonomous works of art (or more precisely, as completely lacking the criteria by which works of art should be judged) was at least as imported as the allegedly derivative conventions used by Egyptian filmmakers. And as time went by it was the film texts that became naturalized, while "revolutionary" criticism remained elite and foreign to most of society. As for the political economy of Egyptian films, Vitalis (this volume) argues convincingly that the global dominance of Hollywood was not as great a problem for Egyptian filmmakers in the 1950s as were underlying structural problems. The inability or unwillingness of Egyptian entrepreneurs to expand the local film presence in the market crippled the industry, and even more so the disjunction between financiers, producers, and distributors. Furthermore, political priorities veered from suspicion of the industry as a whole to a comprehensive intervention in the market that in the long run proved economically disastrous.

30. Even in 1949, more than a decade before the actual nationalization of the Egyptian cinema, Abu Sayf's call for government intervention in the industry was not new. Shalash (1986, 80–85) traces calls for government support of the cinema back to the 1920s.

31. 'Ukasha was not in office when the nationalizations took place, although he was reinstated as minister of culture after the 1967 war. 'Ukasha characterized his intentions toward the cinema industry as limited—more along the lines of Abu Sayf's program outlined in 1949:

> The Ministry of Culture set limited goals, including raising the artistic and professional standards of the cinema by giving increased attention to those working in it, the award-

ing of prizes for the best works and workers in the field, sending missions abroad to study the art of cinema, giving opportunities for cinema workers to expand the range of their knowledge by participating in international conferences and film festivals, establishing festivals ["weeks"] for Arab and foreign films at home, giving financial help to filmmakers working on "committed films" [*al-intaj al-hadif*], financing studios through guaranteed loans, and encouraging the exhibition of Egyptian films at home and abroad. ('Ukasha 1990, 486)

32. For an accounting of public-sector losses in the nationalized period (1963–71), see "al-Nass al-kamil . . . " 1993. Defenders of the public sector such as Salah Abu Sayf challenge the accounting methods used in this report, claiming that the losses were far less, or even that there were no losses (pers. com. June 17, 1994). Abu Sayf, however, allowed that there were significant problems inherent in the managerial structure of the public sector, which included persons opposed to the very concept of a public sector, as well as enthusiastic supporters of the public-sector project.

33. In his first two films, *The White Rose* (Karim 1933) and *Dumu' al-hubb* (Tears of Love; Karim 1935), 'Abd al-Wahhab plays men of modest means who fall in love with aristocratic girls, but the endings are sad: in *The White Rose* he is forced by her father to step aside in favor of an aristocrat; in *Tears of Love* he steps aside so the girl can marry an aristocratic friend, but the friend turns out to be a libertine who wastes all their money, leading ultimately to the woman's suicide. For more on *The White Rose* and how it and 'Abd al-Wahhab were presented to the public in the 1930s, see Armbrust 1996.

34. *O Life, My Passion* won best actress (Layla 'Ilwi) and best director (Majdi Ahmad 'Ali) at the 1996 Montreal Film Festival.

35. This did not prevent the American government from demanding that Egyptian video distributors respect American copyright laws. In 1994 when I was in Cairo American videos suddenly vanished from the market because the Egyptian government had been forced to crack down on piracy. But there was no quid pro quo. No crackdown on distributors of illegal videos of Egyptian products in the American market ever occurred.

REFERENCES

BOOKS, ARTICLES, AND DISSERTATIONS

'Abd al-Rahman, Mahfuz. 1991. "Al-Tamthiliyya al-tarikhiyya i'dad" (Historical Drama—draft). Paper presented at the Second Literary Gathering for the Countries of the Cooperative Council for the Gulf Arab States, United Arab Emirates.

———. 1996. *Nasir 56.* Cairo: Dar al-Mawqif al-'Arabi.

Abdalla, Ahmed. 1985. *The Student Movement and National Politics in Egypt, 1923–1973.* London: Al Saqi Books.

Abdel-Fadil, Mahmoud. 1980. *The Political Economy of Nasserism.* London: Cambridge University Press.

Abdel-Moteleb, Fikri. 1993. "Public Sale Becomes Public Debate." *Al-Ahram Weekly,* August 19–25.

Abou Saif, Layla. 1969. "The Theater of Naguib al-Rihani: The Development of Comedy in Modern Egypt." Ph.D. dissertation, University of Illinois.

Abraham, Nabeel. 1989. "Arab-American Marginality: Mythos and Praxis." *Arab Studies Quarterly* 11: 17–43.

Abraham, Sameer, and Nabeel Abraham. 1983. *Arabs in the New World.* Detroit: Wayne State University Press.

Abu al-Fath, Ilham. 1996. "Mathaf al-thawra lil-jamahir—1997" (A Museum of the Revolution for the Masses—1997). *Al-Akhbar,* July 24.

Abu Jalala, Khalid. 1995. "Saraqat al-musiqa al-Misriyya" (The Theft of Egyptian Music). *Ruz al-Yusuf,* March 28, pp. 62–63.

Abu Sayf, Salah. 1949. "Inqadhu sina'at al-sinima" (Save the Cinema Industry). *Al-Kawakib,* September 8, p. 17.

Abu Shadi, Ali. 1996. "Genres in Egyptian Cinema." In *Screens of Life: Critical Film Writing from the Arab World,* vol. 1, ed. Alia Arasoughly, 84–129. St.-Hyacinthe, Quebec: World Heritage Press.

Abu-Lughod, Janet. 1971. *Cairo: 1001 Years of the City Victorious.* Princeton: Princeton University Press.

———. 1989. *Before European Hegemony: The World System, A.D. 1250–1350.* New York: Oxford University Press.

Abu-Lughod, Lila. 1993a. "Editorial Comment: On Screening Politics in a World of Nations." *Public Culture* 5: 465–67.

———. 1993b. "Finding a Place for Islam: Egyptian Television Serials and the National Interest." *Public Culture* 5: 493–513.

———. 1995a. "Movie Stars and Islamic Moralism in Egypt." *Social Text* 42: 53–67.

———. 1995b. "The Objects of Soap Opera: Egyptian Television and the Cultural Politics of Modernity." In *Worlds Apart: Modernity through the Prism of the Local,* ed. Daniel Miller, 190–210. London: Routledge.

AbuKhalil, As'ad. 1993. "A Note on the Study of Homosexuality in the Arab/Islamic Civilization." *Arab Studies Journal* 1 (2): 32–34, 48.

ACCESS Cultural Arts. 1994. "Creating a New Arab World: A Century in the Life of the Arab-American Community in Detroit," a grant submitted to the National Endowment for the Humanities.

Adwy, Awad Al. 1999. "Zaki to Make 'Sadat' on His Own Terms." *Middle East Times,* May. http://www.metimes.com/issue99–18/cultent/zaki_to_make.htm.

Agassi, Tirzah. 1997. "Peace of Her Heart." *Jerusalem Post,* April 4, p. 3.

Ahmad, Aijaz, ed. 1992a. *In Theory: Classes, Nations, Literatures.* New York: Verso.

———. 1992b. "*Orientalism* and After: Ambivalence and Metropolitan Location in the Work of Edward Said." In *In Theory: Classes, Nations, Literatures,* ed. Aijaz Ahmad, 159–219. New York: Verso.

Aijazuddin, F. S. 1991. *Lahore: Illustrated Views of the 19th Century.* Ahmedabad, India: Mappin Publishing.

Aksüt, Sadun. 1994. *Şarkılarda . . . Istanbul* (Istanbul in Songs). Istanbul: Altın Kitabları Istanbul.

Alatraqchi, Firas. 1996. "Tied in a Knot." *Pose* (March-April): 21–22.

Alcalay, Ammiel. 1993. *After Jews and Arabs: Remaking Levantine Culture.* Minneapolis: University of Minnesota Press.

Allen, Roger. 1992. *A Period of Time.* Reading, U.K.: Ithaca Press.

And, Metin. 1959. *Dances of Anatolian Turkey.* Dance Perspectives 3. Brooklyn: Dance Perspectives.

———. 1976. *Pictorial History of Turkish Dancing.* Ankara: Dost Yayınları.

Anderson, Benedict. 1991. *Imagined Communities: Reflections on the Origin and Spread of Nationalism.* London: Verso.

Ang, Ien. 1985. *Watching Dallas: Soap Opera and the Melodramatic Imagination.* London: Routledge.

Anjavi Shirazi, Sayyid Abu al-Qasim. 1973. *Baziha-yi namayishi* (Theatrical Plays). Tehran: Amir Kabir.

Appadurai, Arjun. 1990. "Disjuncture and Difference in the Global Cultural Economy." *Public Culture* 2 (2): 1–24.

———. 1991. "Global Ethnoscapes." In *Recapturing Anthropology: Working in the Present,* ed. Richard Fox, 191–210. Santa Fe, New Mex.: School of American Research.

———. 1993. "Patriotism and Its Futures." *Public Culture* 5 (3): 411–29.

————. 1996. *Modernity at Large: Cultural Dimensions of Globalization*. Minneapolis: University of Minnesota Press.

Arasoughly, Alia, ed. 1996. *Screens of Life: Critical Film Writing from the Arab World*. Vol. 1. St.-Hyacinthe, Quebec: World Heritage Press.

————. n.d. *Screens of Life: Critical Film Writing from the Arab World*. Vol. 2. St.-Hyacinthe, Quebec: World Heritage Press.

Ardener, Edward. 1989. *The Voice of Prophecy and Other Essays*. Ed. Malcolm Chapman. New York: Basil Blackwell.

Aris, Ibrahim al-. 1996. "An Attempt at Reading the History of Cinema in Lebanon." In *Screens of Life: Critical Film Writing from the Arab World*, vol. 1, ed. Alia Arasoughly, 19–39. St.-Hyacinthe, Quebec: World Heritage Press.

Armbrust, Walter. 1995. "Terrible Terrorist: How the Egyptian Establishment Declared Victory in the War against Islamists." Paper presented at the annual meeting of the American Anthropological Association, Washington, D.C., November 17.

————. 1996. *Mass Culture and Modernism in Egypt*. Cambridge: Cambridge University Press.ß

————. 1998. "Veiled Cinema: An Interview with Yousry Nasrallah." *Visual Anthropology* 10 (2–4): 381–99.

Armes, Roy. 1987. *Third World Film Making and the West*. Berkeley: University of California Press.

Asad, Talal, ed. 1973. *Anthropology and the Colonial Encounter*. London: Ithaca Press.

————. 1993. *Genealogies of Religion*. Baltimore: Johns Hopkins University Press.

Ashcroft, Bill, Gareth Griffiths, and Helen Tiffin. 1989. *The Empire Writes Back: Theory and Practice in Post-Colonial Literatures*. London: Routledge.

Assif, Guy. 1995. "Yesh Tisporet Yesh Haverim" (When There's a Haircut There Are Friends). *Tarbut Ma'ariv* 82 (October): 13.

Assiouty, Mohammed el-. 1996. "In the Can." *Al-Ahram Weekly*, May 23–29.

Aswad, Barbara. 1974. *Arabic-speaking Communities in American Cities*. New York: Center for Migration Studies and the Association of Arab-American University Graduates.

————. 1992. "The Lebanese Muslim Community in Dearborn, Michigan." In *The Lebanese in the World: A Century of Emigration*, ed. Albert Hourani and Nadim Shehadi, 167–88. London: I. B. Tauris.

Aswani, Ahmad al-. 1983. *Al-Samt al-marfud* (The Refused Silence). Cairo: n.p.

Augé, Marc. 1995. *Non-Places: Introduction to an Anthropology of Supermodernity*. London: Verso.

Ayalon, Ami. 1995. *The Press in the Arab Middle East: A History*. New York: Oxford University Press.

'Azzam, Nabil Salim. 1990. "Muhammad 'Abd al-Wahhab in Modern Egyptian Music." Ph.D. dissertation, University of California, Los Angeles.

Badawi, al-Said M. 1973. *Mustawayat al-'Arabiyya al-mu'asira fi Misr* (The Levels of Modern Arabic in Egypt). Cairo: Dar al-Ma'arif.

Badr, 'Abd al-Muhsin Taha. 1984. *Tatawwur al-riwaya al-'Arabiyya al-haditha fi Misr (1870–1938)* (Development of the Modern Arabic Novel in Egypt [1870–1938]). Al-Tab'a 4. Cairo: Dar al-Ma'arif.

Bahra, Nasr al-Din al-. 1992. *Dimashq al-asrar* (Damascus of Secrets). Damascus: al-Jumhuriyya Press.

Baker, Raymond William. 1974. "Egypt in Shadows: Films and the Political Order." *American Behavioral Scientist* 17 (3): 393–423.

Bakhtin, Mikhail. 1984. *Rabelais and His World*. Trans. Helen Iswolsky. Bloomington: Indiana University Press (1965 in Russian).

Bakri, Mahmud. 1995. "Bi-al-'aql" (By Reason). *Al-Ahrar*, July 12.

Bakri, Mustafa. 1995. "Kalima sariha" (Plain Talk). *Al-Sha'b*, July 14.

Bandari, Muna al-, et al. 1994. *Mawsu'at al-aflam al-'Arabiyya* (Encyclopedia of Arab Films). Cairo: Bayt al-Ma'rifa.

Barber, Karin. 1995. "African-Language Literature and Postcolonial Criticism." *Research in African Literatures* 26 (4): 3–30.

Barnouw, Erik, and S. Krishnaswamy. 1963. *Indian Film*. New York: Columbia University Press.

Barthes, Roland. 1975. *The Pleasure of the Text*. Trans. Richard Miller. New York: Hill and Wang.

Basch, Linda, Nina Glick-Schiller, and Christina Szanton Blanc. 1994. *Nations Unbound: Transnational Projects, Postcolonial Predicaments, and Deterritorialized Nation-States*. Langhorne, Pa.: Gordon and Breach.

Basila, Nazik. 1960. *Mudhakkirat Badi'a Masabni* (Memoirs of Badi'a Masabni). Beirut: Dar Maktabat al-Hayat.

Bateson, Gregory. 1972. "Toward a Theory of Schizophenia." In *Steps to an Ecology of Mind*, 201–27. New York: Ballantine.

Baudrillard, Jean. 1995. *The Gulf War Did Not Take Place*. Trans. and introd. Paul Patton. Bloomington: Indiana University Press.

Beeman, William O. 1976. "You Can Take Music Out of the Country, But . . . : The Dynamics of Change in Iranian Musical Tradition." *Asian Music* 7 (2): 19.

———. 1981. "Why Do They Laugh?" *Journal of American Folklore* 94 (374): 506–26.

Behnam, M. Reza 1986. *Cultural Foundations of Iranian Politics*. Salt Lake City: University of Utah Press.

Behrens-Abouseif, Doris. 1985. *Azbakiyya and Its Environs, from Azbak to Isma'il, 1476–1879*. Cairo: Institut Français d'Archéologie Orientale.

Beinin, Joel. 1998. *The Dispersion of Egyptian Jewry*. Berkeley: University of California Press.

Belge, Murat. 1983. "Türkiye'de Günlük Hayat" (Daily Life in Turkey). In *Cumhuriyet Dönemi Türkiye Ansiklopedisi* (Encyclopedia of Turkey in the Republican Period). Istanbul: Iletişim.

Ben, Avishay. n.d. "Sa'adia Brothers—Lior & Shmulik." http://www.nuts.co.il/dana/danai.html.

Ben-zvi, Yael. 1998. "Zionist Lesbianism and Transsexual Transgression." *Middle East Report* 206: 26–28.

Benjamin, Walter. 1969. "Art in the Age of Mechanical Reproduction." In *Illuminations*, 217–42. Trans. Hannah Arendt. New York: Schocken Books.

———. 1983. *Charles Baudelaire: A Lyric Poet in the Era of High Capitalism*. London: Verso.

Berger, Bennet. 1995. *Essay on Culture: Symbolic Structure and Social Structure*. Berkeley: University of California Press.

Berque, Jacques. 1972. *Egypt: Imperialism and Revolution.* New York: Praeger.

Berry, Ahmad. 1995a. "Banurama . . . li-madha?" (Panorama . . . Why?). *Panorama,* no. 1, June 1995, p. 3.

———. 1995b. "Kalimat sharaf" (Word of Honor). *Panorama,* no. 2, August 1995, p. 4.

Bhabha, Homi, ed. 1990. *Nation and Narration.* New York: Routledge.

———. 1994. *The Location of Culture.* London: Routledge.

Bhatia, Shayam. 1997. "Sex-Change Singer Offbeat for Egypt." *The Guardian* (London), May 20, p. 14.

Birenberg, Yoav. 1996. "What Can I Tell You, Yoav, We Have a Wonderful State and a Wonderful People" [in Hebrew]. *Yediot Aharanot* weekly supplement (7 *Nights*), August 23, pp. 6–7.

Blanc, Cristina Szanton, Linda Basch, and Nina Glick-Schiller. 1995. "Transnationalism, Nation-States, and Culture." *Current Anthropology* 36: 683–86.

Bodnar, John. 1992. *Remaking America: Memory, Commemoration, and Patriotism in the Twentieth Century.* Princeton: Princeton University Press.

Boroujerdi, Mehrzad. 1996. *Iranian Intellectuals and the West: The Tormented Triumph of Nativism.* Syracuse: Syracuse University Press.

Bourdieu, Pierre. 1977. *Outline of a Theory of Practice.* Cambridge: Cambridge University Press.

———. 1984. *Distinction: A Social Critique of the Judgment of Taste.* London: Routledge & Kegan Paul.

———. 1991. *Language and Social Power.* Cambridge, Mass.: Harvard University Press.

Bradbury, Ray. 1983. *Something Wicked This Way Comes.* New York: Simon & Schuster, 1962; New York: Knopf.

Breckenridge, Carol, and Arjun Appadurai. 1988. "Editor's Comments." *Public Culture* 1 (1): 1–4.

Broughton, Simon, et al., eds. 1994. *World Music: The Rough Guide.* London: Penguin Books.

Bulletin of the Israeli Academic Center in Cairo. 1988. Vol. 10 (July).

Burroughs, William S. 1967. *The Ticket That Exploded.* New York: Grove Press.

———. 1973. "Face to Face with the Goat God." *Oui* 2, no. 8 (August).

Carroll, Noël. 1985. "The Power of Movies." *Daedalus* 114: 79–103.

Castells, Manuel. 1989. *The Informational City: Information Technology, Economic Restructuring and the Urban-Regional Process.* Oxford: Blackwell.

———. 1996. "The Net and the Self: Working Notes for a Critical Theory of the Informational Society." *Critique of Anthropology* 16 (1): 9–38.

Caton, Margaret Louise. 1983. "Classical Tasnif: A Genre of Persian Vocal Music." Ph.D. dissertation, University of California, Los Angeles.

Çelik, Zeynep. 1986. *The Remaking of Istanbul: Portrait of an Ottoman City in the Nineteenth Century.* Seattle: University of Washington Press.

Chakravarty, Sumita S. 1993. *National Identity in Indian Popular Cinema, 1947–1987.* Austin: University of Texas Press.

"Change Is Good." 1998. *Wired* 6.01 (January): 182–83.

Chardin, Sir John (Chevalier Jean). 1987. *Travels in Persia 1673–1677.* New York: Dover Publications.

Chatterjee, Partha. 1993. *The Nation and Its Fragments.* Princeton: Princeton University Press.

Chelkowski, Peter. 1991. "Popular Entertainment, Media and Social Change in Twentieth-Century Iran." In *Cambridge History of Iran,* ed. Peter Avery et al., 7: 765–814. Cambridge: Cambridge University Press.

Choudhury, M. L. Roy. 1957. *Music in Islam.* Calcutta: H. B.

Christgau, Robert. 1996. "That Old-Time Religion." *Village Voice,* January 30.

Cleveland, William L. 1985. *Islam against the West: Shakib Arslan and the Campaign for Islamic Nationalism.* Austin: University of Texas Press.

Clifford, James. 1988. *The Predicament of Culture: Twentieth-Century Ethnography, Literature and Art.* Cambridge, Mass.: Harvard University Press.

Clifford, James, and George Marcus, eds. 1986. *Writing Culture: The Poetics and Politics of Ethnography.* Berkeley: University of California Press.

Cole, Juan. 1988. *Roots of North Indian Shi'ism in Iran and Iraq: Religion and State in Awadh, 1722–1859.* Berkeley: University of California Press.

Couch, John. 1997. "Culture Incorporated." *Wired* 5.12 (December): 214.

Crofts, Stephen. 1993. "Reconceptualizing National Cinema/s." *Quarterly Review of Film and Video* 14 (3): 49–67.

Danielson, Virginia. 1991. "Shaping Tradition in Arabic Song: The Career and Repertory of Umm Kulthum." Ph.D. dissertation, University of Illinois.

———. 1996. "New Nightingales of the Nile: Popular Music in Egypt Since the 1970s." *Popular Music* 15 (3): 299–312.

———. 1997. *The Voice of Egypt: Umm Kulthum, Arabic Song, and Egyptian Society in the Twentieth Century.* Chicago: University of Chicago Press.

Davis, Eric. 1983. *Challenging Colonialism: Bank Misr and Egyptian Industrialization, 1920–1941.* Princeton: Princeton University Press.

Davis, Stephen. 1993. *Jajouka Rolling Stone: A Fable of Gods and Heroes.* New York: Random House.

de Man, Paul. 1983. *Blindness and Insight: Essays in the Rhetoric of Contemporary Criticism.* 2d ed. London: Methuen.

Docker, John. 1994. *Postmodernism and Popular Culture: A Cultural History.* Cambridge: Cambridge University Press.

Douglas, Allen, and Fadwa Malti-Douglas. 1994. *Arab Comic Strips: Politics of an Emerging Mass Culture.* Bloomington: Indiana University Press.

Douglas, Mary. 1966. *Purity and Danger: An Analysis of Pollution and Taboo.* New York: Praeger.

Dresch, Paul. 1995. "Race, Culture and—What? Pluralist Certainties in the United States." In *The Pursuit of Certainty: Religious and Cultural Formulations,* ed. Wendy James, 61–91. New York: Routledge.

du Plessis, Nancy. 1995. *Notes des cahiers marocains/Notes from the Moroccan Journals, suivi de Art New York.* Paris: Editions l'Harmattan.

Duben, Alan, and Cem Behar. 1991. *Istanbul Households: Marriage, Family, and Fertility, 1880–1940.* Cambridge: Cambridge University Press.

Dunne, Bruce. 1990. "Homosexuality in the Middle East: An Agenda for Historical Research." *Arab Studies Quarterly* 12 (3–4): 55–82.

———. 1998. "Power and Sexuality in the Middle East." *Middle East Report* 206: 8–11.

During, Jean, Zia Mirabdolbaghi, and Dariush Safvat. 1991. *Art of Persian Music.* Washington, D.C.: Mage Publishers.

Dyson, Esther. 1995. "Intellectual Value." *Wired* 3.07 (July): 136–41, 182–84.

"Editorial." 1996. *Cineaste* 22 (1): 1.

"Egyptian Workers in Israel." 1996. UPI, August 19.

"Egyptians Were Stoned on Israeli-Supplied Hashish." 1996. *London Sunday Times,* December 22.

"Egypt's Jewish Community Dwindling." 1998. Reuters, September 27. http://www. arabia.com/content/culture/9u98/Egyptu27.9.98.shtml.

Eickelman, Dale F. 1991. "Traditional Islamic Learning and Ideas of the Person in the Twentieth Century." In *Middle Eastern Lives: The Practice of Biography and Self-Narrative,* ed. Martin Kramer, 35–59. Syracuse: Syracuse University Press.

El Charkawi, Galal. 1966. "History of the U.A.R. Cinema." In *Cinema in the Arab Countries,* ed. Georges Sadoul, 64–97. Paris: UNESCO.

El-Messiri, Sawsan. 1978. *Ibn al-Balad: A Concept of Egyptian Identity.* Leiden: Brill.

El Shawan, Salwa Aziz. 1981. "Al-Musika al-'Arabiyya: A Category of Urban Music in Cairo, Egypt, 1927–1977." Ph.D. dissertation, Columbia University.

Engel, Richard. 1997. "Egyptian Paper Sees Zionist Stars over Egypt." *Middle East Times,* June 6–12: 2.

Erlich, Haggai. 1989. *Students and University in 20th-Century Egyptian Politics.* London: Frank Cass.

Errington, Shelley. 1994. "What Became of Authentic Primitive Art?" *Cultural Anthropology* 9 (2): 201–26.

Essam El-Din, Gamal. 1997. "Visions of October." *Al-Ahram Weekly,* March 13–19.

Fabian, Johannes. 1983. *Time and the Other: How Anthropology Makes Its Object.* New York: Columbia University Press.

Fardon, Richard, ed. 1995. *Counterworks: Managing the Diversity of Knowledge.* New York: Routledge.

Farhat, Hormoz. 1965. "Dastgah Concept in Persian Music." Ph.D. dissertation, University of California, Los Angeles.

Farid, Samir. 1977. *Dalil al-sinima al-'Arabi: Khamsin 'aman 'ala awwal film Misri tawil* (Guide to Arab Cinema: Fifty Years after the First Egyptian Feature Film). Cairo: n.p.

———. 1986. "Surat al-insan al-Misri 'ala al-shasha bayn al-aflam al-istihlakiyya wa-al-aflam al-fanniyya" (The Image of the Egyptian on the Screen between Commercial and Artistic Films). In *al-Insan al-Misri 'ala al-shasha* (The Egyptian on the Screen), ed. Hashim al-Nahhas, 205–14. Cairo: al-Hay'a al-'Amma lil-Kitab.

———. 1994. "Misr wa-Lubnan, wa-al-sinima" (Egypt and Lebanon, and Cinema). *Al-Sinima wa-al-tarikh* 11: 83–92.

———. 1996. "Periodization of Egyptian Cinema." In *Screens of Life: Critical Film Writing from the Arab World,* vol. 1, ed. Alia Arasoughly, 1–18. St.-Hyacinthe, Quebec: World Heritage Press.

Farman Farmaian, Sattareh. 1992. *Daughter of Persia.* New York: Doubleday.

Faubion, James. 1993. *Modern Greek Lessons: A Primer in Historical Constructivism.* Princeton: Princeton University Press.

Fayyad, Sulayman. 1993. *Voices.* Trans. Hosam Aboul-Ela. New York: Marion Boyars Publishers.

Featherstone, Mike. 1995. *Undoing Culture: Globalization, Postmodernism and Identity.* London: Sage.

———. 1996. "Localism, Globalism, and Cultural Identity." In *Global/Local: Cultural Production and the Transnational Imaginary*, ed. Rob Wilson and Wimal Dissanayake, 46–77. Durham: Duke University Press.

Featherstone, Mike, and Scott Lash. 1995. "Globalization, Modernity and the Spatialization of Social Theory: An Introduction." In *Global Modernities*, ed. Mike Featherstone, Roland Robertson, and Scott Lash, 1–24. Thousand Oaks, Calif.: Sage.

Feld, Steven. 1994. "From Schizophonia to Schismogenesis: The Discourses and Practices of World Music and World Beat." In *Music Grooves: Essays and Dialogues*, by Charles Keil and Steven Feld, 257–89. Chicago: University of Chicago Press.

Ferguson, Marjory. 1992. "The Mythology about Globalization." *European Journal of Communication* 7: 69–93.

Film Daily. 1960. *1960 Year Book of Motion Pictures.* 42d annual ed. New York: World's Films and Film Folk.

Finkelstein, Joanne. 1989. *Dining Out: A Sociology of Modern Manners.* New York: New York University Press.

Fischer, Michael M. J. 1980. *Iran: From Religious Dispute to Revolution.* Cambridge, Mass.: Harvard University Press.

Fishman, Joshua. 1972. *Language and Nationalism: Two Integrative Essays.* Rowley, Mass.: Newbury House.

Fisk, Robert. 1996. "Massacre Film Puts Israel in Dock." *The Independent*, May 6.

Friedman, Jonathan. 1995. "Global System, Globalization and the Parameters of Modernity." In *Global Modernities*, ed. Mike Featherstone, Roland Robertson, and Scott Lash, 69–90. Thousand Oaks, Calif.: Sage.

Fuller, Mia. 1996. "Wherever You Go, There You Are: Fascist Plans for the Colonial City of Addis Ababa and the Colonizing Suburb of EUR '42." *Journal of Contemporary History* 31: 397–418.

Fussell, Paul. 1989. *Wartime: Understanding and Behavior in the Second World War.* New York: Oxford University Press.

Gabler, Neal. 1988. *An Empire of Their Own: How the Jews Invented Hollywood.* New York: Doubleday.

Gaffney, Jane. 1987. "The Egyptian Cinema: Industry and Art in a Changing Society." *Arab Studies Quarterly* 9 (1): 53–75.

Gaffney, Patrick D. 1994. *The Prophet's Pulpit: Islamic Preaching in Contemporary Egypt.* Berkeley: University of California Press.

Gellner, Ernest. 1983. *Nations and Nationalism.* Ithaca: Cornell University Press.

Gershoni, Israel, and James Jankowski. 1995. *Redefining the Egyptian Nation, 1930–1945.* Cambridge: Cambridge University Press.

Ghayti, Muhammad al-. 1995a. "Ahmad Zaki wa-'uyun al-saqr allati zalzalat al-Gharb" (Ahmad Zaki and the Hawk's Eyes That Shook the West). *Al-Idha'a wa-al-Tilifizyun*, July 15, pp. 12–14.

———. 1995b. *Fadiha ismuha Sa'ida Sultan: Dana mutribat al-jins al-Isra'iliyya* (A Scandal Named Sa'ida Sultan: Danna the Israeli Sex Artist). Cairo: al-Markaz al-'Arabi lil-Sahafa wa-al-Nashr wa-al-I'lam.

"Ghazal al-banat." 1949. Review of the film *The Flirtation of Girls. Al-Kawakib* 9 (October): 38–39.

Ghosh, Amitav. 1989. "The Diaspora in Indian Culture." *Public Culture* 2 (1): 73–78.

Giddens, Anthony. 1990. *The Consequences of Modernity.* Oxford: Blackwell.

Gilsenan, Michael. 1982. *Recognising Islam: Religion and Society in the Modern Arab World.* New York: Pantheon.

Givens, David, and Timothy Jablonski. 1995. "The 1995 Survey of Anthropology Ph.D.s." *Anthropology Newsletter* 36 (6): 11–12.

Glick-Schiller, Nina, Linda Basch, and Christina Szanton Blanc. 1992. *Towards a Transnational Perspective on Migration: Race, Class, Ethnicity, and Nationalism Reconsidered.* New York: New York Academy of Sciences.

Godfried, Nathan. 1987. *Bridging the Gap between Rich and Poor: American Economic Development Policy Toward the Arab East, 1942–1949.* New York: Greenwood Press.

Goldberg, David Theo, and Abebe Zegeye. 1995. "Editorial Note." *Social Identities* 1: 3–4.

Goodman, Jane. 1995. "'Mr. Joe Saint: Where Were You When . . . ?': Reflections on Islamic Premises and Practices in Contemporary Berber Song." Paper presented at the annual meeting of the American Anthropological Association, November 15.

Gordon, Joel. 1992. *Nasser's Blessed Movement: Egypt's Free Officers and the July Revolution.* Oxford: Oxford University Press.

———. 1997a. "Becoming the Image: Words of Gold, Talk Television, and Ramadan Nights on the Little Screen." *Visual Anthropology* 10 (1): 247–63.

———. 1997b. "Secular and Religious Memory in Egypt: Recalling Nasserist Civics." *Muslim World* 87 (2): 94–110.

Görmüş, A., and A. Baştürk. 1987. "Bülent Ersoy Sahne'ye. . . . " (Bülent Ersoy to the Stage). *Nokta* 20: 13–19.

Grendzier, Irene. 1997. "Following the Flag." *Middle East Report* 205: 10–11.

Grynberg, Daniel. 1996. "A Natural Woman." *Jerusalem Report*, February 22, pp. 34–35.

Guback, Thomas H. 1985. "Hollywood's International Market." In *The American Film Industry*, 2d ed., ed. Tino Balio, 163–86. Madison: University of Wisconsin Press.

Gysin, Brion. 1973. *The Process.* 2d ed. Frogmore, U.K.: Panther Books. (1st ed. Jonathan Cape, London, 1969.)

Hadari, Ahmad al-. 1989. *Tarikh al-sinima fi Misr: al-Juz' al-awwal min bidayat 1896 li-akhir 1930* (The History of Cinema in Egypt: Part 1, From Its Beginnings in 1896 to 1930). Cairo: Nadi al-Sinima.

Haeri, Shahla. 1989. *Law of Desire: Temporary Marriage in Shi'i Iran.* Syracuse: Syracuse University Press.

Hajjar, Lisa, and Steve Niva. 1997. "(Re)Made in the USA: Middle East Studies in the Global Era." *Middle East Report* 205: 2–9.

Hakim, Ayman al-. 1995. "Mahfuz 'Abd al-Rahman yaltaqi bi-Nasir 67" (Mahfuz 'Abd al-Rahman Meets Nasser 67). *Al-Idha'a wa-al-Tilifizyun*, November 4.

Hakim, Tawfiq al-. 1966. *Bird of the East.* Trans. R. Bayly Winder. Beirut: Khayats.

———. 1990. *Sijn al-'umr* (Prison of Life). Al-Fajjala [Cairo]: Maktabat Misr.

Halliday, Fred. 1993. "Orientalism and Its Critics." *British Journal of Middle East Studies* 20: 145–63.

Hammoudi, Abdellah. 1993. *The Victim and Its Masks: An Essay on Sacrifice and Masquerade in the Maghreb.* Chicago: University of Chicago Press.

Hamri, Mohamed. 1972. *Tales from Joujouka.* Santa Barbara, Calif.: Capricorn Press.

Handler, Richard. 1985. "On Having a Culture: Nationalism and the Preservation of Quebec's Patrimoine." In *Objects and Others: Essays on Museums and Material Culture,* ed. George W. Stocking, Jr., 192–217. Madison: University of Wisconsin Press.

Hani, Muhammad. 1995. "Ansar al-malakiyya 'ala al-shasha" (Royal Companions on Screen). *Ruz al-Yusuf,* May 8, pp. 35–42.

Hannerz, Ulf. 1992. *Cultural Complexity.* New York: Columbia University Press.

Haqqi, Yahya. 1973. *The Saint's Lamp and Other Stories.* Trans. M. M. Badawi. Leiden: Brill.

Hardy, Susan. 1994. "Imagining the Last Days: The Politics of Apocalyptic Language." In *Accounting for Fundamentalisms: The Dynamic Character of Movements,* ed. Martin E. Marty and R. Scott Appleby, 57–78. Chicago: University of Chicago Press.

Harris, Nigel. 1986. *The End of the Third World: Newly Industrializing Countries and the Decline of an Ideology.* London: Penguin.

Harvey, David. 1989. *The Condition of Postmodernity: An Enquiry into the Origins of Culture Change.* Oxford: Blackwell.

Hasan, Fatima. 1993. "Jadal fi Misr hawla hazr 199 ughniya li-54 mutriban wa-mutriba" (Controversy in Egypt about the Banning of 199 Songs by 54 Male and Female Artists). *Al-Hayat,* July 1, p. 23.

Hasan, Ilhami. 1986. *Muhammad Tal'at Harb, ra'id sina'at al-sinima al-Misriyya, 1867–1941* (Muhammad Tal'at Harb, Pioneer of the Egyptian Cinema Industry, 1867–1941). Cairo: al-Hay'a al-Misriyya al-'Amma lil-Kitab.

Hasanayn, 'Adil. 1993. *Layla Murad.* Cairo: Amadu.

Hattox, Ralph S. 1985. *Coffee and Coffeehouses: The Origins of Social Beverage in the Medieval Near East.* Seattle: University of Washington Press.

Herzfeld, Michael. 1991. *A Place in History: Social and Monumental Time in a Cretan Town.* Princeton: Princeton University Press.

———. [1987] 1992. *Anthropology through the Looking Glass: Critical Ethnography in the Margins of Europe.* Cambridge: Cambridge University Press.

———. 1995. "It Takes One to Know One: Collective Resentment and Mutual Recognition among Greeks in Local and Global Contexts." In *Counterworks: Managing the Diversity of Knowledge,* ed. Richard Fardon, 124–42. New York: Routledge.

Hinnebusch, Raymond A. 1991. "Class and State in Ba'thist Syria." In *Syria: Culture, Society and Polity,* ed. Richard T. Antoun and Donald Quarteret, 29–47. Albany: State University of New York Press.

———. 1993. "Class, State and the Reversal of Egypt's Agrarian Reform." *Middle East Report* 184: 20–23.

Hoffman, Abbie. 1971. *Steal This Book.* New York: Pirate Editions.

Hoggart, Richard. 1958. *Uses of Literacy.* Middlesex: Penguin.

Holbrook, Victoria. 1994. "Philology Went Down the Crossroads of Modernity to

Meet Orientalism, Nationalism and Ottoman Poetry." *New Perspectives on Turkey* 11: 19–41.

Horowitz, Amy, and Reuven Namdar. 1997. "Overcoming Music Ghettos: An Interview with Avihu Medina, Mizrahi Musician in Israel." *Cultural Survival Quarterly* 20 (4): 53–59.

Hourani, Albert. 1946. *Syria and Lebanon: A Political Essay.* London: Oxford University Press.

———. 1968. "Ottoman Reform and the Politics of Notables." In *Beginnings of Modernization in the Middle East: The Nineteenth Century,* ed. William R. Polk and Richard L. Chambers, 41–68. Chicago: University of Chicago Press.

Husayn, Taha. 1932. *An Egyptian Childhood: The Autobiography of Taha Husayn.* Trans. E. H. Paxton. New York: Routledge.

Ibn Kannan, Muhammad. 1994. *Yawmiyyat Shamiyya: 1111/1699–1153/1740* (Levantine Diary: 1111/1699–1153/1740). Ed. Akram 'Ulabi. Damascus: Dar al-Tabba.

Ibn Khaldun. 1958. *The Muqaddimah: An Introduction to History.* Trans. Franz Rosenthal. New York: Pantheon Books.

Ibrahim, Saad Eddin. 1982. "Egypt's Islamic Militants." *MERIP Reports* 103: 5–14.

Ibrahim, Sonallah. 1971. *The Smell of It, and Other Stories.* Trans. Denys Johnson-Davies. London: Heinemann Educational.

———. 1997. *Sharaf.* Cairo: Dar al-Hilal.

"Isra'il tuharib Misr bi-al-jins fi al-tilifun" (Israel Wages War on Egypt by Telephone Sex). 1995. *Ruz al-Yusuf,* August 21, pp. 18, 20–22.

Issari, M. Ali. 1989. *Cinema in Iran, 1900–1979.* Metuchen, N.J.: Scarecrow Press.

Jacquemond, Richard. 1997. "In the Middle East Deadlock, Egypt's Intellectuals Rediscover   Nasser."   *Le   Monde   Diplomatique   (English   Edition),*   July. http://www.monde-diplomatique.fr/md/en/1997/07/egypt.html.

Jameson, Fredric. 1986. "Third-World Literature in the Era of Multinational Capitalism." *Social Text* 15 (Fall): 65–88.

Jarvie, Ian. 1988. "Dollars and Ideology: Will Hays' Economic Foreign Policy 1922–1945." *Film History* 2: 207–21.

———. 1990. "The Postwar Economic Foreign Policy of the American Film Industry, Europe 1945–1950." *Film History* 4: 277–88.

———. 1992. *Hollywood's Overseas Campaign: The North Atlantic Movie Trade, 1920–1950.* Cambridge: Cambridge University Press.

Jehl, Douglas. 1995. "In a Smutty War, Egypt Says, Israel Exports Sex." *New York Times,* October 10.

———. 1996. "Mansura Journal: Of College Girls Betrayed and Vile Chewing Gum." *New York Times,* July 10, p. A4.

Jenkins, Richard. 1992. *Pierre Bourdieu.* New York: Routledge.

"Jins silah Isra'il al-jadid didd Misr, al-." (Sex Is a New Israeli Weapon against Egypt). 1995. *Al-Hayat al-Misriyya,* December 31, p. 4.

Kabbani, Rana. 1998. "Global Beauty: Damascus." *Vogue* 164, no. 2394 (January): 134–35.

Kearney, Michael. 1995. "The Local and the Global: The Anthropology of Globalization and Transnationalism." *Annual Review of Anthropology* 24: 547–65.

Keeps, David A. 1998. "Sabbath Night Fever." *Details* (November): 110, 112, 117–18, 120.

Kerem, Shay. n.d. "35 Personal Questions to Danna." http://www.nuts.co.il/dana/danai.html.

Keyder, Çaglar. 1987. *State and Class in Turkey: A Study in Capitalist Development.* London: Verso.

Khafaji, 'Amr. 1994. "Al-Tatbi': Ghazw Isra'ili lil-sinima al-Misriyya!" (Normalization: An Israeli Assault on Egyptian Cinema!). *Ruz al-Yusuf*, November 21, pp. 68–71.

Khaleqi, Ruhollah. 1974. *Sarguzasht-i musiqi-i Iran* (History of the Music of Iran). Vol. 1. Tehran: Safiali Shah.

Khalifa, Ayman M. 1995. "The Withering Youth of Egypt." *Ru'ya* 7 (Spring): 6–11.

Khalil, 'Abd al-Nur. 1996. "Wathiqa siyasiyya min tarikh sha'b wa-za'im" (A Political Document from the History of a People and a Leader). *Al-Musawwar*, August 9, p. 50.

Khalil, Nevine. 1996a. "Drama by the Thousands." *Al-Ahram Weekly*, June 6–12.

———. 1996b. "Heritage of a Revolution." *Al-Ahram Weekly*, January 24–31.

Khan, Mohamed. 1969. *An Introduction to the Egyptian Cinema.* London: Informatics.

Khayati, Khemaïs. 1996. *Cinémas arabes: Topographie d'une image éclatée.* Paris: Editions l'Harmattan.

Khayri, Badi'. n.d. *Mudhakkirat Badi' Khayri: 45 sana tahta adwa' al-masrah* (Memoirs of Badi' Khayri: 45 Years under the Lights of the Stage). Interview by Muhammad Rif'at. Beirut: Dar al-Thaqafa.

Khelil, Hédi. 1994. *Résistances et utopies: Essais sur le cinéma arabe et africain* (Resistances and Utopias: Essays on Arab and African Cinema). Tunis: Editions Sahar.

Khomeini, Ruhollah. 1971. *Kashf al-asrar* (Discovery of Secrets). Tehran: Nashr-i Falaq.

Khoury, Philip S. 1983. *Urban Notables and Arab Nationalism: The Politics of Damascus 1860–1920.* Cambridge: Cambridge University Press.

———. 1987. *Syria and the French Mandate: The Politics of Arab Nationalism, 1920–1945.* Princeton: Princeton University Press.

Khust, Nadiya. 1989. *Al-Hijra min al-janna* (Exodus from Paradise). Damascus: al-Ahli Press.

———. 1993. *Dimashq: Dhikrat al-insan wa-al-hajar* (Damascus: Memory of Man and Stone). Damascus: Dar Daniya.

King, John. 1990. *Magic Reels: A History of Cinema in Latin America.* London: Verso.

Kirshenblatt-Gimblett, Barbara. 1996. "The Electronic Vernacular." In *Connected: Engagements with Media*, ed. George Marcus, 21–66. Chicago: University of Chicago Press.

Kitab al-dhahabi, al-. 1972. Cairo: Ittihad al-Sina'at al-Misriyya.

Krämer, Gudrun. 1989. *The Jews of Modern Egypt.* Seattle: University of Washington Press.

Kulin, Ayse. 1996. Bir Tatlı Huzur: Fotoğraflarla Münir Nureddin Selçuk ("A Sweet Repose": Münir Nureddin Selçuk in Photographs). Istanbul: Sel.

Kurd 'Ali, Muhammad. 1944. *Dimashq: Madinat al-sihr wa-al-shi'r* (Damascus: City of Enchantment and Poetry). Egypt: Matba'at al-Ma'arif.

La Guardia, Anton. 1997. "Transsexual Pop Singer Proves Too Unorthodox." *Daily Telegraph*, November 25, p. 16.

Lahore Development Authority. 1980. *Lahore Urban Development and Traffic Study*. 4 vols. Lahore: Lahore Development Authority.

Landau, Jacob M. 1958. *Studies in the Arab Theater and Cinema*. Philadelphia: University of Pennsylvania Press.

Langlois, Tony. 1996. "The Local and Global in North African Popular Music." *Popular Music* 15 (3): 259–73.

Laughlin, Kim, and John Monberg. 1996. "Horizons of Interactivity: Making the News at Time Warner." In *Connected: Engagements with Media*, ed. George Marcus, 249–70. Chicago: University of Chicago Press.

Lavie, Smadar. 1990. *The Poetics of Military Occupation: Mzeina Allegories of Bedouin Identity under Israeli and Egyptian Rule*. Berkeley: University of California Press.

———. 1996. "Blow-Ups in the Borderzones: Third World Israeli Authors' Gropings for Home." In *Displacement, Diaspora and Geographies of Identity*, ed. Smadar Lavie and Ted Swedenburg, 55–96. Durham: Duke University Press.

"Layla al-Muslima." 1948. *Al-Ithnayn*, no. 737, July 26, pp. 8–9.

Leary, Timothy. 1970. *Jail Notes*. New York: Douglas Books.

Levine, Lawrence W. 1988. *Highbrow/Lowbrow: The Emergence of Cultural Hierarchy in America*. Cambridge, Mass.: Harvard University Press.

Lewis, Geoffrey. 1967. *Turkish Grammar*. Oxford: Oxford University Press.

Litweiler, John. 1992. *Ornette Coleman: A Harmolodic Life*. New York: Da Capo.

Lorius, Cassandra. 1996. "Desire and the Gaze: Spectacular Bodies in Cairene Elite Weddings." *Women's Studies International Forum* 19 (5): 513–23.

Low, Setha M. 1996. "The Anthropology of Cities: Imagining and Theorizing the City." *Annual Review of Anthropology* 25: 383–409.

Lowenthal, David. 1996. *The Heritage Crusade and the Spoils of History*. London: Viking.

Lüders, Michael. 1989. *Gesellschaftliche Realität im ägyptischen Kinofilm: Von Nasser zu Sadat 1952–1981* (Social Realism in Egyptian Cinema: From Nasser to Sadat, 1952–1981). Frankfurt am Main: Peter Lang.

Lyotard, Jean-François. 1984. *The Postmodern Condition: A Report on Knowledge*. Minneapolis: University of Minnesota Press.

McGlone, Robert E. 1989. "Rescripting a Troubled Past: John Brown's Family and the Harpers Ferry Conspiracy." *American Historical Review* 75: 1179–1200.

Macleod, Arlene Elowe. 1991. *Accommodating Protest: The New Veiling in Cairo*. New York: Columbia University Press.

Majdi, Tawhid. 1994. "'Busni ya Susu' yuba' sirran fi Misr bi-khamsin ginayh" ("Kiss Me Susu" Is Sold Covertly in Egypt for Fifty Pounds). *Ruz al-Yusuf*, December 12.

Malkmus, Lizbeth, and Roy Armes. 1991. *Arab and African Film Making*. London: Zed Books.

Marcus, George, ed. 1993. *Perilous States: Conversations on Culture, Politics, and Nation*. Chicago: University of Chicago Press.

———. 1996a. *Connected: Engagements with Media*. Chicago: University of Chicago Press.

———. 1996b. Introduction to *Connected: Engagements with Media*, ed. George Marcus, 1–18. Chicago: University of Chicago Press.

Margolis, Maxine. 1994. *Little Brazil*. Princeton: Princeton University Press.

Markoff, Irene. 1990. "The Ideology of Musical Practice and the Professional Turkish Folk Musician: Tempering the Creative Impulse." *Asian Music* 22 (1): 129–45.

Martin, Emily. 1996. "Flexible Bodies in a Society of Flows." *Critical Anthropology* 16: 49–56.

Mazzoleni, Donatella. 1993. "The City and the Imaginary." In *Space and Place: Theories of Identity and Location*, ed. Erica Carter, James Donald, and Judith Squires, 285–302. London: Lawrence and Wishart.

Mehrez, Samia. 1994. *Egyptian Writers between History and Fiction*. Cairo: American University in Cairo Press.

Melucci, Alberto. 1985. "The Symbolic Challenge of Contemporary Movements." *Social Research* 52 (4): 789–816.

Menicucci, Garay. 1998. "Unlocking the Arab Celluloid Closet: Homosexuality in Egyptian Film." *Middle East Report* 206: 32–36.

Mernissi, Fatimah. 1975. *Beyond the Veil: Male-Female Dynamics in a Modern Muslim Society*. New York: John Wiley and Sons.

Metcalf, Thomas R. 1994. *Ideologies of the Raj*. Cambridge: Cambridge University Press.

"Middle Eastern Popular Culture, Proposal for an International Conference on." 1998. http://users.ox.ac.uk/~neareast/middle.htm. Last updated December 14, accessed December 17, 1998.

Miller, Daniel. 1994. *Modernity, an Ethnographic Approach: Dualism and Mass Consumption in Trinidad*. Oxford: Berg Publishers.

———. 1995a. "Introduction: Anthropology, Modernity and Consumption." In *Worlds Apart: Modernity through the Prism of the Local*, ed. Daniel Miller, 1–22. New York: Routledge.

———, ed. 1995b. *Worlds Apart: Modernity through the Prism of the Local*. New York: Routledge.

Miller, Lloyd Clifton. 1995. *Persian Music: A Study of Form and Content of Persian Avaz, Dastgah & Radif*. Salt Lake City: Eastern Arts.

Miller, Neil. 1993. *Out in the World: Gay and Lesbian Life from Buenos Aires to Bangkok*. New York: Vintage.

Mina, Hanna. 1989. *Nihayat rajul shuja'* (The End of a Brave Man). Beirut: Dar al-Adab.

Misri, Husayn Shafiq. 1980. *Adventures and Opinions of Hadji Darwis and Umm Isma'il: Dictations Taken by Hisen Safiq il-Masri*. Preface by Karl-G. Prasse. Copenhagen: Akademisk Forlag.

"Misriyyun murtishun yabi'un ayya shay' wa-yu'ashiqun al-shudhudh, al-" (Bribe-taking Egyptians Will Sell Anything and Love Perverts). 1996. *Ruz al-Yusuf*, August 5, n.p.

Mitchell, Timothy. 1988. *Colonising Egypt*. Cambridge: Cambridge University Press.

Mitchell, Timothy J. 1994. *Flamenco Deep Song*. New Haven: Yale University Press.

Monaco, Eitel. 1966. "Merchandising, Distribution and Import of Films in the Arab World between 1958–1962." In *Cinema in the Arab Countries*, ed. Georges Sadoul, 137–45. Paris: UNESCO.

Mora, Carl. 1982. *Mexican Cinema: Reflections of a Society, 1896–1980.* Berkeley: University of California Press.

Morgan, Ted. 1988. *Literary Outlaw: The Life and Times of William S. Burroughs.* New York: Henry Holt.

Morley, David. 1995. "Where the Global Meets the Local: Notes from the Sitting Room." *Screen* 32 (1): 1–15.

Mumtaz, I'tidal. 1985. *Mudhakkirat raqibat sinima 30 'aman* (Memoirs of a Cinema Censor for 30 Years). Cairo: al-Hay'a al-Misriyya al-'Amma lil-Kitab.

Munro, J. Richard. 1990. "Good-bye to Hollywood: Cultural Imperialism and the New Protectionism." *Vital Speeches of the Day* 61 (June 15): 524–27.

Muntasir, Salah. 1996. "Al-Ziham 'ala Nasir" (The Crowds for Nasser [56]). *Al-Ahram,* August 21.

Murray, Stephen O., and Will Roscoe. 1997. *Islamic Homosexualities: Culture, History and Literature.* New York: New York University Press.

Naficy, Hamid. 1993. *Making of Exile Cultures: Iranian Television in Los Angeles.* Minneapolis: University of Minnesota Press.

Najmi, Kamal al-. 1995. "Da'wa hisba didd fann al-ghina': Hakadha kan al-amr" (The Charge of Hisba against Singing: The Matter Was Thus). *Al-Hayat,* November 18, p. 20.

Nashashibi, Nasser Eddin. 1990. *Jerusalem's Other Voice: Ragheb Nashashibi and Moderation in Palestinian Politics, 1920–1948.* Exeter: Ithaca Press.

"Nass al-kamil li-taqrir al-niyaba al-'amma bi-hifz al-tahqiq fi qadiyat khasa'ir al-qita' al-'amm, al-" (The Full Report of the Public Prosecutor on the Precise Verification in the Matter of Losses in the Public Sector). 1993. *Al-Sinima wa-al-tarikh* 7: 77–91.

Nassaj, Sayyid Hamid. 1984. *Tatawwur fann al-qissa al-qasira fi Misr* (Development of the Art of the Short Story in Egypt). al-Tab'a 2. Cairo: Dar al-Ma'arif.

Nelson, Kristina. 1985. *The Art of Reciting the Qur'an.* Austin: University of Texas Press.

Nettl, Bruno. 1970. "Attitudes Toward Persian Music in Tehran in 1969." *Musical Quarterly* 56: 183–97.

———. 1972. "Persian Popular Music in 1969." *Ethnomusicology* 16 (2): 218–31.

———. 1992. *Radif of Persian Music: Studies of Structure and Cultural Context in the Classical Music of Iran.* (Revised edition of *Radif of Persian Music,* 1987.) Champaign, Ill.: Elephant & Cat.

Ngugi wa Thiong'o. 1986. *Decolonizing the Mind: The Politics of Language in African Literature.* Nairobi and London: James Currey and Heinemann.

Nieuwkerk, Karin van. 1995. *A Trade Like Any Other: Female Singers and Dancers in Egypt.* Austin: University of Texas Press.

Nora, Pierre. 1989. "Between Memory and History: Les Lieux de Memoire." In *Representations: Special Issue on Memory and Counter Memory,* ed. Natalie Davis and Rudolph Starns, 26: 7–25.

"Official Egyptian Newspaper: Israel Spreads AIDS and Hepatitis in Arab Countries." 1998. Israel/Wire, September 4.

Olearius, Adam. 1977. *Voyages and Travels of the Ambassadors sent by Frederick Duke of Holstein, to the Great Duke Muscovy, and the King of Persia. Begun in the year M.DC.*

XXXIII and Finish'd M. DC. XXXIX. London: Thomas Dring and John Starkey, 1662. Reproduction of original in Huntington Library. Microfilm. Ann Arbor, Mich.: University Microfilms.

Oomen, M. A., and K. V. Joseph. 1991. *Economics of Indian Cinema.* New Delhi: Oxford University Press.

Ossman, Susan. 1994. *Picturing Casablanca: Portraits of Power in a Modern City.* Berkeley: University of California Press.

Paidar, Parvin. 1995. *Women and the Political Process in Twentieth-Century Iran.* Cambridge: Cambridge University Press.

Palmer, Robert (Bob). 1971. "Jajouka/Up the Mountain." *Rolling Stone,* October 14.

————. 1989. "Into the Mystic." *Rolling Stone,* March.

Pamuk, Orhan. 1991. *The White Castle: A Novel.* Trans. Victoria Holbrook. New York: Braziller.

————. 1995. *Kara Kitab* (The Black Book). Istanbul: Iletişim.

————. 1996. *The Black Book.* Trans. Güneli Gün. London: Faber.

Pandey, Gyanendra. 1990. *The Construction of Communalism in Colonial North India.* Delhi: Oxford University Press.

Parkinson, Dilworth. 1991. "Searching for Modern Fusha: Real-Life Formal Arabic." *Al-'Arabiyya* 24: 31–64.

Pechey, Graham. 1989. "On the Borders of Bakhtin: Dialogisation, Decolonisation." In *Bakhtin and Cultural Theory,* ed. Ken Hirschkop and David Shepherd, 39–67. Manchester: Manchester University Press.

PEPAC (Pakistan Environmental Planning and Architectural Consultants, Ltd.). 1993. *The Walled City of Lahore.* Lahore: Lahore Government Authority.

Pieterse, Jan Nederveen. 1995. "Globalization as Hybridization." In *Global Modernities,* ed. Mike Featherstone, Roland Robertson, and Scott Lash, 45–68. Thousand Oaks, Calif.: Sage.

Pines, Jim, and Paul Willemen, eds. 1989. *Questions of Third Cinema.* London: British Film Institute.

Portelli, Alessandro. 1991. *The Death of Luigi Trastulli, and Other Stories.* Albany: State University of New York Press.

Prindle, David F. 1993. *Risky Business: The Political Economy of Hollywood.* Boulder, Colo.: Westview Press.

Qadeer, Mohammed A. 1983. *Lahore: Urban Development in the Third World.* Lahore: Vanguard Books.

Qassab Hassan, Najat. 1988. *Hadith Dimashqi* (Damascene Talk). Damascus: Dar Talas.

Qureishi, Jamil A. 1981. *Socio-economic Profile of a City Slum.* Lahore: Punjab Economic Research Institute.

Rabinow, Paul. 1986. "Representations Are Social Facts: Modernity and Post-Modernity in Anthropology." In *Writing Culture: The Poetics and Politics of Ethnography,* ed. James Clifford and George Marcus, 234–61. Berkeley: University of California Press.

Racy, 'Ali Jihad. 1977. "Musical Change and Commercial Recording in Egypt, 1904–1932." Ph.D. dissertation, University of Illinois, Urbana-Champaign.

————. 1991. "Historical Worldviews of Early Ethnomusicologists: An East-West Encounter in Cairo, 1932." In *Ethnomusicology and Modern Music History*, ed. Stephen Blum, Philip V. Bohlman, and Daniel M. Neuman, 68–91. Urbana: University of Illinois Press.

Radi, Lamia. 1997. "Star of David 'Threat' Sweeps Egypt." Agence France Presse feature, June 13.

Rafael, Vincente. 1993. *Contracting Colonialism*. Durham: Duke University Press.

Rahim, Ilham. 1995. "Shara'it fi al-mamnu'" (Forbidden Cassettes). *Al-Shabab* 219 (October): 54–55.

Ramadan, Tariq. 1995. "Sha'art bi-al-yatim yawm wafat 'Abd al-Nasir" (I Felt Like an Orphan the Day Abdel Nasser Died). *Al-Siyasi al-Misri*, July 30.

Ramzi, Kamal. 1984. "Thawrat Yulyu wa-harb al-Suways fi al-sinima al-Misriyya" (The July Revolution and the Suez War in Egyptian Cinema). *Al-Funun* (May–June): 82–88.

Rasim Bey, Ahmad. 1941. "Santis wa-al-mumaththilun 'ala masrahih." *Al-Ithnayn*, no. 347, February 3, pp. 11–13.

Rasmussen, Anne. 1996. "Theory and Practice at the 'Arabic Org': Digital Technology in Contemporary Arab Music Performance." *Popular Music* 15 (3): 345–65.

Redfield, Robert. 1956. *The Folk Culture of Yucatan*. Chicago: University of Chicago Press.

Regev, Motti. 1995. "Present Absentee: Arab Music in Israeli Culture." *Public Culture* 7 (2): 433–45.

———. 1996. "*Musica Mizrakhit*, Israeli Rock and National Culture in Israel." *Popular Music* 15 (3): 275–84.

Rihani, Najib al-. 1959. *Mudhakkirat Najib al-Rihani* (Memoirs of Najib al-Rihani). Cairo: Dar al-Hilal.

Rizq, Hamdi. 1995a. "Sa'ida Sultan tuthir dajja fi Misr wa-juhud amaniyya li-muwajahat 'al-ghazw al-jinsi' al-Isra'ili" (Sa'ida Sultan Stirs Up a Clamor in Egypt and Security Efforts to Counter the Israeli "Sexual Invasion"). *Al-Hayat*, October 4, p. 1.

———. 1995b. "Shaykh al-Azhar yufti bi-jawaz tahwil al-jins" (The Shaykh al-Azhar Gives a Formal Legal Opinion Permitting Sex Change). *Al-Hayat*, November 10, p. 24.

Robins, Kevin, and Asu Aksoy. 1995. "Istanbul Rising: Returning the Repressed to Urban Culture." *European and Regional Studies* 2 (3): 223–35.

Rogan, Eugene. 1997. "No Debate: Middle East Studies in Europe." *Middle East Report* 205: 22–24.

Rojek, Chris. 1995. *Decentring Leisure: Rethinking Leisure Theory*. London: Sage.

Rosenberg, Emily. 1982. *Spreading the American Dream*. New York: Hill and Wang.

Ross, Andrew. 1988. *No Respect: Intellectuals and Popular Culture*. New York: Routledge.

Rouleau, Eric. 1998. "Netanyahu Drove Levy to Resignation Because of His Treacherous Betrayal." *Daily Star* (Beirut), January 21. http://www.dailystar.com.lb/opinion/022198.htm

Rouse, Roger. 1995. "Thinking through Transnationalism: Notes on the Cultural Politics of Class Relations in the Contemporary United States." *Public Culture* 7 (2): 353–402.

———. 1996. "Questions of Identity: Personhood and Collectivity in Transnational Migration to the United States." *Critique of Anthropology* 15 (4): 351–80.

Royal Government of Egypt, Ministry of Social Affairs. 1950. *Social Welfare in Egypt, 1950*, sec. 7, "Mass Media Propaganda."

Rubin, Gayle. 1984. "Thinking Sex: Notes for a Radical Theory of the Politics of Sexuality." In *Pleasure and Danger: Exploring Female Sexuality*, ed. Carol S. Vance, 267–319. Boston: Routledge & Kegan Paul.

Rushdi, Fatima. 1971. *Kifahi fi al-masrah wa-al-sinima* (My Struggle in the Theater and Cinema). Cairo: Dar al-Ma'arif.

Rydell, Robert. 1987. *All the World's a Stage.* Chicago: University of Chicago Press.

Saad, Rehab. 1996. "Nasser 56 and Beyond." *Al-Ahram Weekly*, August 22–28.

Sa'd, 'Abd al-Mun'im. 1986. *Mujaz tarikh al-sinima al-Misriyya* (Survey of the History of Egyptian Cinema). Cairo: Matba'at al-Ahram al-Tijariyya.

Sa'dani, 'Ala' al-. 1996. "Nasir 56—na'm, al-Sadat 73—la'" (Nasser 56—Yes, Sadat 73—No). *Al-Ahram*, September 2.

Sadoul, Georges. 1966. *The Cinema in the Arab Countries.* Paris: UNESCO.

Said, Edward. 1978. *Orientalism.* New York: Pantheon Books.

———. 1990. "Figures, Configurations, Transfigurations." *Race and Class* 32, no. 1 (July–September): 1–16.

———. 1993. *Culture and Imperialism.* New York: Vintage.

Salamandra, Christa. 1997. "Moustache Hairs Lost: Ramadan Television Serials and the Construction of Identity in Damascus, Syria." *Visual Anthropology* 10: 227–46.

Salih, Muhammad. 1995. "Hikaya" (Story). *Al-Ahram*, July 14.

Salih, Tawfiq. 1986. "Al-Waqi'iyya . . . 'sinima al-shabab' wa-mashakil al-qita' al-'amm: hiwar ma' Tawfiq Salih" (Realism . . . "Youth Cinema" and the Problems of the Public Sector, an Interview Conducted by Sa'id Murad). In *Maqalat fi al-sinima al-'Arabiyya* (Articles on Arab Cinema), by Sa'id Murad. Beirut: Dar al-Fikr al-Jadid.

Salim, Ahmad. 1996. "The Tiwanas of Sarhodha." *Friday Times*, August 26, p. 134.

Sarris, Andrew. [1962] 1994. "Notes on the Auteur Theory in 1962." In *Film Theory and Criticism*, ed. Gerald Mast and Marshall Cohen, 527–40. New York: Oxford University Press.

Savigliano, Marta E. 1995. *Tango and the Political Economy of Passion.* Boulder, Colo.: Westview Press.

Schattner, Marcus. 1995. "Un certain Israel en danger de paix." *Liberation*, December 13, p. 2.

Schuyler, Philip D. 1983a. "The Master Musicians of Jahjouka." *Natural History* 92 (10): 60–69.

———. 1983b. Script for *The Master Musicians of Jahjouka.* Long Beach, Calif.: Mendizza and Associates.

Schwartzman, Karen. 1995. "National Cinema in Translation: The Politics of Film Exhibition Culture." *Wide Angle* 16 (3): 66–99.

Seufert, Günter, and Petra Weyland. 1994. "National Events and the Struggle for the Fixing of Meaning: A Comparison of the Symbolic Dimensions of the Funeral Services for Atatürk and Özal." *New Perspectives on Turkey* 11: 71–98.

Shafik, Viola. 1998. *Arab Cinema: History and Cultural Identity.* Cairo: American University in Cairo Press.

Shah, Pann. [1950] 1981. *The Indian Film.* Westport, Conn.: Greenwood Press.

Shalash, Ali. 1986. *Al-Naqd al-sinima'i fi al-sihafa al-Misriyya* (Cinema Criticism in the Egyptian Press). Cairo: al-Hay'a al-'Amma lil-Kitab.

Sharaf al-Din, Duriyya. 1992. *Al-Siyasa wa-al-sinima fi Misr: 1961–1981* (Politics and Cinema in Egypt: 1961–1981). Cairo: Dar al-Shuruq.

Sharrock, David. 1997. "Real Lives: The Very Other Dana." *The Guardian* (London), December 31.

Shay, Anthony. 1995a. "*Bazi-ha-ye namayeshi*: Iranian Women's Theatrical Plays." *Dance Research Journal* 27 (2): 16–24.

———. 1995b. "Dance and Non-Dance: Patterned Movement in Iran and Islam." *Iranian Studies* 28, nos. 1–2 (Winter–Spring): 61–78.

Sherrard, Geoffrey. n.d. "The Illustrious Industrious Bill Laswell." *Glow Magazine* (New York).

Shiner, Larry. 1994. "'Primitive Fakes,' 'Tourist Art,' and the Ideology of Authenticity." *Journal of Aesthetics and Art Criticism* 52 (2): 225–34.

Shohat, Ella. 1988. "Sephardism in Israel: Zionism from the Standpoint of Its Jewish Victims." *Social Text,* no. 19–20: 1–35.

———. 1989. *Israeli Cinema: East/West and the Politics of Representation.* Austin: University of Texas Press.

Shohat, Ella, and Robert Stam. 1994. *Unthinking Eurocentrism: Multiculturalism and the Media.* London: Routledge.

———. 1996. "From the Imperial Family to the Trans-national Imaginary: Media Spectatorship in the Age of Globalization." In *Global/Local: Cultural Production and the Transnational Imaginary,* ed. Rob Wilson and Wimal Dissanayake, 145–70. Durham: Duke University Press.

Shryock, Andrew. 1998. "Mainstreaming Arabs: Film Making as Image Making in *Tales from Arab Detroit.*" *Visual Anthropology* 10 (2–4): 165–88.

Sid-Ahmed, Mohammed. 1995. "Marketing the Solution." *Al-Ahram Weekly,* November 9–15.

Simmel, Georg. 1978. *The Philosophy of Money.* London: Routledge.

Sipra, Imtiaz. 1993. "A City Where Spirits Are Mature and Hearts Understand." *The News* (Lahore), November 18, p. 3.

———. 1994. "Let Lahore Express the Humanism of Lahorites." *The News* (Lahore), April 19, p. 3.

Sipress, Alan. 1995. "Long Dead, but Better Than Ever in Egypt, Nasser Still Works His Magic." *Philadelphia Inquirer,* November 24.

Somekh, Sasson. 1987. "Participation of Egyptian Jews in Modern Arabic Culture, and the Case of Murad Faraj." In *The Jews of Egypt: A Mediterranean Society in Modern Times,* ed. Shimon Shamir, 130–39. Boulder, Colo.: Westview Press.

Soueif, Ahdaf. 1992. *In the Eye of the Sun.* London: Bloomsbury.

Sperber, Dan, 1985. *On Anthropological Knowledge.* Cambridge: Cambridge University Press.

Stallybrass, Peter, and Allon White. 1986. *Politics and Poetics of Transgression.* Ithaca: Cornell University Press.

Stam, Robert. 1989. *Subversive Pleasures: Bakhtin, Cultural Criticism, and Film.* Baltimore: John Hopkins University Press.

Stead, Peter. 1981. "Hollywood's Message for the World: The British Response in the 1930s." *Historical Journal of Film, Radio and Television* 1: 18–32.

Stewart, Susan. 1993. *On Longing: Narratives of the Miniature, the Gigantic, the Souvenir, the Collection.* Baltimore: Johns Hopkins University Press.

Stokes, Martin. 1992a. *The Arabesk Debate: Music and Musicians in Modern Turkey.* Oxford: Clarendon Press.

———. 1992b. "Islam, the Turkish State and Arabesk." *Popular Music* 11 (2): 213–27.

———. 1995–96. "'Alaturka Fantasies': Deceit, the Voice and the Arabesk Stage in Turkey." *New Formations* 27: 42–58.

———. 1996. "Nostalgia, History and Memory in Contemporary Turkish Musicology." *Music and Anthropology* 1 (electronic publication).

Strathern, Marilyn, ed. 1995. *Shifting Contexts: Transformations in Anthropological Knowledge.* New York: Routledge.

Strinati, Dominic. 1995. *Introduction to Theories of Popular Culture.* London: Routledge.

Susser, Ida. 1996. "Anthropological Perspectives on the Informational Society." *Critical Anthropology* 16: 39–48.

Swedenburg, Ted. 1995. *Memories of Revolt: The 1936–1939 Rebellion and the Palestinian National Past.* Minneapolis: University of Minnesota Press.

Swirski, Shlomo. 1989. *Israel: The Oriental Majority.* Trans. Barbara Swirski. London: Zed Books.

Tamari, Steven. 1998. "Teaching and Learning in Eighteenth-Century Damascus: Localism and Ottomanism in an Early Modern Arab Society." Ph.D. dissertation, Georgetown University.

Tamawi, Ahmad Husayn. 1992. *Al-Hilal: Mi'at 'am min al-tanwir wa-al-tahdith* (*Al-Hilal:* One Hundred Years of Enlightenment and Innovation). Cairo: Dar al-Hilal.

Tapper, Nancy. 1981. "Direct Exchange and Brideprice: Alternative Forms in a Complex Marriage System." *Man* 16 (3): 387–407.

———. 1988–89. "Changing Marriage Ceremonial and Gender Roles in the Arab World: An Anthropological Perspective." *Arab Affairs* 8 (Winter): 117–35.

Tavernier, John Baptista. 1961. *Six Voyages of John Baptista Tavernier, A Noble Man of France Now Living Through Turkey Into Persia, and the East-Indies, Finished in the Year 1670.* Trans. John Phillips. London: 1678. Reproduction of original in University of Michigan Libraries. Microfilm. Ann Arbor, Mich.: University Microfilms.

Taylor, Charles. 1992. *The Ethics of Authenticity.* Cambridge, Mass.: Harvard University Press.

Taylor, Timothy D. 1997. *Global Pop: World Music, World Markets.* New York: Routledge.

Teachout, Terry. 1996. Review of *The Yellow Admiral,* by Patrick O'Brian (Norton). *New York Times Book Review,* November 3, p. 9.

Tehrani, Faramarz. 1991. *Ritm-ha-ye varzeshi* (Exercise Rhythms). Tehran: Pars Press.

Thomas, Bob. 1984. *Astaire, the Man, the Dancer.* New York: St. Martin's Press.

Thompson, Kristin. 1985. *Exporting Entertainment: America in the World Film Market.* London: British Film Institute.

Thorval, Yves. 1975. *Regards sur le cinéma égyptien* (Glances at Egyptian Cinema). Beirut: Dar el-Mashreq.

Tilmisani, Kamil al-. 1957. *Safir Amrika bi-al-alwan al-tabi'iyya* (American Ambassador in Technicolor and Cinemascope). Cairo: Dar al-Fikr.

Tomlinson, John. 1991. *Cultural Imperialism.* Baltimore: Johns Hopkins University Press.

Tsur, Shai. 1998. "Why People Agree on Zehava." *Jerusalem Post,* November 1, p. 7.

Turjuman, Siham. [1969] 1990. *Ya mal al-Sham* (O Wealth of Damascus). Damascus: Alif Ba al-Adib.

———. 1994. *Daughter of Damascus.* Trans. Andrea Rugh. Austin: University of Texas Press.

"2500 Misri mujannidun fi al-jaysh al-Isra'ili" (2500 Egyptian Recruits in the Israeli Army). 1996. *Ruz al-Yusuf,* August 5, pp. 20–23.

Twitchell, James B. 1992. *Carnival Culture: The Trashing of Taste in America.* New York: Columbia University Press.

'Ukasha, Tharwat. 1990. *Mudhakkirati fi al-siyasa wa-al-thaqafa* (My Memoirs on Politics and Culture). 2d ed. Cairo: Dar al-Hilal.

United Nations Development Programme. 1995. *Human Development Report, 1995.* Oxford: Oxford University Press.

Viswanathan, Gauri, 1989. *Masks of Conquest: Literary Study and British Rule in India.* New York: Columbia University Press.

Vitalis, Robert. 1995. *When Capitalists Collide: Business Conflict and the End of Empire in Egypt.* Berkeley: University of California Press.

———. 1996. "The End of Third Worldism in Egypt Studies." *Arab Studies Journal* 4 (1): 13–33.

———. 1997. "The Closing of the Arabian Oil Frontier and the Future of Saudi-American Relations." *Middle East Report* 204: 15–21.

Wahba, 'Abd al-Latif. 1995. "Tashilat Isra'iliyya li-jadhb al-shabab al-Misri" (Israeli Facilitations to Attract Egyptian Youth). *Al-Ahali,* November 8, p. 2.

Wahbi, Yusuf. 1973. *'Ishtu alf 'am* (I Have Lived a Thousand Years). Vol. 1. Cairo: Dar al-Ma'arif.

Wallerstein, Immanuel. 1974. *The Modern World-System: Capitalist Agriculture and the Origins of the European World Economy in the Sixteenth Century.* New York: Academic Press.

"Waqaha Isra'iliyya fawq 'ulbat saja'ir: 'Al-khayl 'Arabi' . . . wa-'al-kurbaj Misri' . . . wa-'al-qa'id Amriki' . . . !" (Israeli Impudence on a Cigarette Packet: "Arab Horses" and "Egyptian Whip" and "American Commander"!). 1996. *Al-'Arabi,* February 19.

Wassef, Magda, ed. 1994. *Égypte, 100 ans de cinéma.* Paris: Institut du Monde Arabe.

Watrous, Peter. 1995. "By an Exotic Touch of Moroccan Spice." *New York Times,* October 18.

Weiss, Anita M. 1992. *Walls within Walls: Life Histories of Working Women in the Old City of Lahore.* Boulder, Colo.: Westview Press.

Westermarck, Edward. 1968. *Ritual and Belief in Morocco.* New Hyde Park, N.Y.: University Books. Originally published by Macmillan, London, 1926.

White, Hayden. 1987. *The Content of the Form.* Baltimore: Johns Hopkins University Press.

Wilk, Richard. 1995. "Learning to Be Local in Belize: Global Systems of Common Difference." In *Worlds Apart: Modernity through the Prism of the Local*, ed. Daniel Miller, 110–33. New York: Routledge.

Williams, Raymond. 1973. *The Country and the City*. London: Chatto and Windus.

Wilson, Rob, and Wimal Dissanayake, eds. 1996. *Global/Local: Cultural Production and the Transnational Imaginary*. Durham: Duke University Press.

Wittgenstein, Ludwig. 1989. *Philosophical Investigations*. Trans. Gertrude Elizabeth Margaret Anscombe. Oxford: Basil Blackwell.

Wolf, Eric. 1982. *Europe and the People without History*. Berkeley: University of California Press.

Wright, Gwendolyn. 1991. *The Politics of Design in French Colonial Urbanism*. Chicago: University of Chicago Press.

Yusuf, Fatima al-. [1953] 1967. *Dhikrayat* (Memoirs). Cairo: Dar Ruz al-Yusuf.

Zinder, Jac. 1992. "Eternal 6/8 Groove: In the San Fernando Valley, the Persian Hit Factory Lives On." *LA Weekly*, January 17–23, pp. 33–37.

Zukin, Sharon. 1991. *Landscapes of Power*. Berkeley: University of California Press.

ARCHIVAL SOURCES

National Archives and Record Administration, Washington, D.C. Record Group 59. General Records of the Department of State.

SELECT DISCOGRAPHY

Apocalypse Across the Sky. 1992. The Master Musicians of Jajouka featuring Bachir al-Attar. Produced by Bill Laswell. Notes by William Burroughs and Brion Gysin. Axiom/Island Records 314–510 857–2.

Bachir Attar: The Next Dream. 1993. Bachir al-Attar: *ghaita, gimbri, lira*, percussion. Aiyb Dieng: *chatan*, congas, *doff*, bass drums, tom toms, gongs, metal percussion. Maceo Parker: alto saxophone, flute. Produced by Bill Laswell. Notes by David Silver. CMP Records CMP 57.

Bande Original du Film Latcho Drom. 1993. KG Production/Virgin 72438 392492 9.

Brian Jones Presents the Pipes of Pan at Joujouka. 1971. Produced by Brian Jones. Notes by Brion Gysin and Brian Jones. Paintings by Mohamed Hamri. Rolling Stones Records/Atco (Atlantic) COC 49100 (ST-RS-712309). [Recorded in 1968. 12" 33 1/3 rpm record. New compact disc edition in 1995.]

Brian Jones Presents the Pipes of Pan at Jajouka. 1995. Produced by Brian Jones. Executive Producers: Philip Glass, Kurt Munkasci, and Rory Johnston. Notes by Bachir al-Attar, Paul Bowles, William Burroughs, Stephen Davis, Brian Jones, Brion Gysin, and David Silver. Point Music (Philips Classics/PolyGram) 446 487–2. [Reissue of 1971 Brian Jones recording. Deluxe edition (Point Music 446 825–2 and 446 826–2) includes additional graphics, more extensive notes by David Silver and William S. Burroughs, and a second CD, produced by Cliff Mark, with two "full-length remixes."]

Danna International. 1993. Sa'ida Sultan (Danna International). Produced by IMP Dance, Tel Aviv.

Diva. 1998. Sa'ida Sultan (Danna International). Produced by IMP Dance, Tel Aviv.

Egypt: Les Musiciens du Nil. 1987. Ocora (Radio France) C559006.

Global Meditation: Authentic Music from Meditative Traditions of the World. 1993. Produced by Bill Laswell. The Relaxation Company/Ellipsis Arts. [Four-CD set. Disc 2, "Harmony and Interplay," includes examples of Gnawa and Jajouka.]

Jajouka between the Mountains. 1995. The Master Musicians of Jajouka featuring Bashir al-Attar. Produced by Eric Sanzen, Cherie Nutting, and Steve Carnaby. Real World Records/WOMAD Select WSCD001.

Joujouka Black Eyes. 1995. The Master Musicians of Joujouka. Produced by Frank Rynne. Notes by Joe Ambrose and Frank Rynne. Sub Rosa/le coeur du monde SR87.

Maganona. 1996. Sa'ida Sultan (Danna International). Produced by Helicon/Big Foot Records, Tel Aviv.

The Master Musicians of Jajouka. 1974. Produced by Joel Rubiner. Notes by Robert Palmer. Adelphi Records. [Recorded in 1972. 12" 33 1/3 rpm disc. Reissued on compact disc in 1995. Genes GCD 3000.]

Musicians of the Nile: Charcoal Gypsies. 1996. WOMAD Productions for Real World Records 2366 2.

Ornette Coleman: Dancing in Your Head. 1977. Produced by Ornette Coleman. A&M Records. [Band 3, "Midnight Sunrise," includes "Ornette Coleman (alto saxophone), Robert Palmer (clarinet), featuring the Master Musicians of Joujouka." Recorded in 1973. Reissued in 1988(?). A&M Records (Japan) POCM-5044.]

Salamat Meet Les Musiciens du Nil. 1994. Piranha PIR0936.

Steel Wheels. 1989. Rolling Stones. Produced by Chris Kimsey and the Glimmer Twins. Promotone/Rolling Stones Records 45333. [Band 10, "Continental Drift," includes "Moroccan Instruments by The Master Musicians of Jajouka with Bashir al-Attar."]

SUFI: Moroccan Trance Music II. 1996. The Gnoua Brotherhood of Marrakech/The Master Musicians of Joujouka. Produced by Frank Rynne. Notes by Joe Ambrose, Mohamed Hamri, and Frank Rynne. Painting by Mohamed Hamri. Sub Rosa/le coeur du monde SR97.

Tampa. 1995. Sa'ida Sultan (Danna International). Produced by IMP Dance, Tel Aviv.

Umpatamba. 1994. Sa'ida Sultan (Danna International). Produced by IMP Dance, Tel Aviv.

FILMOGRAPHY

Abu Sayf, Salah. 1956. *Shabab imra'a* (A Woman's Youth). Cairo: Wahid Farid, Ramsis Najib.

Ahmad, Majdi 'Ali. 1996. *Ya dunya ya gharami* (O Life, My Passion). Cairo: Ra'fat al-Mihi.

'Ali, Muzaffar. 1981. *Umrao Jaan* (Dear Umrao). India: Integrated Films.

Badr Khan, Ahmad. 1941. *Intisar al-shabab* (The Triumph of Youth). Cairo: Sharikat Aflam al-Nil.

———. 1943. *Shahr al-'asal* (Honeymoon). Cairo: Studiyu Misr.

———. 1955. *Allah ma'na* (God Is with Us). Cairo: Studiyu Misr.

Barakat, Hinri. 1961. *Fi baytina rajul* (There Is a Man in Our House). Cairo: Hinri Barakat.

Berger, Ludwig, and Michael Powell. 1940. *The Thief of Baghdad*. Hollywood: United Artists.

Bishara, Khayri. 1990. *Kaburya* (Crabs). Cairo: Hurus lil-Fidyu wa-al-Sinima.

Boleslawski, Richard. 1932. *Rasputin and the Princess*. Hollywood: MGM.

Boughedir, Férid. 1995 *Un été à la Goulette* (Summer in La Goulette). Paris: Cine Tele Films.

Brooks, Richard. 1950. *Crisis*. Hollywood: MGM.

Chahine, Youssef. 1958. *Bab al-hadid* (Cairo Station). Cairo: Jibra'il al-Talhami.

———. 1963. *al-Nasir Salah al-Din* (Saladin the Victorious). Cairo: Aflam Asiya.

———. 1978. *Iskandariyya layh?* (Alexandria Why?). Cairo and Algeria: Aflam Misr al-Alamiyya wa-al-Tilifizyun al-Jazairi (RTI).

Dhulfiqar, 'Izz al-Din. 1957a. *Bur Sa'id* (Port Said). Cairo: Aflam al-'Ahd al-Jadid.

———. 1957b. *Rudd qalbi* (Return My Heart). Cairo: Aflam Asiya.

———. 1958. *Shari' al-hubb* (Street of Love). Cairo: Hilmi Raflah.

Douglas, Gordon. 1951. *I Was a Communist*. Hollywood: Warner Brothers.

Endfield, Cy. 1950. *The Sound of Fury*. Hollywood: United Artists.

Fadil, Muhammad. 1995. *Nasir 56* (Nasser 56). Cairo: Egyptian Radio and Television Union.

Fawzi, Husayn. 1958. *Ahibbak ya Hasan* (I Love You, Hasan). Cairo: Husayn Fawzi.

Fleming, Victor. 1943. *A Guy Named Joe*. Hollywood: MGM.

Fu'ad, Ahmad. 1992. *Al-Hubb fi Taba* (Love in Taba). Cairo: Sharikat GYS lil-Intaj al-Fanni.

Fusco, Coco. 1993. *Couple in a Cage: A Guatinaui Odyssey*. New York: Authentic Documentary Productions.

Gatlif, Tony. 1993. *Latcho Drom* (Safe Journey). France: Michèle Ray-Gavrus.

Imam, Hasan. 1972. *Khalli balak min Zuzu* (Pay Attention to Zuzu). Cairo: Takfur Antuniyan.

———. 1975. *Badi'a Masabni*. Cairo: Ahmad al-Haruni.

Jalal, Nadir. 1994. *Al-Irhabi* (The Terrorist). Cairo: Mustafa Mitwalli.

Kamal, Husayn. 1969. *Shay min al-khawf* (A Bit of Fear). Cairo: al-Mu'assasa al-Misriyya al-'Amma lil-Sinima.

Karim, Muhammad. 1933. *Al-Warda al-bayda'* (The White Rose). Cairo: Aflam Muhammad 'Abd al-Wahhab.

———. 1935. *Dumu' al-hubb* (Tears of Love). Cairo: Aflam Muhammad 'Abd al-Wahhab.

———. 1938. *Yahya al-hubb* (Long Live Love). Cairo: Aflam Muhammad 'Abd al-Wahhab.

———. 1946. *Dunya* (World). Cairo: Aflam Raqiya.

Khan, Muhammad. 1988. *Zawjat rajul muhimm* (Wife of an Important Man). Cairo: al-Sharika al-'Alamiyya lil-Sinima wa-al-Tilifizyun.

Lama, Ibrahim. 1927. *Qubla fi al-sahra'* (Kiss in the Desert). Cairo: Kundur Film.

Lloyd, Frank. 1935. *Mutiny on the Bounty*. Hollywood: MGM.

Mendizza, Michael. 1983. *The Master Musicians of Jahjouka*. One-hour documentary film. Long Beach, Calif.: Mendizza and Associates.

Mizrahi, Togo. 1941a. *Layla bint al-rif* (Layla, Daughter of the Countryside). Cairo: Aflam Togo Mizrahi.

———. 1941b. *Layla bint madaris* (Layla, Daughter of Schools). Cairo: Sharikat al-Aflam al-'Arabiyya.

Mustafa, Niyazi. 1957. *Sijin Abu Za'bal* (The Prisoner of Abu Za'bal). Cairo: Aflam al-Najm al-Faddi.

Nasrallah, Yusri. 1993. *Mirsidis* (Mercedes). Cairo: Aflam Misr al-'Alamiyya (Youssef Chahine).

Rafla, Hilmi. 1962. *Almaz wa-'Abduh al-Hamuli* (Almaz and 'Abduh al-Hamuli). Cairo: Sharikat Misr lil-Tamthil wa-al-Sinima.

Robbins, Tim. *Dead Man Walking*. Hollywood: Gramercy Pictures.

Rusti, Istifan. 1927. *Layla*. Cairo: Isis Film ('Aziza Amir).

Salih, Tawfiq. 1955. *Darb al-mahabil* (Fools' Alley). Cairo: Aflam al-Najah.

Salim, Kamal. 1939. *Al-'Azima* (Resolution). Cairo: Studiyu Misr.

Salim, Muhammad. 1963. *Muntaha al-farah* (The Utmost Joy). Cairo: al-Sharika al-'Amma lil-Intaj al-Sinima'i.

Scorsese, Martin. *The Age of Innocence*. Hollywood: Columbia Pictures.

Shaykh, Kamal al-. 1954. *Hayat aw mawt* (Life or Death). Cairo: Aflam Asiya.

———. 1970. *Ghurub wa-shuruq* (Sunset, Sunrise). Cairo: al-Mu'assasa al-Misriyya al-'Amma lil-Sinima.

Stone, Oliver. 1994. *Natural Born Killers*. Hollywood: Warner Brothers.

Tayyib, 'Atif al-. 1992. *Didd al-hukumah* (Against the Government). Tamidu lil-Intaj wa-al-Tawzi (Midhat al-Sharif).

Templeton, George. 1951. *Quebec*. Hollywood: Paramount.

Tilmisani, Kamil al-. 1945. *al-Suq al-sawda'* (Black Market). Cairo: Studiyu Misr.

Volpi, Mario. 1936. *Malikat al-masarih* (Queen of Theaters). Cairo: Badi'a Masabni.

Wajdi, Anwar. 1945. *Layla bint al-fuqara* (Layla, Daughter of the Poor). Cairo: Sharikat al-Aflam al-Muttahida.

———. 1946. *Layla bint al-aghniya'* (Layla, Daughter of the Rich). Cairo: Sharikat al-Aflam al-Muttahida.

———. 1949. *Ghazal al-banat* (The Flirtation of Girls). Cairo: Sharikat al-Aflam al-Muttahida.

Wellman, William. 1948. *The Iron Curtain*. Hollywood: Twentieth Century-Fox.

CONTRIBUTORS

Walter Armbrust is visiting assistant professor of anthropology at the Center for Contemporary Arab Studies, Georgetown University. He is the author of *Mass Culture and Modernism in Egypt* (Cambridge University Press, 1996) and editor of *The Seen and the Unseeable: Visual Culture in the Middle East* (a triple issue of the journal *Visual Anthropology*, vol. 10, nos. 2–4). He writes on modernity, nationalism, and popular culture in the Middle East. He is currently working on a cultural history of the Egyptian cinema.

Roberta L. Dougherty is the Middle East bibliographer at the University of Pennsylvania's Van Pelt Library. In 1986 she performed with the Reda Troupe for Folkloric Arts in Cairo, Egypt. She writes about the arts in Arab societies and is currently conducting research on the social construction of performance in modern Egypt.

Joel Gordon is associate professor of history at the University of Arkansas. He is the author of *Nasser's Blessed Movement: Egypt's Free Officers and the July Revolution* (Oxford University Press, 1992). He is currently writing a book on popular civic culture during the Nasser era.

Richard McGill Murphy is a New York City–based writer and documentary filmmaker. He holds a D.Phil. in social anthropology from Oxford University; his work focuses on popular culture, politics, and the rhetorical construction of modernity in urban South Asia. His work has appeared in the *Times* (London), the *New York Times Magazine,* and the *New Republic,* among other publications. Murphy is the founder and president of Walled City Media, an independent film and television production company.

Christa Salamandra is a research associate at the Institute of Social and Cultural Anthropology, University of Oxford, and book review editor of the *Journal of the Anthropological Society of Oxford (JASO)*. She writes about public culture in Damascus and is interested in cities, media, and consumption. Salamandra is currently working on a project examining transnational processes among Gulf Arabs in London.

Philip Schuyler received his undergraduate degree from Yale and his Ph.D. from the University of Washington. An ethnomusicologist specializing in North Africa and the Middle East, he has lived and worked for extended periods in Morocco and Yemen. His special interests are the ethnography of performance and the interrelationship of the arts. Among his publications are an ethnographic film, field recordings for UNESCO and various American publishers, and numerous articles in both professional journals and the general-interest press, including the *New York Times* and the *New Yorker*. He is currently associate professor and chair of the Ethnomusicology Division in the School of Music at the University of Washington.

Anthony Shay is the founder/director of the AVAZ International Dance Theater, a company devoted to the performance of dances from the Iranian world, which includes Central Asia and the Caucasus. He was honored by President Bill Clinton for his forty years as a choreographer. He holds a Ph.D. in dance history and theory from the University of California, Riverside.

Andrew Shryock is a cultural anthropologist who works in Jordan and Detroit. He is especially interested in modernity, identity politics, and historical ethnography. His book *Nationalism and the Genealogical Imagination* (University of California Press, 1997) received the Albert Hourani Award of the Middle East Studies Association. His most recent essays on Arab-American identity appear in *Arab Detroit: From Margin to Mainstream* (Wayne State University Press, 2000), a volume he edited with Nabeel Abraham. Shryock is assistant professor of anthropology at the University of Michigan, Ann Arbor.

Martin Stokes received a D.Phil. from the University of Oxford in 1989. Currently he is associate professor in the Department of Music at the University of Chicago. He is the author of *The Arabesk Debate: Music and Musicians in Modern Turkey* (Oxford University Press, 1992) and various articles on music, popular culture, and the Middle East.

Ted Swedenburg, assistant professor of anthropology at the University of Arkansas, is the author of *Memories of Revolt* (University of Minnesota Press, 1995) and coeditor of *Displacement, Diaspora and Geographies of Identity* (Duke University Press, 1996). He also serves on the editorial committee of

Middle East Report. He is currently working on a book manuscript, titled *Sounds from the Interzone,* that deals with "border" musics from or connected to the Middle East.

Robert Vitalis teaches in the Department of Political Science and is director of the Middle East Center at the University of Pennsylvania. He works in the areas of historical comparative theory, the political and cultural economy of business-state relations, and the history of international relations and development theory. His first book is *When Capitalists Collide: Business Conflict and the End of Empire in Egypt* (University of California Press, 1995). His second book, *America's Kingdom,* will look at the United States and the opening of the Saudi Arabian oil frontier.

Katherine E. Zirbel is a cultural anthropologist and performer who studies narrative, experience, spectacle, and political economy in the context of expressive culture in the Middle East. She has taught at Rhodes College and the University of Michigan, where she received her Ph.D. in 1999. She is currently an adjunct professor at New York University.

INDEX

Page numbers in *italics* refer to illustrations or photographs.